Mastering
ENVY/Developer

Advances in Object Technology Series

Dr. Richard S. Wiener
Series Editor and Editor
Journal of Object-Oriented Programming
101 Communications, Inc.
New York, New York

and

Department of Computer Science
University of Colorado
Colorado Springs, Colorado

Additional Volumes in Preparation

Mastering
ENVY/Developer

JOSEPH PELRINE
ALAN KNIGHT
ADRIAN CHO

 CAMBRIDGE
UNIVERSITY PRESS

 SIGS
BOOKS

CAMBRIDGE
UNIVERSITY PRESS

32 Avenue of the Americas, New York NY 10013-2473, USA

Cambridge University Press is part of the University of Cambridge.

It furthers the University's mission by disseminating knowledge in the pursuit of
education, learning and research at the highest international levels of excellence.

www.cambridge.org
Information on this title: www.cambridge.org/9780521666503

© Cambridge University Press 2001

Any product mentioned in this book may be a trademark of its company.

First published in 2001

A catalogue record for this publication is available from the British Library

ISBN 978-0-521-66650-3 Paperback

≡≡Contents≡≡

Chapter 4: Advanced Development 73

Chapter 5: Formal Concepts 99

Chapter 7: Extending the System

Chapter 8: Administration

Appendix: A Selected Annotated API of ENVY System Classes

≡Foreword≡

This book describes ENVY/Developer and its use by three very experienced professional software developers who have used it to build both successful products, including Top Link and VA/Java, and applications for numerous customers. Their unique user-oriented perspectives give developers and managers insight into how to use the product successfully in team development projects.

ENVY/Developer began as Orwell (OOPSLA reference), a research prototype developed in the Object Oriented Research Group, at Carleton University. It was built as part of the Actra project; a multiprocessor embedded Smalltalk, funded by the Defense Research Establishment Ottawa. Orwell addressed the problem of coordinating multiple developers working in the OO RAD environment of Smalltalk.

In designing Orwell, we sought to address the needs of our funding agency DREO, in particular Dr. Brian Barry who would later become CTO, then CEO of Object Technology International (OTI) and was interested in versioning configuration management for Smalltalk. Our goal was to meet the needs of our development team, which meant preserving the incremental nature of the Smalltalk programming environment.

What we developed at Carleton, then quickly re-implemented at OTI, was a strong specific solution for Smalltalk. Little did we know at the time how strong and specific it was to be! It was developed as an internal tool to support building embedded systems, hence the strict rules for compatibility, which were designed to reduce the downstream problems of the packaging or roaming engineer.

ENVY/Developer evolved to meet the needs of software engineers both inside and outside OTI. Although designed for internal use, Orwell escaped under customer pull to become the widely used ENVY/Developer product first for OTI's embedded ENVY/Smalltalk, then Digitalk's Smalltalk/V family, then PPS VisualWorks, followed by IBM's VisualAge for Smalltalk Team, and finally VisualAge for Java Enterprise Edition. It was also customized and built into numerous CASE and test environments. It provides a unique, although sometimes controversial approach to addressing the problem of team development and versioning an incremental object-oriented environment.

Kent Johnson implemented the initial design, and became the lead developer for the product. Kent translated my white board dialogs into working code initially in Smalltalk/V and then V286. During the early years he not only developed ENVY/Manager he managed ENVY/Smalltalk image. We introduced what at that time were some simple packaging notions called applications, and prerequisites, which are now, of course, as commonplace as packages in Java or assemblies in .Net. Soon Kent moved to OTI, Mike Milinkovich joined him, they introduced the concepts of configuration maps (known more commonly today as manifests) and subapplications, which allowed the isolation of platform specific code. In later years, Adrian Cho, one of the co-authors of this book, made substantial contributions in numerous areas such as required maps, an ENVY API, and almost single-handedly supporting the VisualWorks platforms, as well as far too many EMSRV platforms and VA/Java.

Pete Lord of NCR, was one of the first to appreciate that ENVY could be extended to support non-Smalltalk artifacts such as test scripts and was in a large part responsible for pulling ENVY/Developer out of OTI engineering. The initial implementation used a C Btree library; the library was as large as the Smalltalk image! In order to satisfy our commitments to the Tektronix oscilloscope team (our first embedded Smalltalk customer) and NCR, Dave Thomson and I quickly tossed the Btree and designed a simple method-specific, lock-free atomic update protocol, while Kent rewrote the persistent dictionary above Dave. The solution was originally designed to use client side locking because we used NetWare file servers; however, Tektronix was developing using Smalltalk/V on Sun workstations with NFS (stateless is not a feature!). John Duimovich and Dave Thomson hacked together a Unix server for ENVY/Manager called EMSRV, which supported the same protocols as the client side locks.

ENVY/Developer has an attitude which some may say reflected it's inventor. While most version management systems use a sign in/sign out approach and user conflict/merge tools, ENVY opted instead for a human-centered model of component ownership. This was intended to eliminate the low personal commitment we found when programmers checked out modules with no owner, inserted their fixes or updates, and then released them back into the library with little concern for who these changes impacted. Component ownership, in particular class ownership was advocated in the Orwell paper, and became a controversial matter.

In 1987 when OTI started working with Digitalk, "NV" was the code name for New V, the portable 32 bit, generation scavenging Smalltalk implemented by Mike Wilson and John Duimovich, with assistance from Peter Shipton and Dave Thomson. NV was released by Digitalk as Smalltalk/V Mac and sold by OTI as ENVY/Smalltalk to embedded customers who developed using Sun and Apollo workstations as well as PCs. The words NV made it into the Tektronix contract, and not liking acronyms, I decided in a moment of haste that we were building environments and so the English word "envy" was chosen. Being a small company, we trademarked only ENVY; hence all of the products became ENVY/something... The name ENVY/Developer was cleverly chosen by Mike Milinkovich, who was then product manager. He needed a way to package ENVY/Manager, ENVY/Packager, and ENVY/Stats into a single product that would be easy to market.

In practice ENVY allows many styles. Component ownership is often collective during the evolution of a new component and then becomes more static through the life of a component. We are also not religious about the use of merge tools, which are highly appropriate for distributed development of more loosely connected teams. ENVY/Developer's evolution suffered largely due to the fact that it was the stable foundation for the development of Babel, OTI's multi-platform standards-based library, which allows common native widget GUI code on ParcPlace, Digitalk, and ENVY/Smalltalk embedded platforms. It also supported the development of IBM Smalltalk, VisualAge, and VA/Java.

Concurrently OTI maintains versions of ENVY/Developer for ParcPlace Smalltalk. Sadly, much of the best developer time went into debugging socket libraries, LAN locking problems and Smalltalk vendor platform portability issues. Likely the best kept secret is that OTI has more criticisms, feature requests, and wishes for ENVY/Developer than any of our customers and users.

ENVY/Developer's stability is a testimony to the dedication of the engineering team; its lack of evolution is a testimony to the futility of our industry where vendors take smart talented people and condemn them to platform hell.

The authors have in-depth experience using ENVY/Developer. They have also developed extension tools and best practices to allow it to be used in different settings and tailored for specific needs. The authors' experiences span three continents. Alan has worked both as a consultant and product developer with Object People and now Cincom in Canada. Joseph has been involved as a consultant on numerous Smalltalk and Gemstone projects in Europe. Adrian had his own Smalltalk business in Sydney, Australia and later joined OTI as the technical lead for ENVY/Developer. We at OTI appreciate their efforts in describing ENVY/Developer from their perspective. Both novice and expert ENVY/Developer users will benefit from their expert user views.

≡Acknowledgments≡

Like any book, this one is not an individual achievement and could not have happened without the help and influence of many people.

We would like to give our most sincere thanks to all of those who helped us. First of all, we thank everyone at Cambridge University Press and SIGS Books, particularly our editor Lothlórien Homet for her tremendous patience and commitment to this project.

Dave Thomas provided the original inspiration for ENVY, founded and led OTI, and of course wrote the Foreword. Without him, none of this could have happened. We'd also like to thank everyone at OTI for producing ENVY, and for their invaluable help and cooperation in getting this book written. The VisualAge team at IBM, the VisualWorks team at Cincom, and all the other Smalltalk vendors helped make our programming lives a little bit brighter.

Eric Clayberg, at Instantiations/Smalltalk Systems, contributed the piece of Chapter 9 on renaming versions and hiding source code, and has generally been a cool guy to exchange ideas with as well as an outstanding contributor to the Smalltalk community. Paul Baumann, at Gemstone, provided some very useful input based on his real-life job using ENVY to delivery high quality, multi-dialect, and -platform software product. Jan Steinman, cofounder of Bytesmiths, was a source of inspiration and helped with the outline. Don Roberts and John Brant created the Refactoring Browser and were very helpful in the port to the ENVY browsers.

We have benefited enormously from the feedback we've received on the book from many sources, both from those who reviewed the text and those we've discussed the issues with. We'd particularly like to single out Stephane Ducasse for his tireless review of the text, and to specifically acknowledge Anthony Lander, Donald Smith, and Didier Besset.

We'd like to thank the Smalltalk user community as a whole for its endurance and support, and we'd particularly like to thank those who ordered the book on faith long before it was finished. There are too many people to mention who pestered us to write and finish this book, and of course we've worked with countless people over the years who have asked for and helped shape the things we've implemented here.

In addition to these people, Joseph would like to specifically thank Alan and Adrian for agreeing to work with him on this project, and also (in alphabetical order) Kent Beck, Stefan Bosshard, Kyle Brown, Thorsten Dittmar, Joachim Geidel, Justin

Hill, Ralph Johnson, Daniel Jutzi, Eliot Miranda, Jeff Odell, John Sarkela, Renate Schirmer, Bobby Woolf, all the guys at Daedalos, Camp Smalltalk, and the cast of thousands who kept screaming "when's it gonna be done?"

Alan would like to thank Kirsten Carlson for her near-infinite patience and love, for putting up with all those times he disappeared to work on the book, and for her help and advice on writing. He would, of course, also like to thank Joseph and Adrian for their work on the book. He would also like to thank everyone at The Object People for the wonderful and supportive environment there, the opportunity to work on ENVY with a wide variety of customers, and for many stimulating discussions on ENVY features and usage. In particular, he'd like to thank Wayne Beaton, Dave Buck, Ron Charron, Martin Kobetic, and Anthony Lander. Finally, he'd like to thank Annick Fron and the European Smalltalk User Group for inviting him to speak and making him come up with a topic where he thought he could contribute something.

Adrian would like to thank Joseph and Alan for inviting him to participate in this project. He would also like to thank Dave Thomas and everyone at OTI for their work on ENVY and for their support and encouragement in writing this book.

≡Introduction≡

Smalltalk was first built as a personal computing environment. Most systems at that time were time-sharing, with character-based terminals. In contrast, Smalltalk provided a high-resolution graphical screen and a mouse to maximize the power available to the one user actually sitting at the machine. Smalltalk was designed so that every component in the system was accessible to the user and could be understood by one person.

This was an outstanding vision, and one that remains both important and ahead of the mainstream even today. However, this emphasis on the personal meant that cooperative development issues were less well represented.

Individuals could be incredibly productive, but the code resided in each developer's image and was not directly visible to other team members. The code could be filed out and exchanged between developers but on an ad hoc basis. The way Smalltalk represented code, and the development practices that Smalltalk encouraged were not a good match for the file-based version control systems of the day. As Smalltalk became more widely used in industry, the need for support of large teams became more critical.

Different schemes were attempted that built relatively lightweight Smalltalk layers on top of existing team programming systems. Finally, in the mid-1980s, Carleton University Professor Dave Thomas and some of his students broke the mold and came up with Orwell, a repository-based system that was tightly integrated with the Smalltalk environment. This was later commercialized as ENVY/Developer, and it rapidly became the dominant team development system for commercial Smalltalk work. In recent years, the same ideas have been the basis for the team environment in IBM's VisualAge for Java and VisualAge Generator products.

Although ENVY has long been widely used, no books have been available on it. Developers using ENVY were forced to rely on courses, magazine articles, and folklore to understand how to use and extend the system. This book was written to help fill that void. We hope to provide an introduction that lets new users quickly come up to speed and be productive, a reference that will let experienced users and administrators find the information they need, and information to help toolsmiths and power users extend the system in the ways they need. We also hope to provide the community with some useful tools we have built and described in this book.

Structure of This Book

This book is divided into two major sections. The first section (Chapters 1 through 6) is about standard ENVY usage. It introduces ENVY concepts and practices in both a tutorial and more theoretical format. The second section (Chapters 7 through 10) is devoted to particular issues and to extending and enhancing the ENVY system. This section includes many different topics, appropriate for system administrators, advanced developers, and toolsmiths.

Who Should Read This Book

This book will be useful to anyone who works with ENVY, or who is interested in team programming mechanisms, particularly as they are applied to object-oriented languages and interactive development environments. The book is primarily aimed at three audiences.

The first, and perhaps the most important, are those learning ENVY or developing with it on a day-to-day basis. For these readers the tutorial chapters and explanation of ENVY concepts will be most useful. Basic knowledge of Smalltalk is assumed, but no prior knowledge of ENVY is required. For these readers, Chapters 1 through 4 provide an ENVY tutorial with examples and advice. A quicker and more formal summary of ENVY concepts is provided in Chapter 5: "Formal Concepts." It may also be useful to read Chapter 6: "Packaging and Delivery," Chapter 8: "Administration," and Chapter 10: "Troubleshooting," but these are not necessary for basic ENVY usage. A subset of this audience consists of project managers using ENVY who want to understand the concepts and how they affect work processes but who don't need to use the tool. For these readers the most useful resources will be Chapter 5: "Formal Concepts," Chapter 8: "Administration," and Chapter 10: "Troubleshooting." The tutorial Chapters 1 through 4 may also be of use, although the setup and installation portion of Chapter 1 will be unnecessary.

The second audience administers an ENVY project or a portion of it. These users might be more experienced developers or nonprogramming system administrators charged with maintaining an ENVY system. These readers will probably find Chapter 5: "Formal Concepts" useful for quickly understanding the ideas behind ENVY, and will definitely want to read Chapter 8: "Administration."

Finally, there are power users and toolsmiths who understand and use ENVY routinely and want to understand the implementation, advanced features, or ways to customize and extend the system for their needs. For these users the later chapters will be most valuable, particularly Chapter 7: "Extending the System" and Chapter 9: "Goodies." Chapter 6: "Packaging and Delivery" will be useful for anyone involved in delivering an application, and the tools described in Chapter 8: "Administration" are also valuable for power users and tool builders. Advanced users may also want to skim the tutorial chapters for useful tidbits. Of particular use may be the advice on setting up complex configurations in the "Installation and Setup" portion of Chapter 1.

Conventions

For the most part, the typographical conventions in this book should be straightforward for anyone used to reading Smalltalk code. Code embedded in the text, including the names of classes, methods, and applications, is shown in a different font. For example, we might talk about the method printOn: in the class Question. The same convention is used for the names of menu items.

We will discuss both Cincom's VisualWorks and IBM's VisualAge Smalltalk. Most of what we will say applies to both of these implementations equally, but from time to time you'll encounter implementation-specific sections. We highlight these as follows.

VA This paragraph is specific to IBM's VisualAge. It might be talking about menus in the VisualAge organizer, features that are supported only in VisualAge, or some other aspect of the system that does not apply to VisualWorks.

VW This paragraph is specific to Cincom's VisualWorks. It might be talking about parcel integration, features that are supported only in VisualWorks, or some other aspect of the system that does not apply to VisualAge.

One particular stylistic convention for the code deserves note, that of ending methods with a period. The issue of whether to include or omit a closing period is as contentious and emotional as only trivial issues can be. In this book we have opted to include the period, for the following reasons:

- It's more consistent to always end statements with a terminator (except in the presence of brackets). Some people argue that the period is a separator, not a terminator. In our opinion they spend too much time thinking about parser theory and not enough time about the simplicity of day-to-day work.

- It is less error prone. One of the standard Smalltalk errors is to add a line at the end of a method only to discover that the method will not compile because the previous line has no period. This doesn't happen if we consistently terminate statements with a period.

- Finally, and perhaps most important, it is more consistent with natural language. One of Smalltalk's virtues as a computer language is that many of its statements can easily be read as if they were English sentences. I believe the designers of Smalltalk deliberately chose the period because it is the way we end sentences in English.

Software for This Book

This book does not include a CD-ROM containing the software, and this is a deliberate choice. In this era of the Internet, any frozen medium will quickly be out of date. Instead, copies of the accompanying software, along with updates, new goodies, and code contributed by the community will be available at the book's Web sites.

- *www.us.cambridge.org/titles/0521666503*
- *www.envymasters.com*

Links to other software mentioned in the book will be available at these sites. We also list references for the most important outside tools mentioned in the book:

- The SUnit unit testing framework is available at *www.xprogramming.com*.
- The Refactoring Browser is available at *www.refactory.com*.
- VA Assist Pro is available at *www.smalltalksystems.com*.

For Smalltalk software in general, the following links may also be of use:

- IBM's Smalltalk Web site is at *www.ibm.com/software/ad/smalltalk*.
- Cincom's Smalltalk Web site is at *www.cincom.com/smalltalk*.

VisualWorks and VisualAge are the only Smalltalk implementation currently supported by ENVY but by no means the only Smalltalks available. We list URLs for most of the other Smalltalks so that readers can see some of the other possibilities and breadth of the available implementations, as follows:

- **Dolphin:** A Windows-specific Smalltalk, which is inexpensive, simple to use, and has a very nice user interface. An excellent introduction to Smalltalk is available at *www.object-arts.com*.

- **Gemstone:** An active object-oriented database that includes its own Smalltalk running on the server. An integration is available that lets you use ENVY on the client to control GemStone code. You can access Gemstone at *www.smalltalk.gemstone.com*.

- **Pocket Smalltalk:** An open-source Smalltalk for the Palm hand-held computer. It produces extremely compact programs (~45K) and is available at *www.pocketsmalltalk.com*.

- **Object Studio:** A Smalltalk that comes out of a more 4GL tradition. It is widely used in corporate environments. This Smalltalk is also owned by Cincom and is available at *www.cincom.com/objectstudio*.

- **Smalltalk MT:** A Smalltalk implementation very tightly integrated with Windows that provides high performance, native Windows threading, DLL creation. It is available at *www.objectconnect.com*.

- **Smalltalk/X:** Despite the name, a version for both UNIX and Windows NT, with some very sophisticated features. It is available at *www.exept.de*.

- **SmallScript:** While information on this is scarce at the time of publication, this will be a Smalltalk implementation integrated with the Microsoft .NET platform and will be available at *www.smallscript.com*.

- **Squeak:** An open-source implementation with some very sophisticated graphical features, coordinated by a team at Disney that includes Alan Kay. Squeak boasts a very strong user community and is available at *www.squeak.org*.

- **Visual Smalltalk:** Once one of the primary commercial Smalltalks, this was abandoned by ParcPlace-Digitalk after an attempted merger. It's still in use, but new development is minimal. This Smalltalk was acquired by Cincom as part of the VisualWorks acquisition and is available at *www.cincom.com/vse*.

As with anything on the web, these addresses are subject to change, so if you have problems with them check the main web site for links or use a search engine.

The Story of This Book

The idea for this book started back in 1998, when Stephane Ducasse of Bern University suggested to Joseph Pelrine that he write a book on ENVY. Soon thereafter, Lothlórien Homet, then struggling to get the SIGS Publications book division back on its feet, sat in on Joseph's Smalltalk Solutions talk on ENVY and proposed the same thing. Joseph, feeling a bit uncomfortable, agreed on the condition that he could convince one of his colleagues (who knew a lot more about ENVY than he did) to contribute. After some cajoling, Alan Knight agreed to work on the project. While Joseph prepared the book proposal (thanks, Joseph), Alan convinced Adrian Cho of OTI to act as technical editor. Organizing, writing, and many schedule slips ensued. Part way through the project Joseph talked Adrian into coming aboard as an author. After the first draft was written, Alan spent months revising and refactoring. The reason the tome you hold in your hands reads as easily as it does is due in large part to Alan's work (thanks, Alan). Adrian's depth of ENVY knowledge, both technical and philosophical, was invaluable and he contributed one of the most useful ENVY utilities to ever see the light of day, the checkpoint mechanism (thanks, Adrian). All this time, Lothlórien Homet has had the patience of a saint, deftly and adroitly juggling carrot and stick to get all of us to finally finish this manuscript (thanks, Lothlórien).

Basel and Ottawa, September, 2000

═Chapter 1═

Getting Started

To start with, we'll introduce ENVY/Developer, go over enough of the basic ENVY/Developer architecture to get you started, and describe in some detail how to set up the environment and configure the options available. All readers will want to review the architecture section. The setup sections will be of particular interest to new users and to administrators responsible for the maintenance of an ENVY installation.

Overview

First, let's identify what ENVY/Developer is, where it comes from, and what it's good for. This information will help you understand the architecture and where ENVY's concepts come from.

What Is ENVY/Developer?

ENVY/Developer is a software engineering environment for Smalltalk programming. Specifically, it provides facilities for team programming and delivering significant-sized applications, built on top of the regular Smalltalk development environment. Smalltalk is widely recognized as being very productive for individual developers, but the standard Smalltalk environment was not designed with the idea of collaborative development in mind. ENVY/Developer extends the basic Smalltalk environment to include facilities for team programming and configuration management.

Technically, *ENVY* is a generic term that refers to a family of products and technologies. These include ENVY/Smalltalk, ENVY/Developer, ENVY/Replicator, and others. However, ENVY/Developer is the most widely used of these products, and it is common usage to use just the term "ENVY" to refer to ENVY/Developer, or even more specifically to ENVY/Manager. Although this is technically incorrect, it is the common usage and is the standard we follow for this book.

At various points, ENVY implementations existed for all three major commercial Smalltalk platforms. We describe these as follows:

- **VisualWorks:** This includes ObjectWorks/Smalltalk and its successor VisualWorks. These are the direct descendants of the original Xerox Smalltalk and were and are currently owned by Cincom Systems.

- **IBM Smalltalk:** This includes OTI's ENVY/Smalltalk, IBM's IBM Smalltalk, and IBM's VisualAge/Smalltalk products. These products are currently made by IBM and their OTI subsidiary.

- **Digitalk:** This includes Smalltalk/V DOS, Smalltalk/V Windows, and Visual Smalltalk. These products are also owned by Cincom Systems, but have not had ENVY support for some time. We will not consider Visual Smalltalk when talking about ENVY implementations.

The full suite of ENVY products comprises the folowing modules:

- **ENVY/Developer** is a toolset that exists in a Smalltalk image, implemented in Smalltalk code. For the IBM Smalltalk platform, it consists of four separate products. Currently, only ENVY/Manager is supported for the ParcPlace platform.

- **ENVY/Manager** provides configuration management and version control facilities. This product is the focus of this book. As a product, it is transparent to the user because it is tightly integrated into the development environment. It is not normally possible to load or unload ENVY/Manager.

- **ENVY/Packager** is an image packaging or "stripping" tool used to create a deliverable application out of a development image. This is used within products in the IBM Smalltalk family, and also existed historically for Digitalk Smalltalk.

- **ENVY/Swapper** is an object dumper and loader. It can be used to serialize a network of object instances to a file or an arbitrary stream. This is nominally a separate component, but one that must be loaded because ENVY/Manager makes use of it. On VisualWorks platforms, the equivalent BOSS facility is used instead.

- **ENVY/Stats** is an execution profiler that analyzes the time and/or memory used in executing a piece of Smalltalk code.

History

ENVY/Developer originated in the late 1980s as a research project at Carleton University in Ottawa, Canada. The project, known as *Orwell*, was led by Dave Thomas, founder of OTI, and a professor at the School of Computer Science. The concepts introduced in Orwell have served as the foundation of ENVY/Developer for over a decade.

ENVY/Developer was first implemented on Digitalk's Smalltalk/V for MS-DOS, and subsequently evolved to support other members of the Digitalk product family.

It was ported to ParcPlace's VisualWorks, and was used as an integral piece of ENVY/Smalltalk, which then served as the basis for IBM Smalltalk and VisualAge. Ultimately, OTI was acquired by IBM, becoming a wholly owned subsidiary of IBM Canada.

Architecture

This section describes the fundamental architecture of ENVY/Developer, and how it differs from both traditional Smalltalk environments and traditional file-based source code control systems.

The Repository

A classical Smalltalk environment is intended for an individual developer. The system consists of a collection of files:

- **One or more image files:** These files hold the complete state of a development environment, including all of the compiled code.

- **A sources file:** This contains the source code to the base system. In normal usage, there is only one sources file, and it does not change until there is a new version of the base Smalltalk system.

- **One or more change logs:** For each image file, there is a corresponding change log. Every time code is compiled in the image, the corresponding source code is saved into the appropriate change log. A pointer into the change log is saved with the compiled code, so that its source can be retrieved.

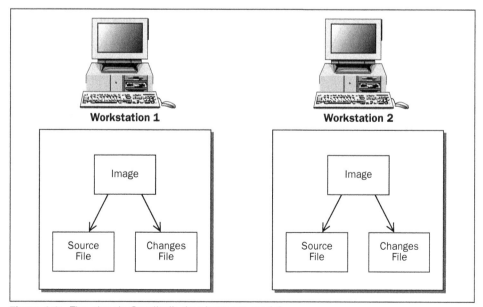

Figure 1-1: The classic Smalltalk development model.

In this model, developers work individually. To collaborate with other developers, they would "file out" the relevant code in source code format and send it to them. This allows for collaboration, but does not maintain version information, requires a manual process, and allows information to be lost.

ENVY/Manager augments this model by providing configuration management and version control facilities. All code is stored in a central database rather than in files associated with a particular image. Developers are continuously connected to this database; therefore, changes are immediately visible to all developers. Because all changes are centralized, it is much less likely for code to be lost.

This centralization is very powerful, but it requires significant changes to the basic environment. ENVY cannot be delivered as a traditional standalone component, or as a set of file-ins. Rather, OTI provides a new base image in which fundamental changes have been made to the underlying system. These changes replace the usual change log and sources with an interface to the ENVY/Manager library where all code is maintained. It also structures all source code into one of several types of

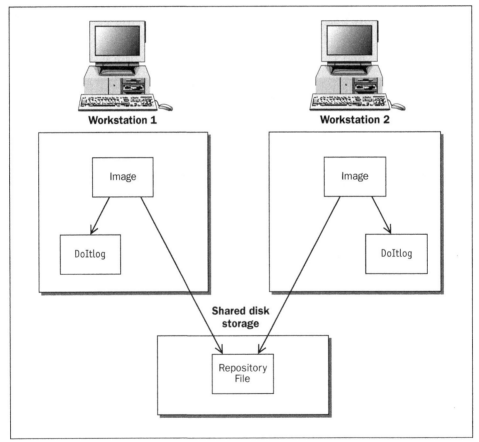

Figure 1-2: The ENVY development model.

components, and provides a complete set of browsers to develop, maintain, and configure these software components. These replace the normal development browsers.

This has important implications for the work process. In the classical model, development was image-centric. With ENVY/Manager the image becomes a discardable by-product of development, secondary to the repository that stores and coordinates all work. An image serves as a private workspace where a user can develop, test, and execute code. The library, to which all users are connected, serves as a shared workspace where users can work separately or cooperatively on the same projects and components.

Concurrent Development

The ENVY model of development is also distinct from traditional file-based version control systems, which typically rely on a check-in/check-out development model. With file-based tools the team programming environment looks like some form of shared directory structure. Users check files out into a local directory, then check them back into the system. In Smalltalk, the primary representation of a program is as objects, with text files used only as a backup and interchange form. The ENVY repository acts as an object-oriented (OO) database to hold and recreate these objects. The image serves the purpose of the directory structure, holding together the current state of the various components.

This fine granularity of components enables highly concurrent development because changes can be tracked down to the individual method level, with no necessary correspondence between any of the software components and a disk file. ENVY enables developers to manage components in the repository at any level, ranging from individual methods to entire subsystems, further increasing concurrency. Rather than managing conflicts using a file-based differencing mechanism, it uses component ownership as a fundamental mechanism. Any number of developers can work concurrently on a single component, but one developer is designated as owner of that component and the owner must approve any changes. For more information on this model, see Chapter 3.

In addition to being a multi-user product, ENVY is a multi-platform product. Any ENVY image may be connected to a library, and browse and possibly load components created using other ENVY images running on different platforms or different Smalltalk base images or virtual machines. In fact, sites with multiple users will typically be running images on multiple platforms and sometimes multiple Smalltalk releases, all connected to the same library.

ENVY Concepts

This has been a quick overview of the ENVY architecture. For more information about ENVY concepts and architecture in a more formal setting, see Chapter 5. The following sections start to apply these concepts in a more detailed and tutorial style. These are appropriate for new users, or any users who would like the concepts and development process further explained, with examples and detailed advice.

Installation and Setup

This section talks about installation and setup procedures for ENVY in some detail, including a number of different configuration options. This section isn't intended to replace the setup instructions that come with the product, but rather to supplement them with explanations and advice on the various options available. You should consult the installation instructions and release notes that came with your ENVY installation and your Smalltalk programming environment. We cover both server and client setup. If you are working on an existing project, it's likely there is a preexisting server setup, and you will simply need to consult with your system administrator on what the appropriate client options are.

Note that some variation exists between different versions of ENVY, and here we primarily discuss the current versions, specifically VisualAge 5.0 and VisualWorks 3.0 and 5i. We discuss both versions of VisualWorks because both are in common use right now and some differences exist between them. Almost all of what we say for VisualAge 5.0 also applies to Versions 4.5 and 4.0.

As a new user, you'll want to read the sections here to get you up and running as quickly as possible, then move on to Chapter 2, which covers some basic concepts. As an ENVY administrator, you may want to read this section to examine the possible choices you face in configuring the setup for your users. All readers may want to go over this section briefly for things they may not have known about ENVY configuration.

Client Backup

It's always important to have good backup procedures. When installing ENVY, one of the first things you should do is ensure that you have access to a copy of the Smalltalk image as it was distributed (a *clean image*). One way to do this is to keep a compressed copy somewhere easily accessible. If something goes wrong with your ENVY environment, a clean image is the best place to recover from.

The Repository

As described previously under "Architecture," ENVY uses a central database to store source code. This is normally called the *repository* but may also be called the *ENVY database*, the *manager file*, or *manager.dat*. A number of these terms come from the repository's implementation as a single large file, which may be named either manager.dat or with a name encoding the version number, for example, mgr50.dat. This file acts as a database to store the source code and data associated with the various software components.

> **Performance Tip**
>
> Give the ENVY repository its own disk partition. This solves two problems.
> First, you won't have to worry as much about running out of disk space and
> crashing your library. Second, ENVY works by successively appending very
> small chunks to this very large file. This can cause disk fragmentation if other
> programs use the same partition. This is a particular problem when using NTFS,
> but is much less severe on other systems, so you may want to avoid using NTFS
> partitions for ENVY repositories.

Accessing the Repository

In the single-user or standalone version of ENVY, the repository file is stored on a
local disk and accessed directly. In a team environment, the repository is shared,
either through a network file system or the EMSRV server process (the preferred
mechanism).

The mechanism used is determined at startup by information specified in the configuration file.

The Configuration File

The configuration file is a simple text file that specifies many important startup
parameters for ENVY. The configuration file may be set up automatically as part of
your installation, or you may need to edit it manually. In either case, it can be important to look at this file if you need to change or debug your setup.

This file has two primary formats depending on which version of Smalltalk you're
using. In VisualWorks, the configuration file is named ENVY.CNF and contains
Smalltalk source code, which is read in, compiled, and executed at startup. Note that
the exact contents of this file are different between VisualWorks 3.0 and VisualWorks
5i. In VisualAge, the configuration file is in Windows .INI format, with the same
name as the development environment executable (for example, ABT.INI).

At startup, the system reads this file and uses it to set various parameters, including directories to search for various resources. For our purposes, the most important
settings are the location of the repository file, whether it is accessed locally or over
the network, and optionally the name or IP address of the machine running the
ENVY server.

Access Methods

ENVY can access the repository in two different ways: through direct file access (possibly networked) or through a server process called EMSRV.

In direct file access, the Smalltalk image directly accesses the repository file and
manipulates it, including obtaining locks. This is most commonly used in a single-
user installation, where the file is stored on a local hard drive. In older versions of
ENVY, it was also possible to access the repository using network file and locking

services, although not all networks were supported, and UNIX NFS was specifically not supported because it did not support the required locking mechanisms.

EMSRV is an acronym for the ENVY/Manager Server. When using EMSRV access, ENVY does not access the repository file directly, but goes through a server process running on the machine that holds the repository file. This is the preferred mechanism in current versions of ENVY (VisualAge 4.5 and later, VisualWorks 5i and later). Consequently, EMSRV must be used whenever an ENVY repository is to be shared by more than one user or when the repository file is not stored locally on the machine running ENVY. There are several reasons for this change. Not all networks provide reliable locking services, and many subtle bugs can arise with different combinations of networking software and operating systems. Furthermore, the server process can also be more efficient because it can combine multiple file operations into a single request. The biggest disadvantage of this mechanism is that it makes installation significantly more complex.

File Access

File access is extremely simple to set up. You simply need to specify the location of the file. The exact technique for doing this varies depending on your ENVY dialect and version.

Using file access in VisualWorks 5i, the relevant part of your configuration file would look something like this:

```
ENVY.EmLibrary
defaultName: 'D:\apps\vw5i\envy\manager\manager.dat';
serverAddress: nil.
```

This specifies the local file path to the ENVY repository, and that there is no server in use. Using file access in VisualWorks 3.0 adds some additional options, so the relevant part of your configuration file would look like this:

```
EmLibrary
defaultName: 'C:\APPS\VW30\SERVER\MANAGER.DAT';
serverAddress: nil;
releaseLockMode: true;
singleUserMode: true.
```

We have again specified the file name and a nil server, but we have also specified additional options that have become obsolete in VisualWorks 5i. The first of these is releaseLockMode, which was essentially obsolete even in earlier versions but was used to indicate to ENVY that the file system could be relied upon to release locks when the library was closed. Otherwise, the ENVY system would have to manually release any locks. You should leave this setting as true unless the ENVY documentation indicates otherwise for your platform. The other option is to specify whether we're a single user, and don't need to worry about contention in the database. If we are, then ENVY can run a little bit more efficiently. Note that if you've set this option to true, and someone else attempts to access the database, the attempt will fail.

In VisualWorks 3.0 and earlier, the configuration file also contains the names of shared libraries to be used for network file access and password checking. These will vary by platform, and you should consult the ENVY release notes for which libraries to use.

Using file access in VisualAge, the relevant portion of your configuration file would look like this:

```
[EmLibraryInterface]
DefaultName=C:\apps\va50\mgr50.dat
ServerAddress=
OpenReadOnly=false
```

This specifies the local file path to the ENVY repository, and that no server is in use. Further, we can specify that we wish to open the repository in read-only mode. This might be appropriate for browsing a repository to which we do not have write access, either because we have insufficient privileges, or because it's on a network partition.

Tip

Even in ENVY versions that supported repository access over a network file system, you are better off using EMSRV. It's more stable and reliable.

EMSRV Access

Using EMSRV in VisualAge, the relevant part of your configuration file might look like this:

```
DefaultName=F:\VISUALAGE\MGR50.DAT
ServerAddress=JUPITER
```

This specifies the server file path (see below) and the name of the server, which is a computer on the LAN with the name Jupiter.

Using EMSRV access in VisualWorks 5i, the relevant part of your configuration file would look something like this:

```
ENVY.EmLibrary
defaultName: 'F:\VISUALWORKS\MANAGER.DAT';
serverAddress: '172.30.1.25'.
```

This specifies the server's file path to the ENVY repository, and the IP address of the server. Using EMSRV access in VisualWorks 3.0, some additional options exist, and the relevant part of your configuration file might look like the following:

```
EmLibrary
defaultName: 'F:\VISUALWORKS\MANAGER.DAT';
serverAddress: 'JUPITER';
releaseLockMode: true;
singleUserMode: false.
```

Here we have specified the file name and a named server, but we've also specified additional options, which have become obsolete in VisualWorks 5i. The first of these is releaseLockMode, which was essentially obsolete even in earlier versions, but was used to indicate to ENVY that the file system could be relied upon to release locks when the library was closed. If not, the ENVY system would have to manually release any locks. You should leave this setting as true unless the ENVY documentation indicates otherwise for your platform. The other option is to specify whether we are a single user, and don't need to worry about contention in the database. In this case, because we are setting up with EMSRV, it's unlikely that we intend to use this as a single-user database.

In this example, it's important that the path we provided to the repository is a *server* path, in terms of the server's drives. So in this example we expect the server to have a *physical* drive F: with an F:\VISUALAGE or F:\VISUALWORKS directory on it. We don't care if the *client* has a drive F:, whether physical or networked. Although the configuration file is on the client machine, the repository file path isn't used on the client but is sent directly to the EMSRV process, which runs on the server. The repository path is then used by EMSRV, which interprets it in the context of the server machine it is running on. If, instead of an absolute path name, we used a relative path, such as ..\manager.dat, then this would be interpreted relative to the home directory of the EMSRV process on the server. Note that it is not even necessary for the client to have network access to the repository file when using EMSRV.

The address of the server can be specified either by name or by IP address. In the preceding examples, we have either used the local network name Jupiter, or the IP address of the corresponding machine. We recommend using the IP address. This is less convenient if your networking setup changes, but we have found it more robust in the presence of a variety of network issues.

Also note that when using EMSRV, the repository file must exist on a hard drive that is physically attached to the computer running the EMSRV process. That is, it is *not* possible to use EMSRV when the directory containing the repository file is network mounted. You should be sure that EMSRV is run on the machine that physically contains the hard drive with the repository file.

Troubleshooting Installation

If you can install your basic Smalltalk environment, relatively few things can go wrong with the basic ENVY install. The most common cause of problems is with the EMSRV installation, and that's what we mostly address in this section.

This is not to imply that EMSRV is unstable. As mentioned previously, EMSRV is both more stable and better optimized than file access, and is generally to be preferred. The biggest disadvantage of EMSRV is that there are more things that can go wrong. This section discusses some of the problems that can arise, and provides approaches to debugging them.

General Issues

One area of confusion with EMSRV is the relationship of the server process to the repository. Users tend to work in a single repository, and to think of EMSRV as being associated with that repository. In fact, EMSRV has no inherent knowledge of what repository files it can access. The client provides that information based on its configuration file. In fact, a single EMSRV can access many different repositories, as long as they are all on the server. You can even run a single EMSRV process to handle repositories for VisualAge for Smalltalk, VisualWorks, and VisualAge for Java.

Remember that the repository file must be physically located on the same machine as the one running EMSRV. EMSRV cannot access the repository over a network.

Once you understand what the setup parameters should look like, it's just a matter of getting it working. The documentation on installing EMSRV is quite good, but it can still be a frustrating process, as with anything involving closed-box programs trying to communicate. It's really simple as long as we have someone who thoroughly understands the operating system, its services, the TCP/IP implementation, the network configuration, Smalltalk, and the error messages produced by all of these. If we're not lucky enough to have a person like that, then we'll just have to do it ourselves.

Installation Options

Under UNIX, there are few installation options. EMSRV can be run interactively from the command line, or automatically launched at startup by the operating system, but there is little distinction between the two modes of operation.

Under Windows NT, EMSRV can also be run in two different ways: from the command line or by installing it as an NT service. Unfortunately, services that fail to start up do not typically provide any error messages, making it very difficult to debug. Once you are up and running, it's simpler to run EMSRV as a service, but it's easier to debug from the command line. Typically, try running it from the command line until you're sure it's up and running and you know what arguments to specify, then install it as a service.

Furthermore, under Windows NT, you need to be careful about users and passwords. If you want to use native password checking, you will need to create a special user for EMSRV and give it the advanced privilege to "act as part of the operating system." This is necessary because, as a security measure, NT does not allow most programs to check passwords other than by logging in. By acting as part of the operating system, EMSRV gains the capability to check passwords. One problem to watch out for in this situation is that the EMSRV user has valid login privileges. You may not be able to successfully start EMSRV until the user you've created has interactively logged in at least once. Furthermore, Windows NT typically sets user passwords to expire. If your special EMSRV user's password expires, you will not be able to restart EMSRV until it has been reset, and the error messages will not be terribly informative. We recommend either setting the special EMSRV user's password not to expire, or changing it regularly.

The EMADMIN Utility

Once you have set up the server process, you need to be sure you can connect to it. Rather than testing this by starting up a development environment and waiting for it to succeed or fail, consider using the EMADMIN utility instead. This is a simple command-line utility that performs a number of useful functions for monitoring and administering EMSRV. The simplest use of this utility is to get basic statistics, using

```
EMADMIN STAT 127.0.0.1
```

which, if EMSRV is running on our local machine (using the localhost IP address 127.0.0.1), produces output like the following:

```
EMADMIN 6.22
Copyright (C) IBM Corporation 1989-1998
Server Type    : EMSRV
Server Version : EMSRV 6.22 for Windows NT Apr  4 1998 15:36:56 (AEST)

=========================================================

EMSRV Statistics for: localhost

-------------------------------------------------

EMSRV 6.22 for Windows NT Apr  4 1998 15:36:56 (AEST)


Total Connects: 1  Total Disconnects:     0
Total Opens: 0  Total Closes:     0
Active Locks:     0  Unexpected Connection Closes: 0
Total Locks: 0  Total Unlocks:          0
Total Reads: 0  Total Writes:     0
Total Reads Failed On Lock:          0
Total Locks Failed On Lock:          0
Times Lock Limit Hit:                0
Total Requests Serviced:             5
Requests in last interval:           0
Largest Packet Sent:   70 Largest Packet Received:  12
Server Has Been Alive For: 0 Days 1 Hours 4 Minutes 38 Seconds
Server Working Directory : D:\apps\va45

-------------------------------------------------

=========================================================
```

If EMSRV is not running or is inaccessible, the utility produces something like

```
EMADMIN 6.22
Copyright (C) IBM Corporation 1989-1998
Error Querying Server
```

First run EMADMIN on the server machine, which should verify if the process is running. Then try running it from the client workstation. If both the server and client can find it, there's a good chance you can connect from a development environment. Remember to specify the correct host name, and try using an IP address if you have trouble with the host name.

Common Problems

The most common EMSRV problems are either that the server just won't start, or that once it has started the client can't connect to it. This covers a lot of ground, but it does help narrow the problem down. Server failure is most frequently due to either directory or account setup/login problems. Inability to connect from the client is typically due to networking problems.

You'll need to debug your configuration, which is like any debugging or detective effort. Don't take anything for granted. If you can run EMADMIN from the server but not from the client, test to be sure you can ping the server. We've been in situations in which, after considerable frustration, someone finally remembered the network reorganization that left the client machine with an invalid IP address for the server in its hosts file. Once we changed it, everything worked.

Make sure the software is being found, and that the versions are consistent. If the ENVY shared libraries are unreachable, you may not get an informative error message. If you have multiple versions of ENVY installed, you need to be careful that the shared libraries and executables that are found are consistent. If you've installed EMSRV correctly but an older version of EMADMIN is first in your path, then it may fail to find the server even though everything is running correctly. EMSRV has good backward-compatibility, so it should be fine to run a more recent version of EMSRV than was distributed with your installation, as long as you have the right version of the corresponding tools. Always check the release notes for any possible incompatibilities.

Another common problem arises after the initial setup, when doing import/export. If you are exporting, it might be to a file on the client, or to one on the server, depending on a number of factors. It's easy for a user to try to import/export to a floppy drive that turns out to be on the server rather than his or her local machine. On an NT server, if there is no floppy disk in the drive, the entire EMSRV process freezes while it waits for one. This locks out all other users, and can be very frustrating.

Multiple Images

Many developers have multiple images installed in their machine, some of them connected to different repositories. This is actually quite easy to do, and most of the files involved can be shared. There are several different cases, including

- multiple images in one directory
- multiple images in different directories
- multiple repositories

Multiple Images in One Directory

This is the simplest case because all the directory structures remain the same. Set up shortcuts or scripts that invoke the executable, supplying the name of the image as a parameter.

In VisualAge you would do the following:

> abt.exe –imyProgram.icx

or simply create another copy of the VisualAge executable, whose name is the same as the image you are launching.

> myProgram.exe

 In VisualWorks, if the last command-line argument has no leading "-", it is automatically treated as the name of the image file.

> visual.exe myProgram.im

Multiple Images in Different Directories

It can be less confusing if images for separate projects have their own directory structures. This is more complicated to set up, but helps avoid problems later. For these purposes, we're assuming all these images share a common repository.

First, make sure that all the associated executables and libraries can be found from each directory. This can be accomplished by copying them into each directory, at the cost of some space usage, or you can set up your PATH so that they are correctly found by the operating system.

You will need to copy certain files into each directory, and the exact files vary by dialect.

 In VisualAge, if you have the ABT.EXE executable in the same directory as your standard configuration files, you do not need a copy of either ABT.CNF or ABT.INI files.

> ABT.ICX – the image
> ABT.CNF – (optional) this doesn't hold anything useful, but is still read in VA 4.5. It is
>   not required in VA 5.0.
> ABT.INI - (optional) the configuration information

 In VisualWorks, if you have the VISUAL.EXE executable in the same directory as your standard ENVY.CNF file, you do not need a copy of ENVY.CNF in your directory. Otherwise, you will need to copy it.

> VISUAL.IM – the image
> ENVY.CNF - (optional) the configuration information
> Any shared libraries not visible to the executable (e.g., not in the PATH)

Set up shortcuts or scripts as in the single-directory case, but be sure to set the working directory to the one containing the image, and to explicitly specify the image with a command-line argument. If you do not specify it, the system may decide to use the image from the same directory as the executable, defeating this setup. In any case, verify that you have two independent images by running each, opening a workspace with some distinctive text, and saving it. Then run the other image and be sure you don't see that text.

It's also usually a good idea to name the images differently, making it easier to tell which one you're dealing with. There are few situations as confusing as having launched two different development images and trying to sort out which windows belong to which one, and which context you're working in right now.

Finally, under Windows it's possible to associate the image file type with the executable so that you can launch the environment just by double-clicking on the image file. This is convenient, but can be a problem if you have multiple different versions of your environment installed.

Different Repositories

You can also set up images in different directories to access different repositories. One circumstance where this is very useful is with a laptop computer that uses both a shared repository and one on the local hard drive.

This setup requires some additional files to be copied.

 In VisualWorks, use the same setup as in the case of multiple images in different directories, but be sure to copy the ENVY.CNF file into the image directory and edit it to access the correct repository, and possibly change the shared libraries used for access (VisualWorks 3.0 only) if the repositories are accessed differently. The files required are:

- VISUAL.IM — the image
- ENVY.CNF — the configuration information
- Any shared libraries not visible to the executable (for example, not in the PATH)

 In VisualAge, you will need the following:

- ABT.ICX — the image file
- ABT.CNF — the old configuration file; not used, but still required in VA 4.5 (not required in VA 5.0)
- ABT.EXE — the executable
- ABT.INI — the configuration information
- RGB.TXT — definitions associating color names to RGB values

You will need to edit ABT.INI to access the correct repository, and possibly change the server name.

Passwords

In ENVY, it's important to know who the current user is. Users can only version class editions they've created, can only release classes they own, and can only create editions of applications they manage. Most of the time, developers will work as themselves, but occasionally it's useful to change identities and work as a different user. For example, a class owner may be unavailable, or an operation may require library supervisor privileges.

In these types of circumstances, changing users is justified, but it can also cause many problems. The most common of these is changing users and forgetting to change back, doing work as the other user. You end up having to retrace the chain of operations, switching users along the way. Worse yet, if developers are working as users other than themselves, you lose traceability and can disrupt the regular ENVY development process. In general, we recommend avoiding changing users unless it's really necessary.

By default, ENVY does not require any authentication to change users. For the reasons previously described, you may want to turn on password checking. The most common mechanism is "native passwords," in which ENVY requests the password for the corresponding network account to change to that user. Under UNIX, you also have the option to use "shadow" passwords.

A distinction also exists between the treatment of passwords in VisualWorks 3.0 and that in VisualWorks 5i and VisualAge. In VisualWorks 3.0, password checking is controlled from the client by specifying the shared library to use. Another DLL controls the mode of access to the repository. This is both insecure and awkward to configure. Users with access to the ENVY installation could easily switch DLLs on their client and circumvent password checking. With the more recent versions password checking is controlled from the server, and no mechanism exists for turning off password checking from the client.

The ENVY password-checking mechanism should not be seen as high-security, and would be unlikely to exclude malevolent users, but it does provide some ability to control access, and can motivate developers who might otherwise ignore the established procedures to follow a more defined process. Many organizations do not require password checking, either because they rely on programmer discipline or because they follow a different process. This is entirely reasonable, but it's a choice that should be made consciously. For more discussion of passwords and ownership, see Chapter 3. For information on exactly how to enable and configure password checking, see the documentation for your version of ENVY.

VisualAge Features

VisualAge uses the idea of "features," packages not in the base image or even the base repository, which can still be loaded at will. A feature is specified by a .CTL file, which lists the configuration maps it uses and the ENVY export files they are stored in. The user can see a list of all available features, and choose to load one, at which point it automatically is imported and loaded, along with any prerequisite features.

Features are built on top of the normal ENVY application and configuration map environment. They provide two major additional features. First, a feature can be loaded as a single step, even if it includes many different ENVY components. Second, those features don't even have to be imported into the repository. The feature load will search for the .DAT files and automatically import them. This lets us distribute add-on products that install themselves into a directory, but don't require the user to import them before loading.

During normal development, you will not create features unless you are building a third-party product for distribution to VisualAge developers. The main thing you

(VA) need to ensure is that you can correctly access and load features. The main details to check here are the two feature-related directories specified in the configuration file.

- installationPath — the path on the client to find the .CTL files. This must *not* contain a trailing separator.

- importDirectory — the path on the server to find the .DAT files. This *must* include a trailing separator.

It's important not to confuse these directories, and these are settings that may require manual customization. In a team environment, you typically want a single import directory on the server, rather than duplicating import files on client machines. The setup program makes it easy to install the import files on the client, and then manually copy them to the server and adjust each client's importDirectory.

Customizing Setup

Once you have a basic setup, you may want to customize it. As a user, you may have additional configuration options you want to specify. As an administrator, you may want to create a custom base image for developers. This can include preloading commonly used code and setting up some of the environment options in the image. These options are found in the settings dialog boxes or in the special predefined workspace known as either the Preferences Workspace (VisualAge) or the ENVY Workspace (VisualWorks).

This is a large predefined workspace containing Smalltalk code that can be evaluated to customize features of the environment. There are many useful options here and you may want to change your settings from the system defaults. Here are some of the most useful, with the settings we recommend.

EtClassBrowser methodFiltering: #ShowPublicPrivateAll
> By default, the browsers show only public methods, and if you want to see private methods you need to toggle the browser to show only private methods. This option makes the browsers default to showing both public and private methods.

EtAbstractMethodsBrowser showPrivatePublicOnOpen: true
> This option makes the browser display "(public)" or "(private)" after the name of a method, most useful in combination with the previous option.

EmImageBuilder cancelIfMethodsCollide: false
> By default, ENVY cancels an entire load if any method is defined in more than one application. This helps ensure no conflicts exist, but makes it very difficult to resolve conflicts that arise. Setting this option makes the most recent load overwrite any previous definitions of the method, which lets you get on with what you're doing. It's important to pay attention, though, and go back and fix the problem later because this option opens up the possibility that the state of the image can change depending on the order in which components were loaded.

EmImageBuilder cancelIfMethodsDoNotCompile: false

> Similarly, ENVY cancels a load if any method cannot be compiled, most likely due to class extensions or subclasses that rely on a different definition of the base class than what is loaded. This situation may also arise due to incorrect prerequisites. Again, you usually want the load to go ahead so you can fix the problem, either now or later.

EmTimeStamp showVersionTimeStamps: true

> Normally, in a browser, open editions show their timestamp (time of creation) and versions show their version name. Sometimes it's also useful to know the timestamps of versions, and this option lets you see them. This one is a matter of personal preference. It gives you useful information, but makes it harder to pick out open editions in the application manager.

EmClassEditionEntry compareMethodSource: true

> When comparing changes in a changes browser, the system normally goes only by method timestamp. This is faster, but means that methods with identical source code may still compare as different. If you transfer code through file-out/file-in, rather than through export/import, set this option to true.

EtClassBrowser showListHorizontalScrollBars: true

> If you have a smaller screen, this option is very useful for seeing the full names of components displayed in list panes.

Resetting the Image Owner

Finally, there's one very useful expression to know when customizing setup.

> EmUser resetImageOwner

When we first start up a clean ENVY image, the first thing it asks is the name of the image owner. If we distribute our own base image to developers, we'd like it to do the same thing. Otherwise they'll all get an image set up for Library Supervisor and must remember to change the user. If we evaluate this expression, the image reverts to being unowned, and starts up like it was a clean image.

Summary

This chapter has helped get you on your way with ENVY. For developers, we have explained the basic architecture of the tool, and how to get yourself set up with a development environment, including perhaps more options than you really wanted just yet. For administrators, we have reviewed the architecture, and looked at how you can configure the environment for your developers. The toolsmiths probably already knew all this stuff, but perhaps they found a few new things to learn about setup.

Some of the important details to remember from this chapter are:

- ENVY is a generic term for many of OTI's products. Typically, when people say ENVY they refer to ENVY/Developer, or specifically to ENVY/Manager, the team-programming tool.

- ENVY replaces the traditional Smalltalk change log with a unified database of all source and object code.

- ENVY puts in place a disciplined team-programming approach, based on software components and component ownership.

- ENVY can access the repository using either direct file access or a server process (EMSRV).

- You have a number of issues to watch out for with EMSRV installations.

- You can configure ENVY in a variety of ways to support multiple development environments on the same workstation.

- Password checking is an important option, and one that should be evaluated early in a project's life.

- You have many different ways to configure the ENVY image, some of which should be site-wide, and others of which are developer preferences.

═Chapter 2═

Basic Concepts

Before you can start to use ENVY effectively, many questions need answering, even if you already understand Smalltalk development. How do I write code using ENVY? How is that code organized? How do I coordinate with other team members? What's a configuration map?

This chapter sorts out the basic concepts in ENVY, and starts you on the path toward being a productive developer. We start out by discussing development as an individual. In Chapter 3 we move on to team development, and Chapter 4 covers more advanced topics.

The discussion here is aimed at a new user who has at least some experience with Smalltalk development. We'll discuss not only the features but their motivations and best practices, illustrating with examples. The chapter starts out simple, but things will get complicated quickly. Be patient; it'll take some time to become familiar with all of these concepts. More experienced users will find the best practices most interesting, if only to find things they disagree with. Those users looking for a shorter, more formal description of ENVY concepts should see Chapter 5.

Questions and Answers

The example project we'll be using is a simple questionnaire application. There are questions, and there are answers. Questions are strung together into groups, and depending on the answers to one question, the follow-up questions may change. For example, suppose we asked the question, *How would you rate this book?* If the response was *Poor*, then we don't need to ask any more questions because the user clearly has bad judgment. On the other hand, if the response was *Excellent*, then the system needs to ask a number of other questions to determine exactly which parts of the book were most appreciated.

We will use this software to gather user satisfaction and feature information on our other projects. It should be able to function either interactively or over the Web, and we may eventually want it to connect to an interactive voice response system ("If you liked the book, press 2"). Of course, we will also define a test suite for the software to ensure that it is working correctly. This will be based on the open source SUnit testing framework (*www.xprogramming.com*). The system will have to work on multiple different platforms, and we may need to introduce some platform-specific code to facilitate this.

Software Components

Before we can do anything in ENVY, we need to understand the ENVY concept of *software components*. This is a formal term that describes the ways ENVY organizes software. Four main types of components exist: methods, classes, applications, and configuration maps. Methods and classes are treated more or less the same way as they are in regular Smalltalk, so let's start out by considering applications.

Applications

In ENVY, *applications* are what we use to organize classes and methods into larger groupings. They correspond to what are often called *modules* or *packages* in other systems. In fact, the term "application" can be misleading because it implies that an entire program should be built with a single application. In fact, any reasonable-sized programs will have code organized into several different applications, and large projects may have dozens or hundreds.

An application contains both classes and methods, and is said to *control* them. In an ENVY image, classes and methods cannot exist outside an application, and each must be uniquely controlled by one application (although we'll see later how classes can be split up between applications).

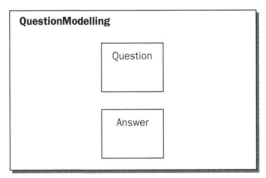

Figure 2-1: Applications and classes.

Example: Creating an Application

We can create an application in several different places, including the Applications Browser, the Application Manager, and the VisualAge Organizer. Let's create a new application called *QuestionModelling* (see the "Application Naming" section). We may be asked in which namespace we want the Application class (VisualWorks 5i). If so, choose either namespace; the choice doesn't matter right now. In either dialect, we will see a complex dialog box asking us to select prerequisites for this application. We haven't looked at prerequisites yet, so just use the defaults.

If we created this application from the Application Manager or the VisualAge Organizer, we should now have our application selected, and we will want to browse it. This is available as a pop-up menu item called either Browse Application (from the Application Manager) or Open (from the VisualAge Organizer). Note that in the VisualAge Organizer you will need to have Full Menus enabled on the Options menu to make the Open menu item visible for applications.

Once we can browse the QuestionModelling application, we can create a new class Question to start our domain model. We'll create it as a subclass of Object. In VisualAge we can do this by selecting Object in the browser, and using the pop-up menu item Add→Subclass.... In VisualWorks, we cannot select the class Object directly, but we can just fill in the class definition template appropriately and save it. You may notice that our application also contains a class QuestionModelling, which is a subclass of something called Application. We can ignore this class for now, but if you're curious about it, see the "Application Classes" section later in this chapter.

Classes and Extensions

In ENVY, software components form a hierarchy. Applications organize classes, and classes organize methods. However, classes in this hierarchy can be divided among multiple applications. This lets us organize individual methods or groups of methods, which turns out to be tremendously useful. It lets us add functionality to system or other classes, while still managing that functionality in the module where it belongs. This gives us enormous flexibility while maintaining a disciplined approach to development.

Exactly one application will be the *controller* of a class, and the class is described as being *defined* in that application. This *class definition* holds not only the literal class definition (for example, variables, class variables, and so forth), but typically holds most of the methods. The definition and the methods defined with it cannot be changed or extended in other applications. Nevertheless, we can add methods to the class in another application, in what is called a *class extension*.

To see why this is important, consider the class Object. This is the most fundamental class in the system, and it is defined in the Kernel application. However, there are many different methods added to Object, supporting a variety of add-on tools. EtBaseTools is the application that holds most of the standard development tools. One of the methods that it defines on Object is inspect. Without class extensions, we would have to either add a method, which assumes both a GUI and a development environment into the most basic system class, or else we would have to dispense the ability to send #inspect to any object.

This ability to divide a class has significant effects on the browsers. When you browse an application, you may only see some of the methods for classes within it, specifically those methods defined in that application. If you browse a class, you will see a pane in the browser listing applications. If multiple applications exist, you can select one or more of them, and this will show methods only in the applications you have selected.

We can think of a class and its extensions as being written on sheets of paper or transparencies. At the bottom level is the class definition, written normally. Above that, we can layer additional methods, written on onionskin paper or a transparent slide. We can see the extensions, but we can also see through them to the definition below, and together they form the entire class. We can layer as many different extensions as we like this way, and when we load a new application it may add new layers to some of our existing classes. This does not affect the functionality that was there before, but may add new methods. From Smalltalk's point of view, it's all a single class, but as the developer, we can pull out any layer and examine or modify it separately.

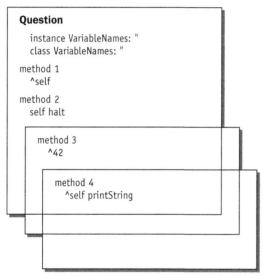

Figure 2-2: Classes and extensions.

Methods

ENVY also treats methods as separate components, in the sense that version control and loading can operate down to the method level, but for the moment we will ignore that aspect and treat classes as the lowest-level component.

Configuration Maps

The largest software component ENVY defines is the *configuration map*. If applications are analogous to modules, then configuration maps are project or program specifications. A configuration map can also be thought of as a complete *bill-of-materials*

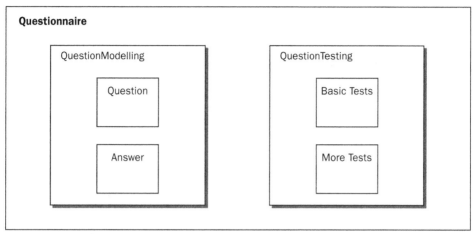

Figure 2-3: The Questionnaire project setup.

for a project because it specifies applications, which in turn specify classes and class extensions, which in turn specify methods.

A small project may not need the organizational features of configuration maps, and be able to fit everything within a single application. Although our example application is definitely small, we're going to set it up as a full-blown configuration map with three different applications.

Example: Creating a Configuration Map

Let's step through the process of creating a configuration map. From the main ENVY menu, select Browse Configuration Maps. This opens a browser with several different panes. In the Names pane at the far left, use the pop-up menu to create a new configuration map, called Questionnaire. This automatically selects an edition from the Versions and Editions pane, and enables you to add applications from the pop-up menu in the Applications pane (upper right). Add the QuestionModelling application we created earlier.

Prerequisites

Applications have various properties, the most important of which is their list of *prerequisites*. A prerequisite is a way of defining exactly which other code an application expects to access. In Java, this sort of information is provided through import statements listing the used classes or packages, and in C/C++ through included header files. In ENVY individual classes do not specify this information. Instead, it is maintained at the application level. This helps keep the amount of information more manageable, and it means that ENVY applications tend to be closely related to the program's overall structure.

Code in a particular application can only use classes and methods that are defined within that application or its prerequisites. Of course, these prerequisites may have their own prerequisites, and that code can also be used. The set of all classes reachable through this tree of prerequisites is referred to as the *visible* classes.

Information on prerequisites and class visibility may be used when trying to package an image into a minimal run-time. It can also be used in configuration management to determine which other components depend on a changed component.

ENVY imposes the rule that the tree of prerequisites must strictly form a tree. That is, all applications must have at least one prerequisite, except Kernel. All chains of prerequisites will thus end at Kernel. For example, if we decide that our VisualAge GUI for our Questionnaire application will use text widgets with monetary amount formatting support, we might include the application EwMonetaryTextSupport as a prerequisite. This in turn has a prerequisite of ScaledDecimalMath, which in turn has a prerequisite of Kernel, which has no prerequisites.

Furthermore, ENVY imposes the restriction that cycles are not permitted in the graph defined by prerequisite relationships. I cannot have QuestionModelling be a prerequisite to QuestionTesting and simultaneously have QuestionTesting be a prerequisite

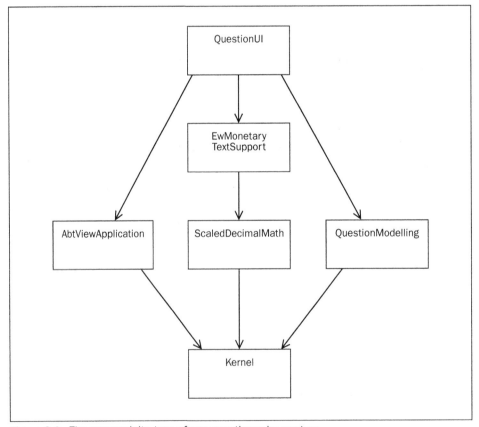

Figure 2-4: The prerequisite tree of our questionnaire system.

to QuestionModelling. All chains of prerequisites must lead directly back to Kernel, without circling back on themselves. This is probably not a major concern right now, but it does mean that we will have to exercise some thought in partitioning our application into layers.

Prerequisite Enforcement

Note that these prerequisite relationships are not necessarily enforced and may not even be enforceable. In Smalltalk, any method can use any class or method that's available in the image. Because there is no compile-time type information and a rich reflection facility, the system has no way of guaranteeing in advance exactly which classes and methods will be accessed. ENVY enforces the prohibition on circular dependencies, and detects most static violations at the class level.

For example, if we're working in VisualAge and we subclass our class Question from AbtAppBldrNonVisual (roughly equivalent to the VisualWorks class Model), then the system knows we depend on the application AbtRunNonVisualApp that contains that class. This class is part of the VisualAge visual tools, so it would not be present in a plain IBM Smalltalk image. ENVY detects and enforces this dependency, so it will not let us add our subclass unless AbtRunNonVisualApp is included in the prerequisites for QuestionModelling. Once we have added the application to our prerequisites, we will not be able to load our QuestionModelling application into an IBM Smalltalk or VisualWorks image because one of its prerequisites would be missing.

ENVY treats class extensions similarly to subclassing. It reliably detects the prerequisites and ensures that we have the application with the class definition included in our prerequisite list. References to nonvisible classes, however, are treated as a warning, with number 49.

```
Warning: 49   Question>#invalidAnswer should not reference
        QuestionUI::InvalidAnswerDialog.
```

One problem is that this is only a warning, and it's easy to make the mistake of ignoring it. Other dependencies may also be introduced by using reflection to construct class names from strings, perform arbitrary symbols, or otherwise use classes and methods dynamically. This code may run correctly during development, but will generate errors in packaging or fail to run in a packaged form. This is a good reason (if you didn't have enough already) to ensure that your code is thoroughly tested in a deployment environment. Note that if we load our code into a clean image, the Transcript will once again show the compilation warnings, and we can review them at that time.

Prerequisites and Loading

Internally, ENVY also uses prerequisites to determine which applications need to be loaded and the order in which to load them. Before explaining this, we should make a short digression to explain loading.

The ENVY repository holds many different components, far more than are normally in the image. We refer to the components in the repository that have an executable form in the current image as being *loaded*. The traditional way of recreating executable classes and methods from secondary storage is to compile Smalltalk source code from files, called *file-in*. Loading a component in ENVY is significantly different from this filing-in. For one thing, the repository stores compiled code as well as source code. This means that code can be loaded very quickly, and that source code is not required for loading.

Another difference from file-in is that the loads are *atomic*. This means that, like a database transaction, the load will either complete successfully, or fail gracefully by returning us to the same state we were in before it began. In comparison, if we file in code using the regular Smalltalk mechanisms, it may make some changes to the state of an image, and then encounter an error and terminate. At that point, we are left with part of the changes loaded and part of them missing, with our environment in an inconsistent state. Note that other mechanisms exist to allow fast, atomic loads, including VisualWorks parcels and VisualAge ICs, but these are dialect-specific and are used for different purposes than the ENVY loading mechanism.

Prerequisites are used in the loading process to ensure that code is correctly brought into memory. When we attempt to load an application, all of its prerequisites must already be loaded or must be in the process of loading. If a prerequisite is missing, the system prompts to see if we want to load it as well. If we choose not to, or if the prerequisite is unavailable, the load will fail.

Unloading

ENVY enables us to manage components, and so components that have been loaded can be unloaded. This is also a significant difference from file-in, where code, which has been loaded, becomes intermingled with the base system code and cannot be removed. Because ENVY knows the component boundaries, it can unlink and remove code just as easily as it can load it. Note that unloading code from an image does not mean that this code is deleted from the repository. Ordinarily, things are never deleted from the repository, so it's always possible to reload.

There are some restrictions on unloading that can make it more difficult than loading in practice. The primary restriction is that it is not possible to unload a class with instances. For example, if we have created instances of our Question class, and have an inspector open on a collection of them, we will not be able to unload the QuestionModelling application. Unloading in this circumstance would leave active objects with no corresponding class to define their structure or behavior, and this is not permitted by the system. Similarly, you cannot unload an application that is a prerequisite of some other loaded application unless you first unload the other application. In this case, ENVY tells you which applications are causing a problem, but does not automatically unload them, so getting the order of unload correct can be tedious when we have a deep tree of dependencies.

Review and Example

Let's briefly reiterate what we have read. Applications contain classes and/or class extensions. Class extensions let us split up a class into multiple pieces, adding methods in other applications. Relationships between applications are structured in two different ways. First, prerequisites determine which other applications are required for this one to operate. Configuration maps let us add a higher-level structure to organize multiple applications into an entire project.

Consider our Questionnaire project. In some of the earlier sidebars in this chapter we created the basic application and a configuration map. Let's look at what our complete structure will be (see Figure 2-5).

We have a domain model in the application QuestionModelling. Its prerequisites are minimal, just Kernel. This is appropriate because right now the domain model does not require any classes other than the basic Smalltalk system classes.

We will also need to test our domain model. For this purpose, we will use the open-source testing framework SUnit, and assume that we have loaded it into an application called SUnit. To hold our tests we'll create a QuestionTesting application. This application will need to make use of the testing framework code, and it will also need to exercise the code it's testing, so we'll add the prerequisites QuestionModelling and SUnit. If you want to follow along with these steps but don't have SUnit, you can either create an empty SUnit application as a temporary placeholder, or you can download the SUnit code as described in the section on "Downloading the Code."

Finally, we'll need a configuration map so that we can easily load all of our components together. We'll call it Questionnaire, and add QuestionTesting and QuestionModelling to it. Eventually, we'll want a user interface for this application, but we'll ignore that for now.

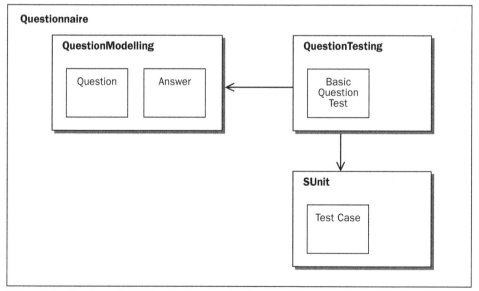

Figure 2-5: The Questionnaire project organization.

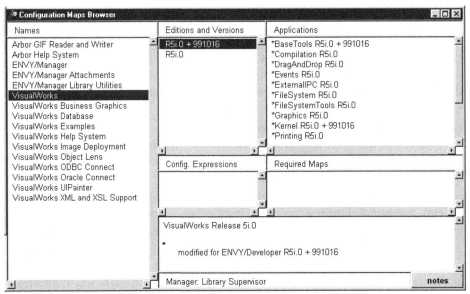

Figure 2-6: The Configuration Maps Browser.

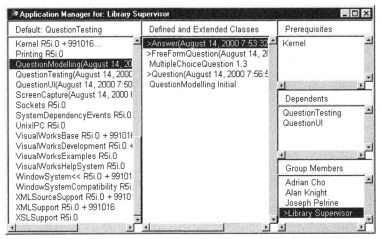

Figure 2-7: The Application Manager with our Questionnaire project.

Version Control

Components don't give us all that much by themselves. We can organize our code within an image, but we haven't seen how to coordinate among users or to how deal with different versions of code. We've been dealing with a subset of ENVY that follows more or less the same image-based model as a standalone environment. We can identify any component completely, just by knowing its name and the type of component it is. Now we are going to introduce some complications because ENVY also works as a version-control system, which allows different editions of components to coexist.

Editions

So far, we've thought of a software component as a single, unified thing — a class, a method, or an application. In fact, multiple different copies of the same component can exist, and we call these *editions*. Each edition is a completely separate copy of the same component, and is distinguished from other editions by a timestamp. For example, in setting up our application, we might have created an edition of the class Question with the timestamp (November 3, 1999 7:51:35 p.m.). So far, this is the only edition, but later we might create another one with the timestamp (November 4, 1999 9:07:35 a.m.). These will be two separate copies, and operating on one of them will not change the other.

There are many reasons we might have multiple editions of a component, but the main reason is to provide version control. We may use different editions to represent a history of development over time (editions for each release of our system) or to represent different streams of development (an edition for bug fixes to our initial Questionnaire system and a separate edition for new development on Questionnaire Pro 2000).

We identify different editions of components by their *signature*, which is the combination of the name and timestamp. For example, the application with the signature Kernel (10/4/97 15:00:01) is an application with the name Kernel that was created on the 10th of April 1997 at 3:00:01 p.m.

Note that edition timestamps indicate the time of creation of an edition, and never change. For example, with our Question class edition, created at 7:51:35 p.m., it does not matter how many changes we make to that class; over that period, the timestamp remains the same. This is different from using timestamps for things such as files, where the timestamp normally tracks the last modification to the file rather than its creation.

Versions

The editions we have described so far are *open editions*. These are identified purely by their timestamp, and can be modified at any point. For version control, we'd like to be able to freeze an edition in a particular state, give it a name, and know that it won't change from that point forward. We can do this by making the edition into a *version*.

A version is an edition that also has a name, for example, Version 1.0.2. By giving it a name, we make it immutable — a permanent snapshot of the component at the time of naming. Versions are generally shown with their name and no timestamp, although the timestamp is still recorded. For example, if we take Question (November 27, 1999 7:51:35 p.m.) and version it, it will have the new signature of Question 1.0. We can still determine the timestamp, but it's easier to think about a version in terms of its name. Figure 2-8 shows a variety of versions and editions in the Application Manager.

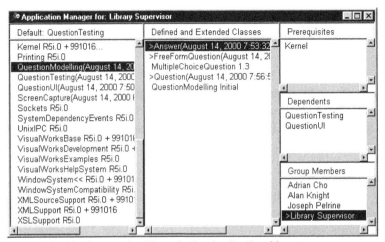

Figure 2-8: Versions and editions in the Application Manager.

While the essential concepts are the same for all components, we will see a number of cases in which ENVY treats different types of components slightly differently, in the interests of streamlining the development process. These differences are usually based on how coarse or fine-grained a component is, and whether we expect it to be shared or private. An example of this occurs with method editions, where ENVY streamlines their treatment to avoid some of the overhead associated with explicitly versioning and naming components. Accordingly, methods are always open editions, and it's not possible to version or to name a method edition. On the other hand, we'll also see later that in some ways method editions behave more like versions.

Edition Lifecycle

When we first create a component, it exists as an open edition. After that, we will normally make versions of these editions, and create new editions from these versions indefinitely, until we stop working on this component.

In this process it's important to distinguish operations that makes copies from operations that modify components in place. If we have a version and we create a new edition from it, we are making a copy of that version into a new open edition.

Creating a Class Edition

ENVY offers two ways to create a new class edition. There's a menu item called Create New Edition that explicitly creates one. Usually this is too much work, so if you simply go ahead and start modifying a class, ENVY automatically creates a new edition for you. You'll see an informational message on the Transcript telling you that this happened.

Info: 109 Made Question (1/16/00 4:08:58 p.m.) from Question 1.0 in
QuestionModelling(12/19/99 10:43:30 a.m.).

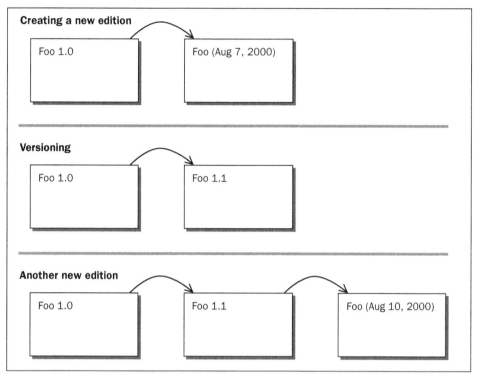

Figure 2-9: Changing versions into editions and then versioning those editions. Note that copying occurs only when creating new editions.

The initial state of that open edition will be exactly the same as the state of the version. In contrast, when we version an open edition, we are assigning a name to that edition and freezing it. No new copy is made. In general, we always create a new edition from a version, although we will see an exception to that in the section on "Checkpointing." We can also make as many new editions as we like from a particular version, which allows for branching streams.

When we create a new edition, it is based on the version from which it was created. There doesn't have to be a previous version (for example, if it is a new component), but if there is one, ENVY can use that information to easily load or compare to the previous edition.

Versioning of a component typically takes place for one of two reasons. Sometimes there are many changes being made to a component over a long period. It can be very convenient if there is at least one point in the history of those changes to which the user can return if development hits a dead end. This is often called *freezing* or *baselining* and it is a technique we discuss in detail later on. In addition, there is the obvious case when changes to a component within a project release cycle have been completed. It is then appropriate to freeze those changes. Versioning brings the added benefit that the changes may be labeled with a version name such as *1.1 [Fixed PR 13459]*. In that example, PR 13459 might be a report submitted by a user of the system or product, describing a defect.

Version Naming Options

When you version a class, you are presented with several different menu options, which could use a bit of explanation. All of these make use of the standard ENVY naming conventions. For more information on these conventions and on alternatives, see the "Naming Conventions" section.

- **Version->Name Each:** This option prompts for a name for each selected class individually. This option provides the most control but can rapidly become tedious if we have many different classes to version.

- **Version->One Name:** This option prompts for a single version name, which it attempts to apply to all of the selected classes. If there are conflicts with existing version names for any of the classes, you will be prompted for a new name, following the default ENVY naming conventions.

- **Version->Use Defaults:** This option applies the default ENVY naming conventions to automatically choose a name for all selected classes. This starts new classes at 1.0, and thereafter increment version numbers automatically.

- **Version/Release All:** This is a separate menu option with three submenu choices corresponding to the preceding items. In each case, it applies the naming option to *all* of the open class editions in that application, *not just the selected classes*. It also releases all of the classes that are not currently released, again ignoring the selection.

Version/Release All

One point in the previous sidebar is worth emphasizing again. When we version using the Version/Release All menu item, it affects *all* classes in that application. It ignores the selected set of classes, applies that version name to all of the open class editions, and releases all unreleased classes. All of the operations work on multiple selections; the point of the All keyword is that you don't need to make a selection. This is a frequent source of confusion.

Terms

ENVY uses many terms in very precise ways, and it's important to make it clear what these terms mean in this context. Because a particular component can have multiple editions, we will use the term *component* to refer to the collection of all editions with the same name for a particular component type. For example, our Question class is a component, and so is our QuestionModelling application.

To specify a particular edition, we will use the term *component edition*. For example, Question 1.0 is a component edition, and so is QuestionTesting (November 27, 1999

7:20:02 p.m.). We may also use the specific name of the component type; for example, we can use *application* to describe an application component or *class edition* to describe a component edition of a class. Note that we will use the term *class edition* to describe either a class definition or a class extension — a fragment of an entire class, controlled by a single application.

The generic term *class* may refer to a class component in all of its editions or occasionally to the more traditional definition of a class and all its methods, regardless of ENVY organization, together in memory.

Finally, when referring to versions and editions, we will use *edition* as the inclusive term for both versions and editions. When we're talking about editions that have been versioned, we will use the term *versions*. When we're talking about editions that have not been versioned, we will use the term *open editions*.

We should also be clear on exactly what it is that makes up a component. Typically, the definition of a component is a specification of a number of subcomponents, forming a tree that ends at method editions, which have no subcomponents. So,

- configuration map editions specify application editions
- application editions specify class editions and prerequisites
- class editions specify instance method editions and class method editions

Releasing Classes

In ENVY, the process of specifying which edition of a subcomponent is used in a parent component is called *releasing*. We are going to talk about releasing different types of components in different sections because this is one of those areas we mentioned earlier in which ENVY treats different component types differently. The reason it does this is to streamline the development process according to the usage patterns of different components. The most frequent releasing operation is releasing classes into applications, so that is where we'll start.

We know that applications reference class editions. How do we know which ones? How do we change them?

Clearly, they have to be able to change. If we create an open edition of an application, and start working on the classes that it contains, then we are creating new open editions of those classes. Our application edition started out holding onto the previous versions of those classes, but it will have to change to refer to our new code.

A particular application edition holds onto a particular class version (it has to be a version, as we'll see later) and this is called the *released* version. The process of making a class the released edition is called *releasing*. Releasing is always relative to a particular edition of the parent component. So, for example, if we release Question 1.0 we are releasing it into one particular edition of the QuestionModelling application. This has no effect on other applications or other editions of the QuestionModelling application.

For example, let's suppose that we've gone through two very short development cycles of our QuestionModelling application. We've created an initial edition, created some classes, written code, versioned the classes, released them, and versioned the application. After that we created a new application edition and class editions and repeated the process. The structure of our application and classes would look something like Figure 2-10.

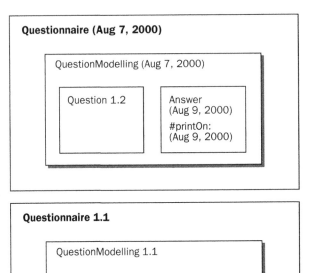

Figure 2-10: Two different versions of the Questionnaire project.

Note that a class version can be released into more than one application, and in fact, this is quite common. If we have two editions of an application, say QuestionModelling 1.0 and 1.1, then any classes we haven't changed between 1.0 and 1.1 will be released into both of them. It is also not necessary that the released edition of a class be the most recent one. We may have a maintenance stream that does not have the most recent versions, or the most recent edition of my application may actually have an older version of some of the classes because the newer versions just weren't stable enough.

Released versus Loaded

The information about which class versions are released into which application editions is stored in the ENVY repository. Just because a version is released doesn't mean it's necessarily the same as what we have loaded into memory.

It helps to understand this if we think about a team environment. So far, we've considered only our own image and the repository, but many other developers may be working on the same project, using the same applications we are. We want to be able to combine the work of others with our own, but we don't want their changes continually appearing in our workspace. To support this, all the changes that any developer makes go into the repository but they are only recorded there, not automatically published to all other developers.

So, how are other people's changes propagated to the group? They are propagated by *releasing* them. In fact, as far as ENVY is concerned, the meaning of *release* is very, very simple. It answers the question, "When I load this application, which versions of the classes should I load?"

The answer is always "the released versions." If a class has been changed, but not yet released into its controlling application, then it won't be loaded when the application is loaded. This means that other developers won't see it if they load, and in fact, if we reload the current application edition, unreleased classes will be replaced by the released version. When we are finished with the class and we want to publish it to others in the group, we need to version and release it.

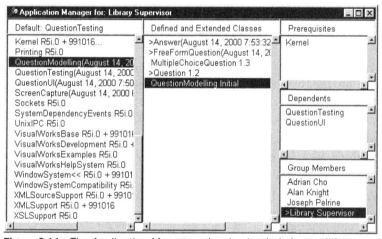

Figure 2-11: The Application Manager, showing loaded class editions including open editions, unreleased versions, and released versions.

Developing with Class Editions

One of the things that affect the way components are treated in ENVY is whether they are considered private or shared in a team environment. In particular, open class editions are considered private to a user. That is, ENVY expects that one user creates an edition and does all the work in it. If multiple users work on the same class at the same time, each gets his or her own private edition, and changes will need to be reconciled later. The idea is that having multiple users in the same class edition at the same time would be too confusing and lead to too much conflict.

The first thing this affects is loading. Normally, any user can browse and/or load any edition of any component. The releasing process defines which editions are loaded automatically when a parent component is loaded, but developers are free to go in and load other editions explicitly. The exception to this is the class edition. Other users can still browse an open class edition in the repository, but only the user who created it can load it. The class edition is said to be *visible* only to the user who created it. This visibility of class editions is a different use of the term *visible* than we saw with class visibility in prerequisite applications. This is potentially confusing, but the meaning is usually clear from the context.

Loading Components

In ENVY, you can load and/or browse any edition of any component from most of the browsers. This is most commonly done from the Application Manager or VisualAge Organizer, but the class and application browsers also support this. Note that if you are browsing in a class-centric view (for example, the hierarchy browser), the menu item to load classes is in the Applications pane. This is because ENVY treats class extensions as separate components, so they are loaded and managed individually in a separate pane.

If we load a component, we usually have several choices, although they don't all apply in every context.

- **Released version:** This option loads the version or edition of the component that is released into the current context. Remember, releasing is always relative to a particular parent, so if the parent you're referring to isn't known in this context, this option won't be available.

- **Previous version:** This option loads the version of the component this one is based on. Previous does not mean "with the next earlier timestamp," but previous in the history of this component.

- **Reload current:** This option loads this version or edition over again. This option is useful for reloading applications to sync up (see the section on "Syncing Up") and in crash recovery.

- **Another edition:** This option is the most general choice, and brings up a dialog box to let you choose which edition to load.

This privacy of open class editions also means they cannot be released. If a class edition is treated as private, then it doesn't make any sense to publish that edition. If other users can't load it, it doesn't make sense for it to be the default when the controlling application is loaded. So, before we can release a class, we have to version it. This makes the typical lifecycle of a class edition as shown in Figure 2-12.

Typically, version and release happen very close together. When we've made a number of changes, and are satisfied that they're ready for others to see, we version

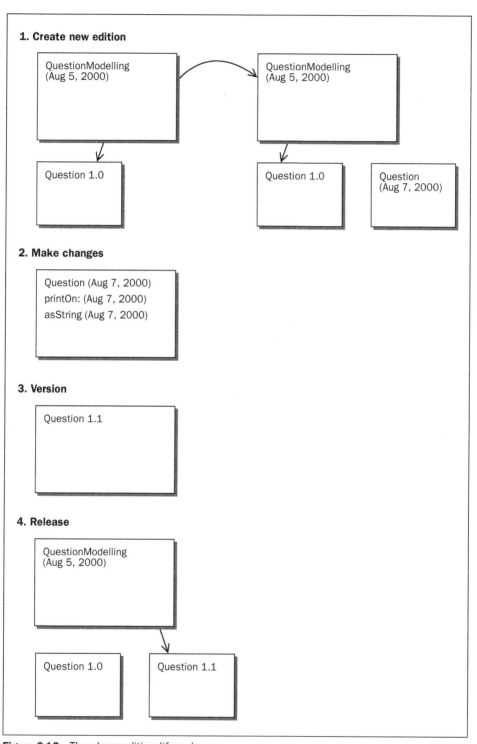

Figure 2-12: The class edition lifecycle.

and release the classes. It's not strictly necessary, though, for version and release to happen at the same time. We might version a class for other reasons. For example, we're about to make some drastic changes, and we want to make sure we can go back to the current state, even if it's not released. We might also version something so that another developer can see it, without making it the default for all developers on the project. For example, we might make a simple workaround for a complex bug and enable other developers to load it, but wait for a more complete fix before publishing. By far the most common case, though, is version and immediate release.

We'll see more about the different roles and privileges for users later, and we'll see how this separation of versioning and releasing is essential to the way ENVY supports team development. We will also see that this treatment of releasing is different for application and configuration map editions, which are not private and are typically shared. In Chapter 3, we will also see what happens when several private editions contain changes to the same class, and how ENVY helps resolve these conflicts.

Complications

This chapter has proviced a basic picture of the development structure in ENVY. With this knowledge you will have enough information to do individual development. There are, however, a few complications you should be aware of.

Application Classes

ENVY provides hooks to run user code in response to various events in the application lifecycle. This lets us do things such as initialize certain classes after an application is loaded, or clean up before it's about to be unloaded. The way this is implemented is by providing a special class inside the application, with the same name as the application. So, our QuestionModelling application will contain a class called QuestionModelling. By default, this class starts out with a version name of Initial. It will be a subclass of the class Application.

For the moment, we don't need to worry too much about this class, but it's important to be aware of it so that we don't get confused by its presence. It's also very important not to confuse the class with the application it represents. Both have the same name, and new ENVY users often make the mistake of subclassing this class, confusing the subclass relationship between classes with the containment relationship between a class and an application. For more information on the events this can be used for, see the "Prerequisites and Loading" and "Unloading" sections earlier in this chapter.

Method Editions

As the most fine-grained components in ENVY, methods are treated specially in a number of respects. Unlike open class editions, method editions are not private to a developer, and can be loaded by any user. This might seem strange because methods are even finer grained than classes, but other factors make it unnecessary to enforce the same sort of privacy we see with open class editions. First, it's very rare to explicitly load

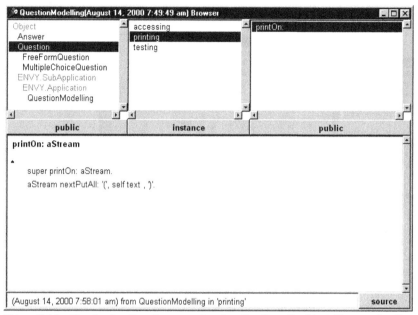

Figure 2-13: The Application Browser showing the QuestionModelling application. Note the class QuestionModelling, which inherits from Application, and that this relationship has no relation to the other domain classes.

a method edition. Users will typically just load the enclosing class edition. Second, method editions in ENVY are immutable objects. If two different users change a class edition, they are both altering the same record in the repository, most likely changing some of the methods that compose that class edition. Because method editions are the most basic component, there's nothing internal to change. Each change to a method edition creates a completely new method edition with a new timestamp and all relevant data. This means that two users can work on the same method without conflicting, and it's not necessary to enforce additional restrictions.

Two other special factors for methods help eliminate unnecessary work for the developer. Because so many method editions exist and they are rarely dealt with individually, method editions are never explicitly given version names, and are always identified only by timestamps. It's also not necessary to release method editions; they are automatically released into the loaded class edition every time a change is made. This eliminates what would be an enormous amount of tedious versioning and releasing of individual methods. In practice what this means is that we normally don't even think of methods as being managed by ENVY, and can concentrate on the class level.

Undefined Classes

We have said that when an application is loaded, ENVY automatically loads the released versions of the classes it contains. What if there is *no* released version of the class, either because no one has released any version of that class, or because the class

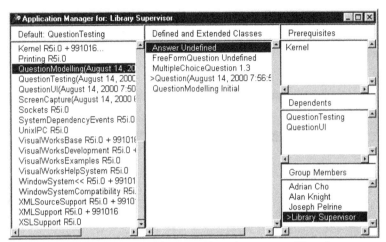

Figure 2-14: The Application Manager. Note that some of the classes are undefined, and that the QuestionModelling application class still has the default version name of Initial. Also note that the prerequisites are listed, but specified only by name.

was deleted from that application edition? In such a case, we refer to the class as *Undefined*. If we look at the class in the context of that application, we will see the version number/edition timestamp as the special string *Undefined*. An example of this is shown in Figure 2-14.

Of course, this applies only to the class in one particular application edition. Other applications may have a definition or an extension to that class, and even other editions of the same application may have it.

Prerequisite Versions

Earlier we said that components specify editions of their various subcomponents. Class editions specify method editions. Configuration map editions specify application editions. Application editions specify class editions and prerequisites. However, the prerequisites are not specified as editions, merely by name.

There's a good reason for this. Consider our QuestionModelling application. It has a prerequisite of Kernel, and let's suppose that it was built using version 5.0 of Kernel. If we specify Kernel 5.0 as our prerequisite, then we cannot load into an image unless Kernel 5.0 has been previously loaded. What happens when we want to move our application to a new version of the system, and only Kernel 5.0.1 is available? We can't possibly have specified Kernel 5.0.1 as a prerequisite because it didn't even exist when we created our version. Because of this difficulty, ENVY keeps track of prerequisites only by name, and will consider any version or edition acceptable. If we attempt to load an application with missing prerequisites where multiple editions of the prerequisites are available we will be asked which one we want to load.

To specify exactly which versions of applications go together, we can use a higher-level component such as a configuration map instead of, or in addition to, prerequisites. For example, if the QuestionModelling application requires a bug fix in Kernel that we don't normally expect to be present, we can make a configuration map containing both our edition of QuestionModelling and the patched version of Kernel.

Residents and Shadows

Earlier, we mentioned that users can browse components in the repository, although they may not be able to load them. A component that is not loaded is called a *shadow*. Components that are loaded are called *resident*. Even without loading the code, it is possible to operate on it, including limited browsing and modifying some attributes. Users cannot change methods, and not all browsing operations are available (for example, senders), but this is still a very powerful mechanism. An extension of this ability is the ability to browse changes between the resident code and some other edition in the repository, or between two different editions in the repository. This will become important when we talk about resolving conflicts (see "Resolving Conflicts").

Trying It Out

Take a deep breath. If you're new to ENVY, you've just had a lot of concepts to absorb at one go. At this point, try some things out to get a handle on these concepts. Working with the tools will help clarify some of these ideas and will also give you a feel for the motivations behind these features.

For example, consider our Questionnaire project and the things we might do with it during development. We have two different applications: QuestionModelling and QuestionTesting. We've set these up with prerequisites based on what other applications they use. We might create open editions of both applications (if they aren't already open) and write some code. When we need a new class, we'll create it in the appropriate application. If we need to extend an existing class, we'll add a class extension to the appropriate application. When we're finished making changes to a particular class or set of classes we can version them, giving them a name, and release them so that other team members can see them.

When we're finished with an iteration or otherwise want to make a snapshot of our application state, we will version the applications. We won't think too much about method editions, although we might notice this is happening behind the scenes. We might also think it's a good idea to define a configuration map to tie the applications together, but with only two applications it's not that important yet.

We may also try loading up a different image and loading our code into it. This helps show the effect of releasing, and simulates multiple developers. We haven't really gotten into the details of team programming yet, but we'll start on that in the next chapter.

Summary

This chapter has described basic ENVY setup and how to organize your code into an ENVY library. Some of the important concepts we've covered are:

- Software components: methods, classes, class extensions, applications, and configuration maps
- The usefulness of class extensions as a code organizing mechanism
- Application prerequisites and their use in layering code
- The concept of versions and editions of components
- How to develop using class editions, including the version and release cycle
- The distinction between released editions and loaded editions

≡Chapter 3≡

Team Development

So far, we've seen ENVY as a code organizing tool and as a version control system. These are powerful facilities, but the most important aspects of ENVY are in its support for working in teams. ENVY differs from traditional team programming tools in many respects. Because it is a Smalltalk-based tool it can deal with software components as objects, rather than working with coarse-grained source files. It also breaks away from the check-in/check-out mechanisms to a more concurrent mechanism in which conflicts are resolved through component ownership and through separation of the versioning and releasing operations. This enables developers to work with maximum concurrency while still providing a disciplined process that maintains the consistency of the system.

Team Development with Class Editions

Recall that applications specify a group of class versions that are loaded when the application is loaded, and that these are called the *released versions*. As we look at team development, this concept becomes more important, and we will see how class and application editions and versions are used to control the team development process.

Before we begin, let's review what it means for a class version to be released:

- When an application edition is loaded, the released versions of its classes are automatically loaded.

- Once an application is versioned, the list of released class versions cannot be modified.

- Most important, the released version is the approved or official edition. If we release a class, we are saying it is stable enough and approved for other developers to use.

Keeping in Sync

One of the big issues in team development is informing developers about new changes that have been published, and letting them painlessly incorporate those changes. In ENVY, this process is usually described as *syncing up*.

Recall the development process for a class: A developer creates a new edition, works on it, and then versions and releases it. Once the version is released, any developer who loads or reloads the application will automatically load this new class version. By loading the released class versions they will automatically see the current published state of the project. So, to synchronize with the other developers on our project, we simply reload the application. As we will see, this idea does not just apply to classes, but also to higher-level components such as applications and configuration maps. The goal is to achieve *one-click loading*, where any developer can immediately get into sync with the rest of the team for all components at all levels simply by loading one top-level configuration map.

Team Development Example

Consider a specific example. We have an ambitious startup company with three developers: Adrian, Alan, and Joseph. All of them are working on the Questionnaire project described in our previous examples. Adrian and Alan are working on the domain, and Joseph is writing tests. The project is structured as a single configuration map, with two applications. They have completed one development iteration, so at the moment all of the applications are open editions, and all of the classes are versioned as 1.0. See Figure 3-1.

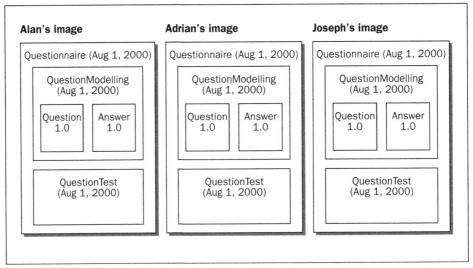

Figure 3-1: Everyone's image at the start of a new development iteration.

We begin with everyone in sync as they start their day. Joseph starts working first, and begins modifying and adding test classes. In the process of doing this he will create new open editions of those classes. Today he begins by adding to BasicQuestionTests and creating a new class MoreBasicQuestionTests. This leaves Joseph with two open class editions in his image.

Adrian will work on the class Answer, creating a new edition and adding some new functionality. Later, Alan will drag himself out of bed and start to work on the Question class, refactoring it to be an abstract superclass with subclasses MultipleChoiceQuestion and FreeFormQuestion. This will create an open edition of Question based on Question version 1.0, and also create open editions of the new classes MultipleChoiceQuestion and FreeFormQuestion.

Up to now, nothing has been released, and so the application editions in the repository haven't changed. If any of our developers reloaded the project, they would revert to the same state that existed this morning, with the same set of loaded classes as version 1.0 of the project.

Now, let's suppose that Joseph versions and releases his changes. Adrian and Alan will notice, the next time they look at an Application Manager or VisualAge Organizer, that released editions in QuestionTesting differ from what they have loaded. Suppose that Adrian reloads the QuestionTesting application to bring himself back in sync. This is shown in Figure 3-2.

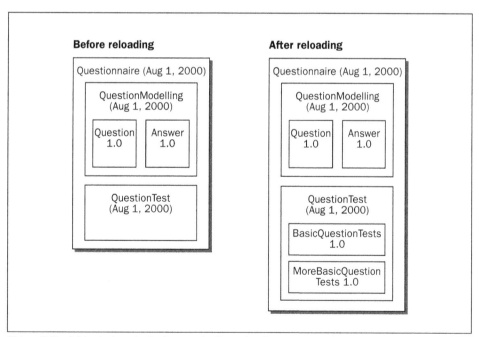

Figure 3-2: Adrian's image, before and after reload.

The "Out of Sync" Indicator

ENVY shows us when a class edition we have loaded is not the same as the released edition, using the "out of sync" indicator in the Application Manager or the VisualAge Organizer. This is shown as a ">" symbol on the left of the component signature. In our example, after a few more tests have been added, Alan's view of the QuestionTesting application might look like this:

```
AdvancedQuestionTests 1.0
>BasicQuestionTests 1.0
>MoreBasicQuestionTests 1.0
QuestionChainingTests 1.0
```

This shows that Alan has loaded version 1.0 of all the test classes. For two of these classes (AdvancedQuestionTests and QuestionChainingTests) this is also the released version, so we are in sync with the repository and the name shows up normally. For the other two classes (BasicQuestionTests and MoreBasicQuestionTests) Joseph has released different editions, and these show up with the ">" sign at the left of their names.

Of course, when we have an open edition that we're working on, it's not the same as the version that's released, and we'll see the out-of-sync indicator beside all of our open editions. For example, this morning, Alan's view of the QuestionModelling application would look like this:

```
Answer 1.0
>FreeFormQuestion (January 23, 2000 2:51:24 p.m.)
>MultipleChoiceQuestion (January 23, 2000 2:57:07 p.m.)
>Question (January 23, 2000 2:23:24 p.m.)
```

In this example, Alan hasn't modified the Answer class, and Adrian hasn't released his changes yet, so there's no out-of-sync indicator. For all the classes Alan is working on, his open edition is not the released one, so there's an out-of-sync indicator. This is expected, and it isn't a reason to sync up.

The Process of Syncing Up

In its most basic form, syncing up is easy. Just reload the component you want to synchronize with. Unfortunately, there's a complication. Consider the ideal development process:

- Write some code.
- Test the code.
- Version the code.
- Load everyone else's most recent code.
- Test again to be sure there are no interactions with other people's recent work.
- Release the code.

For the moment, assume there are no direct conflicts; that is, only one person is working on a particular class at a time. We'll talk about resolving these conflicts later, under the heading of "Class Ownership Details." Note that even with this assumption, conflicts can still arise because changes to two different classes may still conflict, and we will need to test to ensure that this hasn't happened.

Unfortunately, this ideal process is tricky with the standard ENVY releasing mechanism. In particular, if we load everyone else's most recent code by simply reloading an application or configuration map, the reload will remove all our current code because we haven't released it yet. This is undesirable, and there are several ways to avoid this problem:

- **Release our code before we test against other people's most recent work.** If it turns out that problems exist, resolve them and then re-release. This is bad in that we may have released broken code, but it's simple and easy. In our example, Adrian could simply release his changes to the Answer class and then reload the Questionnaire configuration map and retest. If Joseph's new tests interacted badly with Adrian's changes to Answer, Adrian would need to consult with Joseph to correct the problems, and one or both of them would need to re-release. In the meantime, the released code is broken.

- **Load other people's code individually by noting the out-of-sync indicator.** Adrian might note that there were classes he wasn't working on that were out of sync. He could do this by looking for the out-of-sync marker next to class names in the Application Manager or VisualAge Organizer. Alternatively, he might run a query (covered next) to find unreleased classes. He could then load the released versions of BasicQuestionTests and MoreBasicQuestionTests individually, test, and then release his own classes with confidence. He would also take a shortcut by reloading an entire application if he knows he hasn't modified any of the classes in it. For example, Adrian hasn't changed QuestionTesting at all, so he can reload the entire application safely.

- **Load other people's code, and then reload ours.** In a large project, there might be a great many new class editions to be loaded. Even loading entire applications at a time could be tiresome. An alternative approach is to note the classes we have been working on, reload the entire configuration map, and then individually reload our open class editions. This achieves the same effect as above, but may be faster.

- **Change the system to support a sync-up operation that would automate the process and report any potential conflicts.** This is potentially a very useful goodie, and although we don't provide it, the techniques described in "Extending the System," could be used to implement it.

Queries

In the previous section we mentioned running queries to find unreleased classes or classes we're currently working on. These queries are a very valuable facility in

ENVY, and are accessible through the Query submenu from the main ENVY menu. A variety of queries exist; however, two are most useful in daily development:

- **Open Class Editions:** This lists to the Transcript all open class editions currently loaded in the image, grouped by application. Because class editions are private, this effectively tells us what we have been working on and haven't versioned.

- **Unreleased Classes:** This lists to the Transcript all the loaded class editions, which are not the same as the currently released version. This includes all of the open class editions as listed by the previous query, as well as class versions that are not released. With class versions there are two cases: classes that we have versioned but not released, and classes that have been released by someone else. This makes this query less useful in determining what we have done. Because of this ambiguity, it's usually easier to use the open class editions query before versioning, and release classes quickly once we have versioned them.

Aside: Component Relationships

Sometimes, in this and other sections, we refer to components as containing other components. Strictly speaking, this is incorrect. All of the components are independent, and none exclusively contains any of the others. However, it's easier to talk about as a containment relationship, and within a single image it's often the case that components have a unique parent. Here's a summary of the possible relationships among components:

- **Classes and class extensions contain methods.** Within an image, a method must be uniquely contained by a single class or class extension. In the repository, many different editions can contain it. If a method is moved or copied between classes, it's treated as a different method.

- **Applications contain classes and class extensions.** Within an image, a particular class or class extension must be uniquely contained by a single application. Within the repository it can be contained by many different editions. If a class is moved or copied between applications, it is treated as a different class.

- **Configuration maps contain applications.** Configuration maps are not directly represented in an image; consequently, many different configuration maps and different configuration map editions can contain the same application without any problems, regardless of which are loaded.

Integration

What we've been talking about as syncing up is more formally referred to as *integration* — merging changes from multiple developers into a single code base. There are many different possible approaches to integration, and it's worth taking a closer look at ENVY's integration philosophy.

ENVY supports cooperative development in which the essential activity is developing and elaborating a *reference model*. The state of the released code in the library constitutes the published system. In their workspaces, developers maintain their own variations of the model and can privately develop, test, and debug components. When an edition of a component is ready it is released to the reference model in the library, which makes it part of the mainstream of development. Anyone who loads or reloads the reference model will have in their image the current published representation of the system. In this way, the system remains stable while the reference model constantly improves in functionality.

A single library can hold many reference models; typically, there is one per project, development team, or stream of development. The reference model is usually defined by a single top-level configuration map edition that contains specific application editions, which in turn contain versions of classes and class extensions, which in turn contain editions of methods. Each time a developer releases a component, the reference model is altered.

Continuous Integration

An important aspect of the integration process is its frequency. A typical software project has a number of development cycles and each one includes an integration phase. This is where we get phrases like "integration test." Integration can be a very long process, and it's common that various problems aren't detected until integration.

Over time, there has been a tendency to make the integration intervals progressively shorter. Iterative development processes recommend short cycle times, with frequent integrations. Many organizations practice nightly builds. In general, we can achieve significant productivity gains by making integrations short, frequent, and painless. For some points of view on the frequency of integration, see the section "Extreme Programming and ENVY" and McConnell (1996).

While ENVY does not impose any particular timetable or development strategy, its capability to deal with components at a very fine-grained level is supportive of a process called *continuous integration*. In this process, individual developers perform small-scale integrations at will, typically at least once per day. These integrations consist of the steps described previously, testing and releasing their code and syncing up with the published state of the system. This does not require a baselining operation, and baselines will typically occur on a longer time scale. For more information on baselining frequency, see the "When to Baseline" section later in this chapter.

Summary

Before we go further, let's review what we've seen so far:

- Multiple developers can work concurrently in the same application.
- Changes to classes in an image are private to a developer until they're versioned and released.

- There is a reference model of the system represented by the released components in the library. Multiple reference models can exist, each one represented by a configuration map edition.

- Developers work by making incremental changes to that reference model in their own private workspace, and then releasing those changes back into the reference model. In this way, the model evolves without suffering instability.

- Queries and the out-of-sync indicator let developers determine when new changes have been released.

- One-click loading enables developers to easily bring themselves into sync with the reference model.

- When developers frequently release and sync up, the integration process becomes continuous, minimizing later integration problems.

One-Click Loading and Application Editions

We've talked about the goal of one-click loading. A project is defined by a configuration map edition, and at any point developers can reload that edition and bring themselves back into sync with the reference model. However, we're still missing some of the elements that make this possible. In particular, we need to see how application editions are treated differently from class editions.

Application Editions

Earlier we saw that application editions contain class versions. The state of the application edition is controlled by releasing class versions into it. This relationship generalizes to other types of components. Configuration maps contain application editions, controlled by releasing the application editions into the configuration map edition. Later on we'll also see that the same ideas apply to subapplications and required maps.

So far we've seen application editions only in their role as containers, not as the thing contained. Many of the principles of the application-class relationship also apply to the configuration map–application relationship, but there are some important differences:

- ENVY will not automatically create an application edition; developers must explicitly create them.

- Applications are released into configuration maps. Unlike class editions, which can only be contained by one application at a time (in memory), application editions can be shared by multiple different configuration maps, even within an image.

- Applications can be released while they are still editions. This is very, very important, and we'll soon see the reasons for this.

The big difference between class editions and application editions is that we expect open class editions to be private, but open application editions are expected to be shared. During development, if we have two users working on the same class at the same time, we expect them to each have an open class edition and to merge the changes after they're finished. If we have two developers working on the same application at the same time, we expect them to share an application edition and for changes to become immediately visible.

This is a very important difference. The motivation is the granularity of applications compared to classes. A class is a small unit, and two people working on it at the same time seriously risk interfering with each other's work. An application is much coarser, and we often expect multiple developers to be working on an application at the same time. Of course, what those developers are doing is adding and modifying classes, and these changes will be isolated from each other. The idea is that by working in the same application edition, developers quickly become aware of newly published class versions and keep themselves in sync with these changes. At the same time, they will have enough isolation from the work of other developers that they won't feel like they're constantly being interfered with.

Releasing Application Editions

Tip

Read this section! It's very important, and it focuses on one of the most confusing topics in ENVY. It also has some good questions to ask people at job interviews.

Let's think about one-click loading in our example system. We started out with version 1.0, in which all components have been versioned. See Figure 3-3.

Now, we begin to work. Let's say Joseph is going to do the administrative work for this iteration. He will create a new open edition of our Questionnaire configuration map. He'll also create a new open edition of the QuestionModelling and QuestionTesting applications. Adrian and Alan can now load the configuration map edition and start working.

Or not — what's wrong with this picture?

Consider what happens when Alan loads the

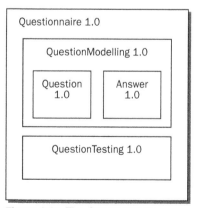

Figure 3-3: The Questionnaire project, version 1.0.

configuration map edition. He will automatically load the released editions of its subcomponents. Which editions are the released ones? The same as they were before, which is to say the same as the previous version. See Figure 3-4.

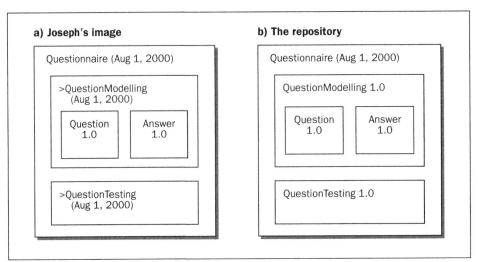

Figure 3-4: The state of our project after creating new application editions. This shows Joseph's image, the repository, and Alan's image after loading the new configuration map edition.

This is a bad situation. Alan cannot one-click load; he'll have to explicitly load all of the open application editions. There are only two right now, but Alan's lazy about this kind of thing, and it's going to get much worse as our application grows.

The problem is that the semantics of releasing that made sense for classes don't make sense for applications. Open class editions are private to a developer. We don't want two people working in the same class edition at the same time; they'll tread on each other's toes constantly. Once someone is finished with a class, he or she can version it so that it's frozen, and then release it so that other developers can see it and use it.

In contrast, open application editions are meant to be shared. If two developers are working on the same application, we *want* them to see each other's class-level changes as soon as they're published. Remember that class releasing always happens with respect to a particular application edition. That means that for two developers to see each other's changes they need to be working on the same application edition. In order for them to have one-click loading and still end up in the same application edition, we need to release the applications while they are still open editions. And that's exactly what we do; developers can't release a class until after it's versioned. They *can* release an application while it's still an open edition, and they should. With this in mind, let's revisit the process our developers went through to start working.

Let's say Joseph is going to do the administrative work for this iteration. He'll create a new open edition of our Questionnaire configuration map. He will also create a new open edition of the QuestionModelling and QuestionTesting applications. He will then *release those open application editions* into the open edition of the Questionnaire configuration map. Adrian and Alan can now load the configuration map edition and start working, and this time it will work. See Figure 3-5 for an illustration.

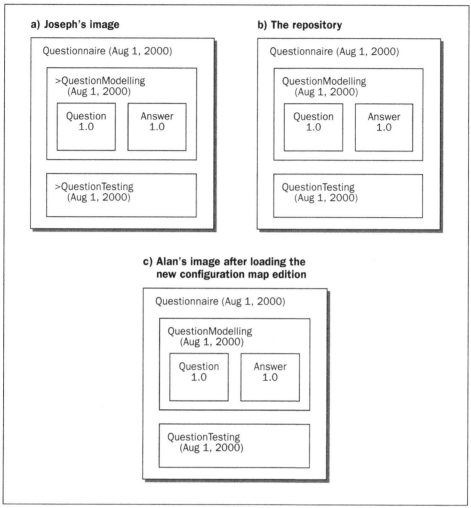

Figure 3-5: The state of our project after creating and releasing the application editions. This once again shows Joseph's image, the repository, and Alan's image after loading the new configuration map edition.

Now our one-click loading process genuinely works. After Joseph works on the QuestionTesting application and versions and releases his class changes, Adrian can reload the Questionnaire configuration map and immediately see those changes.

Developing with Application Editions

In Chapter 2, we saw the typical development process for dealing with class editions. In particular, we saw the repeating cycle of creating a new edition, making changes, versioning, and releasing. See "Team Development with Class Editions" earlier in this chapter. This cycle is different for application editions because we want to release editions as soon as they are created so that other developers can work in them.

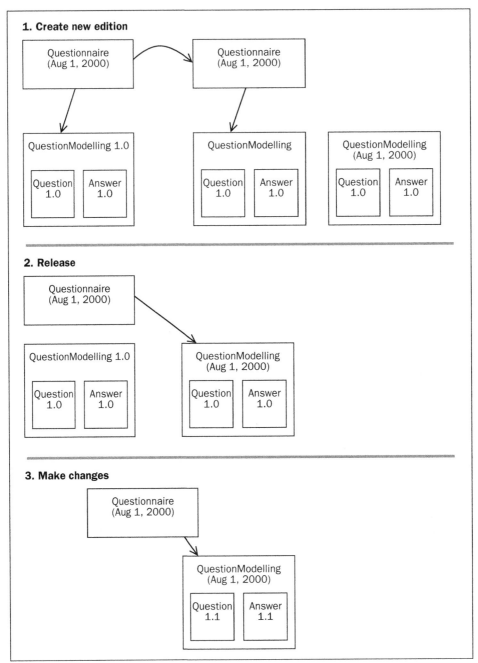

Figure 3-6: The application edition lifecycle.

Releasing a class edition can be thought of as publishing the class as ready for use. Releasing an application edition can be thought of as publishing the application as ready to be worked on.

Baselining

We've now seen how to start working from a fully versioned system, but we haven't really seen how to reach that point. How did we get to this version 1.0, and how do we get to the next version? This process is called creating a *baseline*, and it gives us a frozen version of all of our code. This is also referred to simply as *versioning*. We have several reasons to create a baseline:

- To provide a point of reference
- To enable complete testing of a stable system
- To mark a milestone in development, for example, the end of an iteration

Here we'll be discussing a basic baselining process. We'll describe some additional issues in this process later. Most notably, it will typically take more than one person to do a complete baseline operation, as we will see once we examine user roles (see the "User Roles" section later in this chapter). Class owners will release their classes, application managers will version applications, and configuration map managers will version configuration maps. On a reasonably sized system, it is unlikely that these will be the same person. In larger systems, some degree of tool support may be helpful in baselining. For a discussion of some of these tools, see the sections "A Simple Project Management Tool" and "Checkpointing."

The Baseline Process

Baselining means that we take a reference model and ensure that its components are versioned and released. In order for this to happen, a number of prerequisites must be fulfilled. All open class editions must be versioned and released. All applications must be versioned. (As discussed previously, we expect that the applications are already released into the appropriate configuration map.) As we will see later, sub-applications must also be versioned, and we also expect them to have already been released into their parent application. Finally, all configuration maps must be versioned. Again, we expect that all configuration maps are already released into any appropriate lineups for required maps. For more information on these topics, see the sections on "Conditional Loading of Configuration Maps" and "Subapplications."

The order of these steps is important. When we version a component, we are freezing its state. That state needs to be correct before we version, so anything we are doing to subcomponents has to be completed before we can version the parent component. This means that we have to version and release classes before we can do anything with applications, that applications must be versioned before we can version the configuration maps, and so forth.

For example, consider our Questionnaire project. Go back to the example at the beginning of this chapter (see the "Team Development Example" section). In this example, Joseph was working on the QuestionTesting application, modifying BasicQuestionTests, and creating MoreBasicQuestionTests. Adrian is working on QuestionModelling and modifying the class Answer. Alan is also working on QuestionModelling, modifying Question, and adding new subclasses MultipleChoiceQuestion and FreeFormQuestion.

After a few hours, they decide the system is nearly ready to demo to the venture capitalists, so they decide to make a baseline. Everyone will version and release the classes they were working on. The configuration map will be reloaded and the tests run. In an ideal world, everything runs cleanly because all of the changes have already been thoroughly tested. In a less ideal world, a certain amount of debugging has to be done. Once everyone is satisfied that the code works, both applications are versioned. They are already released into the configuration map because that was essential for our one-click loading. At this point they can now version the configuration map, and have completed a baseline.

Development During a Baseline

One of the things about building a baseline in ENVY is that it interferes with the work of other developers. Remember, open application and configuration map editions are like a shared workspace. We are in the process of freezing that shared workspace, so we can't have other developers releasing classes into it. Otherwise, we might end up testing something different from what we deliver.

During a baseline, developers fundamentally have two options. The first is to do something besides development work. Some developers will be doing the integration, others might be running tests on different configurations, and others might be writing documentation. The second option is to continue developing against the last known state, but not to release code. This can work, but it requires a manual syncing-up process. Once there are new editions, developers note the class editions they were working on, load the new editions, and then manually load their class editions. This can be tedious for a large number of classes, but as long as the time to baseline is relatively short it shouldn't be a big problem. In either case, it should be a well-understood part of the development process that a baseline is occurring and certain restrictions are in effect. It's also helpful if baselines occur at specific times.

Post-Baseline Steps

Just as important as the baseline process are the post-baseline operations. If developers are to work, they need a shared workspace with open editions properly configured for one-click loading. We now need to go through the baseline process in reverse, creating that environment.

For example, in our system, we will create a new open edition of the Questionnaire configuration map. We'll create new open editions of the applications QuestionModelling and QuestionTesting, and we'll release these open editions into the configuration map. Once that's done, we're really finished, and we can alert the developers that new editions are available.

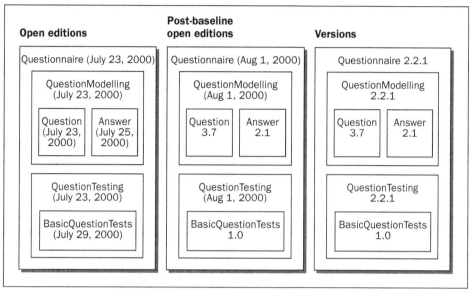

Figure 3-7: Post-baseline steps. We start with open editions, go through a baseline to produce versions, and then create new post-baseline open editions for the next iteration.

When to Baseline

How often should we make a baseline? This depends a lot on the size of the system, the phase of development, and the overall development process. The ultimate answer is, of course, as often as necessary. If we aren't baselining often enough, some of the problems we might see are as follows:

- We don't know when a problem was introduced; that is, we have a feeling this was working last month but we have no way of knowing for sure.

- We don't have a recent, working version we can demo.

- Integration is tedious and difficult. (One benefit of frequent baselines is that it motivates developers to release any pending changes they have, avoiding long-running divergent code bases.)

- We have packaging problems (caused by not packaging intermediate versions, which often accompanies infrequent baselining).

These are warning signs that we should consider baselining more frequently. It's rare that a project baselines too often, but the major warning sign of that is simply:

- Baselining takes up too much of our time.

Baselining more than once a week is probably excessive, except leading up to a release. In most projects, however, the natural tendency is to let baseline frequency slip. If you think you're versioning too often, be sure to look at the "Project Recovery" section. It's possible that the problem is more in the difficulty of integrating changes than the baselining process itself, and the Difficult Integration pattern may apply.

In a spiral development process, an obvious baseline frequency is once per iteration. That's quite reasonable if an iteration is three weeks. If iterations are four months, it's likely a good idea to baseline within an iteration. It's important to keep the baseline process frequent and regular. Baselining is like a heartbeat for a development project. It provides a cadence and an indication of health. The task of baselining and the frequency with which it occurs is an indication of the state and the pace of the project. The frequency of baselines generally increases near the release of a project. This quickening of the heartbeat often occurs once an official code freeze has taken place, with the only changes permitted being bug fixes.

If multiple test and fix passes take place after a code freeze, with each new test and fix pass, the severity threshold for fixing a bug generally increases — only more critical bugs are fixed as system stability becomes more important. For example, there might be three test and fix passes after a code freeze, each with two days of testing and one day of fixing. After the baseline for the third fix pass has been created, the code is released to a production environment (after a short bout of sanity testing).

Component Ownership and Conflict Resolution

One of the things that distinguishes ENVY from other team programming tools is its mechanism for conflict resolution, based on individual ownership of components, particularly classes. This provides a very high degree of concurrent development while maintaining a disciplined process. These sections describe the ENVY principles of ownership, and how these are applied to resolve conflicts.

User Roles

ENVY keeps track of the current user as the *image owner*. When we start up an ENVY image for the first time, we are asked to whom this image belongs. This sets the owner, although it can be changed later, and limits development in that image to operations the owner is authorized to perform.

This authorization is a new concept. So far we've acted as if any developer could perform any operation. This is not the case, and, in fact, ENVY has significant restrictions on what a particular developer can do. These restrictions are based on the *role(s)* a developer plays for a particular component. Five possible roles exist:

- Class Owner
- Class Developer
- Application Manager
- Configuration Map Manager
- Library Supervisor (sort of)

All these roles are important, but for the moment we're going to focus on how these roles affect conflict resolution, and the role of class owner in particular. We'll discuss the remaining roles in more detail in the following sections.

Class Owner

Each class has an owner, with special rights to manipulate that class. In particular, only the owner can release a class version into the containing application. This is an important privilege, which forms the basis of ENVY's conflict resolution mechanism.

Once again we'll go back to the example at the beginning of this chapter (see the "Team Development Example" section) but with a twist. In this example, Joseph was working on the QuestionTesting application, modifying BasicQuestionTests, and creating MoreBasicQuestionTests. Adrian is working on QuestionModelling and modifying the class Answer. Alan is also working on QuestionModelling, modifying Question, and adding new subclasses MultipleChoiceQuestion and FreeFormQuestion. Now let's suppose that Alan also makes some changes to Answer to support his Question changes. Now Alan and

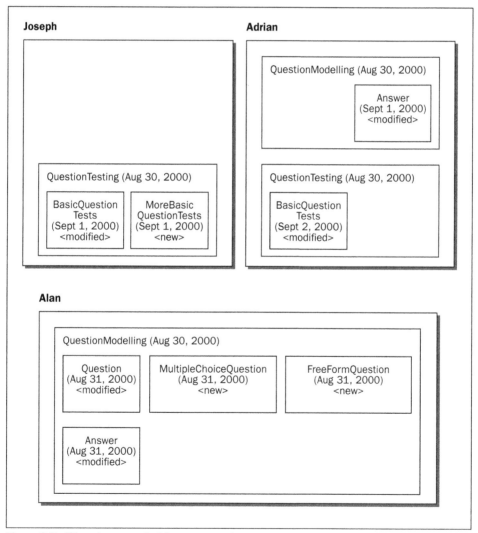

Figure 3-8: Who changes what in our example.

Adrian have both made changes to the same class at the same time. Even worse, Alan also adds some new tests to BasicQuestionTests to support his new functionality, causing conflicts with Joseph. See Figure 3-8.

To resolve these conflicts, we need to know more about the structure of the applications. In particular, we need to know the owner of each class. We list this information below, along with the developers who have modified a particular class.

Class	Owner	Modified By
BasicQuestionTests	Joseph	Alan, Joseph
MoreQuestionTests	Joseph	Joseph
Question	Alan	Alan
FreeFormQuestion	Alan	Alan
MultipleChoiceQuestion	Alan	Alan
Answer	Adrian	Adrian, Alan

Resolving Conflicts

In the previous example, we have two conflicts. Notice both Alan and Joseph have modified BasicQuestionTests. Both Alan and Adrian have modified Answer. These conflicts need to be resolved, which we can do in several different ways. We can characterize these according to who "wins" by having their changes become part of the reference model.

- **Last One in Wins.** There is no conflict resolution mechanism in place, and later changes overwrite older ones. This is like having source files in a directory with no version control.

- **Checked-Out Version Wins.** There is a pessimistic locking mechanism in place. A developer who wants to change a component has to check it out. Once a component is checked out, other developers cannot modify it until after it is checked in. This is the mechanism for many simple source-file–based systems such as SCCS.

- **Last One in Wins, but Has to Merge.** There is a locking mechanism in place but with some degree of optimism. Components must typically be checked out, but multiple developers can modify the same component simultaneously. When the second set of changes is checked in, it has to be merged with the previous changes. In our example, if Adrian checked in his changes first, Alan would need to incorporate Adrian's changes along with his own. Some variation of this mechanism is used in more advanced source-file–based systems such as CVS.

- **Owner Wins.** Components have owners; any change must be approved by the owner. Many developers can modify the component concurrently, but all changes pass through the owner, who must accept and/or merge changes. This is the strategy used by ENVY.

Let's see what this means in our example. Alan made changes to the class Answer. Let's say that he added the method

checkValidityAgainst: aQuestion

and deleted the method

checkMultipleChoiceAnswerWithin: aCollection.

At the same time, Adrian had modified

checkMultipleChoiceAnswerWithin: aCollection

and added several other methods.

Adrian has versioned his changes as Answer 1.2. When Alan goes to version his changes, they are automatically given the name Answer 1.1.1 because ENVY detects the name collision. (For more information on this, see "Default Version Names" later in this chapter.) Now Adrian has to resolve the differences.

The ENVY Strategy

We have said that ENVY implements a strategy in which the owner controls changes to a class. How is this implemented? We've already seen that two developers can be working on the same class at the same time. How does the owner control this development?

In ENVY, the owner exerts control through the *release* step. Only the owner of a class can release a class version into the parent application. Because it is only through releasing that classes become part of the published reference model, this control enables the class owner to verify any changes before they become part of the official system.

Apart from releasing, the owner has few special privileges. Anyone can create an open edition of a class, modify the code, and even version those changes. We refer to someone in this role as a *class developer*. Class developers can make any changes they like, but they cannot release, so their changes will not be the default that is loaded when the parent application is loaded. In other words, class developers can do whatever they like in their private workspace, but it will not become part of the reference model until the owner approves it.

Consider this in our previous example. Adrian and Alan had made conflicting changes. As the owner, Adrian has full control. He can, for example, choose to completely disregard Alan's changes and stay with what was previously released. A more team-oriented approach would be to compare the two sets of changes, incorporate the appropriate pieces from Alan's changes, create a merged edition with both sets of changes combined, and version and release this new edition. This process is shown in more detail in Figure 3-9.

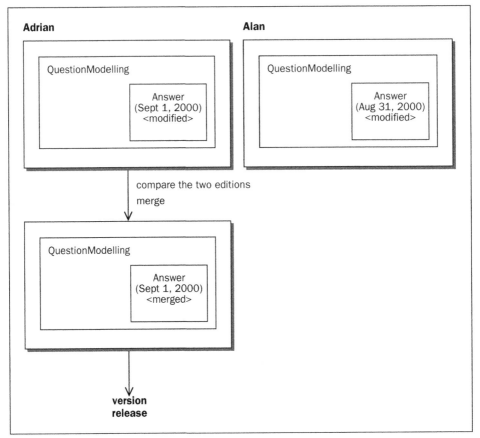

Figure 3-9: The merging process.

This process places a significant burden on the class owner. All changes to the class funnel through the owner, and the owner bears the responsibility for merging in the work of other developers. In practice, this can usually be kept manageable. The owner of a class is typically the person who is doing the most work on it. This means we expect the contributions of other developers to be relatively small. Further, the other developers know who the owner is, and if they plan to make significant modifications to classes they will typically consult the owner(s) and/or work directly with them.

Class Ownership Details

There are some important details regarding class ownership. First, the owner of a class can be changed. The change in ownership affects the current edition and any new editions created from it. This is important because it allows different class owners in different application editions (which typically represent different streams). For example, in the open edition of QuestionModelling, which is developing new functionality for version 2.0, Alan might own the class Question. At the same time, another open edition of QuestionModelling exists for bug fixes to version 1.0, and in that edition, the class Question

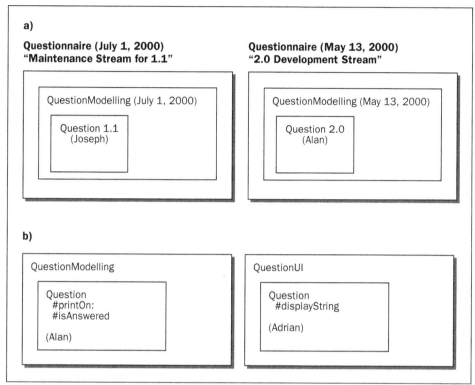

Figure 3-10: Class ownership with streams and extensions.

is owned by Joseph. For more information on maintaining streams of development, see the section on "Streams" in Chapter 4. Second, the owner of the class definition and of its extensions can be different. For example, within the main development stream, Alan might own the class definition for Question in the QuestionModelling application, but Adrian might own a class extension to Question in QuestionUI.

Additional class ownership rights also exist. The class owner is the only one who can delete a class from an application. The class owner can also give away ownership of the class to someone else. In current versions of ENVY, the application manager can also change the ownership of a class within the application, which was not true in earlier versions.

Application Manager

For applications, the role that roughly corresponds to that of class owner is called *application manager*. In the same way the class owner is responsible for the consistency of a class, the application manager is responsible for an entire application. They are called managers rather than owners because the level of control is different. A class owner has complete control over a class, to the point of ignoring the work of any other developers. The manager of an application has less control and a more administrative role. An application acts mostly as a container for classes, and their owners already control those classes. The application manager creates new application editions and controls the versioning of those editions.

This responsibility is more important for application managers because other users do not have the right to create editions or versions. Recall that for classes, any class developer can create a new class edition, and can version that edition. In fact, ENVY creates class editions automatically when a class version is modified. For application editions, only the manager can create a new edition and only the manager can version that edition. The reason for the difference is that applications are shared components. Recall from the discussion on releasing application editions that it's important for developers working on the same application to share the same edition, and that we normally release application editions as soon as they are created. It's the application manager's responsibility to make this sharing happen, determining which editions are in use and when they should be versioned.

Although the title of this role includes the word "manager" and we've referred to it as an administrative role, that doesn't mean the application manager is a manager in the typical sense of the word. An application manager is still very much a software developer, and in a typical project the application manager also owns and develops many of the classes within the application.

Configuration Map Manager

Like applications, configuration maps have managers, whose primary responsibility is creating and versioning editions of these components. Like applications, these editions must be explicitly created, and this can only be done by the *configuration map manager*. We will revisit this role in more detail when we talk about required maps (see "Conditional Loading of Configuration Maps").

Changing Users

At any given time, a development image is associated with a particular user. Typically, this user doesn't change, but it's possible to switch users through the Change User option under the System menu. Depending on the ENVY installation options, you may need to know another user's password to change to that user.

Changing users can be a very powerful facility. For example, by changing to the special user "Library Supervisor," we can do things that are otherwise impossible. However, changing users can also be very dangerous, and it is not recommended unless you know exactly what you are doing. When changing users, make the change for as short a period as possible, and be very sure to change back as quickly as possible. Forgetting to switch back again is a common cause of messy situations and permissions problems, which can be very tedious to resolve.

Library Supervisor

Every application has a manager and every class and class extension has an owner. This naturally leads to the question, who owns the system classes? Who releases changes to classes such as Object or String? In ENVY, the answer is the special user known as *Library Supervisor*. When you first install ENVY, Library Supervisor is the only user and is the owner or manager for all the components that ship with the system.

No single person works as Library Supervisor, but typically one or a few people are authorized to change users (see the preceding sidebar "Changing Users") to Library Supervisor to perform privileged operations. Library Supervisor is the owner of all the system classes, applications, and configuration maps. Most modifications to system components will require someone to act as Library Supervisor. In addition, the Library Supervisor is the only user who can perform certain special operations, including:

- creating, modifying, or purging users
- purging configuration maps or applications
- salvaging configuration maps or applications

Note that Library Supervisor is not the equivalent of a UNIX "root" user. The Library Supervisor is a user like any other, and has no special permissions to affect other users' components. It happens that the Library Supervisor owns or manages the system components, but this does not convey special privileges elsewhere. In some circumstances, it can be useful to have the Library Supervisor act with special privileges to affect any component. This is possible, but requires modifying the ENVY system. VA Assist Pro is an example of a tool that enables these kinds of operations.

Purging

In ENVY, purging refers to the process of removing a component entirely from the repository, something that only the Library Supervisor can do. Ordinary developers can remove components from their image, but those components will always remain in the repository. For example, if we create a class edition, that edition will remain visible in the repository, even if it has been deleted from all images and was never released anywhere. The Library Supervisor can mark a component as purged, at which point it becomes invisible to users, cannot be loaded, and will be permanently deleted the next time the repository is compacted. Up until the repository is compacted, it is possible to retrieve a purged component by salvaging it. The salvage operation is also restricted to the Library Supervisor.

Scratch Editions

We have now seen the basics of how team development works in ENVY. Concurrency in a team is maximized by letting any developer create private class editions to work in, but only allowing release of those changes into the reference model after they are approved by the class owner. Control of shared application editions is centralized through a manager, and other users cannot create editions.

This procedure helps contribute to a stable development environment, but it can also get in the way of doing useful work. The most common problem is creating an open class edition in an application that is currently a version. Normally all the applications we are working on will have open editions, but occasions may arise where we need to modify code that is not part of what we're actively working on. We may only need to change the code temporarily, to insert debugging or exploratory statements without releasing the resulting code. We may want to experiment with a system modification or bug fix without requiring Library Supervisor access. If it works, then it may be worth the trouble of finding the appropriate application manager, but in the meantime, we'd like to be able to just try it.

For example, in developing the QuestionWebUI application, Joseph encounters a peculiar problem. He seems to be making connections from the Web browser properly, but no HTML is coming back. To debug this, he wants to make the low-level socket connection handling code write to a log file so he can tell if the connection is really being made or not. He adds the code, realizes the connection is not being seen at all, and then notices that he has spelled the URL incorrectly. He fixes the spelling and immediately starts seeing correct results. He deletes the logging code by reloading the appropriate system applications and continues to work.

The problem is that the standard ENVY permissions would not allow Joseph to add that code because that application is a version and he doesn't have permission to make an open edition. ENVY gets around this problem by adding the concept of a *scratch edition*. A scratch edition is a temporary edition of an application that can be created by any user, and that exists only in the memory of their image. No record of the scratch edition is created in the database, and it cannot be loaded or viewed by other users.

Scratch editions appear in the application manager or organizer with a special version name, which is the name of the version from which they were constructed with double angle brackets around it. For example, if we had Kernel 5.0 and we made a scratch edition of it we would see Kernel <<5.0>>.

The advantage of the scratch edition is that it helps developers to get on with their work without worrying about the permissions and without disturbing other developers. The disadvantage of the scratch edition is that it lets developers work without worrying about the permissions and without notifying other developers. For small changes, this

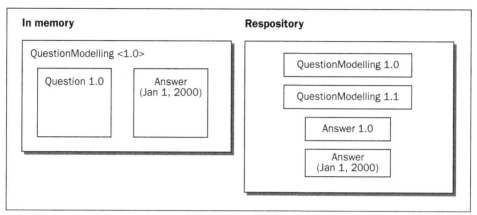

Figure 3-11: Scratch editions in memory and in the repository.

ability is very valuable. On the other hand, making large changes in a scratch edition is almost certainly a bad idea. We won't know what other developers are doing, they won't even know this edition exists, and the changes are harder to recover in the event of a crash. In general, a large number of methods in scratch editions or scratch editions that persist for more than a day or two are likely signs of trouble.

In keeping with their limited function, some operations cannot be performed in a scratch edition. It is not possible to add or delete classes or extensions in a scratch edition. It is also not possible to release classes into a scratch edition. The purpose of releasing is to make classes visible to other team members, and other team members can't see the scratch edition.

If we have done some useful work in a scratch edition and later want to convert it into a real edition, we can simply create a new edition as normal (assuming we are the application manager or have changed the user to become the application manager). Creating an application edition from a scratch edition will preserve all of the changes in the scratch edition. Alternatively, we can simply write down which classes we changed, load an existing open edition, and then load and/or merge our changes into it.

The concept of scratch editions applies only at the application level. The class editions we created are normal class editions, which are visible to other users, can be versioned, and so on. This means it is still possible to recover changes from a scratch edition if our images crash, and that other developers would still be able to see class versions we created within it.

To create a scratch edition, we can either explicitly use the Mark as Scratched menu item, or we can just make a change to a class that is part of an application version. ENVY will tell us the change is not allowed and give us the choice to either cancel the change or automatically create a scratch edition of the application and a regular open edition of the class.

Version Naming Conventions

Version names in ENVY can be very important. They can help distinguish streams, authors, product numbers, and other information. The system includes a default version numbering scheme, but it supports any scheme, and it can often be very useful to use an extended version naming convention to convey more information.

Default Version Names

The default ENVY version naming scheme uses a dotted numbering scheme:

- **1.0:** A major version
- **1.1:** A minor version continuing on from 1.0
- **1.0.1:** Maintenance for version 1.0, not part of new development

This is a common scheme in software, where each level of numbering indicates a branch. In ENVY, the system automatically generates new version names according to this scheme. If the previous version was 1.4, it will automatically choose 1.5. If 1.5 is already taken, then it will assume this represents a branch and will choose 1.4.1.

This scheme works reasonably well, although it can sometimes lead to creating branches without knowing it if we don't pay enough attention to the names the system is generating. Tool support can also help with this, and VA Assist Pro provides a "release only clean" feature that can help circumvent this problem.

Extended Version Names

It's often useful to use an extended naming convention. For one thing, a project may have its own names for releases, and it's better if the component version names follow those names. It may also be useful to track additional information about the component. For example, ENVY timestamps on components only track the date/time at which that edition was created, and there's no information on when a component was versioned. It may also be useful to track class developer information by recording something like developer initials in the version name. Finally, if there's information about a stream of development, we can encode that in the name as well. For example, we might have names like the following:

- **2.0 Beta [AK 7-25-2002a]:** A named stream "2.0 Beta" using user initials and dates to identify versions. Multiple versions on the same date have a letter appended.
- **1.0 Patch3 0.2:** A named stream "1.0 Patch3" with a version number within that stream.

If we have established a project convention for versioning, it can be very useful to change the ENVY version naming convention to automatically use these numbers. This requires extending the system, although again this support is available in VA Assist Pro.

Version Names for Developer Tools

Developers can build two fundamentally different types of products. The first is the "normal" application that ships as some form of executable. For example, we might ship QuestionnaireBuilder, a standalone program that enables users to create questionnaires, deploy them to a Web site, and monitor the results. The second type of product is a development tool whose users are developers, who will see the source code of the tool. For example, we might sell our code as a Questionnaire Framework, which developers can build on and extend for their own systems.

In the first case, it doesn't matter too much what conventions we use for our internal versions. If a configuration map we had internally named as version

> 1.7.4.37 [please, please, work] 2000.2.14 4:03 a.m.

turns out to work and is shipped as part of a packaged executable it's not a problem because the customer will never see that version name.

In the second case, we will likely be shipping our product as an ENVY library, and the end users are developers who will see our version numbers, along with the class owners and other information we might rather not expose. To deliver this, we're going to want to hide the developers and make sure our version names correspond to the overall version name of the product. This involves some advanced ENVY functionality, which we won't cover here, but you should be aware that these are issues and that techniques exist to address them. For more information, see the sections on "Renaming Versions," "Version Naming for Developer Tools," and "Updating Users."

Summary

This chapter has covered a lot of material, explaining in detail the ways in which ENVY supports team development. For developers working in teams, these processes form the basis of many of their day-to-day activities, and a clear understanding of them is very valuable. For administrators, it's important to understand the nature and pace of integration and baselining to know how the project is progressing and how to address integration issues that arise. For toolsmiths, these are fundamental processes that tools need to support.

Some of the important things to remember from this chapter are as follows:

- We can sync up with the current state of the project by reloading a top-level component. This is a fundamental technique in team development, and should be done often.

- ENVY supports a process of continuous integration, where developers constantly make small incremental changes, publish them, and synchronize with the other developers.

- ENVY queries can tell us various things about the image. The most important is the list of open class editions.

- Baselining is the ENVY process for making editions into versions. It freezes the state of an edition and typically marks the end of an iteration.

- ENVY allows concurrent development and resolves the possible conflicts through the class ownership mechanism.

- Various roles and responsibilities are associated with ENVY components, including class owner, class developer, application manager, configuration map manager, and library supervisor.

- Scratch editions let you ignore some of the permissions mechanisms. This can be very useful in the short term but should not be used for large amounts of code.

- It's important to establish consistent naming conventions within a project, and these can be used to convey information.

═Chapter 4═

Advanced Development

In the previous chapters we've rapidly covered almost everything you need to do basic development with ENVY. This chapter deals with some of the more complex issues that arise in a larger project. The two primary issues we'll address are configuration management and project organization. ENVY supports sophisticated configuration management that enables us to write portable software that can also exploit platform features. Project organization includes advice on how to structure the ENVY components that make up a project, a discussion of multi-site development, and ways to manage multiple divergent streams. We also discuss some alternative processes to the standard we've been describing so far, explaining how ENVY can be used as part of an "Extreme Programming" project. Finally, we'll add some miscellaneous topics, tricks, and conventions that ease development.

The discussion here is aimed at someone who has a good understanding of the basic ENVY concepts and has used ENVY at least a little. Much of this advice will be most helpful to someone setting up a larger project. New users should begin by reading some of the previous chapters and working with the concepts discussed in those chapters. Toolsmiths will find this discussion important for ways to organize tools for multiple versions or dialects, and will appreciate some of the tips and conventions.

Configuration Management

The distinction between version control and configuration management is not clearly drawn. However, in our context we will identify configuration management as being concerned with variations in our software due to different configuration information. This might be the host operating system, the Smalltalk dialect, what the customer has paid for, or any other factor. ENVY supports configuration management of this form at two levels: subapplications and configuration maps with required maps. We'll begin by discussing subapplications.

Subapplications

So far we've dealt with the basic software components. These are enough for most development, but in more complex cases important additional mechanisms exist. One of these is the capability to nest applications using subapplications, and to use these subapplications to manage different configurations at load-time.

What Are Subapplications?

In ENVY, applications fill the role of a "module" or "package" construct. Subapplications enable us to refine that concept, adding submodules. While this can be a very useful concept, it is also one that's often misinterpreted; therefore, it's important to be clear about exactly what subapplications are and are not.

In technical terms, subapplications are applications that have the following additional properties:

- They belong to a parent application and cannot be loaded without a parent.

- They are automatically loaded when their parent (sub)application is loaded.

- They have no prerequisites and use the prerequisites from their parent. For prerequisite purposes, all classes in an application and all classes in subapplications may be considered as belonging to the parent application.

- They can be conditionally loaded based on the state of the image when the parent is loaded.

- Their application class inherits from SubApplication rather than from Application (see "Application Classes").

- Note that subapplications can also have subapplications, nested indefinitely.

Subapplication Usage

The concept of submodules is more complex than it appears. Intuitively, it's a way to hierarchically decompose a system, but there are many different kinds of hierarchy, and it's easy to confuse them.

Essentially, ENVY subapplications let us divide a single module into multiple pieces. This is not the same as multiple modules with dependencies between them. An application and its subapplications are more tightly coupled together, in terms of both class relationships and development process.

Two independent applications can have a prerequisite relationship, but it's strictly in one direction. One application uses and depends on the other, and they may be at different layers in the architecture. For example, the QuestionUI application has the prerequisite QuestionModelling. User-interface classes can freely make use of model classes, but the reverse is forbidden. If we want to run a server without a user interface we can easily remove the user-interface classes and still use the model classes.

Two subapplications of the same application, on the other hand, can freely make use of each other's classes, and it can be difficult to separate the two applications. For example, we might break up QuestionModelling into two subapplications Questions and Answers, each containing the classes suggested by its name. We will have many references back and forth between these subapplications. Questions will refer to Answers, and Answers will refer to Questions. It would be very difficult to separate this out to form an image with only Answers and no Questions.

Similarly, with two independent applications, development operations such as versioning and releasing are completely de-coupled. We can load and unload the two applications independently, and mix and match versions. Subapplications have a common parent and that parent can be versioned only when both subapps are versioned, coupling their development. Normally, both will be loaded or unloaded together in the version specified by their parent.

Unfortunately, this distinction doesn't provide much guidance for when to make a component a subapplication rather than an independent application. In general, a good rule of thumb is to use applications by default and only put things into subapplications to use conditional loading for platform-specific code. The following are some additional guidelines for using subapplications.

When to Use Subapplications
Use subapplications to

- organize platform-specific code for conditional loading
- break up a large application without needing to disentangle complex interdependencies
- help reduce namespace clutter and visually group related code together

For example, if we're producing a class library to run in both VisualWorks and VisualAge, we can make most of the code portable, but put small amounts into dialect-specific subapplications.

Another example would be packaging a poorly organized application in VisualAge. There might be many different domain applications, all of which are tightly coupled. Because these are all part of a single project and we don't expect them to exist separately, we can just group them together as subapplications and avoid the need to understand the dependencies. In the long term we'll need to thoroughly refactor the application, but the use of subapplications provides a short-term workaround.

When Not to Use Subapplications
Avoid using subapplications to

- hierarchically decompose an application
- group code that is not otherwise coupled

For example, for the first large ENVY project one of this book's authors worked on, we decided to put our entire project in one application, with subapplications to divide it into subsystems, nested seven layers deep. This seemed perfectly natural, but it turned out to be a very bad idea because it tightly coupled all the different subsystems and made our baseline process much more complicated than it needed to be.

One example where using subapplications might be appropriate is in organizing tests. The question is where to put the unit tests that test a particular domain application. We can put them in a separate application, but then they're not as easy to find. Instead, we can put them in a subapplication of the domain application and have them be conditionally loaded based on the value of some global flag indicating whether this is a development image. This is a questionable case because it's not clear that the value of keeping the tests close to the domain classes outweighs the complexity of the configuration management we need to do. I probably wouldn't do this, choosing instead to keep the tests separate and rely on finding references to a class as a way of seeing which tests use it. For more discussions on possible architectures, see the "Large Projects" section that follows, particularly the "ENVY Implications" subsection.

Finally, note that we also have the option of using configuration maps and conditional loading at that level. This offers many of the same features as conditional loading in subapplications, but can be more flexible because a required map does not need to be uniquely owned by a single parent map. See "Conditional Loading in Configuration Maps" later in this chapter.

The Subapplication Class

Like applications, every subapplication has a special class, with the same name as the subapplication that contains it. For a subapplication, this class inherits from SubApplication. The presence of this class can be confusing, but it is also a very powerful feature. As with application classes, this class receives notification of various system events and can be used to manipulate the subapplication in the repository. This (sub)application class is the reason (sub)application names must follow class naming conventions (start with an uppercase letter; cannot contain whitespace).

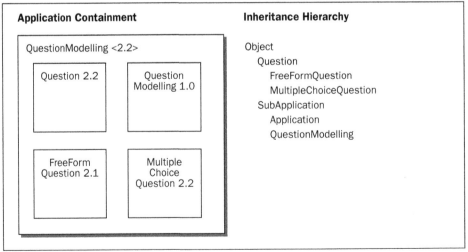

Figure 4-1: The application contains the class and the application class, but the application class has no relationship to the class.

In this context it's important to distinguish between inheritance and containment. The subapplication contains various classes. It's also possible for classes to inherit from the SubApplication class, but that would be an entirely different relationship. For example, if we take our QuestionModelling application and we add the class InvalidAnswer, it will be contained in the QuestionModelling application, but it will not inherit from the class QuestionModelling. This should only be confusing at first. There are no good reasons to inherit from these special classes, so don't do it. If you do find you've done it by accident, it's no problem; just change the superclass to the right one, probably Object.

Conditional Loading of Subapplications

The most important feature of subapplications is the capability to choose at load-time whether they load based on *configuration expressions*. This gives us the ability to programmatically configure our applications for different environments. The most important application of this is in managing platform-dependent code. Smalltalk makes it possible to write completely portable code, but in some situations developers may want to write code specific to a particular operating system, Smalltalk dialect, or system configuration. Conditional loading lets us to do this.

A parent application contains configuration information, which can be viewed using the Application Editions Browser, shown in Figure 4-2. This information includes a list of the following:

- **Configuration Expressions:** Any valid Smalltalk expression returning true or false. This will be compiled and evaluated at load-time.

- **Subapplications:** A list of subapplications with version information. If the

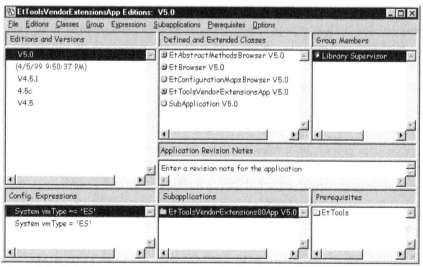

Figure 4-2: This shows the editions of the Application EtToolsVendorExtensionsApp, with conditional loading based on the expression *System vmType ~= 'ES'* to determine whether this is a VisualAge or VisualWorks image.

corresponding configuration expression evaluates to true, then all these subapplications will be loaded.

- ■ **Prerequisites:** A list of prerequisite applications without version information. If the corresponding configuration expression evaluates to true, then these will be treated as the prerequisites of this application during this load.

These three items together are often referred to as an *application lineup*.

Conditional loading can be invaluable when shipping an application with complex configurations. It's most useful for a toolsmith because it's possible to ship a single application or configuration map that automatically configures itself properly at load-time for a variety of different environments.

Conditional Loading Issues

While conditional loading is very powerful, certain issues can restrict its usefulness. This is a complex and heavyweight mechanism. In many cases the configuration-dependent code is relatively small and can be more easily managed in memory. An example of this distinction is shown in the VisualAge and VisualWorks handling of platform-specific widget code. VisualAge has code for native widgets on a wide variety of platforms, and this code is conditionally loaded based on the host operating system. VisualWorks, in contrast, uses its own widget library with a LookPolicy for each operating system. Because this is much smaller, VisualWorks can keep all the widget code in the image and determine the host operating system at run-time. The VisualAge approach gives greater fidelity to the platform, while the VisualWorks approach enables a single image to be binary-portable to all platforms. Both strategies are valid, and the choice depends on our objectives.

Configuration Expressions Must be Robust

Be careful with configuration expressions. These are Smalltalk code fragments that will be compiled and evaluated in the development image as they are loaded. Be very careful to avoid any assumptions about what is or is not present in the image. For example, write

    (Smalltalk at: #Question ifAbsent: [^nil]) version = 3

rather than

    Question version = 3

because the Question class may or may not be present. Any error in a configuration expression can lead to a compile or run-time error at load-time. This is a very undesirable situation, particularly if we are shipping a class library to an end user so that load-time occurs at the customer site.

Order of Evaluation

Configuration expressions are evaluated in order until one of them is true. At that point the configuration information is applied and all other expressions are ignored. While these semantics are clear, they are not intuitive, and they can lead to duplication. For example, it would be useful to create configurations that load the union of the subapplications specified in the configuration expressions in the following table.

Configuration Expression	Subapplications
('WIN-NT' includes: (System subsystemType: 'CG'))	WinNTSubApp 1.0
('MOTIF' includes: (System subsystemType: 'CG'))	UnixSubApp 1.0
Testing = true	TestingSubApp 1.0
True	MainSubApp 1.0, GUISubApp 1.0

Unfortunately, this is not possible with the semantics of configuration expressions. In the previous example, if ENVY detects that the platform is Windows NT, it will load WinNTSubApp, and then stop and not even consider any of the other expressions. Because it will be missing the domain and GUI classes, the system won't work at all.

To load multiple subapplications with different configurations for each platform requires duplicating the list of subapplications in each expression and/or creating more complex expressions as shown in the following example.

Configuration Expression	Subapplications
('WIN-NT' includes: (System subsystemType: 'CG')) and: [Testing not]	MainSubApp 1.0, GUISubApp 1.0, WinNTSubApp 1.0
('WIN-NT' includes: (System subsystemType: 'CG')) and: [Testing]	MainSubApp 1.0, GUISubApp 1.0, WinNTSubApp 1.0, TestingSubApp 1.0

This is tedious and error-prone.

One convention that helps make this more manageable is to "explain" each configuration in a comment at the beginning of the expression. Because they are full Smalltalk expressions, they can contain arbitrary comments, such as:

"NT Normal" ('WIN-NT' includes: (System subsystemType: 'CG')) and: [Testing not]

or

"NT Test" ('WIN-NT' includes: (System subsystemType: 'CG')) and: [Testing]

Editing Configuration Expressions

The previous guidelines tend to make configuration expressions long. One of the secondary problems with extensive use of configuration expressions is that the tools to manage them do not provide good support.

It is not possible to edit a configuration expression once it's created. If we select a configuration expression, and then select Add from the menu, we get the text of the selected expression as the default in the prompter, and can edit it there. This creates, however, a completely new expression and you will need to copy over the configuration information manually and delete the old one. This tends to discourage extensive use of these expressions, or encourages tool building.

Conditional Loading Tricks

These issues tend to discourage use of conditional loading, but we can use some tricks to improve the management or make conditional loading more useful. Thanks to Eric Clayberg for both of these techniques.

Adding a Level of Indirection

There's a saying that all computing problems can be solved by adding another layer of indirection. In this case, adding an extra level of subapplications can greatly simplify loading expressions.

We've already seen that complex expressions require duplicating conditions and subapps in each lineup, as in the following example.

Configuration Expression	Subapplications
('WIN-NT' includes: (System subsystemType: 'CG')) and: [Testing]	MainSubApp 1.0, GUISubApp 1.0, WinNTSubApp 1.0, TestingSubApp 1.0

Now, suppose we break up the subapplications with an additional layer of "shell" subapplications called AlwaysLoadShell, NTShell, and TestingShell. These contain no classes, and are always loaded. The shell subapps contain their own conditions, which are used to determine whether the actual platform-specific code is loaded, as follows.

App/Subapp Name	Configuration Expression	Subapplications
MainApp	true	AlwaysLoadedShellSubApp 1.0, NTShellSubApp 1.0, TestingShellSubApp 1.0
AlwaysLoadedShellSubApp	true	MainSubApp 1.0, GUISubApp 1.0
NTShellSubApp	('WIN-NT' includes: (System subsystemType: 'CG')	WinNTSubApp 1.0
TestingShellSubApp	Testing	TestingSubApp 1.0

What has this accomplished? We've now separated out the conditions and the sub-applications to load so that each can be maintained individually and there's no duplication. This can be a big help with complex loading expressions.

Avoiding Method Conflicts

Another "trick" used for conditional loading is avoiding method conflicts with base class extensions. Tool vendors often want to define simple extension methods in base classes. Methods such as Stream>print:, Object>asString, or Collection>any are very convenient extensions. Unfortunately, if we're a third-party author of development tools we can't just add the method because another tool author may have done the same, and our extension will cause a collision. In addition, these methods may be defined in VisualWorks, but not in VisualAge, or vice-versa.

We can avoid this situation by creating a subapplication for the method in question (it has to be one for each method). Let's suppose the method is Object>asString. In this subapplication's parent, add the condition

```
(Object respondsTo: #asString) not
    or: [(Object>#asString) application name == #MyApp]
```

That is, we're checking that the system does not have this method, or if it does have it, the one that it has is ours. This last point is important because otherwise reloading the application when it was already in memory would cause the method to disappear. Also note that the method > is a handy shortcut for accessing compiled methods. When sent to a class with a selector as the argument, it returns a compiled method.

Conditional Loading of Configuration Maps

Almost all of the concepts we've discussed with respect to conditional loading of subapplications also apply at the level of configuration maps. A configuration map includes a list of

- **Configuration expressions:** Any valid Smalltalk expression returning true or false. This will be compiled and evaluated at load-time.

- **Required maps:** A list of configuration maps with version information. If the configuration expression evaluates to true, then all these configuration maps will also be loaded.

The semantics of required map loading are almost exactly the same as for subapplication loading. Again, the first configuration expression that evaluates to true will be used, and all others will be ignored.

The major difference between configuration maps and subapplications in this respect is that subapplications have a unique parent (sub)application within the image. A particular subapplication can be referenced from more than one parent in the library, but only one of those parents can be loaded at a time in the image. Configuration maps do not have a unique parent, and the same configuration map can be referenced in multiple different ways in configuration maps that are loaded.

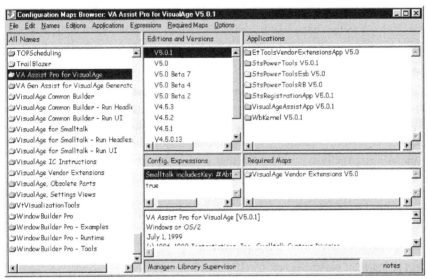

Figure 4-3: The configuration maps browser, showing required maps.

This provides more flexibility, but it does have a downside. If a configuration map is specified differently in different places, then the specification is ambiguous, and what actually gets loaded will depend on the most recently loaded parent map.

Large Projects

Managing a small software project is relatively easy. Things get tough when we try to scale up — sometimes much tougher. There are many issues involved and many different ways to deal with them. In general, this is the subject of software engineering. We can't address all the problems here, but we'll touch on some of the issues and see how the concepts of large project management apply in an ENVY context.

The basic problem is the limit to how much one person can hold in his or her head at one time. A large project, almost by definition, is one that exceeds that limit. If the project is too complex to understand, we need to reduce that complexity to a manageable level. One thing we can do is bring in more developers and partition the project so that each developer only needs to fully understand a small piece. This helps, but if we don't manage the communication overhead it can become overwhelming. If we don't communicate enough — with each other, with management, with the users — we risk losing focus and not delivering the right thing.

Often, the problem is not just a single large project, but many projects — small and large — trying to share resources and get re-use. These projects may be geographically scattered, with remote developers and different ideas and priorities.

Finally, although we may have all the latest software engineering techniques at our disposal, reality may impose less-than-ideal solutions on us in some areas, and we have to deal with the compromises.

Communication

The dominant issue in a large project is communication. There's too much for one person to know and too many people to be kept informed. Poor communication can result in difficult bugs, when changes to one area affect another one that's apparently far removed. Attempts to ensure communication can backfire into endless meetings with no development getting done.

The normal way of dealing with these problems is with *modularity*. We break the system into modules and classes that are isolated from each other's internals. We break the project team down into smaller teams, each working on particular aspects of the system. Because the modules are isolated, changes are less likely to propagate and developers don't need to think about as much at a time, and don't need to communicate with as many people about changes.

Modularity places a lot of importance on an initial architecture to determine how the subsystems are divided and what each one covers. This doesn't mean we should spend enormous amounts of effort up front building the ideal architecture, or that we should hesitate to change one that isn't working for our project. It does mean that we should put some up-front thought into the basic organizing principles we're going to use, and how they affect team and project structures. This will also affect where the most stable interfaces in our system are found.

This isn't the only way of attacking the problem of communication in a software project. The hierarchical breakdown we're discussing more or less mirrors standard software engineering practices. An interesting alternative mechanism is Extreme Programming, which still emphasizes modularity, but instead of trying to limit the scope of communication, integrates it as a fundamental part of development. See the section "Extreme Programming and ENVY," later in this chapter.

Library Architecture

The code within a project will be broken up in a number of ways. At all levels we have a potential division between run-time code and development-time code. Normally the development-time code will be a strict superset of the run-time code, so we will specify the development configuration as an add-on to the run-time configuration.

Projects can also be divided into layers. Within a layer, we partition by subsystem and between run-time and development components. The division within a layer depends on the exact structure of the system, so we'll focus here on the layers we typically see in systems.

Ideally, each layer depends only on layers beneath it, and the lower layers will change more slowly than the upper layers. Multiple projects might depend on the same lower layer, so changes to the lower layer need to be more carefully controlled.

1. Kernel

This layer contains the basic Smalltalk class library. This includes all of the classes supplied by the vendor. Patches and bug fixes to the base libraries are also in this level. Enhancements to the library might be here, but they are more likely implemented as class extensions and are found at higher levels.

This layer is typically maintained by the Library Supervisor. It changes rarely, and any changes should be carefully tested because they may have far-reaching impact. Maintaining the same basic library is important in achieving re-use across projects.

2. Tools

This layer contains the code for third-party products (for example, WindowBuilder runtime, TOPLink, and GemStone libraries) as well as internal system extensions and tools. If we have our own internal tools then they are maintained by the toolsmiths responsible for them. The Library Supervisor is typically responsible for third-party products, although this may also be assigned to developers with detailed knowledge of particular tools. This layer may be divided into two layers, where third-party tools are treated differently from internal tools, particularly if the internal tools are rapidly changing. Within this layer, run-time components are separated from development-time components and can be loaded separately.

3. Domain Objects

This layer contains the business objects used in our application. It is maintained by the project developers and makes use of the run-time portion of the tools layer. All of the domain object code is typically used at run-time, so the development-time portion of this layer consists primarily of tests.

4. User Interface

This layer contains the user-interface logic. This consists primarily of GUI layouts and the "glue" layer between domain models and widgets. In VisualWorks this is represented by ApplicationModel subclasses, and in VisualAge by composition editor parts or by WindowBuilder WbApplication subclasses. In a Web-based system, this might also consist of classes that emit HTML or XML using Web frameworks such as VisualWave, IBM's WebParts, or Swazoo. The project developers also maintain this code. Along with the domain object layer, this is where most day-to-day coding takes place. Again, the only development-time portion of this code usually consists of tests.

ENVY Implications

How do these layers and the division into run-time and development-time code translate into ENVY? At the top level this is almost always done with configuration maps. We need a top-level configuration map so that developers can load the entire project at once.

Given that, we have a choice between organizing the system using configuration maps with required maps or using subapplications with conditional loading. We'll examine both of these alternatives. First, let's look at configuration maps.

In this scheme the main map won't contain anything directly, but will reference each subsystem through required maps. These subsystems may represent entire layers (for example, base fixes) or pieces of a layer representing modules of a project (for example, billing). A layer typically is divided into many different subsystems,

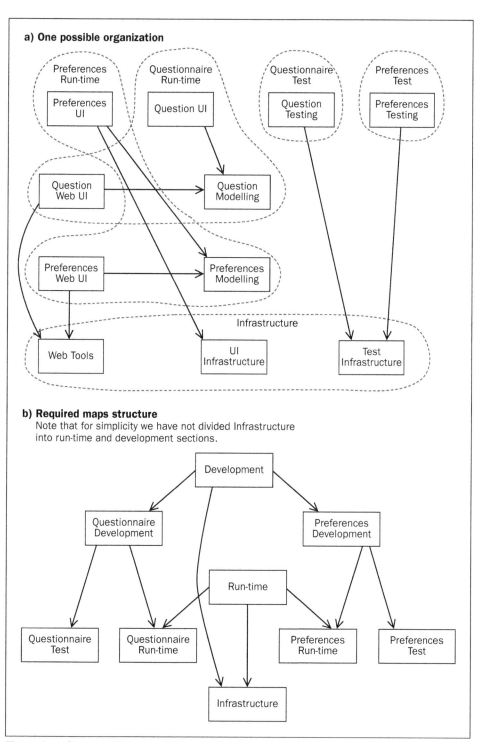

Figure 4-4: One possible organization for the Questionnaire application, using configuration maps as the main unit.

represented by configuration maps and/or applications. We divide into applications for various reasons including maximizing the cohesion of a component, ensuring correct prerequisites within a layer, and minimizing the number of developers working on an application at one time.

For example, over time our Questionnaire project might expand into a larger system. In addition to handling poll-type questionnaires, we can branch out into supporting user preferences. These are special questionnaires in which answers are maintained on a per-user basis and can be modified over time, retaining a history of answers. Figure 4-4 shows one possible project organization and its dependency structure.

This partitioning uses applications as the basic unit, with configuration maps to organize them. Note that we have carefully partitioned the two subsystems of questionnaires and preferences from each other. We have also separated out the run-time classes from the purely development-time classes, and we have separated out the

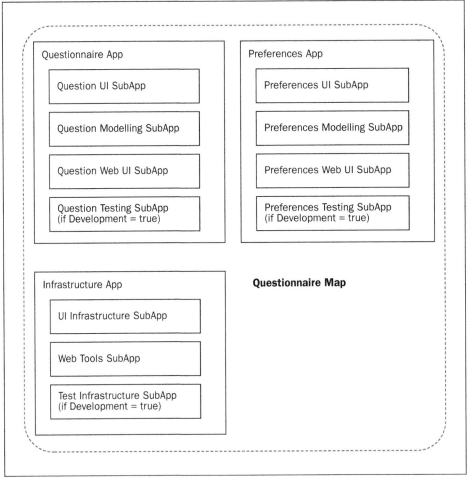

Figure 4-5: Another possible organization for the Questionnaire application, using applications as the main unit and subapplications for divisions within the project.

infrastructure (tools) layer from the domain object and GUI layers. A very large application may have a significantly more complex structure than this, and it can become worthwhile to build tools that help organize these components at a higher level. One such tool is described in the section "A Simple Project Management Tool."

As mentioned previously, it's also possible to use subapplications as the basic unit and have applications that group them using conditional loading (see the "Subapplications" section earlier in this chapter). Both approaches can produce well-organized code (see Figure 4-5). The subapplication approach has the advantage that it can reduce the number of top-level components and group subsystem-related code closer together visually in the Application Manager/Organizer. It can also avoid prerequisite issues because the subapplications of one application are treated as a unit for prerequisite checking. The disadvantages of the subapplication technique are that it requires the use of conditional loading, making it harder to follow the system organization, and that avoiding prerequisite checking can lead to problems that are hidden until packaging-time. The two approaches can also be combined, using subapplications for lower-level groupings and configuration maps for the higher levels.

Manageability

Manageability is also a problem area for large projects. With a large project it's easy for developers to lose focus and not concentrate on what needs to be done. Again, this is primarily dealt with by breaking the system up into smaller units — in this case tangible deliverables. The traditional "waterfall" methodology breaks the project into large deliverables for requirements, analysis, design, implementation, and testing. This helps, but has drawbacks, which have been extensively described elsewhere.

More recent work on "spiral" methodologies tries to break these phases down into many short iterations of the full development cycle. This has several benefits, and one of the most important is frequent concrete deliverables that can be used to measure progress. If we can implement part of the functionality very quickly, we get rapid feedback on whether it was the right thing, what changes we need to make, and where the potential problems are. If a design is flawed or unimplementable, this fact becomes visible very quickly.

These are primarily process issues, so they don't have much effect on our ENVY organization. The primary effect is to push us toward very rapid integration cycles, using the ENVY tools to enable concurrent development with rapid merging. We also want to organize the system so that developers can easily get in sync with the current version. This means we should have a top-level configuration map that enables one-click loading and ensure that it's kept current.

Multiple Projects and Re-Use

Within an organization it's often the case that individual projects are relatively small, but many of them exist, making interproject communication the bottleneck. This is particularly true if projects are trying to re-use infrastructure or domain code.

When we're trying to do this, process issues become critical. One fundamental issue is the motivation for different projects to cooperate with each other. Although the ideal of cooperation is rarely in question, projects are very strongly motivated by their own deliverables and deadlines, and the effects on another project are at best a secondary consideration. Organizational techniques can help address this, but these are beyond the scope of this book.

ENVY Implications

Assuming that projects are interested in cooperating and re-using code, we need to facilitate that communication. One mechanism is to ensure that all projects are using a common development setup. For example, as much as possible, use a single repository rather than one repository per project. In the past, ENVY had issues scaling to support large numbers of users, but the newer versions of EMSRV eliminate this problem. Sharing a repository between projects means that developers have immediate access to code from the other projects, and can re-use code, easily submit bug fixes or enhancements, and browse the library.

A shared repository also makes it easier to ensure that everyone is using the same versions of the basic applications. This is almost a prerequisite for significant re-use. Small differences between the basic toolsets each project is using can lead to subtle errors in the re-used code. An enforced common base standard is important to ensure this doesn't happen.

Multiple Streams

In an ideal world we wouldn't need multiple streams of development. Everyone would work on the same version, updates would be immediate, and we'd stop when we were finished. This is a worthwhile goal to strive for, but unfortunately it's not realistic in most circumstances. Most projects have at least a couple of different streams, representing bug fixes, development for minor releases, and development for upcoming major releases. In some projects much more overlap can exist, and there may be different teams working on the different streams.

This is almost inevitably painful, partly because it violates software engineering principles. We want to express things exactly once, avoiding redundancy. With different streams we have different copies of the code and redundancy between those streams. Some changes will need to be made, validated, and tested in every stream, which is a painful and time-consuming process. Tools can help us, but fundamentally this is a manual process.

There's no magical answer to this dilemma. We need to keep the divergences under control and stay as close to the ideal model as we can. Where we diverge, we need to make sure that processes are in place to keep the streams consistent. We may not be able to avoid parallel streams of development, but we can make sure that we have a clear base and that deviations from that base are as small as possible, last as short a time as possible, are tracked carefully, and are merged into the base as soon as feasible. We should also be sure that testing tracks these streams, so that tests added to a maintenance release also become part of the main regression test suite and ensure that the errors they detect don't recur.

ENVY techniques for developing with multiple streams in ENVY are discussed in more detail in the "Streams" section that follows later in this chapter.

Multi-Site Development

In some cases we may have development at more than one site, either with a distributed team or with individual developers working remotely. This situation becomes a special case of multiple streams, with each site as a separate stream of development, but in this case streams evolve far more rapidly than normal and there's more frequent interaction between streams. The problems are worse with geographically distant sites, particularly if there are time-zone differences.

While distributed development has some big advantages, it is significantly more complex. Integration between multiple sites can become very time-consuming. If possible, it's a good idea to partition the work between sites such that the overlap is minimized. In the ideal case, cross-site integration consists of just loading up new versions of what the other site was working on and testing them. Even if there's overlap, keeping it to a minimum can greatly improve productivity. Typically there's one designated person to do the integration, whether it's one per component, subsystem, or one global "load builder."

An alternative technique is to maintain a single centralized repository and have remote developers connect via a WAN. This is certainly possible, but it can put a serious strain on the network. The protocol between an image and the EMSRV process is communication-intensive. It doesn't use a lot of bandwidth, but it's very sensitive to network latency. Unless we have very good network connectivity, developing this way will likely be frustrating for the remote developers, and should be limited to short or "emergency" sessions.

Beyond integration, many communications issues exist. People at remote sites probably won't talk to one another enough. Therefore, we need to ensure that the developers understand one another, have the same goals, and respond to each other's needs in a timely way. A good communication infrastructure is important. Developers should have good facilities for communicating with each other by telephone, e-mail, and whatever other mechanisms are available. We should be sure there is adequate, reliable bandwidth to quickly transfer large files back and forth. Expect some degree of travel so that developers can have face-to-face time.

Tools exist to help support multi-site development. OTI has a tool called ENVY/Replicator that can manage propagation of components to different repositories. It's a useful tool, but not necessarily appropriate to all development processes. Many projects have built their own tools to partially automate some of the more tedious aspects of keeping different sites in sync. With this book we provide a facility for checkpointing, described in the section "Checkpoints." This enables us to make a versioned copy of a component, suitable for export to another repository, without needing to make a baseline. Essentially it is a snapshot of the current edition's state.

This can speed up cross-site integration. The three-way differences browser (see the section "Three-Way Differences") is a useful tool for merging separate streams.

One problem to watch for when working with sites in different time zones is that ENVY makes extensive use of timestamps for recording component information. If we have developers exchanging components with quick turnaround, the order in which things actually happened can be confusing. One solution is to set everyone's system clocks on one common time.

That's Nice, But...

We've given some advice about how to handle a large project. Unfortunately, one of the other characteristics of large projects is that many development decisions have already been made and cannot easily be changed. We may have an existing process, existing tools, mandated use of a waterfall process, widely distributed development, or other issues. In these circumstances we need to be more creative. If the project is in serious trouble, then it may be possible to make radical changes in the process. If it's not, then we may need to choose our battles. Decide which mechanisms are causing the most problems and focus on those. It may be possible to address the problems while still remaining within the framework that has been dictated, or it may be possible to make a solid business case for moderate change. Other areas may be suboptimal, but still livable. Some things may simply not be subject to change. For example, if the development team is scattered over the country as individual virtual offices, we probably can't change that, and we'll need to adapt our processes to deal with it. See "Troubleshooting" (Chapter 10) for some more concrete advice on dealing with project problems.

Streams

The concept of multiple independent streams of development is fundamental in software. In any system with staged releases we will almost inevitably have development intended to maintain version 1.0, and at the same time different development to support the forthcoming version 2.0. Streams can also appear in support of development for different platforms, development at geographically separated sites, or for other reasons.

On the other hand, developing with multiple streams is almost always painful. Code is duplicated, some changes must be manually propagated between streams, and there is always the possibility of error. For some general discussion of development with streams see the "Multiple Streams" section earlier in this chapter. This section concentrates on the mechanisms of working with streams in ENVY.

In some respects ENVY supports streams well. We can use different open editions to represent different streams of development. There is, however, no explicit notion of a stream in ENVY and some aspects of the process still need to be manually managed with naming conventions and development processes.

Representing Streams

The first question is how to represent streams, and that we can do quite well using component editions. In nonstreamed development we would only ever have one edition of an application open at a time. All developers would load that edition and release their classes into it. Making sure that everyone in a stream uses the same edition makes integration and reloading simple.

With streams we start using multiple open editions. Each edition represents a stream of development. Recall that releasing always means releasing into a parent component, and into one particular edition of that component. By choosing the edition to release into, we're choosing which stream of development we are affecting. Here we can see one of the reasons that ENVY separates versioning and releasing into two separate operations. Versioning gives the component a name but doesn't say anything about which stream(s) it belongs to. Releasing indicates the relationship between components and their parents without saying anything about how they were versioned. This lets us separate the definition of streams and configurations (specified through the release operation) from version control (specified by versioning).

Developers load the top-level configuration map for the stream they're working on and automatically get the right class versions and application editions/versions. They will normally release their changes into the loaded editions, which are then automatically in the right stream. This gets more complicated when a change has to be made in multiple different streams, but it can still be kept manageable.

For example, suppose we have two streams in our Questionnaire project. One represents bug fixes for version 1.0, the other represents new development for version 2.0. Perhaps Joseph makes a change to Question for version 2.0 and releases it into that stream. Alan may make a bug fix for version 1.0 and release it into that stream. He also needs to have a regression test for that bug, and test that it doesn't occur in the 2.0 stream. If that bug occurs there as well, he may need to release his change into the version 2.0 stream, merge his changes with others in the 2.0 stream, or write a different fix that is appropriate for the 2.0 code base. See Figure 4-6.

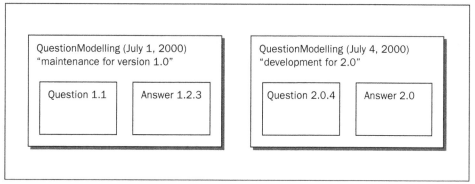

Figure 4-6: The QuestionModelling application with two streams.

Conventions

Using open editions to represent streams works well, but some issues still exist. First of all, we've only talked about maintaining the open editions. What happens when we start versioning off the different streams? We still want to be able to manage separate streams for 1.0 and 2.0, even when they have multiple versions.

ENVY doesn't have support for explicit streams, so we need to designate our streams somehow. The usual mechanisms are comments and version naming conventions. At the configuration-map level we can add comments to indicate the stream, and these are always visible in the browser. For all levels of component, we can provide version names that indicate the stream.

Earlier, we described the default ENVY version naming conventions (see "Version Naming Conventions"). The default convention carries some support for streams, where we can name versions as 1.0.1 to indicate a patch release for version 1.0. A more explicit mechanism is to name the streams. For example, 2.0 Beta [AK 7-25-2002a] could indicate a named stream 2.0 Beta with a version within that stream identified by developer initials, date, and a single letter to indicate one of multiple versions on a single day.

Issues

Using these conventions helps distinguish streams, but there are still issues to be aware of. The top-level configuration map normally indicates the stream, but if we're looking at editions of applications or classes there's no direct way to identify the streams. This is particularly true if subcomponents don't have a consistent naming convention, or for open editions. Classes may quite often be released into multiple different streams, although application and subapplication editions are normally for a single stream. We can flag a particular edition with the ENVY "notes" feature, but notes don't show up by default in most browsers (the configuration map browser is an exception).

In general, any time we're doing a stream-based operation on lower-level components we'll need to manually filter out the editions we're interested in. For example, if we have a list of all the application editions, we can use version naming conventions, notes, or other indications to determine which versions and editions we're interested in. Again, it's possible to build tools that can automate some of these processes. For example, see "Three-Way Differences."

Finally, there are issues in dealing with many independent streams. These issues most frequently arise with small, independent patches. Responsibility for ensuring that patches are applied correctly and that any dependencies are correctly accounted for rests with the user. This can result in unwieldy version names such as 3.1 + patch 345b 98-09-11 + patch 911 99-4-1. In general, this is best addressed with a process issue that tests patches for compatibility, ensures that patches are always applied sequentially, or frequently collects patches together into larger-granularity maintenance releases.

Extreme Programming and ENVY

As much as there is a single "standard" process in software engineering, what we have described is reasonably close to that standard. We have favored the spiral over the waterfall and the lightweight over the heavyweight, but in general this falls well within the boundaries of the standard methodologies.

While ENVY supports this process well, it can also support a much wider range of methodologies. As an example of this, we will describe using ENVY on an Extreme Programming (XP) project. This section is not a tutorial on Extreme Programming or an attempt to justify it. From our point of view, the interesting aspect is how this process can be supported using the ENVY toolset. For more information on the subject, see Beck (2000) or Jeffries et al. (2000) or one of the Web sites www.xprogramming.com, www.extremeprogramming.org, or c2.com/cgi/wiki.

In general terms, Extreme Programming is a lightweight methodology that attempts to reduce the development process to its barest essentials, enabling programmers to concentrate on the important issues. There is a strong emphasis on communication, user involvement, testing, and maintainability of the code, with very little use of traditional design artifacts.

ENVY Issues

Some aspects of Extreme Programming are easily accommodated in ENVY. For example, Extreme Programming attempts to always maintain a running system that passes its regression tests, with very frequent integrations. This fits very well with the ENVY model of continuous integration and the release process. The tests and the code can easily be separated using ENVY applications or subapplications, and ENVY is perfectly happy to let us write the tests first.

Other aspects of this process are very foreign to ENVY. For example, Extreme Programming uses collective code ownership. All developers are free to modify any code at any time and to release those changes. This strongly conflicts with ENVY's ideas on class ownership. Extreme Programming avoids the potential conflicts by practicing very frequent integration and a comprehensive test suite that must be run before release. Developers are less likely to break code they don't understand because they will discover that it's broken when they run the tests. Nevertheless, this has to be reconciled with ENVY's class ownership model.

With collective code ownership comes the possibility of integration conflicts. There are various ways to avoid these conflicts, but a common mechanism is to use sequential integration. Only one pair of developers is allowed to be merging in their changes at any given time. This can be enforced using a physical token that the integrating team holds onto, or simply by designating a particular machine as the "integration machine" where all preintegration tests and releasing takes place. In the latter case it's useful to have tools available that make it easier to load an unreleased configuration onto another machine, as well as to check for conflicts with changes that others have previously released.

Extreme Programming says that all development should be done by pairs of programmers. In effect, code is constantly reviewed, improving quality and productivity. Along with collective code ownership, this is difficult to reconcile with ENVY's ideas of code owners and developers.

Finally, Extreme Programming practices constant refactoring of code. This works well with ENVY, but does run into some limitations of the current versions. ENVY does not gracefully rename components or move components from one parent to another. For example, when renaming a class, ENVY loses the version history for that class. While the older versions still exist, ENVY doesn't know about the connection between them. There's a trick we can use to help with this, described in "Moving and Renaming" later in this chapter.

Extreme Guidelines

The preceding paragraphs might give the impression that it's difficult to use ENVY in an Extreme Programming process. This is not the case. In fact, the "flagship" project for Extreme Programming was the Chrysler Comprehensive Compensation (C3) project, which was built using VisualWorks with ENVY. That project had a team with a maximum of about 14 developers, and used a single integration machine. The following list gives a sample of guidelines used on that project.

- Always work under the name of one of the two people presently pairing. If you are logged in as someone else, everyone will have trouble sorting out where your code is.

- Version frequently. Always version at the end of day to make it easier to bring the code up tomorrow. Don't count on saving the image; you might be working at another machine tomorrow, or someone else might take over because you don't come in.

- Begin each version name with your initials: rej.231, rch.232, and so forth. Optionally use the initials of both team members.

- Use specialized version names sparingly when major changes have been put into a broad-ranging number of classes.

- Use frequent releases.

- Reload frequently. Load at least daily. Ideally, reload immediately before modifying code. Your work will go more easily if you are running and testing on current code.

There are also tools that can be particularly helpful in an Extreme Programming context. These include the following:

- Three-Way Differences Browser (see "Three-Way Differences"): If anyone can change any classes then it's important to be able to see what changed and merge those changes together easily.

- Release Only Clean: VA Assist Pro includes a very useful feature that warns us before we release any class in which the previous version is not the same as the released version. This helps keep us from overwriting other people's changes.

- changeUserTo:while (see "Writing Scripts"): This is a utility method we have provided that's useful for toolsmiths. This method is particularly useful on an XP project where collective code ownership and pair programming must be integrated into the ENVY model.

- Simple Project Management Tool (see "A Simple Project Management Tool"): This tool lets us specify the configuration required to load a project without making as much use of the ENVY conditional loading facilities.

Odds and Ends

A few more things are important to note when using ENVY that haven't quite fit into the categories we've discussed so far. This section gathers these bits and pieces with advice on techniques and conventions.

Application Naming

One of the subtle but contentious issues that comes up is how to name components. One school of thought says that component names should reflect the type of thing that is named. So, in our Questionnaire application we would have a configuration map called Questionnaire Map and the domain model application might be called QuestionModelApp. IBM, for example, has started using this convention for applications within VisualAge. We don't subscribe to this convention because it makes the names of the components more cluttered and it becomes harder to talk about them. Taking this convention to extremes we would start naming classes things like StringClass and DictionaryClass, which is clearly unwieldy.

There is, however, a sound reason behind this convention. All too often, when we first create an application we give it a name that describes the domain and then later on discover that we'd really like to use that name for a class in the domain. For example, we might create a PrintServer application, then later discover that the obvious main class in this application is also called PrintServer. Because this name conflicts with the application class, we can't use it. If we had called the application PrintServerApp, then there would be no problem.

The convention we've used in this book, rather than appending "App" to the name, is to try and use application names that are verb forms rather than noun forms. For example, we might have the Printing application or the PrintServing application. This makes reasonable sense to describe the domain of an application, but it's a form that is very unlikely to be used as a class name. In our domain example we have names such as QuestionModelling and QuestionTesting. Sometimes there isn't a reasonable verb form, so we simply use a name that seems unlikely to be a class name. For example, QuestionUI or TestInfrastructure are very general names, so they're unlikely to be the name of a specific window or test class. If there are naming conventions on the project (for example, window class names are suffixed with "View" or "Screen"), we can choose application names to avoid these conventions. Finally, plural names are unlikely to be class names, so it's relatively safe to name an application something like WebTools.

Moving and Renaming

ENVY does not have good support for renaming or moving classes. We can rename a class, but from ENVY's point of view this is no different from deleting the class with the old name and making a copy of it with the new name. In particular, when we look at the version history of the component, we'll find two separate histories with no connection between them: one with the new name and one with the old name.

ENVY does provide the capability to write "Notes" comments on a component, and these are specific to a particular version or edition. Using this feature we can note that a component was moved or renamed, but only someone who takes the time to look at the notes for each version will see this information. One solution to this problem is to build tools that can examine the notes field or a user field and display a uniform history. This would be ideal, but it is a significant amount of work. For more discussion of these mechanisms, see the "User Fields" section.

It turns out, however, that there's a much lighter-weight solution that makes clever use of version names to make the rename or move more obvious. When we rename a class, we can make a special final version of it that has a special version name indicating what it's been renamed to. When we create the renamed version, we can give the first version a similar special name. This doesn't let us see a uniform version history, and it doesn't let us browse differences between versions with different names, but at least it makes it very obvious what's happened to the history of a component. For example, we might have the version history of a class called Thing:

    Thing (renamed to NewThing)
    Thing [1.1 dev] AC 003
    Thing R 1.0
    Thing [1.0 dev] AC 002
    Thing [1.0 dev] AK 001

The special version name "(renamed to NewThing)" as the last version clearly tells anyone looking at the history where to look for further changes. In the NewThing version history we have the following:

    NewThing [1.1 dev] AC 005
    NewThing [1.1 dev] JP 004
    NewThing (renamed from Thing)

We can use a similar technique when we move classes between applications or subapplications between applications.

Summary

This chapter has covered many different topics, loosely united by the threads of large projects and advanced topics. For developers these are the more advanced topics useful in becoming power users of ENVY. For administrators these will be useful in project setup and in establishing project standards. For toolsmiths this material is important in developing cross-platform tools, supporting complex projects, and understanding the details of ENVY mechanisms.

Some of the important things to remember from this chapter are:

- ENVY supports creating configurations that describe the entire state of a project. This gives us reproducible builds that can be loaded as a single operation.

- Configurations can be defined using either subapplications or "required maps" of configuration maps.

- Subapplications don't have their own prerequisites, but use their parent's.

- It's important to distinguish the different forms of hierarchical decomposition. Subapplication containment is not the same as a prerequisite and is not the same as inheritance. Think carefully about when to use subapplications.

- Conditional loading is supported based on arbitrary Smalltalk expressions. This is a powerful facility, but one that also has drawbacks.

- Lineups are evaluated from first to last and the first configuration expression that evaluates to true will be used. All others are ignored.

- We can simplify configuration expressions significantly by adding an extra layer of subapplications.

- Conditional loading can be used at the single-method level to add common system extensions without conflicting with other applications that might add the same code.

- Large projects may require a more sophisticated organization.

- Multiple streams can be represented in ENVY using top-level components and naming conventions.

- ENVY can support a variety of processes. An alternative to the main process we have described is Extreme Programming. Even though this abandons central ENVY ideas such as code ownership, it can readily be accommodated.

- When naming applications, use names that will not be needed for class names later.

- We can make class renames and moves easier to follow by using special version names to indicate what's happened to the class.

- It can be useful to extend ENVY with tool support. Some of the tools are mentioned here, but detailed information can be found in Chapters 7 and 9 ("Extending the System" and "Goodies").

═══Chapter 5═══

Formal Concepts

The previous four chapters have described ENVY concepts in a tutorial form, helpful for developers getting started with ENVY and advanced developers looking for detailed information and motivation for features. In this chapter we take a different approach, describing the ENVY feature set in a more formal way. This is more appropriate for readers with a background in configuration management seeking to understand the differences between ENVY and other systems. It's also appropriate for users familiar with ENVY who want to understand more about the theoretical motivations behind certain features. This chapter covers most of the material explained in the previous four chapters but in less detail and from a more theoretical perspective.

ENVY Products

Technically, *ENVY* is a generic term for an entire product line from Object Technology International (OTI). Most commonly, it is used to refer to the team programming environment ENVY/Manager. ENVY/Manager has existed for a variety of different Smalltalk environments. It was originally written for Digitalk's Smalltalk/V line, ported to ParcPlace's VisualWorks (now owned by Cincom Systems), and was then tightly integrated into IBM's VisualAge product line, supporting both the Smalltalk and Java versions. In this chapter we use the term ENVY to refer to the ENVY/Manager environment, as it exists for VisualWorks and VisualAge Smalltalk.

Components

The fundamental concept in ENVY is that of software components. We will begin introducing the different types of components: applications, subapplications, classes, class extensions, and configuration maps.

Applications

The most important component type is the *application*. Applications roughly correspond to functional modules. The name can be misleading because a software system (typically referred to as an application) will normally contain multiple ENVY applications. In an ENVY image, classes and methods are always contained in an enclosing application. Applications are said to *control* these classes and methods. An ENVY image contains multiple applications, possibly hundreds of them. In VisualAge the base classes are already divided according to ENVY applications. For other Smalltalk dialects the base class libraries are broken up into ENVY applications as part of the process of creating the ENVY version for that dialect. Because applications are organized along functional lines, the various methods in each class are grouped by functionality.

Every application has a list of other applications, which are its *prerequisites*. The prerequisites specified by the application are referred to as *direct prerequisites* or *immediate prerequisites*. Applications also have implicit prerequisites that are the prerequisites of their direct prerequisites, and so forth. These are referred to *as indirect prerequisites* or *nonlocal prerequisites*. All applications must have at least one prerequisite and prerequisites are not allowed to form cycles. Therefore, the chain of prerequisites defines a hierarchy. At the root of the hierarchy is the system-defined application Kernel, which uniquely has no prerequisites and is a prerequisite of every application, either directly or indirectly. If an application A has a prerequisite B, then A is said to be a *dependent application* of B.

For each application there is a corresponding *application class,* which has the same name as the application. This class serves as a place to put application-level behavior, most commonly associated with application initialization and cleanup.

Subapplications

Applications may contain one or more *subapplications*. In most ways, subapplications are the same as applications, but they can exist only within an application or another subapplication. Subapplications do not maintain prerequisites. By nature, a subapplication's one and only immediate prerequisite is its parent application. Subapplications can also contain subapplications, and there is no theoretical limit to the depth of this nesting, although in practice nestings consisting of more than three or four subapplications are rare.

The primary use of subapplications is in splitting up platform-dependent code that will only be loaded in particular configurations. Subapplications can also be used to partition large applications into smaller subunits. For more information on recommended usage of subapplications, see the "Subapplication Usage" section.

Classes and Class Extensions

Applications exist primarily to control classes. Each class in an image is *defined* in one and only one application, and that application is referred to as the *controller* of that class. The *class definition* contains the definition of that class (name, instance variables, class variables, and so forth) and zero or more class and/or instance methods for that class. Typically most of a class's methods are also contained in the controlling application.

Methods can be added to a class in other applications. This is referred to as *extending* the class, and the resulting collection of methods is called a *class extension*. While classes and class extensions are different, we typically think of them as one type of component. The class in the traditional Smalltalk sense consists of the definition and methods from the class definition and the union of the methods in all class extensions. Note that class extensions can only add methods; they cannot change the definition and they cannot redefine methods. Each method in the image is uniquely controlled by a single application.

Extensions permit developers to group the methods of a class by functionality. More important, extensions enable users to dynamically add functionality to a class. This is a vital facility if the image is to support more than one program, tool, or subsystem because the implementation of almost any program requires not just new classes but typically also new methods added to existing classes. A motivating example is the way in which the EtBaseTools application adds the method inspect to the class Object. This method is used as development-time functionality, so it does not belong as part of the core class Object. Nevertheless, it is enormously useful in development that all objects inherit this method. Adding it in a class extension makes this possible.

Methods

In ENVY, methods are first-class components in their own right. This is notably different from most other team programming tools, where methods are stored and managed only in the context of a larger unit. While ENVY requires methods to exist within the context of a class, each individual change to a method is saved to the repository and can be retrieved individually.

Methods are treated somewhat differently from higher-level components, but these distinctions are mostly to ease development. For example, methods do not have named versions and do not need to be explicitly released.

Configuration Maps

As a top-level component, ENVY defines the *configuration map*. A configuration map is a component that groups together applications.

If applications are analogous to modules, then configuration maps are project or program specifications. A configuration map can also be thought of as a complete *bill-of-materials* for a project because it specifies applications that may in turn specify subapplications, which may in turn specify subapplications, and so forth, down through classes and extensions, and finally methods.

Configuration maps can also specify prerequisites at the map level, using *required maps*. Required maps are configuration maps that will be loaded before this configuration map. They can have configuration expressions attached to them, similarly to subapplications, and in general required maps can serve as an alternative organizing principle to subapplications. For more information on using required maps, see "Conditional Loading in Configuration Maps."

Managing Components

ENVY provides two specific facilities for managing software development in its component-oriented environment — configuration management and version control. Configuration management helps manage complexity and version control helps manage change.

Configuration Management

A component's *configuration* or *lineup* is defined by its relationships to other components. A method is a component but has no configuration because it has no relationships to other components. Applications have a configuration, which is defined by the classes and subapplications it contains. In ENVY, only some relationships are subject to configuration management. For example, in an application we can configure the subapplications of an application differently in different circumstances, but we cannot configure the classes. Of course, we can move any class into a subapplication if we need to make it part of a configuration. The act of modifying a component's configuration is to *configure* that component. Thus far we have described each component as having a single configuration. In fact, ENVY allows configuration maps and applications to have multiple configurations or lineups. Each configuration is identified by a *configuration expression*. This is a Smalltalk expression that is evaluated when the component is loaded. The configuration expressions are ordered — ENVY uses the first configuration for which the corresponding expression evaluates to true and ignores the other configurations. If none of the expressions evaluates to true, then the component cannot be configured for the current environment. This usually means that the component cannot be loaded into that environment.

When components are initially created, they have one configuration with the expression true. When using multiple configurations it's common to leave the last expression in the ordered collection of configuration expressions as the expression true. This ensures that one configuration will always apply. The following table shows the configurable relationships for each component type.

Component	Configurable Relationships
Configuration Map	Required Maps
Application	Prerequisites, Subapplications
Subapplication	Subapplications

Configurations are a powerful facility. They permit configuration of components at load-time to enable the same type of operations more typically performed at compile or link-time in more traditional languages. For example, they permit us to build systems that run on multiple Smalltalk dialects and take advantage of specific features in each. For an example of using configurations for conditional loading, see the "Order of Evaluation" section.

Version Control

So far we have dealt with a two-dimensional world in which components are uniquely identified by their name and component type. A third dimension is added to the picture by ENVY's support for version control and history through multiple *editions* of components. For each component there can be multiple editions, each identified by a timestamp, for example, (9/8/99 12:45:22). The *timestamp* is the date and time the edition was created, and it will never change throughout the life of the component. The component name and timestamp together are known as the *signature*. For example, the application Kernel (10/4/97 15:00:01) is an application with the name Kernel that was created on the 10th of April 1997 at 3:00:01 pm.

Editions can be in one of two states. An open edition has a signature with a name and timestamp. Open editions can be modified. A version has a signature with a name and a version name; for example, in QuestionModelling R1.1, the version name is R1.1. Versions cannot be modified. Most component types can have both versions and editions, but methods are treated specially and are always listed as open editions.

Editions are generally created from versions (or from other editions in the case of methods). An edition is said to be based on another edition, and each edition records the previous edition if it exists. The collection of all previous editions for a particular component shows the history for that component. Development typically proceeds by creating an open edition of a component, making changes, versioning that component, and then creating another new open edition.

Versioning of a component freezes the state of that component and developers can later return to that state. This is useful for marking a particular state in the development process and in particular is useful for recalling the state of software that is to be shipped. This is often called *freezing* or *baselining*. Versioning also enables us to label the edition with a name such as 1.1 [Fixed PR 13459]. In this example, PR 13459 might be a report submitted by a user of the system or product, describing a defect.

Terminology

At this point we should clarify some terms. Considering version control, we will now use the term *component* to refer to the collection of all editions with the same name for a particular component type. We can see that the editions of a component, because they are related by a previous timestamp, can form a tree where editions with no previous edition are the roots of the tree. Editions descended from a particular edition form branches, and the leaves are defined by editions that as yet have no descendants.

We will also introduce the term *class edition*. A class edition is the generic term for either a class or a class extension — effectively a fragment of an entire class that is controlled by a single application.

Previously we defined basic component types. If we now redefine these in the three-dimensional world of component editions, we have the following:

- Configuration map editions specify application editions as well as configurations of required map editions
- Application editions specify configurations of subapplication editions and also specify prerequisites (note that prerequisites are specified only by name, not by edition; for the rationale behind this, see "Prerequisite Versions")
- Subapplication editions specify configurations of other subapplication editions
- Application editions specify class editions
- Class editions specify instance method editions and class method editions

Independence of Relationships

It's important to understand that in ENVY the relationships between components are independent of each other. There is no required progression from oldest to most recent, and multiple components can and often do refer to the same subcomponents.

For example, we might have three different configuration map editions that have elements in common. Two of the maps are different editions of the Questionnaire configuration map. The other is the distribution configuration map for the SUnit testing framework as follows:

Configuration Map Edition	Application Editions
Questionnaire 1.1 Beta 1	QuestionModelling 1.1
	SUnit 2.6
	QuestionTesting 1.1a
Questionnaire (10/8/99 12:01:32)	QuestionModelling (10/8/99 10:56:12)
	SUnit 2.6
	QuestionTesting 1.1a
SUnit 2.6	SUnit 2.6

For subapplications the situation is slightly more complex. Subapplications, as with applications and configuration maps, are independent or are *root* components in the library and can exist independently of any parent component or be referenced from multiple parents. However, when loaded into an image, the subapplication must have a unique parent. Therefore, a subapplication can be referenced from many different parent applications, but only one of those parents can be loaded into an image at one time in configurations that would cause the subapplication to be loaded.

Class editions and methods are not root components, and they cannot exist independently. A class edition is defined or extended in a particular application. A method in a class is also defined in a particular application. Different editions of the application can reference the same class edition, and different class editions of the same class in that application can reference the same method editions. Other applications cannot reference the class editions, and classes in other applications cannot reference the method edition.

The Image and the Library

We've talked about components in the library versus components loaded in the image, and we need to clarify this distinction. Normally all components exist in the ENVY repository, which serves as a database of all possible component editions. These editions may or may not be loaded into a particular development environment or image.

A specific edition in the library is called a *shadow*. A component edition in the image is referred to as a *resident*. Most operations work on resident components, but some operations can work directly on shadows, and the distinction can be important. ENVY also provides browsers specifically for shadows so that we can examine code in the repository without needing to load it.

Shadows can exist with relationships that may not be legal when those components are resident. Resident components must be related according to rules defined by ENVY. For example, suppose we have two applications A and B, where B is a prerequisite of A and A is a prerequisite of B. These two applications can exist in the library in this form, but if we try to load them into an image we will encounter an error because ENVY does not permit circular prerequisite relationships. Similarly, we described the preceding situation where multiple applications contain the same subapplication. This is allowed in the library, but within the image a subapplication must be defined with a unique parent. The same situation can arise with multiple applications defining the same class or method. This is allowed in the library (if it weren't, we would never be able to move a class or method because the new application edition would conflict with old editions in the library). In the image, the restriction is enforced and the applications will not be able to be simultaneously loaded.

We have said that normally all components exist in the library, and we refer to these as *managed* components. It may be possible to have unmanaged components. For example, in ENVY R5i for VisualWorks Release 5i, loading VisualWorks parcels into the image can create unmanaged components. The resulting components do not have any corresponding form in the library and are stored as scratch applications that exist only in the image. If we create an open edition of these applications a corresponding component will be built in the ENVY library and it will become managed code.

Loading Components

Shadows become resident when we load them. In general, loading a component creates a corresponding resident representation (or updates an existing resident representation). Loads are *atomic*, which means they will either succeed or fail in their entirety. If, for any reason, a load does not succeed, then the state of the image will revert to exactly what it was before the load was attempted.

Each component behaves slightly differently when loaded:

- Loading a method creates or updates a corresponding resident method.

- Loading a class definition creates or updates a corresponding resident class and loads all the methods defined in that class.

- Loading a class extension loads all the methods defined in that extension.

- Loading an application creates a corresponding resident application and loads all the classes and extensions it defines. If the application references any subapplications, then these are also loaded. If the application defines any prerequisites that are not currently loaded or are in the process of being loaded, then the user is prompted for the prerequisite edition to load. If the user does not specify an edition the load will fail.

- Loading a configuration map loads all the applications specified by that map but does not create a corresponding resident configuration map. Configuration maps have no resident representation and exist only as shadows.

Required map relationships are slightly different in that they are not enforced by ENVY. When loading a configuration map, a developer may choose to load the configuration map by itself or to load it with all its required maps. The latter choice loads each required map in order, first loading the required maps of each of those maps (and so forth), before finally loading the specified configuration map.

Scratch Editions

Shadows are editions that exist in the library but are not loaded in the image. There are also editions that exist only in the image, but not in the repository. These are *scratch editions*, and they are created so that a developer can work outside of the normal ENVY restrictions in a temporary edition. For example, we might want to add a printing statement into a method in the Kernel application for debugging purposes of some other code we're writing. We don't have permission to make an edition of Kernel, and we don't really want to make a full edition. We do not intend to ever release this code, but we need the right to make a temporary change to it in our image. A scratch edition lets us do this. A scratch edition can be changed into a real edition if we have the right privileges and later decide that we want to preserve that code after all.

Scratch editions are a valuable tool, but should be used sparingly. If significant development happens in scratch editions, it likely indicates that they are being used incorrectly.

Cooperative Development

One of the powerful features in ENVY is its support for concurrent development. Traditional configuration management and version control systems have used a check-in/check-out system where users check out and lock component editions. This prevents other users from simultaneously changing the same component edition. Concurrent file-based systems typically allow arbitrary changes, but then attempt automatic merges. ENVY takes a different approach and uses the concepts of class ownership and releasing as its fundamental mechanisms.

Releasing

Previously we introduced various relationships between component editions. For example, an application contains classes (both definitions and extensions). For each of these classes an application edition specifies a particular class edition. This is known as the *released edition*. The released edition is important for several reasons. First, when an edition of a component is loaded, its related components are also loaded — specifically the released editions of those related components. Second, when a component is versioned and frozen from further changes, all of its subcomponents are also frozen, and it is the released versions that will remain as the referenced components. Third, when we compare two editions of a component, it is the released editions of the referenced components that are compared. Last, the released edition is the approved edition for other developers to use.

Naturally it is possible to change the released edition of a component, and normally this is done explicitly through a *release* operation. We can explicitly release components in the following cases:

- Application editions specified by configuration maps
- Required maps specified by configuration map lineups
- Subapplication editions specified by application lineups
- Class versions specified by application editions
- Instance method editions and class method editions specified by class editions

As we will see, instance method editions and class method editions specified by class editions are also released implicitly during development. This is done to minimize the burden on developers of releasing each change to a method.

Class and Method Editions

Most explicit team programming activities take place at the application and configuration map levels and are relatively rare. Most developers spend most of their time working at the class and method levels. To streamline daily development activities, ENVY treats class and method editions in several ways.

Methods do not have versions. Method editions are always editions and can never be versioned. This saves time by not requiring version names on individual methods. However, method editions are different from all other editions because they have no subcomponents, and every modification creates a new edition. This is in contrast to other components, where new editions can be created only by explicitly creating a new edition out of a version.

For example, if we have an open class edition of Question and we add two instance variables and modify three methods in that class, we still have the same open edition of Question. We have no simple way to retrieve the previous state of the edition. In contrast, if we have an edition of the method Question>questionText and we change the source code and save it, we will have created a new edition of that method. The old edition still exists with its old source code.

In addition, releasing of new method editions happens automatically. Any new method edition created for a resident class will always be released. This is usually what the developer wants, and it saves a great many operations.

Class editions are treated specially in that they must be versions before they can be released, in contrast to all other component types. Methods don't need to be versions before they can be released because there are no method versions. For the higher-level components the rationale is more complex and is described later.

Classes are at a fine enough granularity that we assume the class edition will be private. If two developers are working on the same class at the same time they do not want to see each other's changes immediately but will wait until they're finished and then merge. In contrast, application editions are shared. If multiple people are working in the same application at once, we expect them to at least be notified of each other's changes as soon as they are released.

To support this process, ENVY treats class editions as private. Other developers cannot see our class editions until we have versioned them. Typically we will make a version and very quickly release it into the enclosing application, at which point other developers will load it automatically when they sync up by reloading the application. To achieve this syncing up, it's important that the other developers are using the same application edition we are, so application editions must be released into their higher-level components as editions. For a more detailed description of this process, see the sections "Team Development with Class Editions" and "Releasing Application Editions."

Reference Models

The concept of released editions only makes complete sense in the library. In the library, components only reference released editions because we can only change the reference in the library when we release something new in its place. In the image, on the other hand, an application can reference an open class edition that we're in the process of changing, and this is perfectly normal.

We can think of ENVY team development as a group of developers collectively building a model. Many developers all contribute to create, evolve, and refine a single reference model of the system. A single library can host many different models (one for each project or development team). Each reference model is typically defined by a single configuration map edition that references specific (released) application editions, which in turn reference specific (released) subapplication editions, which all together reference specific (released) class versions, and so forth. Each time a member of the development team releases a component, be it a class version, subapplication, or application edition, the reference model is altered.

Typically the higher-level components are all shared, forming the skeleton of the model. Within their private workspaces, individual developers maintain their own variations of the reference model, primarily as open class editions. This lets them privately develop, test, and debug their own work. When an edition of a class is deemed satisfactory it can be versioned and then released into its parent edition. By releasing to the reference model, members of the development team affect the mainstream of development. If anyone loads or reloads the configuration map edition, they will bring into their image the most current representation of the system. In this way, the reference model is constantly evolving without suffering instability.

Continuous Integration

Through these mechanisms, ENVY supports rapid and frequent integration of changes. While it's certainly possible to defer integration, the common model is referred to as *continuous integration*. Developers constantly perform two tasks. First, they create and/or change components and release them to the reference model. Of course, while they're doing this other developers are doing the same thing. Therefore, as a second task, developers bring their workspace back into sync with the reference model. This is achieved by reloading the released editions for some or all of the system. By reloading the top-level configuration map we can bring ourselves into sync with the entire system in one step. This is known as *one-click loading*. Of course, bringing ourselves into sync with the reference model discards any unreleased changes in our workspace. For more discussion on this point, see "Syncing Up" (both later in this chapter and in the tutorial section).

Developers do not always have to load released editions of components in order to access the most current changes. For example, developers can work privately with each other by loading specific editions of components. This might be done to test a patch or simply to peer review the work of others. For example, Alan might be working on the MultipleChoiceQuestion class defined in QuestionModelling (10/8/99 12:03:00). Adrian is working on the superclass Question in the same application edition. Alan wants to make sure his code works with Adrian's latest changes but Adrian is not yet ready to release because he hasn't finished his own tests. Alan and Adrian can't see each other's open class editions (because they're private to a developer) but Adrian can version his code without releasing it. Once it's a version Alan can load it into his image and try out the changes. As soon as Alan and Adrian are both happy that their changes work together and are stable, they can each version and release their code.

User Roles

ENVY provides user-level control over access to various operations. These are based around the roles that a user plays with respect to particular components. An ENVY image always has an owner, representing the current user. For some actions the current user will be recorded, and for others there is only a single user permitted to take that action. It's also possible to configure at the administrative level how strict the enforcement is and whether passwords will be required when changing the identity of the current user.

Ownership

The most important role in ENVY is that of ownership. Owners are responsible for components or parts of components. When properly assumed, ownership ensures a single point of responsibility for various actions. The fundamental idea is that this encourages higher quality software. The terminology, concept, and the effect of ownership are subtly different for various component types. Configuration map editions and application editions each have a *manager*. Application editions also have development *group members* and *class owners*. We discuss all the responsibilities and roles later, but we'll start by covering *class ownership*, which is the most important role in ENVY.

For each class that is defined or extended in an application edition, a user is responsible for the released version of that class. What the class owner controls is not so much the class itself as the relationship between the class and the application edition. Only the class owner can release a new class version into that application edition. This means that only the class owner can change the reference model with respect to that class. This forms a bottleneck on releasing the class that serves as ENVY's mechanisms for resolving concurrency conflicts. Effectively, any developer can modify the class in any way he or she pleases, but all changes will have to be approved by the class owner before becoming part of the reference model.

For example, the application QuestionUI has various editions of the class or extensions to the class with the name QuestionWindow. One of the editions is the version QuestionWindow 1.2. There is no owner for this version because the owner is not associated with the class edition but with the application edition. Instead, for each edition of the application QuestionUI that has a released edition of QuestionWindow, one user is responsible for that relationship. Adrian Cho might own Question 1.2 in Questionnaire 1.1, while in the application edition Questionnaire 2.0 Joseph Pelrine might own the same class version.

An Example of Class Ownership at Work

Let's say, for example, that Adrian Cho owns Question in QuestionModelling (5/7/99 12:03:22). The currently released edition of Question in QuestionModelling (5/7/99 12:03:22) is 1.2. A bug in validating multiple-choice answers has been reported. Adrian fixes this by creating a new edition of Question in QuestionModelling from (based on) the released edition 1.2. The new edition is Question (12/9/99 17:22:55). Adrian tests the change and verifies that it not only fixes the bug but that it has no unwanted side effects (such as introducing new bugs). Adrian subsequently versions the class edition so that it becomes Question 1.3 [Fixed multiple choice validation] and then releases that class version.

The next day Joseph Pelrine is analyzing performance of the entire polling system for which QuestionModelling is just one application. In particular, users are not happy with the performance of the system. Joseph discovers that multiple-choice validation is slow and that when the changes for many thousands of users are calculated, it can take an extraordinarily long time. Joseph finds a way to improve the performance without changing any of the behaviors or introducing any new bugs. He has a new version of the class Question 1.4 [Improved performance]. However, he does not have the permission to release the new version of this class in Question (12/9/99 17:22:55) because he is not the owner of the class. What he must do is tell Adrian that the new version of the class exists because only Adrian can release it. Adrian does not just immediately release the class version. He instead looks at the changes Joseph has made, using one of ENVY's comparison browsers to compare Joseph's new version of Question with the currently released version. He then loads Joseph's version of Question into his image and runs tests to ensure there is indeed some improvement in performance and that otherwise, the behavior is the same. When he does this, Adrian actually finds that he can make additional performance improvements. So he makes some additional changes, performs further testing, and then versions his new class version (based on Joseph's version) as Question 1.4 [Improved performance 2]. Finally, Adrian releases this version of the class.

Adrian's role as the owner of Question in this edition helps ensure the quality of that class because he must approve any changes made to that class before they are released. ENVY's development model enables other developers to make whatever changes they like to Question and to test those changes in their image. They may even version those changes and ask other users to load the changes and test them. What they cannot do, however, is release those changes to the reference model of the system they are working on.

Remember that what Adrian owns may only be a fragment of the class. If Question is extended in another application a different user might own that extension.

Roles in Detail

This section describes all of the roles and their specific rights and responsibilities. In this section we will use the phrase "you must be ..." when referring to a user role. This means that the owner of the ENVY image in which the operation is being performed must fill this role with respect to the component in question. Correspondingly, the phrase "become ..." when referring to a user role means that it's necessary to change the image owner to be the appropriate user. This is sometimes useful when working in a group, when someone is filling in for a user who is unavailable, or in other cases. Changing users frequently is a sign of problems.

Application Manager

You must be the manager of an application or subapplication edition to perform any of the following operations on that edition:

- add or delete a lineup
- add or delete a subapplication in a lineup
- release another edition of a subapplication in a lineup
- version the application edition
- create an open edition from the application version
- change the privileges
- change the manager to be another user
- add or delete group members
- modify the notes
- modify the comments
- add or delete prerequisites in a lineup (does not apply to subapplications)

Starting with the versions ENVY R4.0 for VisualAge for Smalltalk V4.02 and ENVY R5i.0 for VisualWorks Release 5i.0, under the default privileges for an application edition, the manager of that edition can change the owner of any class entry in that application edition. In previous releases of ENVY, only the class owner could assign ownership to another user.

Development Group Member

You must be a group member of an application edition to perform the following operation on that edition:

- add a class entry (adding a new class, extension, or reserved class name).

In addition, application editions maintain privileges for a number of key application operations. By default, most of these privileges have settings such as *world*, *group*, and *owner*. For example, *create class editions* is usually set to *world*, enabling any user to create editions of classes or extensions in that application edition. If the manager of that application edition changes the setting of that privilege to *group*, the operation will be restricted to group members.

A reserved class name is simply a way to indicate to ENVY that a class by this name is expected to exist in the application at some point. This does not actually create the class but causes the name to appear in the ENVY application manager/organizer with a version timestamp of Undefined. This is rarely used.

Class Owner

You must be the owner of a class entry (class, extension, or reserved name) in an application edition to perform any of the following operations:

- release another edition of the class or extension
- delete the class entry
- change the owner to be another user

Application privileges can also be set so that certain operations are restricted to class owners.

Configuration Map Manager

You must be the manager of a configuration map edition to perform any of the following operations on that edition:

- add or delete an application
- release another edition of an application
- add or delete a lineup
- add or delete a required map in a lineup
- release another edition of a required map in a lineup
- version the configuration map edition
- creating an open edition from the configuration map version
- change the privileges
- change the manager to be another user
- modify the notes
- modify the comment

Starting with the versions ENVY R4.0 for VisualAge for Smalltalk V4.02 and ENVY R5i.0 for VisualWorks Release 5i.0, configuration maps have also had privileges as follows:

Privilege	Settings (default in bold)
Release application editions	**Map manager**/map manager or application manager
Delete application editions	**Map manager**/map manager or application manager

These privileges enable the manager of a configuration map edition to place greater responsibility and trust in the managers of application editions released to the map edition. As an example, Alan Knight is the manager of the configuration map Questionnaire (12/4/99 12:05:05), which has many released applications editions including QuestionModelling 1.1, managed by Joseph Pelrine. Joseph recently found a critical bug in QuestionModelling 1.1 so he immediately created a new edition (16/4/99 1:05:30) and fixed the problem. Normally Joseph would have to wait for Alan to release this new edition of his application because that operation modifies the configuration map edition and Alan is the manager of the map. Alan happens to be at home sick on the day Joseph finds and fixes the bug. Because the bug is critical, Joseph would like to release this fix quickly. One option is to e-mail all developers and tell them the new edition is available and they should manually load it until Alan gets back to work and can release the new edition. However, in this case, Alan has changed the setting of the "release application editions" privilege to be "map manager or application manager." Consequently, Joseph can release the new application edition by himself. Alternatively, Joseph could have changed the user to Alan and released the map as Alan. This might have required using Alan's network password.

Library Supervisor

The *Library Supervisor* is a special user for administering a library. You must be a Library Supervisor to perform any of the following operations:

- purging configuration maps or applications
- salvaging configuration maps or applications
- creating, modifying, or purging users

The Library Supervisor user does not have many special privileges and is not a super user of any sort. However, in addition to these privileges for purging and user management, the Library Supervisor is the default owner of all system components.

Generally the Library Supervisor is also a developer who also has his/her own user in ENVY. He or she toggles between their normal development user and the Library Supervisor user as needed.

Development Process

We've talked about ENVY features and suggested pieces of a development process, but we have yet to fully describe the process. While ENVY can support a variety of different processes, we'll describe a typical process the ENVY mechanisms suggest.

Structuring Components

A project normally starts with a top-level configuration map. For a smaller project, this configuration map might contain all the applications. On a larger project, or one with a strict development/run-time division, this might use the required maps facility to load run-time and development configuration maps. Within the maps will be a set of applications. These applications will have prerequisite relationships among themselves and to system applications. It's generally considered good practice to group these applications into layers, where each layer depends only on the layers below it. For example, a common division is into infrastructure, business logic, and GUI layers. The GUI depends on the business logic and infrastructure layers (as well as the windowing system), the business logic depends only on the infrastructure, and the infrastructure depends only on the base system. This layering enables parts of the system to be easily removed, and also makes it easier to package and deliver the final system.

Each of the applications may also define subapplications with one or more configurations. For example, if the GUI layer contains code which depends on the specific window system (for example, Windows, X, Macintosh) we could define subapplications containing code for each target window system and set up configurations so that only the code appropriate for the current window system would be loaded.

Assigning Roles

Each component larger than a method has an owner or a manager. Typically, the owner is a developer who works on that component. For a class it would be the primary developer for that class. For an application it might be the only person working on that application or a team lead. Alternatively, a project or part of a project might have someone with designated responsibility for baselining and assign ownership of some or all of the applications to that person. Baselining is unlikely to be a full-time occupation on anything but the largest projects; accordingly, this person will also have development responsibilities.

Beginning a Development Cycle

A development cycle begins with open editions of configuration maps, applications, and subapplications, with each of these open editions released into their enclosing components. It's important that the higher-level components are editions because this gives team members a shared workspace. These editions form a reference model of the system. Class editions, on the other hand, will be private to a developer. For further discussion on this issue see "Class and Method Editions" (earlier in this chapter) as well as "One-Click Loading" and "Application Editions" in the tutorial section.

When we first create components they start out as open editions. If we're starting from an existing baseline, we need to create open editions and release them. It's usually easiest to do this top-down, creating the open editions and releasing them as we go. This way when we need to release a component its parent is already an edition we can release into.

It's not necessary for all components to be open editions — only those we expect to modify. If we're not sure which will be modified, it's reasonable to begin a development cycle by creating open editions of the components we're sure will be modified, leaving the others as versions and then creating open editions of the remaining components on an as-needed basis. If we do this, however, it's important to respect the ownership of these applications. If two different developers create two different open editions of the same application or configuration map (for example, by changing user IDs), they can be working in separate streams without realizing it, causing major integration problems.

To work in the shared workspace team members load the open edition of the system configuration map. This loads all the released application editions, their released subapplication editions, and all the released class versions. Once this process is complete the image is synchronized and current with the reference model in the library.

Development

Once we have the latest working environment loaded we can begin working. Typically, most of a developer's time is spent working at the class level. We create new classes or extensions and/or create open editions of versioned classes and extensions. Within these editions we create, update, and delete methods, and change class definitions. Occasionally, developers version their class editions. This might be done for several reasons:

- to release a stable form of the class into the reference model
- to enable other users to load the class edition, perhaps for more thorough testing, without yet releasing it to the reference model
- to freeze changes for ourselves with the intention to immediately continue development (perhaps just before starting a major refactoring)

Getting "Out of Sync"

In the course of development, we expect that many developers will be making changes in class editions and occasionally versioning and releasing those changes. As more and more changes are released, each image gradually becomes more out of date with the reference model. To avoid this problem, we periodically need to resynchronize our workspace with the reference model. Two main mechanisms exist for knowing when we are out of sync: annotations in the browsers and queries.

The ENVY browsers provide annotations to indicate synchronization, which vary depending on the type of browser. Some browsers show information about the image—for example, most development browsers and the Application Manager/VisualAge Organizer. Others show information about the library—for example, editions browsers and the configuration maps browser. In browsers that show library information an asterisk (*) to the left of a component edition indicates that the edition is loaded in the image. For example, when we select a configuration map edition in the Configuration Maps browser, we see a list of the applications released to that map edition. For each application, if that edition is loaded, an asterisk will appear to the left of the application.

The Application Manager and VisualAge organizer primarily show information about the image, but also contain indicators of the library state. In these browsers a greater-than character (>) indicates that a loaded class or subapplication edition is not the one being released into the loaded parent component. If we're modifying a class, we will have our own open edition of it, which is not released. Thus, we expect to see the out-of-sync indicator for our own classes. However, if we see that indicator beside other classes it probably indicates that someone else has released a new version of that class. We may also see the out-of-sync indicator if no released version of a class or subapplication exists, or if we do not have that class or subapplication loaded. If we're following the process as described here it's rare to be out of sync with respect to subapplications, so we normally only have to worry about reloading classes.

Note that ENVY does not use any server-to-client or peer-to-peer broadcast system. Images can only determine which components are released by querying the library. Most shadow browsers will do this for particular components whenever those components are reselected in a browser list. The Application Manager or Organizer queries the library whenever its window gets focus. With slow network connections this can be a bottleneck, so it can be turned off, but doing so is generally not recommended.

A more explicit way to determine how current an image is with the reference model is by performing a query. The ENVY menu has a Query submenu with several image-wide query operations. In particular, one of these operations can report any unreleased classes in loaded applications.

Syncing Up

If the image is out of sync with the reference model then at some point it will need to be resynchronized. You can do this in several different ways, each with different characteristics.

Most obviously, we can perform a one-click load of the entire system. This quickly and easily brings us back into sync with the reference model, but it also loads that reference model over the top of any unreleased changes we have in our image. These changes are not lost; they still exist in the library, but we would need to relocate them and reload them. A complete reload is most appropriate if we don't have any pending changes. For example, if we're returning from vacation and need to get back in sync before starting new work we might use this option.

If we version and release our classes before syncing up we avoid having our changes overwritten, but we run the greater risk of releasing incorrect code into the reference model. Code should not be released until it has been tested against the current state of the system. Further, we should not release code blindly, but should always test it first to make sure all the changes are actually necessary and don't include debugging or other transient code.

A better way to synchronize is to do partial reloading. We could approach this in two ways. The first is to note the changes we have made, do a complete load of the system, and then reload our pending changes. If we have only a few changes, this method is relatively painless. The second way is to check which applications contain new code and reload only those pieces of the system. If we don't have pending changes in an application, we can reload the entire thing; otherwise, we can reload individual classes. We can use the image-wide queries to determine which applications contain new changes. If there are new released versions of classes we have modified, either we or the class owner will have to do a merge.

When to Synchronize

When should we synchronize with the reference model? The simplest answer is "as often as is feasible without disrupting our own work." In general, we always want the entire team to be working on the same code base. On the other hand, we don't want to see code that's broken, and we don't want to interrupt our own work just to incorporate new changes that don't affect us. As soon as it's convenient we want to make sure we have the most up-to-date code from the other developers. Typically, this means we will synchronize more than once a day. If we're approaching release, with many small bug fixes and frequent testing, we may synchronize many times a day. If we're doing a major refactoring of some piece of the system we might not synchronize for a couple of weeks. In general, though, the less time between synchronizations the better.

The most important rule is that we should always synchronize before releasing work. There's no point releasing code based on assumptions that may have changed, and if we haven't checked our work against what other developers have released, we don't know that our assumptions are still valid.

When to Release

From time to time we will release our own changes to the reference model. One important question is how often we should release. This is hard to answer in general, but as a rough guideline we suggest once a day. Like synchronizing, timing and frequency will vary depending on the code we are writing, how disruptive our changes could be, what other developers are doing, and how close we are to iteration boundaries or a release of the software.

We should *not* release unless we are sure that our changes will improve the stability and functionality of the system. This means we should have confidence that the code works, that it should be tested against the current state of the system, and that it adds functionality.

Releasing may also be dictated by what other developers are doing, particularly if a set of changes affects classes owned by multiple different developers. For example, let's say Adrian owns the class Question, and Joseph owns the class Answer. Adrian changes Question so that it becomes an abstract class with the subclasses MultipleChoiceQuestion and FreeTextQuestion. Joseph makes appropriate changes to Answer, which depends on Question. Adrian releases his classes. Joseph must also release Answer to ensure that the reference model is consistent. If Joseph doesn't release, then someone loading the reference model would have code that doesn't work.

Baselining

At the end of a development cycle we create a *baseline*. A baseline is a named version of all the components involved in our project, which is frozen and represents the state of the project at a particular time. This is important to provide a point of reference for later comparison, to provide a stable set of code that can be thoroughly and systematically tested, and to provide a milestone within the overall project.

Baselines can be the basis of demos to customers, and some of them will even be put into production.

To baseline we version all of the components that form our system. This is usually done bottom-up, versioning and releasing classes, then versioning subapplications (recall that they have already been released at the beginning of the iteration), applications, and configuration maps. We can only version an application or subapplication when it is loaded, so we will need to load all of the different configurations to version those subapplications. We will also, of course, need to load them in order to test the different configurations.

Once we've made a version, we need to create new editions of these components so that developers can resume working. This brings us back to the beginning and we start the next development cycle.

When to Baseline

How often should we make a baseline? Again, this is a difficult question to answer in general. It depends on the size and complexity of our application, how rapidly development is proceeding, overall system stability, and the development milestones.

We want to baseline regularly because it provides us with known stable versions of the code. It's not unreasonable to baseline once a week, which also gives us the advantage of having the weekend to do emergency fixes. This is a particularly useful interval if we're doing distributed development because it gives us time to distribute the baseline to other sites. At a minimum, we want to baseline once per iteration because the baseline provides a clear demarcation point between the iterations and lets us measure progress accurately.

Baselining is like a heartbeat for a development project. It provides regularity and an indication of health. A regular schedule for baselining provides developers with a cadence to work to. If it takes a long time to create a baseline or if baselines turn out not to be very stable this can indicate problems with the project. Baselining also tends to speed up as a system nears the release stage.

Baselining can sometimes be a very heavyweight operation. The primary factors are the size and complexity of the system (in terms of ENVY). If multiple lineups exist, this complicates the loading and testing procedures. The more different owners and managers need to interact, the more time this takes. In general, we want to streamline this process as much as possible to make baselining a smooth, painless, and frequent part of the development cycle.

Baselining with Ongoing Development

ENVY doesn't provide a facility to lock out developers from the library during integration. This means that, at least in theory, developers could be releasing classes while we're doing our baseline or integration testing. We want to avoid that, and the easiest way to do it is simply by telling the developers not to do it. If a baseline is taking place, developers should ensure that all code for that build has been released, and once that's happened they should not release additional changes without consulting the people in charge of the baselining operation.

It's also more difficult for developers to do coding work during a baseline because there is no shared workspace. When we version, we freeze all of the current application and subapplication editions. We will shortly create new open editions, but in the meantime developers don't have a shared workspace, and they will need to load the new open editions before they can work. For these reasons, it's easiest for developers if they use this time working on the baseline or doing other nondevelopment work.

Sometimes we can't avoid having development work continue during a baseline operation. It's possible to continue development. Developers continue to work in the previous open editions. Once these have been versioned, ENVY will notify the developer the next time they try to use it, and will make those applications into scratch editions in their image. At some point, once the new editions exist, developers should note the classes they've modified, reload the new reference model, and load their changes into it.

Multiple Streams

ENVY does not have an explicit concept of multiple development streams. Generally, streams are indicated using version naming conventions. For more information on managing multiple streams and on remote development, see the "Multiple Streams" section in Chapter 4.

Code Reviews

A development process may include provisions for code reviews. The ENVY releasing process helps support this mechanism. Let's consider an example.

Adrian owns the class Question and recently he has made some major changes to that class. He wants Alan and Joseph to check those changes for him and provide feedback. He begins by versioning the class edition as Question 1.0 [For review] 005. This serves two purposes. First, Adrian has a snapshot of the code so it's clear that everyone is looking at the same thing. Second, open editions are private, so by versioning the code he enables Alan and Joseph to view and load the code. If Adrian wishes, he can continue development on Question in a separate edition. Meanwhile, Alan and Joseph independently load Adrian's class edition into their images and begin by comparing the edition with its previous version. They don't even have to know what the previous version was because the ENVY browsers provide specific operations to compare and load previous versions.

Alan and Joseph examine Adrian's changes, and run tests on them. They can also make their own changes by creating new editions based on Adrian's edition (this happens automatically if they modify Adrian's version). They can also elaborate on their changes by adding details in the Notes field of a method or the class edition. Once the changes are complete they can version them. Alan versions first so he uses the version name Question 1.0 [Reviewed by Alan] 006. Joseph uses the version name

Question 1.0 [Reviewed by Joseph] 007. They may notify Adrian when they are done or just leave it to him to notice the new editions in the library. Regardless, when their versions are available, Adrian can compare his current edition (which may not be the same as the one reviewed) to Alan's version. He looks at the changes Alan has made and can discuss them with Alan. Because Adrian is the owner of the class, it's up to him to accept or reject any changes Alan has suggested. Once Adrian has processed Alan's changes, he does the same with Joseph's.

In practice, the unit of review will likely be larger than a single class, and there will likely be a more formal review meeting, but the same principles apply.

Libraries

The foundation of ENVY is the library — a multi-user component database designed specifically for maintaining Smalltalk code. The format of the library is not unlike that of a Smalltalk image. Objects in the library are records and each record has a header similar to the header of an object in an image. Records contain 32-bit pointers (of which two bits are used as status bits), which are references to other records in the same library. The available 30 bits, denoting the position of a record in the library, yield a maximum library size of 1GB.

Starting with versions ENVY R4.0 for VisualAge for Smalltalk V4.5 and ENVY/Developer R5i.0 for VisualWorks Release 5i.0, a second format has been available where the records are written on 16-byte boundaries. With this format, the 30 bits in each 32-bit pointer are shifted by four bits, yielding a maximum library size of 16GB (although this is ultimately limited by the file system hosting the library file). In a typical library, the wastage resulting from this technique is less than 5 percent of the library size.

At the time of this writing, most file systems supported by ENVY (and EMSRV) support 16GB files, including the latest releases of Solaris, HP-UX, AIX, Windows NT, and Windows 98. File systems that cannot handle such large files include:

- NetWare (currently limited to 4GB using NWFS with the promise of 16GB files using NSS whenever Novell releases the API)
- OS/2 (limited to 2GB using FAT or HPFS)
- Linux (limited to 2GB using EXT2)

Library Growth

An ENVY library contains many different types of records, typically numbered in the hundreds of thousands. Most of these records are very small (fewer than a hundred bytes), although a handful of the more frequently used records can sometimes occupy hundreds of kilobytes. ENVY clients constantly update the library (directly in a single-user environment or via EMSRV in a multi-user environment). Updates are made by either appending new records to the library or modifying existing records in a strict transaction protocol. The result of this is that the library is being constantly updated with a large number of very small write and append operations, resulting in library growth. There's no easy way to estimate how much the library will grow because so many variables exist. As a very rough guide, 1MB per developer per day is a reasonable estimate.

In a library that has been in use for some time, most of the space will be occupied by records that are no longer necessary. We can reduce the size of the library by compacting out these unneeded records. This is referred to as *cloning*.

Cloning is effectively a garbage collection operation. Beginning with a set of root records, all records reachable from those initial roots are copied to another library. The roots include all configuration map and application versions, and the set of open editions currently in the image. Typically, the size of the library is reduced by two-thirds to three-quarters.

The most important reason for cloning is if the library is in danger of reaching its maximum size. However, libraries are often cloned far before they reach this point. Files of many megabytes in size require not only a large amount of storage space but take a long time to back up. In a library with many developers and a lot of activity, the number of editions of many components will increase to the point where there is just too much noise and clutter in editions lists. Although almost all configuration map and application versions will represent valid baselines, a lot of class versions and a much greater number of method editions will only represent work in progress. If these editions are not ultimately referenced by a baseline they will be left behind in a clone.

Sometimes, it makes sense to further restrict the component editions that will be cloned. You have two easy ways of doing this:

- Purge editions before beginning the clone.
- Do not use the clone operation but instead manually export all the desired configuration maps.

The last option is becoming increasingly more valid as very few projects or tools do not have a configuration map. Often the best way to proceed is to use a combination of these techniques, as follows:

- Purge any configuration map versions you do not want cloned.
- Note any applications that are not referenced by configuration maps. Often the best thing to do is to create configuration maps for these orphan applications.
- Manually export all the configuration map versions or use a script to do this.

Summary

This chapter has covered the major topics in ENVY from a less tutorial and more theoretical perspective. We have presented the fundamental concepts and the reasoning behind them, with a minimum of examples and advice. This chapter is most useful for readers with a background in team programming systems attempting to understand the ENVY concepts, and for more advanced developers who want to understand the reasoning behind certain features.

Some of the important things to remember from this chapter are as follows:

- ENVY divides software into components: configuration maps, applications, subapplications, classes, and methods.

- Classes are defined in only one place but can be extended in many places.

- ENVY manages configurations using conditional loading of subcomponents based on configuration expressions.

- Components can be either versions or editions. Versioning does not imply publishing into a build, which is separated out into a release operation.

- Concurrent development is controlled through control of the releasing operation via class ownership.

- ENVY is a repository-based system. We distinguish between code in the image and code in the repository. There are no source files, and all code remains in the repository.

- The development cycle begins with the creation of new open editions (and possible release of those editions to their parent components) and ends with a baselining operation.

- Throughout the cycle, developers version, release, reintegrate, and test.

- At the end of a cycle, we perform a baseline operation to freeze the current state of the software and prepare for the next iteration.

≡Chapter 6≡

Packaging and Delivery

In a software project, as in any large project, a significant amount of work is needed to close the project. Teams often defer the hard issues of finally delivering a product until much too late in the process, leading to trouble when the time finally arrives.

This chapter examines the ENVY notion of prerequisites in depth, sees how it can affect packaging, and looks at resolving various prerequisite problems. We will look at various alternatives for the packaging and delivery process and their relative advantages and disadvantages. We'll describe in some detail the packaging and delivery process for both VisualAge and VisualWorks. We'll look at application attachments, an ENVY mechanism for keeping track of external files associated with our program. Finally, we'll address some additional delivery issues and strategies for ensuring that packaging does not become a bottleneck.

Prerequisites Revisited

Before we examine program delivery strategies, it's worth revisiting some of the concepts we've previously seen that have a significant effect on delivery. Regardless of our strategy, knowing what other code our program relies on is important if we are to produce a simple, standalone program. Recall that ENVY provides the notion of application prerequisites to help formalize this information. Some packaging strategies, particularly those using the VisualAge packager, rely heavily on correct prerequisites to determine which components need to be linked and which classes and methods can be discarded. Even if we're not using such a mechanism, ENVY prerequisites can help define a layered architecture with all the dependencies made clear. With these uses in mind, let's revisit the ENVY concept of prerequisites in more detail, particularly as it applies to packaging. We'll see some of the problems that can arise with incorrect prerequisites along with possible remedies.

Prerequisites

An application A is said to be a prerequisite of another application B if application B requires code from application A to execute. Application B is said to be a dependent of application A.

Less formally, one application is a prerequisite of another when it contains something the other application needs to use. In the typical case this is a class, and the dependent application subclasses extend or use one or more classes from the prerequisite. Declaring an application as a prerequisite ensures that the prerequisite is loaded into the image before the application that requires it. This process is recursive because the prerequisite application may also have its own prerequisites, which need to be loaded. The prerequisites referenced directly from an application are called *direct* prerequisites. The prerequisites of the direct prerequisites (and their prerequisites, and so on) are called *indirect* prerequisites. The chain of direct and indirect prerequisites dictates the order in which applications are loaded.

Because prerequisites determine the load order, the chain of prerequisites is not allowed to have cycles, either directly or indirectly. The prerequisites must form a tree so that a valid load order can always be computed. Every tree needs to have a root, and the prerequisite tree terminates at the application Kernel, which has no prerequisites. As you might imagine, Kernel is the application that defines Object and the other fundamental system classes. Because every other class in every other application subclasses Object (directly or indirectly), every application has Kernel as a direct or indirect prerequisite.

Class Visibility

In order to subclass, extend, or reference a class, it must be *visible*. Classes visible to an application include:

- all classes in this application
- all classes in subapplications (or their subapplications, recursively) of this application, or in other subapplications of this application's root application
- all classes visible in applications that are prerequisites of the root application

The root application for an application is itself. The root application for a subapplication is its parent application, or the root of its parent subapplication. In other words, subapplications form a tree descending from a single parent application, which is the root of that tree.

Prerequisites apply only at the application level. Subapplications have no prerequisites, but are controlled by their parents' prerequisites. Because we cannot load a subapplication without also loading its parent application, it inherits the prerequisites of its parent.

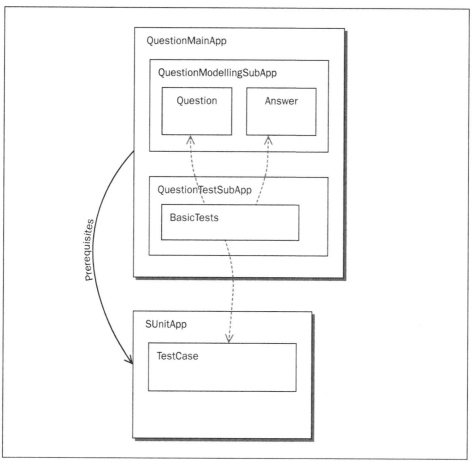

Figure 6-1: Subapplications and their root application. The class BasicTests can see Question and Answer because they are part of a subapplication with the same parent application. It can see TestCase because it is part of a prerequisite of the root application QuestionMainApp.

Some prerequisite relationships can be detected at compile time, and ENVY will enforce those relationships. In particular, ENVY will not permit an application or subapplication to subclass or extend a nonvisible class. Referencing a nonvisible class is a prerequisite violation, but is treated as a warning.

Setting Up Prerequisites

Prerequisites are required when there is a dependency between two different applications. We should be aware of how these dependencies can arise, and what to do to set up the prerequisites properly. We need to be concerned about two different types of dependencies: immediate and hidden.

Immediate Dependencies

An immediate dependency between two applications occurs when a class in the dependent application references a class defined in the prerequisite, either by subclassing, extending, or referencing in a method. For example, in QuestionTesting we subclass the class TestCase from the application SUnit, creating an immediate dependency through subclassing. In QuestionTesting, we reference the class Question in one of our test methods, creating an immediate dependency based on a method reference. This tells us that QuestionTesting requires prerequisites Sunit, and QuestionModelling. QuestionTesting might also define a convenience method as an extension to Collection, introducing an immediate dependency through extension on Kernel. We don't need to explicitly add Kernel as a prerequisite to QuestionTesting because Kernel is already an indirect prerequisite of QuestionTesting.

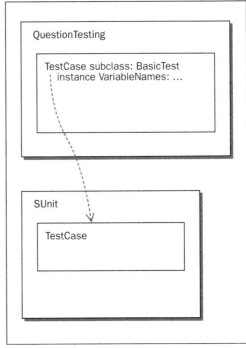

Figure 6-2: Immediate dependencies

Hidden Dependencies

Hidden (or method) prerequisites are more difficult to notice. They occur when a method defined in one application calls a method defined in an extension of the same class in another application. Because of Smalltalk's inherent polymorphism, not even ENVY can be sure that exactly *this particular* implementation of the method is the one that will be called at run-time. These prerequisites tend to cause trouble at packaging time because there is no way to guarantee that they will be detected by the packager.

Here is a somewhat contrived example. In VisualWorks, there's a method

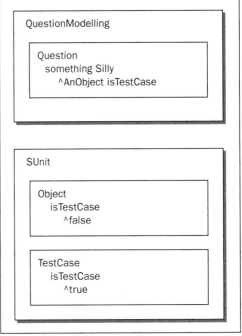

Figure 6-3: Hidden dependencies

Number>isReal. If our QuestionModelling code calls the method isReal on a number, there's no problem because that's implemented and part of the prerequisites. However, if we also had an application loaded (but not listed as a prerequisite), which included a class extension that implemented isReal in Object, then our code, running in the development image, could send 'abc' isReal. This will work in development, but it will not work in the run-time because the method is not included, and the packager only checks to see if there is some implementation of the messages we send. Packaging the image and testing the result are the only possible test for this problem. The SmallLint tests (see the SmallLint sidebar later in this chapter) may help, but they cannot catch all occurrences.

Another way that hidden dependencies can arise is through meta-programming. If we construct and use either class references or message selectors dynamically, the dependency can't be detected. For example, if we write code such as

```
anAppointment perform:
('scheduleFor', Date today monthName) asSymbol.
```

the packager will not know that we should include the selectors scheduleForJanuary, scheduleForFebruary, and so on.

Prerequisite Problems

In an ideal world, everyone would maintain his or her prerequisites correctly at all times. In reality, this is seldom this case. Prerequisite problems typically only manifest as a serious issue when doing packaging with an aggressive packager. If this packaging step is rarely done, then any prerequisite problems will most likely not have been dealt with for some time. In extreme cases many dependencies among applications may not be well reflected in the prerequisites, and these can take significant work to resolve.

Prerequisite Errors

First, let's examine what might be wrong with our prerequisites. Only a few categories of errors exist, though their combinations can become complex.

Missing Prerequisite

A prerequisite can be missing altogether. For example, we might have a QuestionTestingUI application that uses the ENVY vendor extensions code to automatically add itself to some of the standard ENVY menus. This vendor extensions code is not part of the base ENVY libraries, but is an add-on that adds several new methods. Our application might call those methods without adding EtToolsVendorExtensionsApp to its prerequisites. This example is a benign prerequisite violation because our testing user interface is not intended to be packaged. With development-time-only code, the worst thing that is likely to happen is a walkback when we load our code into a clean image. This would still be very confusing to a new user, and is something we should correct. With run-time code, much worse errors could occur, including unexplained crashes in the deployed program.

Over-General Prerequisite

Often, we're not sure exactly what our application depends on, and we may err on the side of caution. This ensures that we will not have mysterious errors in our run-time code, but can cause too much to be included in a packaged image. It can also cause us to be unable to package, if the application we included causes other packaging errors.

An over-general prerequisite occurs when an application references a prerequisite that it does not actually require, when only some of the prerequisites are really necessary. For example, we may have a QuestionnaireUI application that contains a user interface for our Questionnaire project. When we were first setting it up, we modeled our basic UI on the ENVY browsers, and so we included EtBaseTools as a prerequisite. After doing some development, we discovered that this wasn't really a very good idea, and switched to building our own windows from scratch in code. Now, however, we're trying to package, and we still have a prerequisite of EtBaseTools. This is causing us all kinds of packaging problems because this application has prerequisites that are development-time-only code. We need to make use of window code, and we're building this particular UI in VisualAge, so we need a prerequisite of EsWindowSystem, but EtBaseTools is much too general.

Easily Eliminated Prerequisite

Sometimes our application prerequisites are technically correct, but with a small change to our code we could eliminate a large dependency. For example, in our QuestionUI application we might want to have a progress dialog box while we consider the user's answer. We know that ENVY has a progress dialog box, and so we decide use it. The ENVY progress dialog code is a method (execLongOperation:message:allowCancel:showProgress:) in the class EtWindow, which is the superclass of the ENVY browsers. Using this method introduces a dependency on EtBaseTools, which will cause problems when we try to package.

This is a completely legitimate dependency. Our code will not run without this method, and it requires the presence of EtBaseTools. However, if we implement our own progress dialog box, even if we do it by copying the code from EtWindow, we can eliminate this dependency, making our packaging job much easier and our resulting image smaller.

Circular Dependency and Circular Prerequisites

These are two slightly different circumstances. In a circular dependency, two applications are mutually dependent on each other, but may not have each other as prerequisites. This is the most common situation because ENVY attempts to enforce the prohibition on circular prerequisites. However, it is possible to create circular prerequisites, particularly if we use conditional prerequisites (see "Using Configuration Expressions to Set Prerequisites" that follows) or if we modify prerequisites directly in the library (see "Residents and Shadows").

In this case, we have two fundamental choices. The most desirable is to eliminate the circularity by finding easily eliminated prerequisites as described previously in one or the other direction. If we cannot remove the circularity, then we can try reorganizing the code into subapplications, as described later.

Resolving Prerequisite Problems

Let's assume that we've tested our applications and attempted to package, and this process has turned up a number of prerequisite problems. A number of simple techniques exist to set up the prerequisite chain correctly. Let's look at our options in roughly the order in which we might want to consider them.

Add Missing Prerequisites

If our situation corresponds to the preceding missing prerequisite case, then the simplest thing to do is to just add it. Include the missing class or the method's defining application as a prerequisite for the application in question. This is by far the simplest technique, but don't just do it automatically. Think about whether this application actually makes sense as a prerequisite. Adding a bad prerequisite can just make the situation more complicated. For example, if we see that our QuestionTesting application does not have QuestionModelling as a prerequisite, but constantly references classes in that application, the correct answer is to just add it. If we see that QuestionTesting appears to have a dependency on EtBaseTools, we don't want to add it, and we will need to consider other options.

Changing Prerequisites

It's easiest to change prerequisites using either the Application Manager or the VisualAge Organizer. Depending on which one we use, the technique varies slightly. In the Application Manager, select the application. If it's versioned, create a new edition because we can't change prerequisites on a version. Move the mouse to the prerequisites pane and, on the pop-up menu, choose Change. You'll see a dialog box with available prerequisites on the left-hand side and the current direct prerequisites on the right-hand side. Items can be moved from side to side by selecting them and using the double-arrow buttons in the center of the window. Note that only items that are not already prerequisites of the current application will appear on the left-hand side. This includes both direct and indirect prerequisites.

In the VisualAge Organizer, first make sure that full menus are enabled. In the Applications menu, choosing the Prerequisite option opens a dialog box showing the current prerequisite and dependent applications of the selected application. Press the Change button and the same dialog box previously described will open.

Remove Extra Prerequisites

The reverse is also true. If our situation corresponds to the over-general prerequisite case just described, then we should eliminate the redundant prerequisite. In the preceding example, we had QuestionnaireUI with a prerequisite of EtBaseTools. This wasn't necessary, and we could eliminate most of our packaging problems by switching the prerequisite to be just EsWindowSystem. Unfortunately, it's not quite that easy.

Invalid Intermediate States

One of the important lessons in software design is that enforcement of constraints shouldn't be too aggressive. All too often, we see systems that prevent users from performing perfectly reasonable operations because they would violate a system constraint. The users know that the operation violates a constraint, but it's fine because they're about to do another operation that puts the whole system back into balance, and the constraint should be checked then. For example, a beta version of WindowBuilder Pro enforced the constraint that widget names could not be empty strings. If a user went to change the name of a widget, selected the entire string and typed over it, everything worked. If the user went to change the name of a widget, selected the entire string and hit backspace, they got a constraint violation dialog box. Fortunately, this was quickly remedied. ENVY is good about enforcing constraints only at the end of its internal transactions, but sometimes the database-level transactions don't correspond to the user's concepts.

In our example, when we select EtBaseTools from the prerequisite list, we find that the << button to remove the prerequisite is grayed out. ENVY will not allow us to remove EtBaseTools as a prerequisite of QuestionUI; because it detects that this would leave the prerequisites invalid. We know that, and all we want to do is immediately add in EsWindowSystem, but ENVY enforces the constraint at the individual operation level for components in memory. There's no way to get to the state we want without passing through an invalid intermediate state, at least for the objects in memory. We do, however, have the option to use the Application Editions Browser and modify the structure directly in the library. See the "Changing Prerequisites in the Repository" section that follows.

Move Code

Sometimes, we may not be able to simply add a prerequisite (see Figure 6-4). For example, the application we want as a prerequisite may already have *our* application as a prerequisite. Suppose that we wrote a method in the class Question called testConsistency, and this referenced the class BasicQuestionTests in the application QuestionTesting. We can't add QuestionTesting as a prerequisite to QuestionModelling because QuestionModelling is already a prerequisite of QuestionTesting; we would be creating a circular prerequisite. The alternative is to treat this as an easily eliminated prerequisite, and remove it by moving the testConsistency method into the QuestionTesting application. This also makes sense in terms of our design because it appears that the testConsistency method is really a testing support method that was put into the wrong application in the first place.

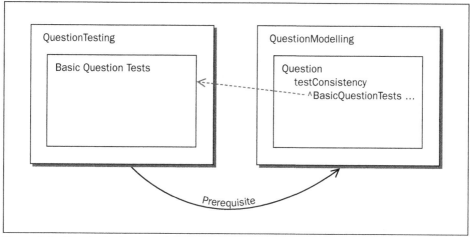

Figure 6-4: The desired prerequisite is unavailable.

In other circumstances, the application may be available, but adding it as a prerequisite doesn't make sense (see Figure 6-5). Suppose that, in the preceding circumstances, the testConsistency method only referenced the class TestCase from the SUnit application. There's no circularity there, so we could add SUnit as a prerequisite to QuestionModelling, but it doesn't seem to make sense. Again, the right thing to do is to move the method into QuestionTesting. We could conceivably move it into SUnit instead, but because it's one of our methods, it doesn't seem to make sense to add it as an extension to third-party software.

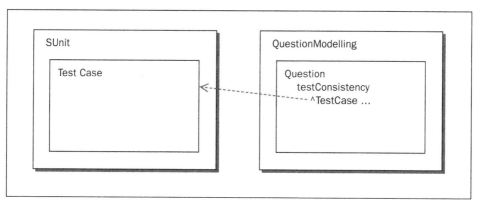

Figure 6-5: The desired prerequisite is available but doesn't make sense.

In general, any time we have an easily eliminated prerequisite we can try to eliminate it by moving methods around. This can solve many prerequisite problems, but it still shouldn't be done blindly. Think about where the methods should go in terms of our design and the layers of our architecture.

Copy Code

As OO developers, we have an instinctive desire not to copy code. Cut and paste reuse is a bad thing, and we try to refactor to eliminate duplicate code whenever possible. Unfortunately, sometimes we don't have the option to refactor, and it's a lot simpler to copy a small piece of code into applications we control than it is to try to sort out prerequisites in applications we don't. This could be copying a class, or just a method or two. Insert the copy either into our application or into an application in the prerequisite chain that we control. In our own work we have often found a class that provides behavior we needed and that itself had only system-level dependencies. In this case, the advantages of copying the class greatly outweighed the problems of including the defining application of the original class as a prerequisite. An example of this is the progress dialog box described previously. Rather than reference EtWindow in EtBaseTools, we can copy the progress dialog box code, which has no real dependency on the ENVY development-time tools, into our own application and use it from there.

Modify Code

Still on the theme of the easily eliminated prerequisite, we may be able to modify our code to eliminate the use of a particular prerequisite. Often we can do this by going one or two steps beyond the high-level methods we call to get to lower-level base system objects. For example, in VisualAge, the browsers in EtTools provide a number of prompting methods. If we follow the call tree, we can see that all these prompter methods eventually call simple methods in CommonWidgets. By directly calling these methods we can avoid needing EtTools as a prerequisite.

Reorganize

Sometimes we really do have two applications that are codependent. It's not reasonable to load one without the other, and neither can reasonably be seen as a lower or higher level. We can decide to reorganize the applications and/or the classes to eliminate the prerequisite problem. Two basic approaches exist. One option is simply to combine the two applications into one, and if both are reasonably small and truly related, this may be the best approach. Another way to make ENVY accept the codependence situation is to reorganize our code into two subapplications with the same root application. This approach works because ENVY does not have prerequisite relationships between subapplications, but simply inherits the prerequisites from the root application. Two subapplications of the same root parent can happily have cross-references back and forth between each other without causing any prerequisite or packaging problems.

Reorganizing can eliminate a number of difficulties, but it's also a drastic step. The applications will no longer be able to be loaded independently, so we must be sure that they are truly tightly coupled. ENVY is also not very helpful in moving code between applications and subapplications. It's not possible to change an application into a subapplication or vice-versa, so we'll need to create a new subapplication and move all of our classes into it. Because classes moved between applications do not know about their earlier editions, this procedure creates a disruption in our version history. For this reason, some people advocate always putting code in subapplications with an empty root application. For information on ways of rearranging ENVY structures while preserving some indicators of version history, see "Moving and Renaming." For more information on subapplications, see "Subapplications."

For example, suppose that our Questionnaire system had not initially been set up as a general system for questions and answers. In fact, two different groups had been developing two independent applications, WebQuestionnaireApp and IVRQuestionnaireApp.

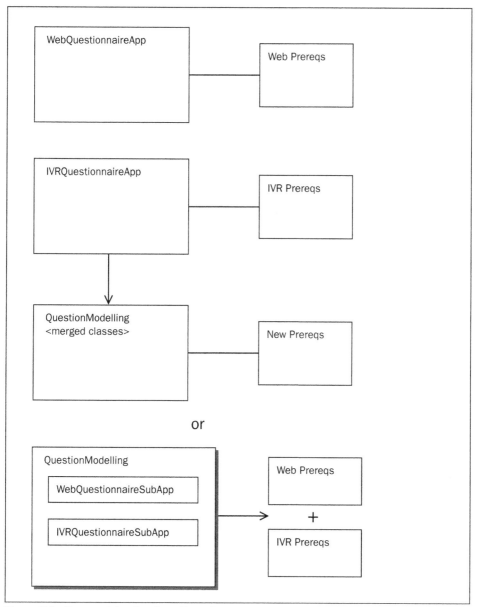

Figure 6-6: Reorganizing the Questionnaire system

Over time, management realized that these two projects were very similar, and the two groups began working together and consolidating their code. Now there is significant reuse between the groups, and most of the domain model is in common, but it remains split between two applications. The prerequisite problems are beginning to be an issue, and we need to consolidate. We could create a new generic QuestionModelling application and move all the code into it. Alternatively, we could create QuestionModelling as an empty application, create WebQuestionnaireSubApp and IVRQuestionnaireSubApp as subapplications of QuestionModelling, and move classes into each respectively.

Mass Cleanup

If the situation is sufficiently bad, the type of incremental fixes we've been talking about may be too slow and painstaking. Even figuring out which applications are mutually dependent can be an enormous amount of work. One drastic step is to simply create a new application, which has all of the problem applications as prerequisites, then as any problems are observed, move the methods involved into this new application. This technique might not be the cleanest or most elegant, but it should be able to eliminate any prerequisite problem. Once we have a set of prerequisites that is at least consistent, development can go forward and we have the ability to do small-scale reorganizations at our leisure.

For example, we might have developed our Questionnaire project as a set of 29 different applications, many of which have complex interlocking dependencies. It works fine in development, but the VisualAge packager won't let us package at all. We simply don't have time to refactor it all right now, so we'll create a QuestionnaireDumpingGround application, and for each packager error we'll move any methods or classes we think might be causing the problem into it. Once we have a running program we can show to management, we can do a proper reorganization. We recommend this technique in only desperate situations. The most common problem that can arise out of this technique is that, with the emergency averted, the proper reorganization will never get done.

Live With It

Depending on the situation, prerequisite violations may be more of a nuisance than something that absolutely must be dealt with. The VisualAge packaging mechanisms are very fussy about prerequisites, whether we're packaging reduced run-time images or ICs. The VisualWorks mechanisms are much more forgiving, and we may be able to be much looser about prerequisites without suffering too much. This does not mean that we should ignore prerequisite problems. Even when they don't immediately affect our program, they can tell us important things about the structure of our design. It does mean that we can deal with them as one problem among many, rather than as an overriding priority.

Meta-Programming

ENVY does its best to detect prerequisite errors, but because of the nature of Smalltalk it cannot detect all of them. If our application makes use of reflection or meta-programming facilities, then ENVY may not be able to detect the need for a prerequisite relationship. For example, rather than referring to a class directly in code, we could reference it as

    Smalltalk classAt: 'Question' asSymbol

Do *not* do this as a way of avoiding prerequisite problems! Because the class is not directly referenced, this introduces a hidden dependency. The packager may now decide to omit the class Question from the run-time image, causing run-time errors. In effect, this treats the immediate symptom but does not cure the disease. Meta-programming simply to circumvent ENVY's prerequisite error messages is a bad use of meta-programming, and should be avoided.

Summary

We've seen a number of possible sources of prerequisite problems, and techniques for dealing with them, ranging from the relatively simple to the extremely drastic. Which technique is appropriate will depend on the circumstances, though we always want to aim for the minimum disruption of development.

Changing Prerequisites in the Repository

Sometimes we need to reorganize prerequisites in a significant way, and the constraints ENVY imposes will not let us do it. For example, see the preceding section titled "Remove Extra Prerequisites." Fortunately, there is a way around this, which is by operating directly on the repository.

Two basic types of browsers exist in ENVY:

- Browsers that work on the contents of the image. All application and class browsers belong to this group, and this is how we normally think of browsers as working.

- Browsers that work on the contents of the repository. These browsers let you manipulate the repository directly, without passing through the in-memory representation. Browsers in this category include Shadow Browsers, Editions Browsers, the Configuration Map Browser, and the Application Editions Browser.

Fewer restrictions are placed on manipulating components in the library than in memory, so we should be able to do whatever's necessary, up to and including removing all the prerequisites and building them from scratch. Once we've changed the prerequisites, we can reload and ensure that they're valid.

Be careful when manipulating prerequisites this way. Because the normal integrity constraints are not applied, it's possible to put components into a state where they cannot be loaded. Let's look at how to use the Application Editions Browser to change prerequisites, while we contemplate a difficult configuration problem.

Using Configuration Expressions to Set Prerequisites

Recall that we can use configuration expressions to conditionally load subapplications. This is useful for automatically loading code that depends on the operating system, the Smalltalk dialect, or anything else we choose. In some circumstances, we may also need conditional prerequisites.

For example, consider the SUnit testing framework. It consists of domain classes, written in standard Smalltalk, and GUI classes, which are written using the dialect-specific GUI framework. As described in "Conditional Loading of Subapplications," we can factor out the GUI code into subapplications, which will conditionally load when the appropriate configuration expression holds. However, we also need to control the prerequisites of the root application because these different subapplications require different prerequisites. The VisualWorks version requires VisualWorksBase, and the VisualAge version requires AbtViewApplication.

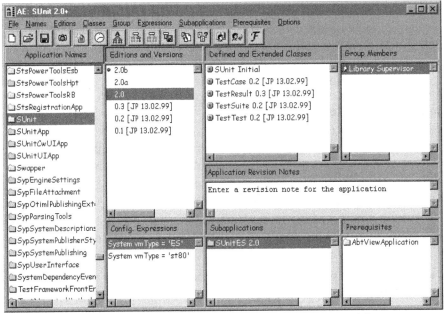

Figure 6-7: The Application Editions Browser with a VisualAge prerequisite

We can set up different prerequisites using the Application Editions Browser. In this browser, when we choose an application and edition, we can see the defined configuration expressions for that edition in the configuration expression pane. If we have not defined any, the default expression will be true, meaning that the expression is valid in any case. To the right of this we see the subapplications (if any) defined for this configuration expression, and further to the right is a pane listing the prerequisites for the selected configuration expression.

To change prerequisites in the library, we just change the prerequisites listed in the browser. Note that, as described previously, we are directly modifying the library.

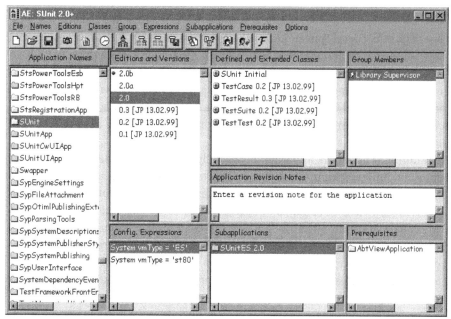

Figure 6-8: The Application Editions Browser with a VisualWorks prerequisite

In addition, we can only change the prerequisites for open editions. By selecting each configuration in turn and setting the prerequisites appropriately, we can set them up however we like.

Delivering

At some point, every project has to either deliver something or be cancelled. Clearly, this is extremely risky because this code that we've worked so hard on has to actually function. We can deal with this risk in two fundamental ways. The first is to put it off as long as possible. In this mode, we avoid dealing with items that have perceived risk, and concentrate on finishing the things we know we can do. This is an all-too-common strategy that works well in the short term, but in the long term leaves us with all the hard items and no time left to complete them. I have spoken to clients who literally and with a straight face assured me that they were more than ninety percent done, with only a few action items to complete. These items included actually reading the data out of two different databases and using real data instead of their example data sets with a dozen or so items.

A better approach to delivery and risk is to identify and deal with risky items as early as possible in the process. If we're not sure if we can solve a particular problem, we need to find out as early as possible. If we really can't solve it, then we either have to do something different, or we can stop now and save a lot of money. For a discussion of this in the literature see the "Risk Management" chapter in McConnell (1996).

Delivering in Smalltalk

How does this affect development in Smalltalk, and particularly ENVY development? Smalltalk is unusual as development environments go because it is written entirely in itself, and the system we are developing includes code from the development environment. If we're writing C++ or Java code, our development environment may or may not be written in C++ or Java. Whether it is or not doesn't matter very much to us because the development environment and the program under development are completely separate.

The traditional Smalltalk approach is radically different. The development environment is not only written in Smalltalk, it reflects back on itself in a very direct way. The classes that represent the browsers, the compiler, and the debugger are part of the same environment that contains our project classes. We can extend them, we can make them part of our application, and we can even replace them. This is tremendously powerful, and makes for a very rich environment. The programming environment provides not just a set of base classes, but a multitude of tools and examples.

The problem that arises with this rich environment is how to separate out what constitutes our program. There are a variety of different approaches to this, and deciding on and validating the approach we will take is an important step in development. Once we know how we intend to deliver, we should regularly run through the process to ensure that we understand all the steps and that unexpected difficulties are dealt with as early as possible.

The following sections review the various possible mechanisms for delivering programs in Smalltalk, with the advantages and disadvantages of each. Where the details are dialect-specific this will be indicated.

Basics

To start with, here's a list of the basic things we need to do to deliver an application, regardless of the mechanism we're using. Some of these steps will be performed automatically by some of the standard packaging mechanisms.

- **The first step is to ensure that the program can be loaded into a clean image.** Over time, it's easy to introduce dependencies on the state of the image in which development is occurring, causing problems when we need to load in a new image. Good organization and/or a project management tool such as that described in the section "A Simple Project Management Tool" can help reduce image building to a simple, reproducible process, which is conducive to its being done on a regular basis. It's a good idea to make this part of your project culture. Developers should become aware of the advantages of working with fresh images, and attempt to move away from the laziness of always using the same image. In an extreme example, at one project, a series of developers had been using the same image for more than three years! The application was for internal use, and was never packaged. When it finally came time to upgrade to a new version of the dialect, they found that it was next to impossible to do.

Regardless, the packaging process should always start from a clean image. All steps of the packaging process must be reproducible, from the beginning, and artifacts of the development process may cause very difficult-to-trace packaging problems. For example, development mechanisms such as code profilers, breakpoints, and testing tools may modify bytecodes in compiled methods. These modifications are generally transparent, but if we package a development image that contains these modified bytecodes, the run-time may crash without warning. When building a new image from scratch, pay attention to any messages on the Transcript. They are often warnings of problems that may need to be corrected before packaging.

SmallLint

A number of quality assurance tools for Smalltalk code are available. One tool that is both useful and free is SmallLint. This is available as part of the Refactoring Browser, which can be downloaded from the following site:

http://st-www.cs.uiuc.edu/~brant/RefactoringBrowser/

SmallLint can check for more than 60 common bugs in Smalltalk programs. The Refactoring Browser itself is discussed in more detail in "ENVY-izing the Refactoring Browser." Among the many tests that SmallLint offers, one is particularly relevant in packaging: methods sent but not implemented in the application.

This tests a group of classes or applications and checks whether there is at least one implementor for every message sent. If checking classes, it looks at the entire image. If checking applications, it looks in the prerequisite chain. This test can show whether there is at least one implementor of all messages we send that will be packaged in a stripped run-time image. This is not a guarantee that it's the right implementor, or that all the implementations we need will be packaged, but it's a good sanity check.

While running this tool, we may also want to pay attention to some of the other diagnostics. For example, Methods Implemented But Not Sent is a good way to find dead code, or code that is only ever called reflectively.

- **Check for Errors:** Before packaging we need to be sure that our code works, so we should check for errors. A good regression-testing suite is essential for delivering software with confidence. If someone can't test their software, they will have problems delivering. As well as doing explicit testing, it's a good idea to use some sort of code quality checker at this stage. See the preceding sidebar on SmallLint for an example.

- **Exception Handling:** Make sure that any unhandled exceptions will be trapped by a default handler, which does something more useful at run-time than bringing up a debugger (or at least something else in addition to bringing up a debugger). Some possibilities are logging the exception stack trace, e-mailing a message to a maintainer, and putting up a "Fatal Error" dialog box for the user.

- **Error logging:** Enable some degree of error logging, including redirecting Transcript messages to a log file.

- **Launching the application on startup:** Make sure that when the program is launched the application code will run automatically.

- **Test in deployed mode:** We'll assume a reasonable regression test suite. Run that test suite with the version that's been prepared for deployment.

- **Initialize image state:** Make sure that variables of all types (instance variables, globals, class variables, class instance variables, and pool dictionary entries) are all correctly and consistently initialized. We should not, for example, depend on whether they were initialized in the development image before packaging.

- **Provisions for update:** We may want to have a mechanism in place for updating the program with patches and new versions.

- **Remove ENVY/Manager:** This is a little bit more aggressive than simply nonpackaging, but if we don't plan to pay for ENVY licenses for end users and have the run-time image connected to the ENVY repository, we'll want to remove the ENVY code from your image. In VisualWorks, there's a simple way to do this, by running the method Kernel>removeEnvyManager. In VisualAge this option is not available as a separate option, but is done automatically by the VisualAge packager.

Given the preceding basics, what additional steps do we need to take to deliver? The following sections go through a number of possibilities.

Meta-Programming

Smalltalk has a very rich reflection and meta-programming protocol. This enables the entire Smalltalk programming environment to be written in Smalltalk and to support changes to that environment while it is running. These facilities are extremely important, but it is also tempting for developers to overuse them. It's relatively rare in normal programming that we need to use reflective techniques, and their use often makes it harder for someone else to read or understand the code. These techniques can also cause packaging errors because they make it difficult to determine exactly which code is required for a program to function. In VisualAge, some reflective techniques may also be impossible to package because VisualAge does not permit run-time programs to use the compiler.

This doesn't mean that we shouldn't use these techniques. They can be phenomenally useful and can enable us to easily achieve things that would otherwise be very cumbersome. The analogy we like to use is that of powerful spices: peppers, cumin, even salt. You'd hate to cook without these spices, and small doses of them applied in the right place can transform a dish. However, if they're used as a main ingredient, the result usually isn't very palatable.

To quote Kent Beck: "Meta-programming is important for mastery of Smalltalk, but it is not important for effective engineering. In fact, it's far more important to know when *not* to use it than it is to know *how* to use it."

Nothing

Not all applications need to separate themselves out from the development environment. If our code is running on a large server, or on well-equipped workstations, and/or the number of users is relatively small, we may be able to get away without any complex packaging step at all. We can simply configure a development image to run in a deployed mode, using the steps described previously in the "Basics" section.

This approach has some definite advantages. Packaging is very simple, and there's almost no risk of running into difficult packaging issues. If there is a problem in the deployed system, it's easy to debug because all the standard tools are there.

This approach also has disadvantages. The deployed image will be much larger than it really needs to be. Depending on the vendor, we may need to pay for development licenses for the run-time image because we're leaving in all the development tools. Our program, although it may be running as a "headless" server, will probably expect to run as a GUI application.

If these obstacles are not major problems, and we would really rather avoid the packaging step, this is a reasonable set of choices. If we need a smaller image or the ability to distribute the run-time to many users, then we need to explore other options.

Package

The most common Smalltalk application delivery process starts from a development environment and a known starting method and then removes all the things that aren't needed. This may be called *stripping* or *packaging*. The approaches to doing this range from ad hoc scripts that remove various subsystems to tools that carefully analyze exactly what can be removed.

These techniques have the potential to produce tremendously small run-time footprints by removing any and all unnecessary code, right down to the individual method and instance variable level. However, they can also be difficult to execute, can be over-aggressive, and problems that arise can be very difficult to debug because most or all of the debug support will have been removed.

Although it is entirely possible to create very compact executables, many developers are not aware of the techniques to keep run-time sizes down. Few guidelines exist to help developers produce a run-time application efficient in its use of memory and other resources. There are a number of reasons for this. Historically, Smalltalk came out of the research community with a focus on the quality of the development environment, not on delivering shrink-wrapped applications. The technology to make very compact applications was added later, and has not received as much attention. Many developers still have an impression of Smalltalk as being slow and requiring large executables, although in fact Smalltalk applications typically run significantly faster and with a lower memory footprint than many of today's technologies, including popular languages such as Java, Visual Basic, and even C++ (see the sidebar "Aside: Memory Footprint").

Aside: Memory Footprint

Many people believe that Smalltalk programs require a very large memory footprint, even though current Smalltalk implementations are competitive with or better than many of today's technologies. While this is not directly related to ENVY, and doing full and convincing benchmarks is well outside the scope of this book, we thought it worthwhile to highlight a couple of data points. One extreme example is Pocket Smalltalk (www.pocketsmalltalk.com), an open source implementation of Smalltalk for handheld devices. A simple Pocket Smalltalk program for a Palm computer is less than 50K, which includes widgets and basic debug support. An example that is perhaps more typical of most development work comes from my own experiences writing a product with mixed Smalltalk and Java. The Smalltalk portion is a sophisticated GUI for a database product, written in VisualAge Smalltalk and packaged. At run-time, under Windows, it has a footprint of roughly 10MB of RAM. The product needs to connect with databases using JDBC, so there is also a Java server, which has no GUI and includes only the database driver and socket communication code. It has a run-time footprint of roughly 13MB of RAM. I measure my e-mail program (Eudora Pro 4.2, presumably written in C or C++) at a memory footprint of 14.5MB of RAM.

History aside, there are legitimate difficulties in building an optimized small footprint production image, particularly using the image stripping approach. Late binding and unbounded polymorphism are key to flexibility and productivity in Smalltalk. It is impossible to perform an automated static analysis of the application classes and be sure exactly what other classes and methods are *not* required. Approximate methods exist, but reflection and other techniques can defeat them and result in errors that are difficult to detect.

All else aside, consider the number of different subsystems that exist in a Smalltalk development environment that may or may not be included in a run-time. This includes basic language classes, meta-programming and reflection, file systems, graphics, widgets, GUI frameworks, applications frameworks, testing frameworks, development tools, GUI construction tools, database connectivity, foreign-language callouts, operating-system interfaces, socket communications, additional libraries, performance profilers, user domain models, user windows, user tests, and user extensions. Merely specifying what's needed is a significant task. Within these subsystems it may also be necessary to divide the code into run-time and development-time components. For example, we don't want to ship our test suites or their support code, and a GUI construction tool will likely consist of both run-time support pieces and development-time-only pieces. See the sidebar on "Loading Only the Run-Time Code" for some advice on partitioning code this way.

Loading Only the Run-Time Code

An important step to take in preparing a minimal image is to load only the code that is required at run-time. We can make this easier by splitting our code into run-time and development-time portions early. For example, we can create a configuration map for all run-time applications, one for development-time add-ons, and a top-level map that contains no applications, but lists both of the other maps as required maps. For example, the Questionnaire Run-Time Only map might contain QuestionModelling and QuestionUI. The Questionnaire Development-Time Only map might contain SUnit and QuestionTesting. The main Questionnaire map would contain no applications, but have required maps of Questionnaire Run-Time Only and Questionnaire Development-Time Only. In normal development, we would load the Questionnaire map, but for run-time packaging we would load only the Questionnaire Run-Time Only map.

An alternative mechanism is to use configuration expressions, and to use some flag to indicate whether an image is development-time or not. For example, we could make a single Questionnaire configuration map and list the required maps in two different configurations, dependent on the value of a global variable IsThisImageForRunTimePackaging. Alternatively, we could organize our code using subapplications, creating an overall Questionnaire application with subapplications for QuestionModelling, QuestionTesting, and QuestionUI. The loading of QuestionTesting would be conditional on the same global variable.

While any of the these solutions would work, we usually prefer the first because it minimizes the number of configurations that need to be kept in sync, and the specific step for loading is slightly simpler. Regardless of our approach, it is important to ensure that we have a clean separation of run-time code from development-time code, and that this is well maintained. For more discussion on application partitioning issues see "Large Projects."

Multiple products fall into the category of "Packaging Tools." We briefly list them here, and they are discussed in more detail in the sections on "VisualAge Packaging" and "VisualWorks Packaging."

- **The VisualAge Packager (reduced run-time mode):** VisualAge Smalltalk includes a sophisticated packager that can operate in one of several different modes. The reduced run-time image mode aggressively removes any unnecessary code, using transitive closure of sent messages and exploiting prerequisite information. This packager came out of OTI's work with embedded systems, and can be used to produce very compact code, with a wealth of optimization options.

- **ParcPlace ImageMaker:** VisualWorks includes a tool called ImageMaker that consists of a number of removal scripts that automatically removes certain subsystems. It does not attempt to detect unused code, and any additional removals require editing the scripts. This mechanism is simple to use, but does not produce the most compact run-times.

- **Runtime Packager:** This third-party product for VisualWorks is available from Advanced Boolean Concepts (www.advbool.com). This stripping tool operates more like the VisualAge packager. It attempts to eliminate unused code based on transitive closure of senders and on monitoring the run-time behavior of the program. It includes a number of other useful tools for creating production run-times. This product is included with the commercial versions of VisualWorks 5i.

Components

Stripping or packaging a development image can present difficulties, as described previously. Within the last few years, new packaging technologies have been developed that attempt to address some of these issues. One such approach is component-based packaging. In this model, we do not try to aggressively remove every piece of unnecessary code. Instead, we create a base system, which includes only the basic functionality, and provide additional pieces as components, which can be dynamically loaded or linked with the program at run-time.

The disadvantage of this approach is that the resulting program will have a larger memory footprint than a packaged image. With reasonable partitioning, though, the additional space requirement can be kept small. Packaging with components may also have a disadvantage in startup time because the components must be linked or loaded on startup. The advantages of this approach are that packaging becomes much simpler, it becomes possible to use the same base runtime image for multiple different programs, and it may even be possible to share memory between multiple programs running simultaneously. It can also simplify distribution of patches because the program can be split up into much smaller pieces.

Products that fall into this category include the following. These are described in more detail in the sections on "VisualAge Packaging" and "VisualWorks Packaging."

- **VisualWorks Parcels:** Parcels are a VisualWorks facility that provide a fast-loading binary representation of code. Rather than aggressively remove unused methods, we can use a tool such as ImageMaker to ensure that only the required subsystems are in the base image. Then we can store our code as one or more parcels, which can be loaded from the command line or dynamically at run-time. There are relatively few ENVY implications to this approach, so it is discussed only briefly.

- **VisualAge Image Components (ICs):** VisualAge ICs are a Smalltalk facility for true shared libraries. They provide a representation of Smalltalk code that can be dynamically linked into an image at run-time. The code is not loaded into the base image, but remains separate and can be unloaded or shared between multiple images. VisualAge provides a version of its base class libraries divided up into ICs. The VisualAge Packager is capable of packaging application(s) into ICs. These can be linked with the image either from the command line at startup or dynamically at run-time. Packaging ICs is a large topic, and while much of what we describe in the "VisualAge Packaging" section that follows applies to both reduced image packaging and to ICs, you should consult the VisualAge documentation for more information on this option.

Separate Run-time and Development Images

The component-based approach to packaging offers advantages in simplicity and other areas, but does not address the problem of debugging problems with the deployed image. An approach that addresses this, along with other issues, is entirely separating the deployed image from the development image. Rather than a single image, which contains all of the development-time tools as well as run-time code, we can run two entirely separate programs — one with development tools and one with only run-time code. The development image can manipulate the run-time image and provide full debugging and development support. This offers a number of advantages. Packaging for deployment becomes trivial because the run-time image is always ready for deployment, and there is no need to remove any code. The development environment cannot be corrupted by changes in the run-time, and can even survive a fatal crash of the run-time image. Finally, in this model, the class libraries of the run-time image do not need to be the same as those in the development image, enabling cross-development.

The disadvantages of this approach are that it requires significant tool support, including distributed programming, particularly if we are to have all of the normal Smalltalk facilities available to us. In addition, running both images and using a distributed programming mechanism communicating between them requires a more high-powered development machine.

Products that fall into this category include the following:

- **VisualAge XD:** The VisualAge Server Smalltalk feature includes a facility called XD. This is primarily targeted at cross-development of headless server applications, but supports more general development in a separate run-time image. This is described in detail in the VisualAge documentation.

- **VisualWorks OpenTalk:** VisualWorks 5i includes a preliminary version of a facility called OpenTalk, which is a distributed framework that includes remote development and debugging of separate images.

Painless Delivery

Operating in a rich development environment can mask potential problems that don't manifest until it's time to deliver. We can deal with this risk by making delivery an incremental process and part of our basic development cycle. If we iterate and make a baseline every three weeks, part of that baselining process should be running through our packaging process and testing the resulting delivered application. If we've introduced a potential delivery problem, we'll know about it almost as soon as it's introduced, rather than at the end of the project. We'll always have a compact and demo-able executable ready, and most important, we'll have confidence in our ability to take the development process through to the end with a systematic and reproducible process.

VisualAge Packaging

Packaging is one of the areas where Smalltalk dialects diverge significantly, and although there are many ideas in common between VisualWorks and VisualAge, the details are quite different. This section addresses some of the VisualAge-specific packaging issues that are the responsibility of the developer and the application manager.

Packaging Concepts

VisualAge supports three different packaging mechanisms. The most common mechanism, and the one generally referred to as "packaging" in a VisualAge context, is the reduced run-time packaging. This starts from a development environment and strips out unused code. The second option is development of Image Components or ICs, shared libraries that can be dynamically linked and unlinked and shared between multiple running images. These are less compact than reduced images, but offer additional capabilities. The third option is XD packaging, in which a completely separate run-time image is built up and packaging is implicit. This produces a standalone image that is also larger than a reduced run-time, but which is much simpler to package. Although the other two options are becoming increasingly important, most VisualAge packaging is still done through a reduced run-time image, and the potential difficulties are the best understood, so we will concentrate on this mechanism.

Packager-Friendly Applications

As application manager for one or more applications, one of our responsibilities is to ensure that these applications can be packaged easily. As application managers, we are in the best possible position to know if any programming techniques were used that might cause problems when packaging. Ideally, if all of the applications correctly supply packaging information, packaging of the entire program should be straightforward. Let's go through a step-by-step procedure to check our code for packager-friendliness. In general, we'll be talking about the reduced run-time packager. Packaging for ICs has similar concepts, but also a number of differences that we won't go into in detail.

The VisualAge Packager API provides several methods, all of which can be used to help the packager do its work. We discuss the most important parts of this API in the following relevant sections. For most of these methods, browsing implementors will provide some examples of usage.

Step 1: Load Into a Clean Image

Standard procedure when packaging from a development image is to minimize the amount of code and/or objects that need to be removed from the image. One simple way to do this is to always start the packaging process by loading a versioned configuration map that contains the code we want to package and as little else as possible into a clean image. This helps make sure that no extraneous code is loaded, and that no unnecessary objects are floating around in the system (background processes, global variables, and debugging information). After packaging, we quit the clean image and test the resulting run-time.

Step 2: Check Prerequisites

Ensure that the prerequisite chain is correct. The packager starts with a small number of "seed" methods, including methods known to be sent by the virtual machine and the method that starts up our program, considering for inclusion *only* the classes and methods in the containing application and its prerequisites. Then, the packager tries to create a call tree starting at the root method, including:

1. Any classes directly referenced in the methods

2. Any methods in the classes found in the first step whose selector is referenced by any methods already known to be included

3. Any methods explicitly listed in the packaging instructions

If a class in not in the prerequisite chain, it and its methods won't be included, even though the class is referenced. Also, if a method is not directly called, it won't be included. This means that those classes or methods that are only referenced through reflection or meta-programming will not automatically be included. This may cause run-time errors in the resulting image.

Step 3: Classes

Classes can be referenced in a number of ways, which may be confusing to the packager. If we're using these methods, we will probably need to use some explicit packager instructions to ensure they're included.

- **Subclasses:** If we use abstract classes whose subclasses are only accessed through methods such as withAllSubclases or allSubclasses, the packager will not include them. We should either explicitly reference the classes or include their names in the packaging instructions.

- **Swapper:** One simple way to maintain objects persistently is to store them in external files using ENVY/Swapper or some other serialization mechanism. If the classes of the objects we have stored this way are not directly referenced from other portions of the code, the packager will not include them. If these classes are not included, then Swapper will read those values as nil. When using serialized objects in this way, be sure that class definitions for all serialized objects are otherwise referenced or included in the packaging instructions.

- **classAt:** Previously, we discussed using Smalltalk classAt: something asSymbol to access classes not included the class in the prerequisite chain. A class solely referenced in this way is not considered by the packager to be explicitly referenced and will not be included in the packaged image.

- **Dictionaries of classes:** One of the common OO design patterns, as described in Alpert et al. (1998) and Gamma et al. (1994), is the *Abstract Factory*. One of the implementation techniques is the use of a part catalog, a dictionary of classes keyed to the different types of objects to be created. If the entries in the dictionary are class names and not classes, or if the dictionary is initialized in a way that does not include explicit class references, these classes could be omitted from the packaged image.

All these techniques have one thing in common: The classes required are not explicitly referenced. If the packager never sees an explicit reference, it will conclude that the class is unused and exclude it from the packaged image.

In an application that uses any of the techniques described previously to reference classes, we need to use the packagerIncludeClassNames method to inform the packager of the names of the classes defined in this application that should be included in the run-time image. For example, to include just the class Answer, we could define this method as follows:

```
packagerIncludeClassNames
"Return the names of all classes to be included"

^#(Answer).
```

To include all classes defined in the application, we could use reflection and define the method as follows. Note that self is an application class, so the method defined will return a list of all classes defined in that application.

```
packagerIncludeClassNames
"Return the names of all classes to be included"

^self defined collect: ( :each | each symbol(.
```

Step 4: Methods

Even if the list of included classes is correct, errors can occur at the method level. Smalltalk is a dynamic language, and it is impossible to be certain which methods are not required. The prerequisite check ensures that the required classes are included in the prerequisite chain, but it cannot guarantee that all methods called will be packaged in the run-time image. For example, if our code calls a method that has no implementation in any of our prerequisites, the packager will complain. However, if the implementation we want is excluded, but another implementation exists, then the packager can't detect the problem. This situation is described in more detail in the "Hidden Dependencies" section earlier in this chapter.

Another problem arises if we don't invoke a method directly, but instead use meta-programming techniques such as perform:. In this case the packager may not recognize that a method is being called and exclude it from the run-time image. The packager assumes that any symbols referenced are message selectors, but a construction such as

```
(self questionType, 'PossibleAnswers') asSymbol
```

won't be recognized as a symbol. If we use these techniques, we should use the packagerIncludeSelectors method to tell the packager which methods are to be included. For example, if we wanted to package a run-time that included our QuestionTesting code so that we could run the unit tests on a packaged image, we would run into the problem that SUnit uses reflection to call any method whose name ends in "test." Because these methods are never explicitly called, the packager would leave them out. We might explicitly include all methods in our classes, whether they're in defined classes or in class extensions, as follows:

```
packagerIncludeSelectors
"Return the selectors for all methods to be included"

^self classes
    inject: Set new
    into: ( :eachClass :set |
        set addAll: class selectors; yourself(.
```

In addition, if we use symbols to define state, this may confuse the packager, which assumes that the symbols are message selectors and will try to include the corresponding methods. For example, in our Question class we might store a state for the question as holding one of the symbols #answerValid, #answerInvalid or #notAnswered. These symbols have no corresponding methods, and we don't want to have to explain this to the packager each time, so we can declare these known nonmessage-send selectors in the packagerKnownSymbols method.

```
packagerKnownSymbols
    ^#(answerValid answerInvalid notAnswered).
```

Atoms

An alternative technique for representing names of states in VisualAge is to use *atoms*. Atoms are similar to symbols, in that two atoms with the same value are guaranteed by the system to be identical, but they are created with ## instead of #, and cannot be used as arguments to perform:. For example, if we stored the atom ##answerValid, the packager would realize that this was not a message selector, and not flag it as a possible problem. This is a preferred technique, whose only major disadvantage is that it makes the code nonportable to other Smalltalk dialects.

Other packager hooks are available, but they are generally less useful. These include packagerIgnoreSelectors and packagerIgnoreReferencesInSelectors. We generally don't recommend using these except in special circumstances because they can easily be misused to mask the symptoms of serious problems that should be dealt with in other ways.

Step 5: Variable Initialization

To reduce image size by not packaging unnecessary objects, it is a good idea to reset the values of singletons, class and class instance variables, globals, and pools. Apart from saving space, this can remove transient information that won't be valid in a run-time (for example, file handles) and large amounts of information that should be filled in at run-time (for example, pools of NLS strings).

We have two ways to handle initialization in VisualAge. The first and the recommended mechanism is to use pragma methods. These provide a declarative syntax for defining global, class, and pool variables in the application. These methods are thoroughly described in the VisualAge documentation.

The second mechanism is to define the method epPreDumpingActionsFor: on the application class. This method is called before packaging begins and provides a hook to do any prepackaging processing of the image. In this case, we will need methods to declare and/or initialize global, pool, and other values. Such methods should be implemented on the classes themselves rather than on the application class. They can be called by the application's loaded method and by the packager's predumping action.

The packager also provides the method epPostDumpingActionsFor:, which provides a post-processing hook. Because, after packaging, artifacts of the packaging process may hang around in the image unnecessarily, we generally exit from the development environment without saving the image when we've finished packaging, and do not implement this method.

Step 6: Packaging

The best test for packaging is packaging. If we follow the preceding tips and keep our prerequisites correct, packaging should be a simple matter of pushing a button, taking a coffee break, and checking the results. In addition, running the packager on our code gives us an increased feeling of security. It also helps isolate problems. If we were able to package cleanly at the end of the last iteration, and we can't package now, then the problem is clearly in the code we've written since then. This helps narrow the possible range of problems considerably.

In our work, we tend to be a bit fanatical about zero packaging errors. While you might not be so strict, the fewer errors permitted to accumulate, the fewer problems you will have later down the road.

VisualWorks Packaging

Packaging is one of the areas where Smalltalk dialects diverge significantly, and although there are many ideas in common between VisualWorks and VisualAge, the details are quite different. This section addresses some of the VisualWorks-specific packaging issues that are the responsibility of the developer and the application manager.

Packaging Concepts

VisualWorks supports two main packaging mechanisms. The most common mechanism is the one generally referred to as "stripping." This starts from a development environment and strips out unused code. The second option is storage of the application code in parcels, which can be rapidly loaded into a running image. This is a less compact form, but offers advantages in flexibility and image size. Traditionally, VisualWorks packaging has differed from VisualAge in that its licensing restrictions were more relaxed. In particular, it was possible to freely include the compiler in a deployed VisualWorks image. As of VisualAge Version 5.5 these restrictions have been removed and these techniques can also be used with VisualAge.

Stripping

VisualWorks offers two different possibilities for stripping an image. The first is the ImageMaker, which is the default mechanism supplied by Cincom. In ENVY, this is located in the ImageDeployment application, which is not loaded by default. The ImageMaker does not attempt to do any computation of what can be removed, but enables the developer to specify which of a variety of features are to be removed. Detailed removal scripts also exist that can be edited manually. This packager is not too aggressive, but is relatively safe because it makes no attempt to prune the user code, and it will only remove subsystems that are explicitly indicated. There are relatively few issues in using ImageMaker to produce a stripped run-time. Note that ImageMaker can also be used to prepare a basic run-time image, which loads parcels representing the application code, as described in the following "Parcels" section.

A more sophisticated tool is Runtime Packager, provided as a third-party product by Advanced Boolean Concepts (www.advbool.com). This adds a number of additional features over the default tools, including simplifying the packaging process, automated tracking of unneeded classes and methods, and much more aggressive image compression. This packager is included in commercial configurations of VisualWorks 5i, and we recommend it as the default packaging mechanism in most circumstances, both for the set of packaging features and for ease of use.

Preparing the Image

Runtime Packager and ImageMaker can operate both with and without ENVY, and so are much less reliant on ENVY information than the VisualAge packager. In particular, the inclusion of classes and methods is entirely based on usage, and they will not be excluded based on prerequisites. While this can potentially lead to inclusion of classes that might be excluded by VisualAge packaging, it means that correct ENVY prerequisites are not particularly important to correct packaging. It is, however, important that the code not include dependencies on ENVY system applications (for example, EtTools), which will always be removed as part of the packaging process. For example, see the "Easily Eliminated Prerequisite" section earlier in this chapter where we discuss how using the ENVY progress dialog box in user code can lead to packaging errors.

The most important step in preparing to package using either ImageMaker or Runtime Packager is to load the minimum necessary code into a clean image. If our project contains development-time-only code, the best policy is to ensure that it's not loaded before packaging. Runtime Packager attempts to clean up the image by removing extraneous variables, closing windows, and so forth, but if we've loaded into a clean image where user code has never been run, then we're guaranteed those things were never there in the first place. For more discussion on this topic, see the preceding sidebar on "Loading Only the Run-Time Code." Once we have loaded all the code into the image, we should save it. This makes sure that, if we encounter problems during the packaging process, we can easily revert back to a clean image in which we've done nothing but load code.

Runtime Packager offers a number of convenient options for how to treat the run-time image. These include excluding or including the compiler, diagnostic dumps for run-time exceptions, packaging "headless," including or excluding an emergency evaluator that can provide access to the internals of a packaged run-time, including or excluding particular UI looks, and others. The packager can also write out parcels, including parcels that have been stripped of any unused methods, which lets us combine stripping and parcel-based delivery.

One VisualWorks option that deserves some further explanation is the *three-step save*. This is an option that can provide performance improvements in a run-time image by optimizing garbage-collector behavior, but it does complicate the packaging process. VisualWorks includes a number of different garbage-collector spaces, one of which is called PermSpace. This includes objects that are never expected to be garbage-collected. The Perm Save As option enables you to save the entire current contents of the image into PermSpace. When packaging, we can assume that all of our classes, methods, and run-time structures that are present in the packaged image will stay there permanently. The three-step save process does the packaging, then saves the entire image to PermSpace. This is still not enough because, in addition to the things we want to keep, there may be transient information (open files, windows, and other temporary artifacts of the image). To get rid of these, we start up the image again and do a full garbage-collect to dispose of the transient objects that are no longer used. Then we save the image again. The result is a compact image in which our permanent objects are not considered by the garbage collector, minimizing its work. For more information on PermSpace, see the VisualWorks documentation.

Variable Initialization

To reduce image size by not packaging unnecessary objects, it is a good idea to reset the values of singletons, class and class instance variables, globals, and pools. Apart from saving space this can remove transient information that won't be valid in a run-time (for example, file handles) and large amounts of information that should be filled in at run-time (for example, message catalogs of NLS strings).

We have two main ways to handle initialization in VisualWorks, depending on the version. The first mechanism is to use ENVY pragma methods. These provide a declarative syntax for defining global, class, and pool variables in the application. These methods are described in the ENVY documentation.

The second mechanism is to specify a PreStrip Class and PreStrip Method in Runtime Packager, which is invoked before the stripping process begins. This provides a hook to do any prepackaging processing of the image. In this case, we will need methods that declare and/or initialize global, pool, and other values. Such methods should be implemented on the classes themselves rather than on the application class. They can be called by the Application's loaded method and by the packager's PreStrip method.

Runtime Packager also provides the method RuntimeManager>postStripBlock:, a postprocessing hook. Because, after packaging, artifacts of the packaging process may hang around in the image unnecessarily, we generally exit from the development environment without saving the image when we're finished packaging, and don't use this hook.

In VisualWorks 5i, it may also be possible to define some things that would normally be variables as *statics*. This is a similar mechanism to ENVY's pragmas, and incorporates a constant value as part of the class definition, which is automatically initialized without any user intervention. In ENVY, these two mechanisms are tied together. When using ENVY, VisualWorks statics should be defined through pragmas, and they will be automatically initialized on component load.

Parcels

In recent releases, VisualWorks has introduced and elaborated the concept of *parcels*. These are a mechanism for organizing code for delivery. They provide a fast-loading mechanism for distributing modules in binary and/or source code form.

Parcels were introduced in VisualWorks 2.5, but it was not until Version 3.0 that they became truly useful. Parcels serve a number of purposes. First, they provide a simple distribution mechanism for code, both binary and source. Within the image they can provide an organizing mechanism for source code. With Version 5i, VisualWorks now includes an alternative team programming tool called StORE, whose packages correspond closely to parcels.

Parcels can also be used as a packaging mechanism. Rather than stripping an image, we can distribute a minimal run-time image and the various parcels it requires. These can be loaded (and unloaded) at run-time, enabling sophisticated code management. It's also possible to combine the two approaches, creating a stripped image with part of the code and other parts loaded through parcels. Using Runtime Packager, it's even possible to create parcels minimized for run-time.

The degree of parcel integration with ENVY varies depending with the version. In VisualWorks 3.0 there were some notable shortcomings, partially due to overlap and mismatches between the concepts. These semantic differences can cause some problems dealing with parcels in ENVY. Fortunately, the integration has greatly improved in ENVY for VisualWorks 5i.

As a unit of code organization, parcels are similar to applications, but the prerequisite relationships among parcels are much weaker, allowing operations that would be impossible in ENVY. Most notably the order of parcel loading is much more flexible, including the capability to load a parcel, which references or extends code that does not exist. This will obviously cause problems with code that tries to use the prerequisite, but other code will run properly. If the prerequisite is later loaded, references will be updated accordingly, code that previously could not be loaded will be installed, and everything will work. Methods in parcels can also modify existing system methods and automatically replace the old version on unload, something that ENVY class extensions do not support.

As a unit of run-time executable code distribution, parcels are similar to VisualAge's ICs. Both are platform-independent ways of distributing bytecodes that can be dynamically linked into a running VM. The main difference is that ICs are shareable between multiple images, and their optimizations and limitations are based around that requirement. Parcels are loaded into a single image, and are not shared. In this respect they are closer to Java .class files, although they are significantly more powerful.

ENVY supports the use of parcels, but in the context that ENVY is the primary code organizing mechanism. We use ENVY to develop code and organize it into applications and configuration maps. We can generate parcels for deployment, but they are generated from the ENVY structures, and conform to the ENVY rules (for example, prerequisites). The exact treatment varies between VisualWorks 3.0 and 5i.

⊘   In VisualWorks 3.0/ENVY 4.0 it's possible to develop with ENVY and save the code out to parcels, with each parcel directly corresponding to a single ENVY application. **Warning:** Do *not* load parcelled versions of code back into an ENVY 4.0 development image! If you do so, the ENVY structures will most likely be corrupted, and you will need to exit from the image without saving. The reason for this is that both ENVY and parcels provide mechanisms for managing code. ENVY intercepts the normal Smalltalk code modification mechanisms of browsing and file-in, but parcel loading goes around these mechanisms. As far as ENVY is concerned, this is loading unmanaged code, and it goes into the appropriate application. This holds even if we are loading classes that already happen to have definitions and methods in ENVY. As a result, loading a parcel can change class definitions or methods for versioned classes and applications without ENVY being aware of it, and any attempt to later change those definitions can very badly confuse the system. This restriction does not apply in VisualWorks 5i in which ENVY fully understands the parcel mechanisms.

In VisualWorks 5i, the parcel integration is significantly richer. It's possible to load parcels into ENVY, and the code will be correctly managed, whether it is new code or a modified version of code already in the image. When we load a parcel, ENVY automatically creates a new application for it, which appears as a scratch edition. If we create a new edition from that parcel, ENVY stores the parcel code into the repository and the code and application can be managed normally. This is very convenient, and enables us to bring non-ENVY-aware parcels into ENVY easily. It's also possible to create parcels corresponding to an arbitrary group of ENVY applications.

In either VisualWorks 3.0 or 5i, parcels that correspond to applications will include the ENVY Application class. This can be a problem when loading these parcels into non-ENVY VisualWorks images because the superclasses Application and SubApplication do not exist. ENVY provides a VisualWorks parcel, which includes stub versions of the Application and SubApplication classes, and you should also load these if you are loading any parcels created from ENVY. This parcel is distributed in the files EMAPPS.PCL and EMAPPS.PST.

Application Attachments

Often it's not until we try to deliver a program that we finally notice how many external dependencies it has. Initialization files, document templates, bitmaps and icons, external libraries, external library source code, and many other files may be necessary for a program to function. Wouldn't it be nice if we could version these all in ENVY, together with the application? Well, the good news is we can — by using *application attachments*.

What are application attachments? They are arbitrary (non-Smalltalk) files stored in the ENVY repository. The word "attachment" means they are not standalone components, but are attached to existing ENVY components — in this case, to applications and subapplications.

Folders

Attachments are stored in *folders*. A folder is simply a way of grouping attachments together. ENVY allows attachments to be moved or copied between folders, similar to categorizing methods. These changes in the internal organizational structure have no effect on the external file path of the attachment, which is also saved.

Folders can be named or renamed to any string containing printable characters. They permit manipulation of groups of attachments. All attachments contained in one folder can be retrieved from the repository with a single action. Also, deleting a folder deletes all attachments in the folder.

Using Attachments

An attachment can be any external file, whether text or binary. ENVY stores attachments in an internal compressed format, with a platform-independent form of the path name. This allows files to be stored on one platform and recreated on another platform. The attachment mechanism offers a number of options to localize the file or path name upon storage and retrieval.

One problem, though, is that attachments are stored internally as a type of user field. The consequence of this is that there is no direct history and only one version (the latest) of a file accessible at any one time.

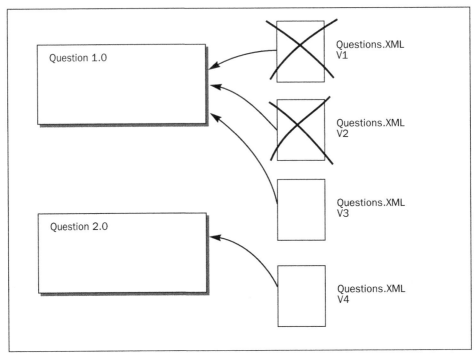

Figure 6-9: Attachments and history

This relationship between attachments (and other user fields) and history is subtle. Anything stored in a user field, including file attachments, is not a first-class ENVY object, and does not have versions, editions, or other history information. However, that object is associated with an ENVY component that does have history information. This means that we do have a partial history for that object, partial in that there is only one copy of the object per edition of the container. For example, if we decide to read our questions out of an XML file, then there will be a corresponding file called QUESTIONS.XML, and we'll attach that to the QuestionModelling application. Regardless of how many times we change this, we will always get the most recent version back from the attachments mechanism. That is, until we make a new edition. At that point, the version of QUESTIONS.XML associated with our version 1.0 application is frozen. Whenever we ask for the file associated with version 1.0, we'll get the last one that was set on version 1.0. If we ask our open edition, we'll get the last one that was set on the open edition.

Why would we want to use the application attachment mechanism? We could duplicate this functionality simply by storing the files into comments or user fields. The application attachments have some advantages. First, they make it easy to recursively store whole directory trees and to have them recreated on retrieval. Second, attachments offer the option of target platform localization. Line delimiter transformation and path name correction can be performed on retrieval.

Issues

The main disadvantage of the attachment mechanism has already been mentioned. No version history exists — the last one checking in an attachment wins. Also, because ENVY is an append-only repository, each storage of an attachment increases the size of the repository by the size of the file being stored and by the small overhead of the record structure size. Although this is not a huge problem with a maximum repository size of 16GB, it is still a critical factor in deciding whether to use attachments.

Another option with attachments is to use an external version control system, but to store ENVY references into that system, essentially paths and version numbers or possibly URLs. This helps keep the repository size down while letting us be sure we have the right versions of corresponding components. It can also provide integration with another team that has its own version control and team programming strategies.

Version Naming for Developer Tools

If we're shipping a packaged image to a customer, there really doesn't have to be any relationship between the internal version names we're using and what the product is called. We can get ready to ship our new update of Questionnaire 1.2 only to discover a few days before launch that marketing has decided to call it Questionnaire Pro 2000, Enterprise Edition. It doesn't matter because we're the only ones who ever see the version names.

The situation is different if we're shipping a development tool. If we're shipping the Questionnaire framework as a Smalltalk development tool, developers are going to see all of our version names, class owners, and maybe even source code. We may not want this, particularly when these were created by last-minute patches. Suppose we've just versioned everything off as version 2.0 and sent it to testing. Testing finds a bug serious enough to warrant a fix. What do we call the new version?

Maintaining Consistent Version Numbers

Let's take a quick look at a mechanism to keep class, app, and map version names in sync. We like this scheme better than most we've seen because it requires much less effort to target a particular number.

The usual problem is that development is iterative, and we don't always know whether we're finished or not. At some point, we decide that all our classes and applications should be called 2.0. The problem is that there will probably be several iterations of fixes before 2.0 is really ready for release. If everything was named 2.0 on the first attempt, then to reuse the name would mean purging code (valuable history) for each of the subsequent attempts until the release.

We could solve this problem using the version renaming tool described in "Renaming Versions." However, we prefer to save that kind of direct repository modification as a last resort. First, it's confusing to other users, and revising our development history this way can cause confusion when trying to track releases later on. If we can manage with a simple naming convention, we prefer to do that.

A different kind of inconsistency arises between class and application version numbers. Typically the version/release cycle for classes is much faster than that of applications, so higher-level components will increment their version numbers much more slowly. The application version 1.2 might easily contain classes versioned 1.34 if we use the default conventions.

We feel that keeping class version names in sync with build/application version names is more trouble than it is worth. Classes should have their own version history with names that are not tied to the version names of applications that contain them. While tying the two together would make it simpler to match up classes and applications, it would make it harder to follow the history of the classes because numbers would change arbitrarily.

There's also an issue with the default ENVY mechanism for detecting conflicts. If we modify version 1.1 and someone else has already made another version from it (called 1.2 by default), then ENVY will suggest version 1.1.1, which hints at the potential conflicts. While this is a weak mechanism, it's one that most developers are used to, and gaps in the version numbering scheme will defeat it.

Naming Convention

What we do is target a particular version name for both classes and applications in the release, but we aren't fussy about matching up version names before that. We also put additional information into the version name besides just a number. This is easier if we can supply our own default naming convention, but can also be done manually.

During regular development, we use whatever versioning scheme we like and take advantage of the ENVY auto-increment feature for version names. For example, if we have an application and are targeting release 5.1, we'll version classes as:

    5.1 dev 11-3-99 AK

When we get relatively close to a release, we'll version applications as:

    5.1 beta1 11-3-99

We'll leave the classes inside those applications with whatever version names they had before.

When we finally have a build that is judged suitable to be a release candidate, we will rename or reversion all of the components at all levels.

Repository Optimization

We can use a number of tricks to manipulate the way code is stored in the repository. These are most often used to minimize repository size, but can also affect loading speed. Repository size is of most importance if we are releasing incremental updates or repositories for multiple versions or dialects. These techniques are unlikely to be useful for a smaller project, but are the sort of techniques that OTI used for its own releases.

- Check if any of the methods had actually changed with the previous release (by comparing the two versions); if not, then release the previous method to save space in a library that shared the two releases.

- Do the opposite of the preceding technique and intentionally resave every single method (using a script) so that the initial set of bytecodes stored in the method edition is the set matching a particular platform. This can save space in the library because the method editions contain only one bytecode set rather than an initial set (whichever platform the method edition was originally saved on) and then one or more additional bytecode sets from later saves. By doing this, each class edition only needs to know one set of bytecodes. This can also be used to speed up loading. If the linker is turned on (which it normally is), and the initial set of bytecodes in the method is correct for the current VM, then that set will be used. If not, we have to do three more reads in the library (one for the dictionary of bytecode types, another for the dictionary of method format timestamps, and another for the record containing the bytecodes) just for that method, to get the correct set of bytecodes. If that is the case for all the methods in a large load, it can make a big difference.

Which of these two options is better depends on how much code has changed since the previous release.

When reversioning or renaming, use a three-part name in the following form:

5.1.3 candidate 1 000

The first part shows the official recognized product name, the second is an optional text field, and the third part shows the revision number for each part of the product. This reversioning step is to happen only once — for the first release candidate.

As is often the case, the release candidate will fail some test several weeks later and require another cycle of changes. When this happens, don't do anything special with any of the version names. Allow the version name to increment naturally (version with defaults). Never be concerned that the revision numbers of subparts (classes, subapps, and apps) increment faster than their higher level parts (maps, apps, and subapps). The revision number of a part should not be forced to coincide with the revision number of the whole (or vice versa).

Each time there is a candidate release, make a copy of the configuration map version that has only the official product release name (for example, create a new map edition based on 5.1.3 005 and then version it as 5.1.3). It is helpful to change the comment of the 5.1.3 map to mention that it was based on 5.1.3 005. The 5.1.3 map serves as a way to identify the code that was actually released. If that candidate fails, then purge the 5.1.3 edition and reuse 5.1.3 for the next release candidate.

Always sanity-test release candidates (and anything else that gets sent out). It's well worth having outside sanity testing to supplement this. Because all release candidates look the same, it's a good idea to destroy any release candidate declared as invalid.

Post-Release

At some point we will have an actual product release. When that happens, don't do anything special. Continue to make changes and version with defaults for the next release (whatever that may be named), using the name of the last release. This is good because we may not know the name of the next release in advance, and we don't want to release patch code that includes the next release name. If we ever have a forked development path because of code incompatibility, we can use the traditional dot notation to indicate where the fork began (that is, 5.1.3 045.0).

One noticeable element that an OTI release has is the "R" in front of it, so ENVY 5i.2 would be 5i.2 001, 5i.2 002, and then R5i.2 for a release candidate. For example, if we looked in the history stream of the ENVY VW 5i development, we would see:

R5i.0
5i.0 [FIX PASS 3] 020
5i.0 019
5i.0 018
5i.0 [FIX PASS 2] 017
5i.0 016
5i.0 [FIX PASS 1] 015
5i.0 014
5i.0 013
5i.0 [CHANGES FROM REVIEW] 012
5i.0 011
5i.0 [FOR REVIEW] 010

With this naming convention we can clearly see the progression of versions and easily find important milestones. The text field may also describe the nature of the changes, as in 5i.0 [Namespace support] 005.

Incremental Updates and Patches

One problem that comes up when deploying a system is distributing updates and patches. The organizational issues of ensuring patch compatibility and of being able to tell which patches are installed in a particular deployment are beyond the scope of this book. We suggest that you ship a new repository with complete configuration maps for each upgrade if you are delivering development tools and frameworks. Both the extra work and the extra size become negligible when compared to questions such as testing every arbitrary combination of patches or ensuring that they be applied sequentially.

Other options you might want to look into, especially if you deliver packaged executables, are tools such as Unity System's SmallCycle product, which manages the deployment process, and even has the option of binary patching executables, or of packaging to ICs (VA) and parcels (VW), both of which increase modularity at the cost of a minor performance penalty.

Summary

We have taken an in-depth look at the process necessary for delivering an application, and the various strategies available for doing this. For developers, it's important to understand which aspects of coding can be problematic in application delivery, and how code organization can influence the packaging process. For administrators, it's important to understand the packaging process, and which aspects need to be addressed early in the development cycle. For toolsmiths, this provides insight into different possible mechanisms, and troubleshooting advice for packaging.

Some of the important details to remember from this chapter are:

- Prerequisites are an important ENVY concept and are critical for VisualAge packaging, regardless of the mechanism. They are used less in VisualWorks packaging, but still convey important information about program structure.

- Prerequisite problems can arise in many ways and can usually be corrected using one of a few simple patterns.

- ENVY browsers can operate either on components in memory, or components in the library. Operating directly on the library presents some dangers but can be important when trying to correct difficult prerequisite situations.

- Three fundamental packaging mechanisms exist. The most common is "stripping" a development image. However, delivery as components and building up a separate run-time image are both increasing in importance.

- SmallLint is a useful tool for checking common errors in your programs before delivering.

- Always package starting from a clean image, with only the run-time code loaded.

- Application attachments enable you to manage non-Smalltalk files within the ENVY environment.

≡Chapter 7≡

Extending
the System

Smalltalk is a wonderfully open environment. Some or all of the source code is available to developers, and can be changed to do almost anything. From an experimental point of view this is wonderful. We can "burn the disk packs" and invent our own new language and environment. Unfortunately, the people who are paying us may have more prosaic goals in mind.

Our changes may need to be reviewed every time there's an upgrade or a patch to the basic class libraries. Inadequately tested extensions can be more trouble than they're worth, and managers of large projects with many developers are often reluctant to have every developer soup up his or her personal environment.

If we make changes to base classes, they may conflict with third-party products, with other teams in the organization, or even with customers if we're distributing development tools. System changes also scatter code around. If we modify a class in Kernel, then our system's configuration map will have to include our special version of Kernel. Before long we're loading dozens of applications, each containing only a few lines of our code. These all have to be managed by Library Supervisor, complicating maintenance.

On the other hand, changing system code offers very significant advantages. Sometimes the system is wrong. It may have bugs, or be missing functionality that requires changes to existing classes. Power-users like to extend their environments because it makes them more productive. We can usually put methods in a helper class, but if OO design says they belong in a system class, then that's where we really want to put them.

There's a tension between two different models of development here. One model is that of components, which says that we should be striving for self-contained, independent units of functionality that are easily composed. On the other side we have the principles of open source, where all system code is exposed for developers to study and enhance, helping the base system evolve. Both models have advantages and disadvantages. Balancing the tension between them requires dexterity on the part of developers. Fortunately, a number of mechanisms can help, by enabling us to modify the system in minimally intrusive ways.

First, we can accomplish a great deal without ever changing system code. The following sections discuss some of the tasks we can do simply by exploiting hooks the system gives us when loading and unloading code. Often, the system's developers have given us additional hooks in the form of policy classes or system overrides that let us change and extend behavior even more radically. Finally, even if we do change code there are criteria that can help us judge how maintainable these changes will be.

This chapter looks at the different mechanisms available to us for extending system behavior. We'll see how ENVY provides hooks on various system actions, particularly loading and unloading code. We'll use these hooks to create a simple query for scratch editions and to hook a workspace editor on a well-known filename into the system menu. Next, we'll look at some of the things we can do by subclassing ENVY policy objects to provide new behavior. This will let us integrate prerequisite checking with our regression tests. With more drastic modifications we'll see how we can use class extensions and other tricks to make drastic changes without ever modifying system code. We'll see how we can use this to automatically release subapplication editions without requiring user intervention, and we'll modify the browsers to provide a standard way for applications to add menu items without ever modifying the browser code itself.

This section covers some topics of interest to all developers, particularly the sections on loading and unloading code. Toolsmiths will find this one of the most valuable sections, showing areas in which the system can be extended with detailed how-to information. Administrators will probably find the most value in understanding the ways tools can make their jobs easier. Many of the extensions we talk about here address problems we've discussed earlier, and some of them are used again or carried forward in the "Goodies" chapter (Chapter 9).

Modify State

The first approach to extending is to see if the developers have already provided hooks for the functionality we're looking for. Often, we can modify behavior significantly simply by changing system state. For example, in ENVY we can evaluate

```
EmImageBuilder cancelIfMethodsDoNotCompile: false.
```

to make the load of a component continue even if it encounters a compilation error (see "Component Loading").

These kinds of behavior changes don't normally cause any problems, and are made without any changes to system code. Potential conflicts can occur if two or more systems want to change the same state in conflicting ways, but this is a rare occurrence and represents a genuine semantic conflict that the user will have to resolve.

The main disadvantage of this technique is that it requires system designers to put in the appropriate hooks. If we're doing something beyond what they anticipated, then we're out of luck. However, these hooks can be quite general, particularly if they enable us to substitute our own classes, as described later.

One of the issues with this approach is that if we're going to modify state we need to decide when we're going to do it. Fortunately, ENVY provides a rich set of hooks on system events so that we can react appropriately. These are important for making state-based modifications and also for making sure that extension code (or any other code) loads and unloads cleanly.

Loading and Unloading

It's always important to be sure that code loads and unloads cleanly. This means we need to be sure that code initializes properly when it's loaded, and cleans up properly before it's unloaded. ENVY provides a variety of hooks to run initialization and finalization code easily. Most of these hooks are associated with the ENVY application class and control initialization at the application level, although a provision also exists for initialization code at the class level. For more information, see "Application Classes."

Initializing Class Variables

If we are loading classes from the repository, we may want to initialize class and class instance variables. This can be done in a number of ways. First, we can use a pure Smalltalk mechanism, access the variables only through methods, and have them initialized lazily on first access. We can also have an explicit initialization method for the class. If we're doing this, we can have ENVY automatically call the method. All we need to do is implement the method initializeAfterLoad as a class method for any class we want initialized. After ENVY loads an application it sends this message to any class in the application that understands it. Note that this method is not triggered on a Re-Load Current operation; ENVY assumes we haven't changed anything that requires reinitialization.

Another alternative is to explicitly initialize our classes as part of the overall application initialization by defining a loaded method in the application class, as described later. Finally, in recent versions of ENVY we can describe initialization for certain types of variables in terms of *pragmas*. Pragmas are particularly useful for pool dictionaries, but can be used for other initialization tasks as well. For VisualWorks 5i, which treats class variables as a special case of class-level statics, pragmas are the preferred initialization mechanism. For more information on pragmas, see the ENVY documentation.

Application-Level Hooks

ENVY provides hooks that allow user-defined code to execute at various points in the lifecycle of an application. These hooks can be used for a variety of purposes. For example, we can declare or remove global or pool variables, initialize object state, add or remove menu items, and generally make sure that our applications initialize correctly and tidy up after themselves. Note that in many cases there are alternative mechanisms for these tasks. For example, as described previously, ENVY provides pragma declarations as the recommended way to declare and initialize pool variables. VisualWorks provides a purely declarative syntax for extending the system menus. If such mechanisms are available, we should take advantage of them.

All of these hooks are defined on a per-application (or subapplication) basis. In the application class we define class methods according to the protocol described later. At the appropriate points, ENVY invokes the methods for all of the applications affected. It's important to note when the actions occur. For example, loaded occurs after the code has been loaded, and removing occurs before the code is unloaded because otherwise the class doesn't exist in the image and couldn't be sent these messages.

Loaded

If we have initialization code that we want executed *after* the application has been loaded, we define it in the loaded method in the application class. This method is sent to an application after it has been loaded or reloaded — for example, as a class method in the QuestionUI application class.

```
loaded
    QuestionnairePreferences initialize.
    self updateSystemMenus.
```

Removing

This method defines cleanup code to be run *before* the application is to be unloaded. The most important task this method normally does is ensure that no instances of any of the classes are defined by this application. ENVY will not unload a class that has instances. This is a sensible restriction because unloading would leave instances in the image without a corresponding class definition. However, this means that if instances of any of the classes being unloaded exist, then the unload will fail. This is one of the most common causes of unload failures. Even instances stored in class variables of the classes to be unloaded will prevent a successful unload, so we should be sure to nil out any possible references to instances in this method. We should also make sure that if we've made changes to system menus or otherwise modified the UI that those changes are undone — for example, as a class method in the the QuestionUI application class.

```
removing
    QuestionnairePreferences release.
    self removeFromSystemMenus.
```

failedRemove

We aren't guaranteed that a remove operation will succeed. In particular, we can't unload an application if that would leave instances or classes in an inconsistent state. As already mentioned, we can't unload the definition of a class that has instances. We can't unload classes with subclasses that would be left in the image because we would then have classes without a superclass.

Also note that, unlike loading, the unload operation is not atomic. We can partially remove an application, which then remains in the image but in an inconsistent state. Most frequently, the preceding removing code will have run so the classes and corresponding structures will not be correctly initialized. To enable us to handle this situation, ENVY defines a failedRemove method, which will be sent if an error occurs while unloading. The default implementation of failedRemove marks the application as a scratch edition. We may also want to invoke the loaded method to reinitialize the application — for example, the QuestionUI application class.

    failedRemove
        self loaded.

Optionally, we could put in a call to super failedRemove. That would mark the application edition as scratched, which we may or may not want. If we believe that we've done all that's necessary to restore the application to a stable state, then we don't need to mark it as scratched.

Also note that usually we don't do any initialization directly in the ENVY methods, but rather have them invoke separate methods that do the real work. This lets us use the code in other places without duplicating it or depending on the ENVY classes in our domain code.

Before and After

We mentioned that the normal mechanisms run *after* code is loaded or *before* it is unloaded. This is adequate for most circumstances, but every once in a while we need to run code *before* code is loaded or *after* it is unloaded. This is tricky. We can't just write that code in one of the classes because they won't exist when the code needs to run.

To deal with this, ENVY lets us store code as strings in the repository, associated with particular components. At appropriate times in the component lifecycle ENVY compiles and evaluates these strings. This is definitely an advanced facility, and one that is rarely used. In older versions this facility was commonly used to define pool dictionaries or globals. If these weren't defined, then the code being loaded wouldn't compile, so the definition needed to happen before loading. More recent versions of Smalltalk and/or ENVY provide facilities to handle most of these cases more cleanly, using mechanisms such as the ENVY pragmas or VisualWorks static declarations.

toBeLoadedCode

If we have code that needs to run before an application is loaded, we can store it as a string in the repository as toBeLoadedCode. For example,

```
QuestionUI toBeLoadedCode: '
    Smalltalk
        declareVariable: "WhyAreWeUsingAGlobal";
        declarePoolDictionary: "ShouldUsePragmasPool";
        declare Variable: "SomePoolConstant"
            poolName: "ShouldUsePragmasPool" '.
```

You need to watch out for a few details when using this mechanism. First, because this is a string to be evaluated, we need to double the quote characters in our code. Also, the declare methods will not overwrite a previous declaration, so any variables that were already defined will not change. This means that if we change the declaration and reload, we won't see the new variable definitions unless we had explicitly deleted them. Second, to set the toBeLoadedCode, we will need to be the manager of the application it's associated with.

Finally, these source strings do not have a version history. The toBeLoadedCode is associated with a particular edition, and if we change it we will wipe out any previous definition for that edition. To preserve the version history of this code we can use a setToBeLoadedCode method as described later.

To remove the toBeLoadedCode from an application, we can just set it to an empty string, as in this example:

```
QuestionUI toBeLoadedCode: ''.
```

wasRemovedCode

Corresponding to the toBeLoadedCode is the wasRemovedCode, which runs after the application has been successfully unloaded. You can use this method to remove globals or pool dictionaries, which cannot be removed while the code that uses it is still in memory. For example,

```
QuestionUI wasRemovedCode: '
    Smalltalk
        undeclare: "WhyAreWeUsingAGlobal";
        undeclare: "ShouldUsePragmasPool" '.
```

Similar to the toBeLoadedCode, the wasRemovedCode strings do not have their own version history, and can only be set by the manager of the application. We can remove this code from an application by setting it to an empty string.

```
MyApplication wasRemovedCode: ''.
```

setToBeLoadedCode

It's easy to forget about toBeLoadedCode or wasRemovedCode because they have no version history and don't show up in the browsers. A useful convention for making this code more visible and providing it with a version history is to explicitly put it into methods. By putting this code into a method, we give it an identity as a first-class code component, with its own version history, for example, as class methods in QuestionUI.

```
setToBeLoadedCode
    "self setToBeLoadedCode"
self toBeLoadedCode: '
    Smalltalk
      declareVariable: "WhyAreWeUsingAGlobal";
      declarePoolDictionary: "ShouldUsePragmasPool";
      declare Variable: "SomePoolConstant"
        poolName: "ShouldUsePragmasPool" '.
```

setWasRemovedCode

```
    "self setWasRemovedCode"
self wasRemovedCode: '
    Smalltalk
      undeclare: "WhyAreWeUsingAGlobal";
      undeclare: "ShouldUsePragmasPool" '.
```

addToSystemMenu

ENVY expects that applications might want to make functionality available on the System or ENVY menu, which is primarily useful for development tools. We might think we could just put this functionality into the loaded method, but the ENVY menus are also rebuilt at startup, so we'd need to use a combination of hooks. To make this common case simpler, ENVY provides the method addToSystemMenu — for example, in QuestionUI.

```
addToSystemMenu
    (System transcriptMenuNamed: #systemMenu)
      add: #openQuestionnaireWindow
      label: 'Questionnaire'
      enable: true
      for: self.
```

This code inserts a menu item labeled Questionnaire into the system menu, which sends the message openQuestionnaireWindow to the application class QuestionUI. Although this method is clearly intended to be used to add to the system menu, we can easily add to other menus as well. For more information on adding items to ENVY menus, see "The Menu Extension API."

If we're adding items to menus, we should also be sure to remove those items when the application is unloaded. Removing items needs to happen only once, on unload, so there's no corresponding removeFromSystemMenu method. Instead, we can just call this code from the removing method in our application.

```
removing
    (System transcriptMenuNamed: #systemMenu)
      remove: #openQuestionnaireWindow.
```

Adding to the Transcript Menu

Rather than adding to the already-crowded system menu, we might want to add an entire new menu into the Transcript. We can do this using the loaded method to call some of the ENVY menu-related hooks — for example, in QuestionUI.

```
loaded
    System
      addTranscriptMenuNamed: #Questionnaire
      title: (DirectedMessage
        selector: #questionnaireMenuTitle
        arguments: #()
        receiver: QuestionUI)
      selectorForBuild: #addToQuestionnaireMenu
      before: #last.
```

This example uses some complex System protocol, particularly the method named addTranscriptMenuNamed:title:selectorForBuild:before:. Let's look at the parameters more closely. The first parameter (the symbol #Questionnaire) is the name by which code can refer to the menu. In particular, we can get back our menu using the method named transcriptMenuNamed:.

The second parameter is the title that will appear in the transcript window. This can be a string, but we've added some complications by using a DirectedMessage, which will be evaluated at run-time. This might be used to enable our tool for multiple languages (for example, Canadian, Swiss-German, and Australian) or to vary the title in some other way.

The third parameter is particularly interesting. In the same way that ENVY defines the addToSystemMenu message, we can allow any application to add items to our menu, and define a standard message for doing so. Following the naming convention, we'll use addToQuestionnaireMenu. This also points out that we need to add our menu only once, in the loaded code, and that ENVY will rebuild the actual menu instance when necessary.

Finally, the before: parameter lets us define where our menu appears in the menu bar. This method has many options, and the method comment clearly explains how to use it. Some other variations are also available that may be useful in different circumstances.

Our loaded method doesn't actually define the contents of the menu, so we'll use the addToQuestionnaireMethod to do that.

Finally, if we're going to define our own Transcript menu we need to clean it up when our application is unloaded, which we can do by implementing the removing method in our application class and using the removeTranscriptMenuNamed:ifAbsent: method.

```
removing
    System
      removeTranscriptMenuNamed: #questionnaireMenu
      ifAbsent: [].
```

Example Utilities

Here's a small but complete example to illustrate the hooks described previously. It adds two small utilities to the system.

- **A notepad.** Many programmers have their monitor covered with a layer of Post-It notes, or have many scattered files with to-do lists and items to remember. We'll add a menu item that opens up a standard file in a well-known place for us to keep these notes instead.

- **A query on scratched applications in our image.** Before finishing work for the day (or night), it's a good habit to check our image for applications we've scratched. This helps us avoid leaving code in scratch editions for a long time, and to get rid of debugging code we no longer need. We'll do this as a simple query that just lists all the scratch editions. This is a simple example, but extending the set of queries provided by ENVY can be extremely useful.

All the following methods are defined in the MedLoadUnloadApp class. First, we define the loaded and removing methods to install and remove the menu properly.

```
loaded
    System
        addTranscriptMenuNamed: #projectMenu
            title: 'MED Examples'
            selectorForBuild: #addToProjectMenu
            before: #last;
        updateTranscriptMenus.
```

```
removing
    System
        removeTranscriptMenuNamed: #projectMenu
        ifAbsent: [].
```

For safety's sake, we'll add a failedRemove method, resetting the menu if the application fails to unload.

```
failedRemove
    self loaded.
```

Next, we define our menu with its individual items. By defining the addToProjectMenu method, any other application can add items to this menu.

```
addToProjectMenu
    self projectMenu
      add: #openNotepad
        label: 'Open Notepad'
        enable: true
        for: self;
      add: #showScratchedApps
```

```
        label: 'Scratched Apps'
        enable: true
        for: self;
    yourself.
```

projectMenu

```
^System transcriptMenuNamed: #projectMenu.
```

Now, all that's left is to implement the functionality necessary for the two mini-tools. First, the notepad. This will be a Workspace that is saved to a known file name, defined by the notepadFileName method. If the file does not exist, we'll get an error trying to open it the first time. Because this is a simple example, we won't deal with the exception handling for that case. It's easiest to get started by opening a Workspace and then saving it as notepad.txt.

openNotepad

```
"VA version"
(EtWorkspace forFileNamed: self notepadFileName) open.
```

openNotepad

```
"VW version"
self notepadFileName asFilename edit.
```

notepadFileName

```
^'notepad.txt'.
```

For the query, we first need to find out which applications (and subapplications) are scratched. To do this, we simply find all the currently loaded applications and select those that are scratched.

scratchedApps

```
^SubApplication currentlyLoaded select: [ :app |
    app isScratch].
```

Once we have the collection, we print it out to the Transcript.

showScratchedApps

```
Transcript
    cr;
    show: 'Scratched apps'.
self scratchedApps do: [:app |
    Transcript
    tab;
    show: app signature.
    app manager = EmUser current)
        ifFalse: [
        Transcript show: ' ',app manager fullName]
    Transcript cr;
Transcript show: 'done'.
```

Policy Classes

Even if we can't change the behavior of the system simply by setting a flag, we may be able to do a more complex override in which we provide a new *policy class*. A policy class is a place where the system's authors have abstracted out system behavior so that it can be replaced by plugging in a different set of policies. For this to work we need not only the abstraction but a public hook so that we can specify that our class is to be used instead of the default. This can happen in a number of ways.

If the system class is used as a singleton, a hook may exist that enables us to replace it. For example, in VisualWorks we can modify input processing by replacing the standard InputState instance.

```
MyExtendedInputState install
```

If the system class is used in multiple places, the system needs to use the "Abstract Factory" pattern (see Gamma et al., 1994) to decouple the class creation from the system class. For example, in VisualAge we can change the classes used for browsers.

```
EtTools browserMappings
  at: #application
put: MyApplicationBrowser.
```

Note that this needs to be sent specifically to EtTools, the application class for the EtTools application. In VisualAge 4.5, the EtBaseTools application also has protocol for browserMappings, which is not used.

As with modifying state, this technique is very powerful and causes few problems. Because the hooks are typically broader, there is slightly more likelihood of conflict between different systems trying to use these mechanisms in conflicting ways. Another potential problem is related to unloading. We always want applications to load and unload cleanly. An application cannot unload if any of its classes have instances. If the system is using instances of our classes, we need to make sure they are removed and the system behavior reset. This can be difficult. For example, if an instance of one of our classes is on the stack, there aren't any safe ways to get rid of it before unloading, and the best we can do is some sort of two-stage unload.

In this section, we'll look at two relatively sophisticated ways we can change system options by replacing the standard classes. We're going to look at two defaults we can change. The first is the error reporter, which generally just logs to the Transcript. We can change this to integrate testing of prerequisite errors into our test suite. The second default is the library interface, which lets us change the way version names are generated.

Changing the Error Reporter

The error reporter is the interface the system uses to tell us about problems. Any time we see a Transcript message starting with "Info," "Warning," or "Error," it has been passed to us through the error reporter.

We can change the error reporter to have a different behavior. It's maintained as a class variable named ErrorReportingDevice in the class EmImageSupport. By default, this is an instance of EmErrorReporter, which holds references to the standard "log devices," for example, the Transcript. We have two different ways to change this. The first is more powerful, but gives us complete flexibility, while the second is simpler and is often enough for what we need.

Heavyweight Override

The first way of changing error reporting behavior we'll call the *heavyweight* way. This is the mechanism documented in the preferences workspace.

First, we'll need to provide our own class to replace the default. We'll probably want to make it a subclass of EmErrorReporter. Second, we'll need to override the standard behavior for the things we want to change. Some of the more useful and interesting messages to override are:

```
logError:withParms:severity:
reportError:withParms:severity:
```

Finally, we need to create and install our new error reporter. Here's an example of the code to do this, assuming that our new error reporter is called MyErrorReporter. If we want to change the behavior permanently, we'll probably want to put this code into something that's called from the loaded method of our application.

```
MyErrorReporter initialize.
EmImageSupport errorReporter:
(MyErrorReporter new initialize).
```

Lightweight Override

Usually, we don't need all of the power of providing our own error reporter. Very often, we can get by with the standard error reporter and by replacing the log device with our own class. We call this the *lightweight* override, and we've found it sufficient for almost all cases.

Typically, the error reporter logs output to the system Transcript, or to a file stream. We can simply replace that stream to achieve a number of interesting effects. The example we'll show here combines a change to the error reporter with prerequisite analysis methods and with the SUnit testing framework to automatically include prerequisite testing in our test suites.

Automatic Prerequisite Testing

Let's look at how the log device is used. If we examine the EmErrorReporter class we find that the instance variable is directly referenced in only two methods — the accessors. If we browse the senders of logDevice, we see that the logger needs to respond to only a few messages: cr, nextPutAll: and flush. If we implement just these three methods we'll be compatible with the standard error reporter. Because the system log device is the Transcript, let's also implement show: and tab in our logger to enhance compatibility.

```
Object subclass: #MedSilentErrorLogger
    classInstanceVariableNames: 'current '
    instanceVariableNames: ''
    classVariableNames: ''
    poolDictionaries: ''
```

nextPutAll: aString
```
(aString
    indexOfSubCollection: 'Warning: 49'
    startingAt: 1) = 1 ifTrue

    self restoreDefaultLogger.
    TestResult exFailure signalWith: aString].
```

restoreDefaultLogger
```
EmImageSupport errorReporter logDevice:
    System errorLog.
```

All we've done here is capture the output to the log device and ignore it. However, if a "Warning 49" came down the pipe, we'd first reset the default error logger, and then trigger a test framework failure exception. The whole test case looks like this:

```
TestCase subclass: #PrereqCheckTestCase
    instanceVariableNames: 'logger '
    classVariableNames: ''
    poolDictionaries: ''
```

testBadPrereqs
```
self should: [MedErrorReporterTestApp badPrereqs].
```

Finding Bad Prerequisites

This logging relies critically on the badPrereqs method called previously. We're expecting this to force the display of any prerequisite errors onto the error reporter. How do we do that?

Well, if we look at where Warning 49 is triggered, we find that after a method is successfully compiled ENVY checks for bad prerequisites by calling the method CompiledMethod>>testVisibilityIn:. All we need to do is to loop through our application, find all the methods controlled by that application, and send this message. We don't even need to do anything to print the results because testVisibilityIn: writes its warnings to the Transcript. So, we define a method on SubApplication (which will be inherited by Application) as follows:

badPrereqs
```
Transcript cr; show: 'Looking for bad prereqs...'.
self withAllSubApplications do: [ :app |
    Transcript cr; show: 'Checking ', app name.
    app classes do: [ :class |
```

```
(class methodsIn: app) do: [ :method |
    method testVisibilityIn: app]]].
Transcript cr; show: 'Done'.
```

This technique works quite well and catches many prerequisite problems, but we can go further. What happens when we unload or delete a class referenced by methods in other applications? Or when we load an application referencing classes not in the image?

In the first case, the symbol representing the class would still be listed, and the value of that key would be nil. Essentially, what once was a class is now a nil global. In the second case, the symbol representing the class would be declared in the unmanaged (VisualAge) or undeclared (VisualWorks) namespace. In either case, the system prerequisite check will not flag this as an error because for all the system knows we *could* be referencing a nil global.

In fact, we ran into this problem developing the code that accompanies this book. This motivated us to put together a simple solution.

Testing for Missing Variables

The method CompiledMethod>>testForNilGlobals works the same way that testVisibilityIn: does. It looks through the method's literal frame and picks out all literal references that are either nil or unmanaged/undeclared. Because this is similar to a missing prerequisite, we decided to use the same error reporting mechanism, and declare this problem as a Warning 49. This version of the method works for VisualWorks 3.0 and earlier and for VisualAge.

```
testForNilGlobals
    self allLiteralsDo: [:literal |
    literal isAssociation ifTrue: [
      | key |
      key := literal key.
      ((self isClassOrPoolVar: key) not and: [
          self isNilOrUnmanaged: key]) ifTrue: [
        | qualifiedName |
        qualifiedName :=
            ' the nil or unmanaged class or global ', key.
        EmImageSupport errorReporter
          logError: 49
          withParms: (Array
              with: self printString
              with: qualifiedName)]]].


isClassOrPoolVar: key
    ^(self methodClass
    variableAssociationAt: key
    using: Smalltalk
    ifAbsent: [nil]) notNil.
```

The method isClassOrPoolVar: makes sure that the slot is not referencing a class or pool variable. Unfortunately, the definition of unmanaged is different between VisualAge and VisualWorks, so we needed to factor out the dialect difference into a separate method.

isNilOrUnmanaged: key
```
"VisualAge version"
^(System image globalNamespace
    at: key
    ifAbsent: [nil]) isNil or: [
        System image globalNamespace unmanagedNamespace
            includesKey: key].
```

isNilOrUnmanaged: key
```
"VisualWorks version"
^(Smalltalk at: key ifAbsent: [nil]) isNil
    or: [Undeclared includesKey: key].
```

Because our version needed to be loadable in both VisualAge and VisualWorks dialects, we put CompiledMethod>>isNilOrUnmanaged: into a separate subapplication, and configured the subapplications to be loaded depending upon which dialect was being used. If you're typing in the code, you might want to in-line the message send with the implementation appropriate for your dialect.

Once we implemented this method, is was logical to go back and change badPrereqs to include our new test.

badPrereqs
```
    Transcript cr; show: 'Looking for bad prereqs...'.
    self withAllSubApplications do: [ :app |
      Transcript cr; show: 'Checking ', app name.
    app classes do: [ :class |
       (class methodsIn: app) do: [ :method |
          method
             testVisibilityIn: app;
             testForNilGlobals]]].
    Transcript cr; show: 'Done'.
```

Missing Variables in VisualWorks 5i

VisualWorks 5i significantly changes the use of variables and classes, introducing full namespaces and changing the internals of the system. This actually simplifies our tests significantly because the model of classes and methods is rich enough to let us ask some of our questions directly. Unfortunately, it changes the code enough that it's not directly compatible and the entire thing needs to be in a new subapplication. With any luck we'll have this refactored by the time you read this.

```
testForNilGlobals
    self allLiteralsDo: [:literal |
      (literal isVariableBinding
        and: [literal binding isForClass])
        ifTrue: [
          (self isNilOrUnmanaged: key)
            ifTrue: [
            | qualifiedName |
          qualifiedName := ' the nil or unmanaged class or global ', key.
            EmImageSupport errorReporter
            logError: 49
            withParms: (Array
            with: self printString
            with: qualifiedName)]]].
isNilOrUnmanaged: binding
"VisualWorks 5i version"
^(binding value isNil
      or: [Undeclared includesKey: binding key].
```

Of course, as discussed in the section on "Hidden Dependencies," some prerequisite errors can't be detected statically at all. We can find most problems, but some coding techniques will require us to do a complete packaging and testing step to find all the correct prerequisites and code to be included.

Changing the Default Library Interface

Another default that we can usefully change is the library interface. One of the major responsibilities of this object is supplying the default version names. By changing it, we can change the version naming mechanism to default to our project's conventions. The library interface is a singleton, which can be accessed as:

```
EmInterface current
```

Let's first define a new library interface, and then override one of the default numbering schemes. We'll call our class MedLibraryInterface and put it in an application called MedLibraryInterfaceApp. In the application class we'll define methods to install and remove our new interface as we discussed at the beginning of this chapter.

```
loaded
    self isInstalled ifFalse: [
      EmInterface current: MedLibraryInterface new]

removing
    self isInstalled ifTrue: [
      EmInterface current: EmInterface new]

isInstalled
^EmInterface current class == MedLibraryInterface
```

So, we have a new library interface defined and installed, but it doesn't do anything yet. Let's look at a simple change we can make — adding user initials to the default version names for configuration maps.

We don't really care how the system normally generates new version numbers. All we need to know is that the method availableConfigMapVersionNameFor: gives us the suggested new name for versioning a configuration map. This name starts at 1.0, and is incremented numerically. To change it to the format X.x Initials (for example, 1.12 JP), all we need to do is override the method, get the default version number, and append the initials of the current user. In our new MedLibraryInterface class we override this method.

availableConfigMapVersionNameFor: aConfigurationMap

```
^(super availableConfigMapVersionNameFor:
aConfigurationMap),
' ',
EmUser current initials
```

EmUser instances don't know how to return their initials, so we'll need to define that as well.

initials

```
^self fullName select: [:c | c isUppercase]
```

This is a little crude, but it will give us something resembling a user's initials. Maybe that's not really what we want, though. It might be nice if we could let people decide their own initials. Maybe they have a name that doesn't abbreviate properly with this algorithm (for example, Andrew MacMillan becomes AMM). Maybe there's more than one team member with the same initials, so they want to add something extra to differentiate them. We can do this using User Fields. We haven't really talked about the API for User Fields yet, but we'll describe it in detail in "User Fields."

initials

```
| initials |
(initials := self record
  inheritedUserFieldAt: #Initials) isEmpty
  ifTrue: [self initials: self createInitials].
^initials
```

initials: aString

```
self updateRecordWith: [:record |
  record
  inheritedUserFieldAt: #Initials put: aString].
^aString
```

createInitials

```
^self fullName select: [:c | c isUppercase]
```

The Art of the Class Extension

We've seen how to extend or change system behavior using various hooks the system provides us when code is loaded or unloaded. We've also seen how we can plug our own policy objects into the system to add some complex behavior. However, sometimes neither of these solutions is enough and we need to get into the system code itself.

Once we've decided to extend the system code, a variety of different mechanisms are still available to us, some more intrusive than others. One of the most flexible is the class extension. In this section we'll look at the pros and cons of actually modifying the system, and the different ways to do it.

Any time we actually change code, we should bear in mind the maintainability issues. In particular:

- At what layer does this change occur? In particular, is it a development-time-only change, or are we introducing code that our run-time code will depend on?

- How fragile is this change? When the vendor releases a new version of the base libraries, how likely are we to have to modify our code?

- How widely used will this be? Should we make this something that is automatically loaded for every developer as part of the project, or should it be separated out as a "goodie" that people can load if they want to? We may also want to ensure that extensions are easily unloadable so we can test our run-time code against a clean image.

With a little thought and planning, we can minimize the difficulties. If we can load and unload our extensions easily we can quickly check whether our code introduces problems or breaks in the presence of a new version, without needing to build a new image. If we avoid directly changing system code, but instead use the hooks provided (and maybe a few tricks) to transparently insert the changes, we'll know exactly where we interface to the system and where to look when checking compatibility with a new release.

Class Extensions

In basic Smalltalk, as it came out of the Xerox labs, there's no concept of a "module." Most commercial Smalltalks have added some equivalent, at least for team programming purposes, and in ENVY it's the application. All classes live primarily in an application, which holds their definition and methods, at least the basic methods.

It's often desirable to be able to have methods for a class distributed across more than one application. In ENVY this is done through class extensions, which hold additional methods for a class that's defined somewhere else. The base application holds the class definition, and extensions can add methods to it. Note that extensions cannot change the definition of a class and cannot change or replace existing methods.

This capability is extremely powerful, and provides lots of opportunities to augment or modify system behavior. The most basic use is simply to add behavior to an existing class. For example, we might add the method any to all collections by providing this code:

```
Collection>any
    ^self detect: [:each | true].
```

This enables us to put methods in the classes where they belong, but still manage them in the appropriate application, making maintenance much simpler.

Advanced Class Extensions

That's the standard use of class extensions, but we can perform several more tricks to make more sophisticated modifications. These are definitely tricks, and aren't going to be as maintainable as a pure class extension, but they may still be better than directly modifying system code.

Recall that the rules for class extensions do not allow for ambiguity in method definitions. Of all the applications loaded into the image, a particular method can be defined in only one of them. However, we have a few ways around this limitation.

If a method is defined in an abstract class and is not overridden in the concrete subclasses, we can add an extension implementing that method. As far as the system is concerned, we have only added methods, not changed them. As far as system behavior goes we have changed the implementation of that method in the concrete classes.

For example, in VisualAge part of the browser hierarchy looks like this:

```
...EtBrowser
    EtAbstractMethodsBrowser
    EtClassBrowser
```

The submenu for finding implementers of the selected method is created using the method EtAbstractMethodsBrowser>>implementorsSubMenu. This provides the options for Local and All implementers. VisualAge Assist Pro adds a class extension in EtClassBrowser, which overrides this method to call

```
    super implementorsSubMenu
```

and then adds several additional options.

This technique can be very powerful, but it relies heavily on the exact structure of the classes we are extending. It works best in a deep inheritance hierarchy with many layers of abstract classes. In Smalltalk, good examples of this are the Number and Collection hierarchies. In ENVY, the best example of this is the browser hierarchy.

This technique can also be combined with subclassing, where some modifications can be made directly in extensions, which can then control which classes are used in other parts of the system.

Other Techniques

Once more, recall the following:

- An extension cannot change a class definition.
- A method in memory must be uniquely defined by a single application.

However, we'll see some ways around both of these rules. Be warned that these techniques start to have considerably greater drawbacks for maintainability and developer sanity. They range from the questionable to the distinctly insane. Use at your own risk.

Doesn't Count If It's Not Loaded

The limitations apply only to methods loaded in the same image at the same time. If we have two applications that we never plan to load in the same image at the same time, we can freely duplicate methods names. This is an unusual circumstance, but one that can happen, for example, with platform-specific code. If we never expect our Windows and UNIX platform-specific code to be loaded at the same time, then we can freely use the same method names in each. This is an interesting technique, but I've never had occasion to actually use it.

Just Load It

When we try to load an application where a method name conflicts with one already loaded, ENVY will normally cancel the entire load. We can avoid this situation by setting the flag.

```
EmImageBuilder cancelIfMethodsCollide: false
```

In this case the new method replaces the old one, and the load will proceed. Normally this is used as a technique to force the load so we can correct the problem. However, we can do this deliberately as a way of forcing a code change. The downside is that if the original application is reloaded, it will reinstate the original code, causing hard-to-find bugs.

Modify in Loaded Code

ENVY lets us specify code to be run before and after an application is loaded. Because it's code, it can do anything, including making scratch editions of other applications and filing in code. This is pretty much the only way we can change class definitions in another application.

Both of the preceding techniques are not recommended for production code. They're acceptable, if extreme, ways to modify a system during development, but both make the state of the system dependent on the order in which applications are loaded. If someone reloads the system application later, they can wipe out our extensions in a way that's very hard to track down.

Slot Stealing

Although it's difficult to actually change a class definition, in practice we can make it behave differently without changing the definition, using a technique called *slot stealing*. Basically, we take an instance variable that stores a single value and make it store multiple values, as follows:

```
BEFORE
    Object subclass: #SomeClass
        instanceVariableNames: 'name address phoneNumber'

    initialize
        phoneNumber := ''

    phoneNumber
        ^phoneNumber

    phoneNumber: aString
        phoneNumber := aString
```

```
AFTER
    Object subclass: #SomeClass
        instanceVariableNames: 'name address phoneNumber'

    initialize
        phoneNumber := IdentityDictionary new

    phoneNumber
        ^phoneNumber at: #phone ifAbsent: ['']

    phoneNumber: aString
        phoneNumber at: #phone put: aString

    vehicles
        ^phoneNumber at: #vehicles ifAbsent: [#()]

    vehicles: aCollection
        ^phoneNumber at: vehicles put: aCollection
```

This one deserves its own special "You did *what*?" category. There are circumstances in which one might have to do this, particularly with class definitions that are known to the VM or in an OO database with poor schema migration facilities. In that sort of circumstance we would do this if we really, really, really couldn't think of any other way. Note that we would have to change the behavior of (at least) the original get and set methods, so we'd need to use at least one other dubious technique to implement this solution.

Why Class Extensions?

Class extensions are an extremely important facility, and there are good reasons for using them that go well beyond the desire to hack the system classes.

Proper Factoring: One of the strengths of OO programming is that methods are placed with the data structures they manipulate. Encapsulation is preserved, method placement makes intuitive sense, and the system is well factored. If we're adding code that manipulates these structures then we want to preserve these properties.

A good example is the method #inspect. This belongs in Object because we can send it to any object. However, it's also closely tied to the GUI and development tools. We don't want to include it in the base system applications because we expect it to be stripped from any deliverable. We can't avoid the problem by subclassing because subclassing Object doesn't give us the ability to send the message to any object. We could force users to write

        Inspector new openOn: anObject

but this is awkward and makes it harder to make custom inspectors for specific classes. A class extension lets us put the method in Object, but group it with the other development tools code.

Prerequisite Conflicts: One of the problems that can arise in ENVY is circular prerequisites. For example, it's not difficult for two applications to each reference classes defined in the other. ENVY does not allow circular prerequisites. Class extensions can be used to break these cycles.

Do We Really Want to do This?

Reviewing these techniques, we can see that they can be very powerful, but we should always think twice before using them. Even though the system may not recognize these as code changes, they effectively are, with all of the maintenance issues that implies.

There are also potential conflicts with third-party products. Our class extensions change system behavior, and those products may rely on that behavior. The result may be very hard-to-find bugs in one or both systems.

Finally, trying to fit modifications inside of class extensions can lead to code that is complex and hard to maintain. If this happens, we're losing many of the advantages of these mechanisms and should probably consider another approach.

Automating Subapplication Release

As an example of the kinds of modifications we can make with class extensions, this next section describes a way of automatically releasing subapplication editions as soon as they are created, without modifying any of the Application Manager code. Before we come to that, though, let's briefly review why we'd want to do it.

Visitor Pattern: One of the more complex patterns defined in Gamma et al. (1994) is Visitor. This defines a mechanism for adding functionality to a complex data structure as a visitor rather than as methods in the class. There are valid uses of this pattern, particularly in compiler techniques, but in systems without a class extension-like mechanism it is often used to solve problems that are more simply addressed by a minimal class extension.

Disadvantages: The use of class extensions also has downsides, some of them significant. They can violate encapsulation because we can add an accessor method to gain access to otherwise private variables in another class. They can make it harder to understand functionality if it is implemented in many different applications. My current VisualAge image has methods in Object defined in 53 different applications, which seems excessive. If developers use methods in system classes without paying close attention to the application that defines them, they risk making prerequisite errors that aren't detected until very late in development. Like any system modification mechanism, the risks depend on what you're building. Extensions for development tools are almost risk-free. Extensions for application development are usually acceptable, but can pose problems when developing components for redistribution. In all cases, it's important to realize that we'll have to reexamine extensions with each new version of the software because they may rely on internal structures that have changed.

In general, think twice before using extensions, but don't be afraid to use them where appropriate.

Recall that releasing subapplications works differently from releasing classes, and that this is one of the most subtle areas in ENVY for novices. See "Releasing Application Editions."

From the system's point of view, releasing has a simple meaning. It answers this question:

When I load a component, which versions/editions of its subcomponents should I load?

The answer is always "the released ones." Because developers are always thinking of what they're doing now and tend to assume there's forward progress in software development, they often think in terms of the most recent versions or editions. ENVY doesn't care which editions are most recent, and pays attention to only what's released. Another mental difficulty is realizing that releasing always means releasing *into* something. Nothing can be released without a parent to contain it.

This is a difficult enough conceptual hurdle, but a greater difficulty lies in the different treatment of classes and applications.* From the system's point of view it's exactly the same, but the role the operation plays in development is very different. The critical difference is how we treat open editions of these different components.

---

* Note that throughout this section we'll use "releasing applications" to mean both releasing a subapplication into its parent application and releasing an application into one or more configuration maps.

Class Editions

An open class edition is private to a developer. You can't even load someone else's open class edition. If two people want to work on the same class at the same time, they each make a separate edition and merge changes later. The idea is that classes are small enough and are edited quickly enough so that we want people to have exclusive access to their copy while they're making their changes.

Because the meaning of *release* is to control what people load, and other people can't load open class editions, obviously we can't release an open class edition.

So, for class development, the normal sequence of operations is as follows:

1. Create an edition.

2. Make some changes.

3. Version it.

4. Release it.

Typically, version and release happen close together, particularly when it's the class owner making the changes.

Application Editions

Application and subapplication editions, on the other hand, are normally shared among developers. Everyone on the team works in the same application editions, and releases their classes into them. The idea is that an application edition stays open for a while, and developers will want to get in sync with other people's class changes on a regular basis, without having to wait for an application version.

To ensure that everyone sees the same thing, and for convenience, we want "one-click loading," where developers load the open edition of the main configuration map and automatically get the current state of the whole system.

When we load the configuration map it will load the released versions/editions of all the applications in it. If we want the latest changes, that means the open application editions have to be released into the configuration map. Similarly, when we load one of these applications it will load the released versions/editions of all the sub-applications in it, so the current open editions have to be released.

So, for application/subapplication development, the normal sequence of operations is as follows:

1. Create an edition.

2. Release it.

3. Make some changes.

4. Version it.

Creating an edition and releasing it happen very close together because there's typically no reason to have a private application edition.

This distinction is one of the most confusing things in ENVY, and novice users often don't realize that application editions need to be released early. I know I didn't realize it, and on my first ENVY project it caused a lot of problems. Even experienced developers can easily forget to release an open edition, particularly when multiple configurations are involved.

Automating Release

All of that is a very long bit of review to describe a system extension that can help reduce the problem. Because we almost always want to release these editions, particularly subapplication editions, as soon as they are created, we can automate the process. This can be done with some simple modifications to the base system.

Applying the principles described in "The Art of the Class Extension" previously, we can see that EtAbstractApplicationsBrowser defines the method newApplicationEditions, which does something like

```
relevantApplications do: [:each |
    each newEdition]
```

but this is an abstract class, and the method is normally only called from EtApplicationsBrowser (the superclass of EtApplicationManager). We can override this method in a class extension in EtApplicationsBrowser to be more like

```
relevantApplications do: [:each |
    each editionAndRelease]
```

and we can define a new method editionAndRelease in Application and SubApplication. Note the loop through the currently loaded applications. Because newEdition creates a new object, our current Application object is no longer valid, and we need to find the corresponding new edition.

Application>editionAndRelease
```
    "This is meaningless for applications,
    so just edition"
^self newEdition
```

SubApplication>editionAndRelease
```
    | newEdition |
    self newEdition ifFalse: [^false].
    newEdition := self allLoadedAppsAndSubApps
      detect: [:each | each symbol == self symbol]
      ifNone: [^false].
    newEdition releaseSubApp.
  ^true
```

We will also define a portability method for returning all of the currently loaded applications, which works in both VisualWorks and VisualAge. This has to compensate for VisualAge code, which allows for the possibility that we are using the XD tools to develop against a remote image. In both cases we ask for the loaded subapplications, which also gives us all the loaded applications as well.

SubApplication>allLoadedAppsAndSubApps

```
"VisualWorks version"
^SubApplication currentlyLoaded
```

SubApplication>allLoadedAppsAndSubApps

```
"VisualAge version"
^self owningImage loadedSubApplications
```

Finally, we define a method for releasing an edition easily, that our editionAndRelease can call.

releaseSubApp

```
| expressions |
expressions := EtApplicationManager new
promptForSubApplicationExpressionsFor: self parent.
expressions isNil ifTrue: [^nil].
expressions do: [:expr |
  self parent
    releaseSubApplication: self
    in: expr]
```

In VisualAge, VA Assist Pro also includes similar functionality. It takes a slightly different approach, adding an item to the Application Manager menu for Create & Release New Edition. The fundamental principle is the same. Unfortunately, this implementation is incompatible with VisualAge Assist Pro because it also overrides newApplicationEditions in the same place. This is an example of conflicting behavior changes using class extensions.

Automating Release with Multiple Configurations

I'm not a big fan of application lineups. The mechanism is awkward, the browser support isn't very good, and they quickly become unmanageable. If another mechanism will do the job I prefer to use it, even at the cost of efficiency. However, for certain jobs there's no substitute for using lineups and conditional loading.

When using lineups, one of the issues is the inevitable confrontation with the dialog box asking which other configurations you want to release this component into (see Figure 7-1). Apart from not necessarily knowing what this dialog box is talking about, the problem is that this is a modal dialog box. Unless we're well versed in the lineup structure we probably don't know the right answer, and a wrong answer can do serious damage to the configuration without being noticed.

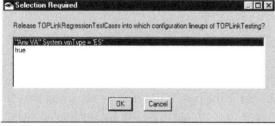

Figure 7-1: Screen shot of the dialog box

Fortunately, this process can be mostly automated. When we release a subapplication into an application, or an application into a configuration map, a reasonable default is that we want the new edition released everywhere that the old edition was already released. So, if we modify the Windows-specific subapplication, we want it released into just the Windows configuration. If we modify something that applies to three out of five configurations, we want it released to just those three. Fortunately, this is not difficult. VA Assist Pro automates this, adding a Release To Existing Configs option. The code is short and is sketched out as follows:

```
| parent configs expressions |
parent := subApp parent
parent isNil ifTrue: [^self].

configs := parent editionRecord
subApplicationConfigurations.
expressionAssocs := configs
select: [:assoc |
assoc value includesKey: subApp name].
expressions := expressionAssocs
    collect: [:assoc | assoc key].

expressions do: [:expr |
    parent releaseSubApplication: subApp in: expr].
```

An Example — The Menu Extension API

The most common system extensions are tools: code generators, formatters, and so on. If we add tools to our environment, we'd like to make them easily accessible for use. The easiest way to do this is by offering them as menu items. Of course, other people also want to add their tools to the browser menus, and collisions are inevitable.

For this reason, we have written a standard API for extending the ENVY browser menus. This API is the same on both VisualWorks and VisualAge. This API is in the public domain and has been adapted by a number of commercial vendors of third-party vendors as a way to avoid menu conflicts. We encourage you to use it in your work. Recent versions of VisualWorks also include an alternative mechanism, based on pragmas for methods defined in the ApplicationModel class, but this is not portable between dialects.

Apart from being a useful tool, this is a good example of how we as third parties can nevertheless make significant changes to basic behavior without changing system code. We'll first take a look at the protocol for the API, and then look at a few examples of using it, and finally, look at the implementation details.

Public Protocol

The EtToolsVendorExtensionsApp offers the following four methods for extending the applications, classes, methods, and text browser menus. These are intended to be implemented by ENVY application classes and will be invoked by the system in the same sort of circumstances that addToSystemMenu would be.

- addToApplicationsMenu:browser:
- addToClassesMenu:browser:
- addToDefaultTextMenu:browser:
- addToMethodsMenu:browser:

Let's look at an example implementation of one of these methods. This is taken from the VisualAge Packaging Assistant application, which includes the badPrereqs method described previously. This is a class method of MedPackagingAssistantApp, and once it's passed the appropriate menu instance it can use standard VisualAge menu protocol to add itself to the appropriate menu.

addToApplicationsMenu: aMenu browser: aBrowser

```
"The default behavior for the receiver is to add
nothing to the applications menu."
"Subclasses can override this message to add items"

aMenu
  add: #badPrerequisiteClasses
  label: 'Bad Prereqs'
  enable: [aBrowser isApplicationSelected]
  for: aBrowser;
yourself.
```

Adding Items to Submenus

Sometimes we want a tool to be installed not on the main menu but on a submenu. For this purpose, VisualWorks provides the menuItemWithValue: method to access submenus. The menu extension API includes an implementation of this method for VisualAge. Here's an example of how to use it:

addToClassesMenu: aMenu browser: aBrowser

```
  | theMenu |
theMenu := aMenu menuItemWithValue:
  #compareClassSubMenu.
  theMenu isNil ifTrue: [^self].
  theMenu subMenu
  add: #diffClass3Ways
  label: '3-way Diff'
  enable: [aBrowser isOneClassSelected]
  for: aBrowser
```

This example is taken from the code for the three-way differences browser goodie presented in "Three-Way Differences." We use menuItemWithValue: because we want the menu item to appear on the Compare... submenu along with all other differencing options.

Controlling Menu Visibility

If there's a public protocol for adding items to the browser menus, people will use it. Because the menus are large already, we also implemented methods to control the visibility of menu items. Similar to the *enable* block that ENVY already offers, we have a *visible* block. This block is evaluated when the menu is needed, and, depending on the block returning true or false, the menu item will be displayed or not. For the sake of ease of use, we have added "visible" versions of all the standard menu hooks.

- add:label:enable:toggle:for:accelerator:acceleratorText:
- add:label:enable:toggle:for:before:
- add:label:enable:toggle:visible:for:
- add:label:enable:toggle:visible:for:accelerator:acceleratorText:
- add:label:enable:toggle:visible:for:after:
- add:label:enable:toggle:visible:for:before:
- add:label:enable:visible:for:
- add:label:enable:visible:for:after:
- add:label:enable:visible:for:before:
- add:label:toggle:visible:for:
- addSubMenu:label:enable:manage:for:
- addSubMenu:label:enable:visible:for:
- addSubMenu:label:enable:visible:for:after:
- addSubMenu:label:enable:visible:for:before:

For example, the Refactoring Browser has context-sensitive submenus attached to the text pane pop-up menu. These vary depending on what text has been selected. If the selection is the name of an instance variable, then various instance variable refactorings will be available. If it's the name of a method, then method-level refactorings will be available, and so forth.

Later in this section we'll describe an integration of the Refactoring Browser with the standard VisualAge browsers. However, VisualAge caches the browser menus upon creating the browser, making dynamic menu changes very difficult. Rather than generating different menus, we generate a menu that is the union of all possibilities and make certain actions visible or invisible based on the selection. This isn't necessary in VisualWorks, but for compatibility's sake, the same protocol is implemented there, giving tool vendors more flexibility when developing cross-dialect tools.

Implementing the Menu Extensions API

The ENVY browsers have a heavily factored hierarchy, with functionality spread out among a number of abstract classes. This offers a number of places for "creative" use of class extensions. In particular, the EtAbstractMethodsBrowser class is a very promising victim.

Hooking a method into the browsers is actually quite simple. For example, let's look at our extension to the classes menu. In our application, EtToolsVendorExtensionsApp, we've extended EtAbstractMethodsBrowser (of course we've declared EtTools as a prerequisite) and overridden the method classesListWidget. This method defines which menu is used for the widget.

classesListWidget
"Return a multiselection list widget for classes."

```
^self
    multiSelectionListWidget: #classes
    changeSelector: #classesSelected:
    menuSelector: #newClassesMenu
    printBlock: self classPrintBlock
    statusBlock: self classStatusIndicatorBlock
    min: 0
    max: -1
    doubleClick: self classDoubleClickSelector
    initialSelection: self selectedClasses
```

Next, we implemented the newClassesMenu method. This grabs the original menu and then iterates through all loaded subapps, offering them a chance to add an item to the menu.

newClassesMenu
"Override the default classes menu. Give all our tools
the opportunity to add themselves to the menu. We do
this by sending all loaded apps the message with the
menu and the browser as arguments. The apps can either
register themselves or the browser as the receiver of
the message. Browse implementors for examples"

```
| aMenu |
aMenu := self classesMenu.
SubApplication currentlyLoaded reverseDo: [:app |
    app addToClassesMenu: aMenu browser: self].
^aMenu
```

The addToClassesMenu:browser: method has two arguments — the menu to be added to and the browser in which the menu appears. Because the browser is a useful source of state information, a menu extension will typically implement its functionality as an extension method in the browser, and have the menu callback be directed to the browser by using one of the many add*for: methods.

addToClassesMenu: aMenu browser: aBrowser
"The default behavior for the receiver is to add
nothing to the classes menu."
"Subclasses can override this message to add items"

Controlling Menu Visibility

We mentioned the implementation of the *visible* block previously. This block is evaluated when the menu is needed, and, depending whether the result is true or false, the menu item will be displayed or not. Let's look at the implementation of one of these methods. Because the underlying mechanism is quite different in VisualAge and VisualWorks, we'll show both implementations.

Here's the VisualAge version, defined on `CwMenu`:

```
add: selector
    label: label
    enable: enable
    visible: visible
    for: anObject

    | entry |
    entry :=
      (CwMenuPushButton
        selector: selector
        label: label
        enable: enable
        owner: anObject)
            manage: visible;
            yourself.
    self addEntry: entry
```

Because VisualAge caches the menu items upon building the browser, it is necessary to use another mechanism to dynamically change menu entries. Because the underlying X/Motif emulation layer allows for "manage" blocks, which are evaluated upon menu display, we use this technique to control visibility.

Here's the VisualWorks version of the same method, defined in `EtHierarchicalMenu`:

```
add: selector
    label: aString
    enable: aBooleanOrBlock
    visible: aBlock
    for: anObject

    ^aBlock value
      ifTrue: [self
        add: selector
        label: aString
        enable: aBooleanOrBlock
        for: anObject]
      ifFalse: [nil]
```

Because the ENVY menus in VisualWorks are not cached, but rather rebuilt every time they're needed, we can have a straightforward implementation of the visibility mechanism.

Summary

This chapter has covered a variety of ways to extend the system, including many different examples. These include:

- Hooks for invoking actions on code load or unload, with examples for installing queries and utility functions in the system menus
- Making new subclasses of policy objects, with examples integrating prerequisite checking into a suite of regression tests
- Using class extensions and other related techniques to modify system code without "really" modifying it
- Automatically releasing subapplication editions as soon as they are created
- Defining a standard API for extensions to the system menus that minimizes conflicts

In this chapter, we've seen a number of ways by which we can extend the ENVY environment without changing base code, and without having harmful effects on the system. In the next chapter, we're going to look at a number of goodies that use these techniques and that illustrate ways of accessing and managing ENVY-internal information.

═══Chapter 8═══

Administration

The administrator of an ENVY system must look after the many necessary tasks to ensure that the system and the development process run smoothly. This chapter describes some of these tasks as well as tools that make life easier for an administrator. We first describe the tasks associated with managing ENVY users, followed by a discussion of moving code between different images, repositories, and development sites. Administration also includes responsibility for the repository — managing its growth and dealing with system upgrades and the needs of remote developers. Many administrative tasks are repetitive, and we include a section on writing scripts using the ENVY API to automate some of these tasks. This is followed by more abstract discussions on organizing an ENVY project and maximizing code re-use. Finally, you'll find some general tips and tricks for keeping an ENVY system running smoothly.

Obviously, this chapter is primarily of interest to administrators. Power users who want to understand more about the details of ENVY will also find it valuable, and toolsmiths may find the process descriptions and tools useful. Also of interest with respect to administration are Chapter 1, "Getting Started," which covers installation and setup of an ENVY system, and Chapters 3 and 4, "Team Development" and "Advanced Development," which address some of the code organization and project management issues that affect the administration of an ENVY system.

Maintenance Operations

It's difficult to define exactly what the job of an ENVY administrator is. Different responsibilities might belong to an administrator on one project but to developers on another project. On a small project, there's no distinction at all between an

administrator and a developer. Depending on the project, there are various operations that involve administrative responsibilities. We list these below, with pointers to
other chapters that describe these activities.

- Setting up a project and establishing development conventions (see Chapter
  1, "Getting Started" and Chapter 4, "Advanced Development")
- Baselining (see "Baselining" in Chapter 3)
- Versioning and releasing, particularly the distinction between releasing
  classes and releasing applications/subapplications (see "One-Click Loading
  and Application Editions" in Chapter 3)
- Adding/removing users and managing user responsibilities (in this chapter)
- Backup (in this chapter)
- Checking library integrity and disk space (see "Repository Recovery" in
  Chapter 10)
- Import/export of code (in this chapter)
- Purging/restoring components (in this chapter)
- System upgrades (in this chapter)

Managing Users

One of the most common tasks in administering ENVY is dealing with users. As
developers arrive and depart or change responsibilities, this process must be managed.
We add or remove users from the repository, grant or remove permissions, and
change the owners or managers of components.

ENVY Users

ENVY has an explicit notion of developers and uses this to implement permissions
and track user activities. For these purposes, a user is defined by three different names:

- **Unique name:** the "primary key" of the user record in the repository
- **Network name:** the username for network login purposes, often the same
  as the unique name
- **Full name:** the name as displayed in the development environment

Any time we look at a list of users in an ENVY tool, we see the users' full names
— for example, "Alan Knight." There's no constraint that says a user's full name has
to be unique, so it's entirely possible to have two different users named "Alan Knight"
in the list of users. The situation is confusing but legal. We probably want to resolve
it by merging the two, but it's not an indicator of problems with the repository. For
an explanation of how this can happen, see "Administering Users" next.

The network name is used only when checking a user's identity or password against
the network. Any ENVY image has an owner, the user who last used it. When the

image starts up, ENVY checks the image owner's network name against the currently logged in user according to the operating system. If the two don't match, ENVY asks us for the password and won't let us proceed without it. For more information on controlling access with passwords, see "Passwords."

The unique name is the name ENVY uses internally to identify this user. It must be unique within this repository. It's common to use the network name as the unique name because network logins are likely unique for each user.

Resetting the Image Owner

In ENVY, an image almost always has an owner. The exception is that, when we get a new, clean image from the vendor, it has no owner. As soon as we start up such an image, we're asked to specify an owner, and we can't proceed until we do.

Sometimes, we'd like to return an image to that unowned state, particularly if we're doing something like building a base image for all of our developers. We can do this using the method System>>resetImageOwner.

Administering Users

At various points, we'll need to maintain the users in our repository. For the most part, these operations are limited to the special user Library Supervisor. When maintaining users, all of the ENVY functions are accessed through the Users submenu under the ENVY System menu. These functions enable us to create, delete, and modify users in our own repository. We can also import users from other repositories or export our own users to other repositories,

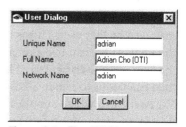

Figure 8-1: The ENVY user-editing dialog box

and this operation is available to any user. Figure 8-1 shows the dialog used for editing user information.

For the most part, user administration is straightforward, but you should be aware of a few points.

When importing or exporting components, the users associated with those components are also transferred. Within an organization this is rarely a problem, but it can lead to some confusion. For example, when importing code from another project, or from a third-party library, it's possible that we will see the developers of that code appear as users in our library. Typically those users will be removed before the software is released, but they may not be. This is particularly common if we're using a beta version of software.

This transfer of users also explains how we can see two different users with the same full name. Suppose a developer is working in a standalone repository and creates a user definition with a different unique name from the main repository. For example, we might have a user with full name "Alan Knight," unique name "alanknight," and network name "alanknight." The network name doesn't matter in the standalone repository because there's no network login to worry about. In the team repository at work there might be a user "Alan Knight" with unique name "alan" and network name "alan." When we transfer code from one repository to the other, we end up with lists that show two different users called "Alan Knight." We could fix this by changing the full name of the standalone user to something like "Alan (Standalone) Knight." A more complete fix would be to remove that user and change ownership of his code to the "real" Alan Knight from the team repository. Or, we could just live with two identities.

Updating Users

Two main circumstances exist where we're concerned with changing ENVY user responsibilities. The first is when a user changes real-life responsibilities or leaves the team, and we need to reassign ownership of their components and remove them from the appropriate groups. The second is when we're shipping a product as a development tool and supplying our users with an ENVY export, which they will load into their environment. In this case we want to remove the names of all our users and make it appear that all components are owned, managed, and developed by the Library Supervisor.

In the first case, we need to track down all the classes and applications owned or managed by that user. This is relatively easy for the current versions (those loaded in the image). We can use a query to find all classes owned by a particular user using the ENVY->Query->Classes Owned By... menu item. Unfortunately, there's no shortcut that then enables us to remap all of those classes to someone else. Fortunately, we can use VA Assist Pro which supplies a Replace option for users. This can quickly replace a user in multiple applications or multiple editions of an application.

In the second case, we're usually exporting code (covered next), which lets us take advantage of a more automated mechanism. In the Configuration Maps Browser, we can set an option to Map Users. When we export code, if this flag is set, ENVY looks for a user field on the configuration map called #userMapping, which is expected to be a dictionary whose keys are unique names of ENVY users. Any occurrences of these users in the code being exported will automatically be replaced with the corresponding value from the userMapping dictionary. Typically, we want to map all of our internal users to Library Supervisor.

Transferring Code

One of the most basic maintenance operations is transferring code in and out of our system. We need to bring in patches, third-party products, code developed elsewhere within the organization, and code from remote sites (which may include the laptops of team members). We can exchange code in several ways. The simplest, most standard mechanism is the file-out, dumping code into a text file that can be read in and recompiled on another system, or even in another dialect. Specific versions of Smalltalk may have additional mechanisms that are faster or preserve more information, for example, VisualWorks parcels. When working with ENVY, the preferred mechanism is the ENVY import/export process. This transfers components, with all the extended ENVY information from one repository to another. These don't have to be full repositories, and one of them can be a smaller, standalone file. We can use this mechanism to distribute software to end users, to back up a subset of the library, or to send code to a remote site.

File-In/File-Out

Smalltalk has long had a "standard" file-in/out mechanism for code, which is based on the format of the original Smalltalk-80 change log. You would think that this would make transferring code in textual format between different systems very easy, but in fact enough incompatibilities exist that apparently simple transfers can be fairly troublesome. These troubles stem both from syntactic differences and from additions or changes to the semantics of the code itself.

The basic file format is very simple, consisting of a series of Smalltalk statements, broken up into *chunks* by exclamation points. Those statements create and manipulate Smalltalk class and method objects, bringing the program they represent into existence. This is often referred to as *chunk format*.

File-Ins

While ENVY has its own file-out format, it also supports the generic Smalltalk "chunk" file-out format. This format is enabled with the following option:

```
System genericFormat: true/false.
```

If we use the ENVY format, we have some additional options available to let us store extra information:

```
System fileOutComments: false "file out comments"
System fileOutDescriptions: false "file out descriptions/notes"
System fileOutCategories: false "file out method categories"
```

VisualWorks File-Outs

Here are some examples from non-ENVY VisualWorks 3.0. We have class definitions, which include the class category, used by the browsers to organize classes into groups.

```
Boolean subclass: #True
    instanceVariableNames: "
    classVariableNames: "
    poolDictionaries: "
    category: 'Kernel-Objects'!

True comment:
'I represent the logical value true.'!
```

Methods are associated with the class, and each has a method category, used by the browsers to group methods logically.

```
!True methodsFor: 'logical operations'!
& alternativeObject
    "Evaluating conjunction -- answer alternativeObject since receiver is true."

    ^alternativeObject! !
```

This is straightforward. The difficulties arise because this format includes assumptions about the way classes and methods are organized. This scheme matches the organization of the image and the browsers in the original Smalltalk-80, but when we add ENVY to the picture significant differences arise. Class categories are effectively replaced by the more sophisticated applications (categories still exist in VisualWorks/ENVY, but don't show up in the browsers). Method categories exist, but a method can exist in multiple categories, and also has a public/private classification.

ENVY File-Outs

To preserve this additional information, ENVY uses its own file-out format, which is significantly different for certain constructs. An example of this format is shown next. The first major difference is that we can file-in an entire application at once. In this case, we must ensure that the application we are filing into exists, creating it if necessary. We also need to set it to be the default application for the rest of the file-in process.

The Default Application

Most of the time ENVY does a good job of choosing which application that code should go into. So, for example, if we're in an applications browser and we add code to a class, it will be placed in the application we have selected. In a few circumstances ENVY can't figure out the right application, and if it can't it will use the default application.

We can set the default application from the Application Manager or Applications Browser by choosing the Set as Default menu item for an application. Afterward, this default application will be used whenever ENVY can't determine another application from the context. We can tell which application is the default by looking in the upper left-hand corner of the Application Manager window or from the bottom status bar of the VisualAge Organizer.

The most common circumstance in which the default application becomes important is in filing-in code. Because there's no browser to provide context, ENVY doesn't know the right application to use, and will often resort to the default.

```
Application create: #SUnitApp with:
   (#( Kernel)
      collect: [:each | Smalltalk at: each ifAbsent: [
      Application errorPrerequisite: #SUnitApp missing: each]])!
```

```
SUnitApp becomeDefault!
```

The basic class definition is the same, although VisualAge omits the class category.

```
Application subclass: #SUnitApp
      instanceVariableNames: "
      classVariableNames: "
      poolDictionaries: "!
```

In the interests of making the file-out code simple, there's some duplication of statements. Setting the default more than once doesn't hurt anything, and doesn't slow things down much.

```
SUnitApp becomeDefault!
```

Method definitions implicitly categorize them as either public or private, and do not include a category, as opposed to the methodsFor: in the normal file-out.

```
!TestCase publicMethods !
```

```
assert: aBoolean
   aBoolean ifFalse: [
   TestResult exFailure signalWith: 'Assertion failed']!
```

Once all of the methods for a class are filed in, they are categorized in one series of statements.

```
TestCase categoriesFor: #'assert:' are: #('asserting')!
TestCase categoriesFor: #'debug' are: #('running')!
```

Portable File-Outs

Of course, it's possible to make file-out code work more portably. ENVY can be configured to use the generic file-out format using the Preferences Workspace (see "Customizing Setup"). This enables the code to file-in to other dialects more easily, but loses the ENVY-specific information, becoming very much a lowest common denominator.

This loss of information becomes even more acute once we consider VisualWorks 5i. This version introduces a number of significant changes, including namespaces for classes, the unification of pool dictionaries and globals as "statics," and the use of XML as the default file format. While these changes help advance Smalltalk, they make VisualWorks 5i incompatible at the file-out level with all other dialects. Naturally, old-format file-outs are supported for backward compatibility, but they don't support all of the new semantics.

Two current mechanisms exist for providing fully portable file-outs. The first is the ANSI-standard Smalltalk Interchange Format (SIF). This is formally standardized, but does not include all of the possible semantic variations. Open-source code implementing SIF for different dialects is available, and can be found at www.pocketsmalltalk.com/sif. Recently, there's been an effort at a unified XML-based interchange format as part of the Camp Smalltalk work (see http://camp.smalltalk.org). These are both important efforts, and we hope to see a unified text format by the time this book is published, but in the meantime we need to consider our options dealing with the current formats.

Because a file-out is parsed and executed as Smalltalk code, we can make some additions to the classes that are being manipulated. By adding just a few methods we may be able to file-in code from a dialect that has a different idea of how code should look.

For example, if we compare VisualWorks chunk format to VisualAge format, the major differences are that the VisualWorks class definitions contain class categories and comments, and that the method categorization is done as part of the method definition, rather than after the fact. Simple support for filing VisualWorks code into VisualAge can be added by defining the methods.

```
Behavior>>methodsFor: aString
    ^self methods.

Class>>subclass: className
    instanceVariableNames: stringOfInstVars
    classVariableNames: stringOfClassVars
    poolDictionaries: stringOfPoolNames
    category: ignoreThis

    ^self
        subclass: className
        instanceVariableNames: stringOfInstVars
        classVariableNames: stringOfClassVars
        poolDictionaries: stringOfPoolNames
```

This gives us basic file-in capability, but it's less than ideal because we will discard the method categories and leave all methods as public. We can preserve the method categories, but it's more work. One way would be to subclass the VisualAge class EmFileOutInterface to add a current method category, and use this to automatically classify methods as they are filed in.

Similar mechanisms can be used to provide file-in and file-out compatibility between almost any other Smalltalk dialects. The VisualWorks 5i XML format is the only major exception, and VisualWorks 5i also supports chunk format.

Dialect-Specific Mechanisms

Different dialects may have their own mechanisms for transferring code between environments. Typically, these aren't portable, but they offer advantages over file-in in certain circumstances. For example, VisualWorks has "parcels," which contain compiled and/or source code and can be very rapidly loaded. This can be used to either transfer code at development time, or to organize the run-time loading of code. Parcels load much faster than source code and also provide atomic loading.

VisualAge includes ICs, which are similar in principle to parcels but with a different emphasis. ICs package run-time code into chunks that are loadable and shareable between images. They are more difficult to create than parcels, but provide true shared library functionality, which can be extremely valuable if we have multiple images running simultaneously on a server.

Neither of these mechanisms requires the compiler in order to load code, which also makes them suitable as a mechanism for distributing run-time updates to code.

ENVY Import/Export

Even if we use the native ENVY file-out format, we lose important information about the components. For example, when we file-out code, we don't know the developer, the edition timestamps, or the version names.

We can transfer components, maintaining all the extended ENVY information, if we use ENVY's own import/export facility. Exporting enables us to transfer a versioned component from one ENVY library to another, complete with all the ENVY-relevant information, including timestamps, names, user fields, and everything else. This is the cleanest way of transferring code between two ENVY-enabled images, and is the most common in daily use. In practice, we would normally use file-out or other formats only to move code to a non-ENVY environment.

One limitation on import/export is that open editions cannot be moved, only versions. There's a good reason for this. The defining characteristic of a version is that it can't be changed. If we're going to make copies of components in other repositories, we want to be sure that we have the same thing in both places. Otherwise, what the customer in New York thinks is version 2.3.4.7 might be subtly different from what the developer in Yellowknife thinks is version 2.3.4.7, and our version control is lost.

When we're transferring code frequently (for example, developers on the road doing work from their laptops), it can be painful to have to version so frequently. One way around this roadblock is to use the checkpointing facility described in the "Checkpointing" section.

Also note that versions aren't completely immutable. The code itself can't change, but some attributes can be tweaked even after a version has been made. For example, we can add and remove group members, change ownership of components, and modify comments and notes. This is typically harmless, but it does mean that some aspects of the components can still get out of sync when we duplicate them between libraries (and these are exactly the sorts of things that won't show up when browsing changes). Typically, we'll want one copy to be the master, and we'll need to be very strict about merging changes into it from other sources.

VisualWorks 5i Compatibility

Unfortunately, because of the extensive changes made in VisualWorks 5i (namespaces, changes in pools, and class variables to statics), it's not as easy to have transparent interchange of code between the different Smalltalk dialects and versions ENVY supports.

In general, it's easy to go forward because VisualWorks 5i can convert classes as they are loaded, whether that's through file-in, parceling-in, or ENVY loading. The difficulty arises because this conversion causes changes that are not easily reversible. For example, both class variables and pool dictionary entries become the more general "statics" and, along with classes, are put into namespaces. There's no fully automatic way of translating these items back into the older form. VisualWorks can file-out in older formats, but even then the process may make invalid assumptions.

For normal development, this is not a huge problem. A project typically uses only one version of software, and a one-time conversion to a new version is adequate. Some problems arise during maintenance when you need to take changes from a newer version and port them to an older version. This is relatively infrequent, though, and having to do some degree of manual reconversion is usually acceptable.

The larger problem arises if we're supplying an infrastructure layer required to support multiple versions of the software. In such a case, the lack of easy portability becomes a more significant issue. Typically, we'd want to share a repository between the different dialects to minimize duplication of code (see "Combined Libraries" later in this chapter). In general, this is possible as long as we observe certain restrictions. Here, we're assuming we want to share code between VisualWorks 2.5 or 3.0, VisualWorks 5i, and VisualAge.

- VisualWorks 2.5 and 3.0 do not support 16GB repositories, so we'll need to use a 1GB repository.

- All of our classes should be kept in the Smalltalk namespace.

- Extensions to classes that aren't in the Smalltalk namespace cannot be shared between VisualWorks 5i and the others. We'll need to put these extensions into separate subapplications and have them loaded conditionally by dialect. Maintenance will have to be performed separately between dialects.

Given these restrictions, it should be possible to do a great deal of code sharing and cross-development between VisualWorks 5i and other dialects.

Managing Libraries

For the most part, ENVY libraries are easy to manage. Developers do their work, and it's automatically stored in the library. The administrator's work is relatively light most of the time. However, we need to be concerned with some administrative tasks, mostly related to compacting the database, transferring components between versions, and managing backup and restore.

Purge

By default, everything that's created within the ENVY environment goes into the repository and stays there. From configuration maps and applications down to individual method editions, everything remains accessible. This makes it easy to ensure that code changes aren't lost, but it can lead to a proliferation of old or unimportant versions lying around.

The purge operation enables us to mark a configuration map, application, or subapplication as deleted, so they won't show up in the editions browsers or any other lists of editions. This is done by just setting a flag in the edition record, so we can also unpurge (restore), as long as the library hasn't been cloned in the meantime. This also means that purge doesn't actually reduce the space usage of the repository; it affects only the user interface. See Figure 8-2 for an illustration of the library structure with purged components.

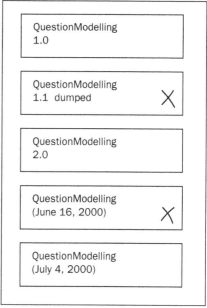

Figure 8-2: The repository with purged editions

Because the purge operation doesn't save space and affects only higher-level components (not classes or methods), it isn't all that useful. In particular, it's not possible to use purge to solve the problem of class edition clutter. In this situation, many class editions are created and then discarded. For example, say developers added a self halt or Transcript show:, and then discarded the edition. From the editions browser there's no easy way to distinguish one of these junk editions from a legitimate open edition, and it will stay open in the library indefinitely. The easiest way to deal with this situation is for developers to follow the convention of versioning these components with a name containing a keyword (for example, "junk") rather than leaving them as open editions.

A few other things to note about purge. Only the Library Supervisor can purge components, and it has to be done from an editions browser. Also, purging one level of component doesn't necessarily purge all of its subcomponents. For example, if we purge one edition of an application, it won't remove any of the class editions from the repository because they may also be referenced by other editions. However, if we purge the entire application, it will also purge all of the class and method editions associated with that application. This is, of course, a very drastic operation and not something to be done lightly, even with the capability to restore.

With these limitations, purge is primarily used to remove old code, that we really don't need any more, or that has been exported to an archival repository and is no longer needed for developers. It can also be used before cloning to indicate which applications and/or editions aren't needed in the cloned library.

Clone

Even if a component has been purged, it's still in the library. There's no way in normal operation to reclaim a component's space, so the repository will grow indefinitely. In earlier versions, this could be a significant problem because the maximum library size was 1GB. A large development project can reasonably reach that limit, particularly if it uses space-intensive features such as library objects. Current versions of ENVY support libraries as large as 16GB, so the compaction is a less serious problem. Still, even with today's machines, we may not have 16GB of spare disk space and it can be worthwhile to reclaim excess space in the repository. This is done by *cloning* the repository to create a newer, smaller version. This process does not touch the source repository, so after cloning we will need to switch over to the new repository and move the old one to archival storage.

The cloning process is invoked from the ENVY System menu. Two options exist, Clone Library and Clone Image and Library.

Clone Library takes all the nonpurged versions of top-level components in a library (configuration maps and applications) and transfers them to a new library, including all the corresponding classes, methods, and library objects. We can think of the ENVY library as containing a few precious gems, which represent our versions, floating in a vast sea of garbage changes. Cloning simply copies over the gems, leaving the rest behind. Figure 8-3 illustrates the cloning process for a repository with versions, open editions, and purged versions.

Clone Image and Library does the same thing as Clone Library but it also transfers any open editions that are present in the image that is performing the clone operation. This enables us to compact while still maintaining open editions. Note, however, that this applies only to the editions in *this* particular image, so other developers with open changes may lose them.

Realistically, it's rarely necessary to clone. Usually, before a library reaches anything close to the size where it would be important to clone it, a new version of the software has been issued, and it's simpler to just export the versions that are worth saving into a new, clean repository, rather than clone the existing repository. See the "System Upgrades" section a little later in this chapter. This is not quite as convenient as cloning because exporting won't preserve open editions, but if we're switching libraries it's normally safest to have everything versioned off anyway.

Managing Disk Space

The ENVY library has a theoretical maximum size of either 1GB or 16GB, depending on the version of ENVY. However, a more practical limit is the available disk space. Running out of disk space on the partition that contains the ENVY repository is a major problem and can lead to repository corruption.

To avoid this problem, one solution is to give ENVY its own partition, and to ensure that there's plenty of space on it. Barring that, we should be careful to monitor the partition with the repository to ensure that there's enough free space, and that the repository isn't approaching its maximum size.

Before

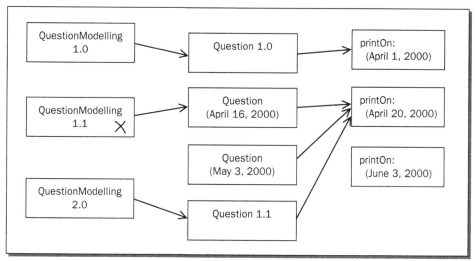

After

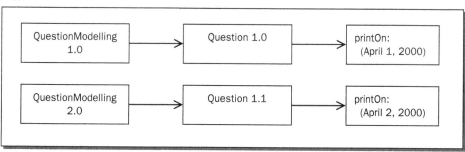

Figure 8-3: Cloning a repository

If we do run into space problems, we'll need to recover the repository, and may lose work. See the "Repository Recovery" section.

Combined Libraries

Often, different projects are working with different versions of Smalltalk, or even different dialects. When working on both VisualWorks and VisualAge, it's often useful to be able to combine the ENVY installations to enable them to work on the same library. This is not difficult, but we have a few things to watch out for, depending on exactly which versions we need to support.

If we're supporting the newest versions, we'll need to use EMSRV to access the library, which is a good idea anyway. EMSRV is fully backward compatible so there shouldn't be any problem running the latest version (6.23 as of this writing) with an older version of ENVY.

We also need to worry about repository formats. Newer versions of ENVY support libraries with a 16GB maximum size, but older versions cannot access these libraries. If we try, we'll see an error reading the library header. If we need to mix newer and older versions, we may need to use a 1GB format library.

It's entirely possible to run both VisualWorks and VisualAge accessing the same repository, and this shouldn't cause any problems. VisualWorks 5i does present some special issues, and these were discussed in "VisualWorks 5i Compatibility" previously.

Backup

The ENVY repository represents a single point of failure for all of our development. Frequent, reliable backup is absolutely critical.

Everybody knows this, but backup procedures still tend to be lax because, under normal circumstances, no one cares about the backup. A typical scenario is that a backup exists, but it can take several days to actually figure out how to restore it the first time a disaster happens.

ENVY presents a minor challenge for backup strategies because of the nature of the repository. Most backup mechanisms are file-centered: they do incremental backup based on which files have changed, and they won't back up a file if it changes during the course of the backup. With ENVY there's essentially only one gigantic file to back up, which defeats incremental backups. Because we can't back up the file if it's changing, we need to ensure that the repository isn't being accessed during the backup. We don't know of a way to do incremental backup of an ENVY repository, but several possible strategies exist for ensuring that the repository isn't changing during backup.

The simplest strategy is just to back up at a time when we're sure no one else is using the repository. Because many backups are scheduled for late-night operation anyway, this is often an easy thing to do. Unfortunately, programmers have a tendency to work unusual hours, and if we allow dial-in access to the repository or have remote users in different time zones this may not be very good protection.

The second strategy involves locking users out. With newer versions of ENVY (VA 4.5 or greater, VW 5i), all shared repository access must go through EMSRV, so it's enough to shut down the EMSRV process. You can do this in two ways:

- emadmin stop: The emadmin program can shut down the EMSRV process, throwing out any users. Doing this automatically requires the password of the user that was specified at EMSRV startup.

- sigquit: Under UNIX, the EMSRV process should respond safely to signals, shutting itself down cleanly.

A third strategy is not to lock users out, but to use ENVY mechanisms to safely make a backup copy of the repository, which is not accessed by users, and then use normal backup mechanisms to access that. The repository can be copied using the emadmin copy command as in the following example:

```
emadmin copy 127.0.0.1:manager.dat 127.0.0.1:backup.dat -o -p mypassword -q
```

This command copies from the manager.dat file accessed through the given EMSRV instance (running on localhost) to the backup.dat file, overwriting files if necessary, using the password "mypassword" and running in "quiet" mode. This copy of the repository will be made by incrementally obtaining and releasing the necessary locks so users can continue to work on the library, even as it's being copied. The backup.dat file can then be backed up normally because it won't be changing.

Typically, both of the more sophisticated mechanisms for controlling access during backup require use of the EMSRV user's password, either to stop/restart the server, or to make a copy. For this reason, it's advisable to run EMSRV with as few privileges as possible. Do not run it as root or administrator, but create a special user with only those privileges necessary to run. Under NT, the only special privilege required is "Act as Part of the Operating System" so that user passwords can be checked. On other operating systems no special privileges are required, other than the ability to access the directory where the repository is kept.

System Upgrades

From time to time new releases of ENVY and/or the underlying Smalltalk system appear, and we need to upgrade our installation. Several components need to be upgraded:

- client installation
- EMSRV
- repository

The client installation is simple. Users using the new version install the new client software, including the VM, image, and supplementary files.

If there's a new version of EMSRV we will normally want to use it in place of the previous version. Typically, a new version of EMSRV is backward-compatible with older versions, so there shouldn't be any issues using it for all clients. Bring down the old EMSRV using emadmin stop, replace it with the newer version, and test that all the different clients we need can still connect to the repository.

The most significant part of an upgrade is the repository. Here we have two options — incorporate the new software into our existing repository or migrate our software into the new repository. Both of these options have advantages.

To incorporate new software into an existing repository, we install the new repository on our server but don't connect clients to it. Instead, we import all of the configuration maps from the new version into our current repository. This enables all current users to continue working without any interruption. Code can be migrated at our leisure. The main disadvantages of this approach are that it doesn't give us the opportunity to condense our repository as we migrate, and it requires someone to manually migrate all of the code from the new repository. This would also be impossible if there's a change of repository format, but this is extremely unlikely.

To migrate our software into a new repository, we need to ensure that we have versions of everything we want to save and then export them into the new repository. Once this is done, users connect to the new repository instead of the old one and continue working. This has the disadvantage that all code has to be versioned and that all development stops briefly before resuming in the new library. It has the advantages that there's no possibility of missing some component from the new version, and that it compresses the library in the process of migrating. Because the export process is quite speedy, it's not a big problem to switch over immediately after a baseline.

A variation of this is to operate for a transitional period with two separate repositories. Migrate code from the old to the new, but allow development to proceed, at least for some period of time, in two separate installations. This is convenient because it minimizes the synchronization that's required, particularly if we have multiple teams using the same repository. At a time that's convenient for project A, one team can migrate to the new repository, but project B can continue in the old repository for a couple of days while that team meets a deadline, then migrates. Continuing in separate repositories for an extended period of time is a bad idea because it starts to cause problems integrating and updating among groups, but for a short period the harm is minimal and it can help keep development flexible.

In most situations, none of these upgrades will be a significant problem, and the most significant effort will be adapting code to changes and new features in the new release. For a major upgrade, we may want to maintain two separate streams (see "Multiple Streams") while we port to the new release.

Remote Work

Ideally, we want all our users to be connected to the central ENVY repository all the time, but in many situations that's not realistic and we will need to support remote work. This is not about a team split between two sites, which is covered in "Multi-Site Development," but rather the more limited case of a single user working remotely.

Within this situation are a few subcases. The first is remote developers telecommuting, such as contractors working off-site. They're doing almost all their work in a remote repository and connecting occasionally. The second case is a developer who normally works in the team repository but is temporarily disconnected. This might happen when one of the team members is travelling and trying to get work done on a plane, in a hotel room, or even on the beach. Finally, you have the case of someone who, for whatever reason, is remote, but can connect over some kind of wide-area network to the remote repository.

All of these subcases can make integration significantly more awkward than normal development, and need to be carefully managed. Nevertheless, these situations arise for good reasons. In some cases it's something the developer wants — "Great! I get to stay in my home town and work on this cool project from my living room." In other cases it's employer-motivated — "Oh great. Work called and I have to dial in and fix an urgent bug. Go on ahead to the beach without me."

When developers work primarily in their own repository (for example, a remote contractor), this is really a special case of multi-site development, where one of the sites has just one person. The same sorts of rules apply. It's much harder to integrate between sites, so as much as possible try to have the remote person as the sole developer of the components he or she works on. Ensure that there's good communication and fast network links between the sites. Expect that some degree of in-person communication will be necessary.

If we start getting thrashing between the sites, with integration and transfer taking up too much time, we should consider repartitioning components or ownership boundaries. We may also want to spend a bit of time on simple tools to manage the integration process, possibly building in some awareness of our situation.

With normally connected users, the difficulties are fewer. If they're working in their own repository we can assume the changes are relatively small, so even if they're scattered over several different applications the integration burden should be relatively light. One of the difficulties in this case is getting the code into the remote repository in the first place. Suppose a developer is going on a trip and wants to work on some code part way through an integration cycle. This means exporting the code to a laptop, but we may not have a version of that code that's current.

In this circumstance basic ENVY functionality gives us few choices. The choices are to work from the old version, file-out the current open edition and file it in on the laptop, or get everyone to help make an unscheduled baseline. None of these is ideal. What we'd really like is the ability to create a temporary version directly from the current open edition. Our developer could export that version directly to the laptop, develop code while on the trip, then merge back in later knowing exactly what the new code is based on. This is exactly the functionality provided by the checkpointing code, described in "Checkpointing."

Finally, we have the situation of a developer who is working remotely but can access the main repository over a network link. For the same reasons outlined earlier, this isn't a very feasible way to work most of the time because network latency severely affects the response time of the ENVY environment. It's workable for short-term connections, but typically not feasible for larger-scale work. For more significant coding, the developer is probably better off working with a local repository and doing frequent integrations.

Writing Scripts

Library Supervisors and ENVY power users often have tasks they need to do on a semi-regular basis. Many of these are repetitive, and it would be nice to have a way to automate them. To help with this, we introduce the idea of an ENVY script, which is roughly equivalent to a batch file or UNIX shell script.

Scripts tend to start out as code in workspaces rather than as methods. Of course, we can make scripts into methods, but in our experience, we've found it's often difficult to find the appropriate class for the method, and we're hesitant to define pseudo-classes that just collect a number of utility methods. However, we have packed some of the necessary infrastructure into a few classes, which you can find in the MedScriptSupportApp.

To do good script writing, we need support in two main areas:

- prompters
- access to ENVY protocol

Judicious use of prompters enables us to quickly choose the components we want to manipulate. It saves us from writing ugly loops like the following:

```
(Application currentlyLoaded select: [ :each |
    (each name copyFrom: 1 to: 3) = 'Foo']) do...
```

This section defines several additional utilities for working with prompters that understand the ENVY components. To help out with ENVY protocol we've provided examples throughout the book, and the Appendix provides an annotated protocol that you can use as a reference.

Prompter Utilities

If we look closely enough, it turns out that, of all the prompters we need to select, most ENVY components are already available within ENVY. For the most part, though, they're hidden somewhere deep in the EtBrowser hierarchy. To make this easier to work with, we've created a façade to this code as class methods in MedPrompters. All of these methods will simply delegate to the appropriate browser or utility class methods as follows:

Applications

- chooseAnApp
- chooseAnAppAndEdition
- chooseSomeApps
- chooseSomeAppsAndEditions

Configuration Maps

- chooseAConfigMap
- chooseAConfigMapAndEdition
- chooseConfigMapEditionFor:
- chooseSomeConfigMapsAndEditions
- chooseSomeConfigMapsAndEditionsSelecting:

Users

- chooseAUser

For example, our implementation of chooseSomeApps creates a new and otherwise unused instance of EtBrowser, so we can use one of its prompter messages. We never open a window for this browser, and in fact EtBrowser is an abstract class, so we could never actually use it as a browser. However, because the method we're invoking doesn't use any of the browser's state, we can safely invoke it. We'll also make use of the currentlyLoaded protocol to find all of the applications currently in the image.

```
MedPrompters class>chooseSomeApps
    EtBrowser new
        prompt: 'Select some Apps'
        chooseMultipleFrom:
            (Application currentlyLoaded asSortedCollection:
                Class sortBlock)
        initialSelection: nil
        printBlock: nil
        statusIndicatorBlock: nil
```

A similar but simpler example for choosing a user makes use of the EtTools application class protocol for choosing a user. This overloads the application class, which is normally used only for application-level protocol and makes it a utility class as well.

```
MedPrompters class>chooseAUser
    ^EtTools promptForUser: 'Choose a User'
```

ENVY Protocol

The most difficult part of writing scripts or any ENVY tools is understanding the relationships between components and finding the methods necessary to manipulate these relationships. This is complicated by a few factors. First, the components are not directly related through instance variables; rather, many of the most important relationships are implicit in methods. Further, these methods are not concentrated in the components themselves, but are spread out over three distinct groups of classes: the browsers, the "helper" classes such as EmInterface, and the components themselves. Sometimes it's not easy to find the right code, even when we know it has to exist somewhere.

In the earliest versions of ENVY almost everything was done directly in the browser code. Over time much of the code was moved to utility classes such as EtTools and EmInterface. This reduced code duplication but the utility classes became very complex, with many methods that manipulate different types of components, making it harder to find any given piece of functionality.

The third place to look for code that manipulates components is the components themselves. Studying the methods in (Sub-)Application, EmConfigurationMap, EmUser, and so on will give a good idea of what's possible. The most useful of these methods are listed in annotated form in the Appendix. You'll also find a diagram showing the relationships between the components and how to navigate among them on this book's inside back cover.

Adding a User

This section shows an example script for adding a user to multiple applications at once. This is typical of the kind of repetitive operations an administrator may need to perform. Each time a new developer joins the team, the Library Supervisor has to define a new ENVY user and ensure that this user is added as a group member in all the applications he or she will be working on. Technically, the correct approach to this is to notify all of the relevant application managers and ask them to add the user. Often, however, people will take a shortcut and have the Library Supervisor directly add the user, changing users where necessary. This is a tedious process, and manually changing users is very error-prone. By automating this process with a script we can both simplify the process and reduce errors.

First, we use two of the preceding prompter methods to choose a user and a group of applications. This gives us our input, but we need some additional facilities to support changing users in order to perform a particular operation. This is provided in the MedPrompters class, implemented as follows.

```
MedPrompters class>changeUserTo: aUser while: aBlock
    | oldUser |
    oldUser := EmUser current.
    [(EmUser classPool declareVariable: 'CurrentUser')
      value: aUser.
      aBlock value] ensure: [
        (EmUser classPool declareVariable: 'CurrentUser')
        value: oldUser].
```

We set the current user in a slightly sneaky way, sending the declareVariable: message to the dictionary of class variables. This lets us work around the fact that there's no setter for the CurrentUser class variable, and this protocol is implemented on all the structures that might be used in the classPool variable in different dialects (Dictionary, EsSmalltalkNamespace, and GeneralNamespace).

Given the preceding methods, writing the script becomes trivial. This version has no error handling, but you often don't need error handling on a script, and it would be easy to make a more robust version.

```
"Add a user to an bunch of apps"
| user apps |
user := MedPrompters chooseAUser.
apps := MedPrompters chooseSomeApps.
apps do: [ :app |
    MedPrompters
    changeUserTo: app manager
    while: [app addGroupMember: user]]
```

Here are some examples of other scripts that could be useful.

- **Load Build Report:** List the names of classes and methods that have changed between two arbitrary editions.

- **Backup:** Export our project to a repository with a file name based on the version string.

- **Import and Load:** For someone who is working remotely. Import all code from a repository file. For each class, check for changes and for conflicts. Specifically, there's a change in the import if a class there is newer than the version released in the previous version of its containing application. A conflict occurs if there's also a version in the repository that satisfies the same conditions. If there's a newer version with no conflict, load and release the class. If there's a newer version with a conflict, open a differences browser.

- **Stale Open Editions:** For one or more applications, find all open class editions in the library with creation dates more than N days ago. List them, grouped by developer. Yell at those developers.

Organizing for Re-Use

In addition to maintenance tasks, an administrator may also be involved in larger-scale organization. Many organizations want to maximize re-use of code developed within and across projects, and the organization of ENVY repositories can have an impact on this.

Re-use is a very broad topic, and goes well beyond the scope of this book. Here, we'll primarily focus on the small-scale and the readily achievable. Very large-scale re-use, enterprise-wide and across organizations, is extremely difficult, and we won't even begin to address it. A more reasonable goal is smaller-scale re-use, mostly within an organization and between projects in similar domains. In particular, this is the level of re-use at which the configuration of our team programming tools can make a difference.

The Ideal of Re-Use

One of the strong selling points for object technology was the potential re-use of code. Unfortunately, over the years this has proven to be more difficult than one might think. Although today significant re-use is common, it's not necessarily in the places where people were looking for it. In hindsight, it's easy to see that re-usable libraries have emerged in precisely those areas that were widely needed, easily abstracted, and common to many different kinds of systems. In these areas, a great deal of re-use has been achieved, even though we now take this for granted and don't consider it "real" re-use.

For example, today a given user-interface widget is normally written once and used in many different applications. The code containing it is most likely in a separate library and dynamically linked at run-time. Instances of the widget are customized through run-time quasi-reflective mechanisms such as events or callbacks. The idea of custom coding even part of a widget seems ridiculous. It *is* ridiculous, but it hasn't been all that long since re-use by subclassing was the state of the art. Subclassing ListView and overriding methods to change its actions seemed like quite a reasonable thing and a definite improvement over other technologies of the time.

Even today this kind of re-use is still a work-in-progress in many mainstream environments. If I have a list that displays a collection of strings, do we have to provide strings and write code to match that string (or its index in the collection) up to the domain object I really want? Or, can I populate the widget with a collection of domain objects and just tell the list how they display? It all depends on the tools we're using.

There's an important idea here. We have a category of objects (for example, widgets) and general APIs that all of them are expected to implement. The widgets have specific behavior and attributes, and the general APIs enable development tools to discover them, manipulate them, and connect them to the domain. This lets us use a list widget within a GUI builder that doesn't have any built-in knowledge of list widgets. New widgets can be added to the palette and used to construct applications without any modification to the underlying framework. This is a very clean, simple model of re-use, which has been very successful.

These days this is referred to as a "component" model, and is the basis of most widely used GUI builders, including the VisualAge composition editor, the VisualWorks canvas tool, WindowBuilder Pro, Java Beans, and Visual Basic. The most successful use of components has been with GUI widgets, but there have also been many attempts to make domain components. This has been successful for domains, which are well abstracted, general-purpose, and can be rigorously specified. For example, components are available for image processing, interfacing to computational engines, and I/O mechanisms such as speech synthesis and recognition. Overall, the most successful applications could be broadly characterized as infrastructure.

The least successful application of components has been in trying to organize more general business models. The problem is that these models are typically concrete, vary greatly between and within organizations, and are rapidly evolving. Another difficulty is that component models typically simplify the underlying object model to make things more manageable for the component assembler. For example, most component models don't support inheritance. The component framework doesn't have to expose the full object model underneath, and often doesn't, simplifying for the benefit of the component assembler. When trying to model a complex domain, it's usually not possible to simplify the features that much. So far these and other factors have hampered the development of a re-usable component market for general business models.

This re-use of business models is what most people want when they talk about re-use. Some have questioned whether it's even worth striving for this kind of re-use, preferring instead to do exactly what is necessary for a particular project and not attempting to generalize for re-use. For example, see "Extreme Programming and ENVY" in Chapter 4. Re-use is often described as essential for software to become an industrial process, or compared to the use of integrated circuits as components in electronics. However, software is in many ways closer to engineering or industrial design than to production processes, and in electronics the component analogy is breaking down as the industry moves more and more toward application-specific integrated circuits (ASIC). Nevertheless, software re-use remains a significant goal in many organizations, and a great deal of work is being done to try and make it a reality.

If we want to achieve re-use, we need to bear in mind the limitations of current approaches and the current best practices. While components have not had great success in business object re-use, the lessons of components are still important. We need to strive for clearly abstracted objects, weak coupling, and simplicity for the user. In later sections we'll talk about some of the concrete steps that can help achieve these goals.

Finally, note that *component* is an overloaded term (much like *object*). In this book we normally talk about two kinds of components. Usually, we say *software components* to mean individual version-controlled elements within ENVY: methods, classes, applications, and configuration maps. These are components in that they are the building blocks of our programs. In this section we're also talking about the more general ideas of re-usable building blocks with a meta-protocol for manipulating them, and we'll refer to that as just *components*.

Economics and Culture

The first thing to recognize is that re-use costs. There are certainly benefits to not having to write the same code twice, but ensuring that code can be re-used is harder than building nonreusable code. The larger-scale the re-use, the harder it gets (although the benefits are also larger).

The second thing to recognize is that the benefits don't come to the person who paid the costs. You spent more time polishing and documenting your code to make it reusable, so that someone else doesn't have to write that functionality. That person saves money and time. You lose money and time, but you get to feel good about your code.

If we're re-using code within a project, or within a small organization, then this is reasonable as long as there's an overall benefit. We have the same boss, so he or she doesn't mind if our work takes a little longer as long as the organization as a whole wins. The larger the scale of the re-use, the harder this becomes to justify. If it's a choice between getting our work done on time or helping support someone on a completely different project, we're going to opt for our work. Upper management has to be more than normally understanding or have an explicit policy in place to encourage re-use. For re-use in the general public we get into a true producer/consumer relationship, where I pay you to use your code and I expect professional-level support.

The user also has costs. If I'm going to re-use your code, first I have to know that it exists, and if it's suitable for my problem. That takes research, and I may have to spend a couple of weeks evaluating your software to know if it's really suitable. That takes time and it's hard to do. Also, as a typical developer, for any given component I probably believe I could write a better version myself in two weeks. Sometimes I may even be right. If my project decides to use your code we become dependent on you for bug fixes and upgrades. If we need additional functionality it's hard or impossible for us to add it, and your schedules may not correspond to ours.

All of these problems get worse the larger the scale. Within a project it's easy. We expect everyone to use the same infrastructure, the same business objects, and the same frameworks. We control everything about the system, and if we find unnecessary duplication we can easily eliminate it. Experts on the system are readily available, as is full source code, and turnaround time for changes is in minutes. The farther away the re-use "customer" is, the more rigid and formalized the interface has to be, and the better the documentation. The producer has to start "selling" to potential users, with everything that entails.

This is not to say that re-use isn't possible, or isn't a good idea. Clearly, getting software that solves a problem without having to write it is a very big win, and worth significant pain. The success of component models, even in limited areas, is proof of that. Even without any kind of infrastructure, developers have sought out software to re-use when the incentive to avoid doing it themselves is sufficiently large. Two good examples of this are parser generators and report writers. Both are messy and complex to implement, and many re-usable implementations exist and are widely used.

This *is* to say that re-use isn't trivial, and that both the producer and consumer have costs, regardless of the technology. The wider the re-use, and the more domain-specific the software is, the greater the difficulty. Be realistic about where re-use is a good idea, where it's achievable, and what it will take to achieve it.

Re-Use Mechanisms

To achieve re-use, we need to define our goals. What scale of re-use are we aiming for? What type of re-use mechanism are we aiming for? What's the granularity of the re-usable units?

In early attempts at re-use, the standard mechanism was inheritance. This tended to lead to large frameworks, where users would create subclasses at particular points in a sophisticated inheritance hierarchy and write methods to specialize their functionality. The framework calls user code at well-defined points, tightly integrating the user functionality with the general framework code.

This kind of re-use is possible, and gives very fine-grained control but it's very difficult to use and makes a lot of demands on the user. Examples of this are frameworks for structured graphics and/or widgets and GUI building. Users often need source code to the framework and/or extremely detailed documentation.

A looser coupling mechanism is through composition. User classes work with instances of the re-usable code. The re-usable code needs clear APIs, but doesn't call out to user code, reducing the complexity.

With composition, it's still useful to be able to receive notification of what's happening within the component code. Unlike inheritance, where code explicitly calls known methods, which users must implement, it's possible to use a more abstract mechanism. In Smalltalk, this can take the form of method selectors to perform or blocks to evaluate (for example, pluggable views). It can also take a more generalized form as events or callbacks, which are less dependent on Smalltalk-specific features.

It's also important to consider the granularity at which re-use occurs. Although these three mechanisms are the basic ones available, the flavor of re-use can be quite different at different scales.

The most basic unit of re-use is the class. Because it clearly defines an interface, it's an obvious mechanism for re-use. For simple applications, such as a single widget, a single class may be adequate, but typically it's not enough. Frameworks normally consist of many classes. Even when doing re-use through composition, it's typical that we have either multiple related classes to deal with, or a single service object acting as a façade to a more complex internal structure.

In general, coarse-grained components can be very simple to use, whereas fine-grained components offer more flexibility. If we consider the single largest issue in re-use to be the cost to the re-user of evaluation and understanding, then we should generally favor composition over inheritance, weak coupling over strong, and coarser-grained over fine-grained. Give users building blocks they can stand on rather than scaffolding they need to build within.

Achieving Re-Use

Enough preaching. We know it's hard. Given that, what are the concrete steps you can take, using ENVY, to encourage re-use? Here are a few:

- Keep components independent.
- Use weak coupling.
- Keep it clear.
- Keep it simple.
- Choose your boundaries and specify them clearly.
- Keep a common infrastructure.

Independence

The most important aspect of achieving re-use is independence. Re-use means taking something out of the context it was originally built for and using it somewhere else. The more dependencies a component has on the original environment, the less re-usable it is.

Obviously, limits exist. By this metric, the ultimately re-usable component is a completely standalone application. Anybody can use it, and it has almost no dependencies. It's true that this mechanism has been phenomenally successful, but it has a few problems. There's a great deal of duplication, inter-component communication is painful, and it's not very flexible.

To get more power, more flexibility, and better communication, we introduce dependencies. Introducing dependencies can be good. It gives us power, letting us use additional facilities. It lets us solve more specific problems, and it lets us make assumptions that make our job easier. On the other hand, it inhibits re-use because all these things tie us to particular infrastructures, particular domains, or particular architectures. These tradeoffs have to be made case-by-case, but if we're aiming for re-use we need to be aware of and explicit about dependencies.

Independence takes many forms, including:

- **Domain-independence:** General code is more re-usable, but over-generalized code is too hard to understand and may not be usable at all.

- **Independence of infrastructure:** Changes to the base library, use of extended libraries, and use of support frameworks all make our code less re-usable.

- **Independence of architecture:** Re-use means people will use our components in ways we never anticipated. Minimize the assumptions.

- **Independence of language:** For truly large-scale re-use, we'll need to make our code available in a language-independent form, using CORBA, COM, or some other wrapper mechanism.

- **Platform-independence:** If our code is tied to a particular operating system, or other system, it's less re-usable. Fortunately, Smalltalk gives us good operating-system independence, although for large-scale re-use we may also need to ensure that we're not tied to a particular Smalltalk dialect.

Within ENVY, we should ensure that our prerequisites are minimal, accurate, and kept up to date to ensure independence of infrastructure.

Clarity and Usability

Components can't be re-used unless they are understood. If users don't know what something does, they won't try to re-use it. There's really no way we can formally specify what a component does, at least not at the level users want. This means we have to use informal mechanisms, and hope they're clear enough.

Naming

Names are magic. They're also domain specific. To really say what something does we would need to give it much too long a name, and a short name can easily be mistaken for something entirely different. This is a hard problem, and naming everything that is known with a short yet unambiguous name is not an easy job. Fortunately, if we're only trying to achieve re-use within a relatively small group, we can assume they all have some similar ideas and terminology.

Within ENVY, ensure that names are well chosen, and that classes and applications have clear, simple comments, with pointers to more detailed documentation and specifications. Because many Smalltalks still don't have full namespace support, prefix your classes with a short, unique name to avoid name conflicts with user code (for example, the code included with this book is prefixed with "Med"). For some discussion on general naming and Smalltalk style, see Beck (1997).

Concepts

Ideas are magic, too. Not only do consumers of our component have to be able to identify it, they have to be able to use it quickly, "out of the box." The harder it is to understand and remember the fundamental concepts, the less likely someone is to use it. Consider the collection library. The method do: is a good example of re-usability, but inject:into: is complicated enough that it's much less used. Ruthlessly prune what a basic user of a component needs to know. If someone just uses everything with the defaults, how likely is it to do the right thing?

Within ENVY, code cleanly and simply. Include a separate Examples application that illustrates standard usage and concepts.

Perspectives

Any software component is built with a particular point of view and a particular usage. If it isn't, that's probably a sign of over-design and nonusability in general. The world is littered with the corpses of solutions designed from scratch to solve very broad classes of problems. The most successful general solutions have arisen by repeatedly solving many specific problems and then generalizing from well-understood, working code. We will always have a perspective, and we should make it as clear as possible as quickly as possible.

Specification

We said there's no way we can completely specify the behavior of these components at the level our users want. This doesn't mean it's not worth trying to specify it at all. In their early stages, knowledge of re-usable components is usually transmitted by sitting down with the designers for a day or two and absorbing their assumptions. In the larger scale, we need to make the assumptions very explicit. Ideally, the structure of the code should make the assumptions clear and impossible to violate. At a minimum, public APIs should check the assumptions and give clear error messages if they're violated. For very large-scale re-use, it's probably worthwhile to have a more sophisticated graphical interface rather than letting users specify details in code. Communicating clearly with the users quickly becomes a lot of work, but there's nothing else that has more effect on re-usability.

Within ENVY, have a regression test suite that fully exercises the software, including error cases and error messages. Outside of ENVY, maintain a good specification of the software and be sure the test suite agrees with it.

Infrastructure

Within an organization, one of the most important factors that facilitate re-use is a common base for everyone to build on. One of the most difficult tasks in making a component re-usable is ensuring that it doesn't depend on details of our installation, tools, or supporting code. The more we can ensure that our target audience shares these characteristics, the easier it will be. To some degree, this requires a common architecture, and to the extent that we can enforce a common architecture, that will also help re-usability.

If we can't dictate the infrastructure, then we need to minimize our reliance on it. We may even need to do this at the expense of writing clean code. Keep the following points in mind:

- Do not modify base classes unless you have absolutely no alternative. Modifications make it much harder to manage code in ENVY and virtually guarantee that users will have to examine the code and resolve it with their own modifications, patches, or other versions.

- Consider using a helper class rather than adding methods to a base class, even though the helper is not as good in terms of OO style. For example, consider writing the procedural HelperClass>anyElementOf: rather than adding Collection>any and risking a conflict with other base modifications.

- If we do need to add methods to base classes, we should consider using a conditional loading technique like the one described in "Conditional Loading Tricks."

- Be careful with "clever" techniques such as #doesNotUnderstand: handlers, reflective modification of classes/methods, and even #perform:. These are very powerful, but can make code harder to manage, harder to understand, and can conflict with other tools.

- Ensure that our prerequisites are minimal, accurate, and up to date. Before distributing the software, load, test, and (if applicable) package it in a minimal install to reveal hidden dependencies.

Packaging

If a component is to be re-used, it has to be distributed. In some ways this is fairly simple, but we can take some additional steps to make components more usable and independent.

Separate out the different aspects of what we're distributing. Generally, these are as follows:

- **Development-time:** what a developer would normally load (includes any editing facilities)

- **Run-time:** what's actually needed in a packaged image

- **Examples:** examples of usage

- **Testing:** the test suites (may or may not be visible to end users)

- **Tools:** any supplementary tools not already part of the development-time code

For a coarse-grained component, a reasonable strategy is to give each of these its own configuration map, potentially with required map relationships between them.

If we're distributing multiple re-usable business classes, it's reasonable to group them together, so that the development-time map would load multiple classes.

For finer-grained components, it's also possible to collapse some of these categories together. We might, for example, group tools with development, and examples with testing. We might also put these components directly in applications rather than in configuration maps.

An alternative strategy is to make a single application, and group the various testing/tools under it as subapplications. In general, we prefer to use configuration maps for this, and in the case of re-usable software this is particularly true because they're more visible to the end user, and handle duplication better. For more information on these tradeoffs, see "Subapplication Usage."

Tips and Tricks

To conclude this chapter, we present a couple of miscellaneous tips and tricks that may be helpful in administering an ENVY system. While they don't fall in the broad categories we've discussed previously, they're things that it might be very helpful to know before starting out on a project.

Fragmentation on NTFS

The ENVY library works by successively appending small records to a single very large file. Depending on the characteristics of the file system it's installed on, this can lead to very serious disk fragmentation. In particular, NTFS drives are very susceptible to this because each record allocates a small amount of additional storage. FAT format drives are less susceptible because the file space is allocated in larger chunks. It doesn't seem to be a big problem on other types of file systems.

The only real strategy (aside from not using NTFS) to avoid this problem is to put the repository on a disk partition of its own, so that successive appends will be allocated sequentially on the drive.

Managing Import/Export Directories

You have a couple of things to watch out for with import and export operations. These are particularly tricky because it varies depending on the version of ENVY and the type of server.

First, it's important to be aware of the directory we're using to import/export, and whether it's on the client or the server.

If we're running with a local repository, or one that is shared over a network file system, then import/export is relative to the *client* system. That is, if we export to C:\TEMP\FOO.DAT, this means the temp directory on the local hard drive of the client computer.

When using EMSRV to connect to the repository (which is the normal mechanism for all current versions of ENVY), then import/export is relative to the *server's* file system. This is where the version matters. For VisualAge 4.5 and VisualWorks/ENVY 4.0, the path is *always* relative to the server; there's no option. ENVY for VisualWorks 5i and VisualAge 5.0 allows the import/export path to be relative to either the server or the client.

This distinction has two consequences. First, it can be painful to import, particularly if the repository is on a secure server. If we have a floppy or CD-ROM with a file to import, and the import is only server-relative, we have to either physically go to the server and load the file, or load it onto a workstation and transfer it over to the server. One way to get around this is to provide a public import/export directory that is well known and has permissions that allow any developer to store and retrieve files. This directory should be on the same server that runs EMSRV because EMSRV can only access directories on drives local to the server.

Second, users can easily freeze the ENVY server. If we're running a Windows server, and a user asks to import or export to a floppy drive, that refers to the server's floppy drive. If the server has a floppy drive, and there's no disk in it, then the EMSRV process freezes, displaying the Abort/Retry/Ignore dialog box and locking out all users until someone physically goes to the server to fix it. If the server isn't close by, this can be a serious problem.

The newest versions of ENVY help resolve the first problem, but not the second. About the only thing you can do for this is run on a non-Windows server, or ensure that the server doesn't have a floppy drive.

Summary

Administration is a broad topic, and the role of the administrator is hard to define. In ENVY, this is even more difficult than normal because the role of the administrator can vary significantly with different projects. An administrator might be the technical lead, doing baselines, user maintenance, and other ENVY operations. On the other hand, part of this role might be filled by a system administrator who is completely unfamiliar with Smalltalk programming but manages the machines on which the repository lives. The remainder of the administrator's role might be filled by one or more team members doing Smalltalk-specific administration.

In this chapter we've covered the essentials of the administration required for a smooth-functioning ENVY system. Some of the important details to remember are as follows:

- ENVY keeps track of users for various purposes, and users are administered by the Library Supervisor.

- Code can be transferred between systems in many different ways, including file-outs, ENVY .DAT files, and dialect-specific mechanisms such as parcels and ICs. With file-outs, it may be necessary to do additional work for portability.

- It's possible and often useful to share a repository between different versions of Smalltalk and even different dialects, although you'll run into some challenges doing this with VisualWorks 5i.

- The ENVY library is noncompacting. Components can be purged, but will still occupy space until the library is cloned. Cloning can greatly reduce the size of a repository and also remove unnecessary editions.

- Many administration tasks can be partially or fully automated using a library of Smalltalk scripts and associated helper code.

- The organization of our code can have a significant effect on re-use, and this should be considered early in the process.

═══Chapter 9═══

Goodies

While ENVY provides an extensive toolset, tools and enhancements can make life easier for a developer or administrator. This section presents a few such tools, with example source code and explanations of the techniques involved. For full code, including complete source code for these tools, see the book's Web site. The tools we will look at are as follows:

- A script manager, which organizes a collection of scripts inside user fields in the repository.

- A three-way differences browser, which streamlines the process of merging two divergent streams together.

- A simple project management tool to support the layered architecture described in Chapter 4.

- A checkpointing facility, which creates versions of a component out of editions without modifying the underlying editions, tremendously simplifying backup, intermediate baselines, and management of multiple repositories. We think this is one of the most useful and important ENVY add-ons we've seen.

- An integration of the Refactoring Browser facilities into the standard ENVY browsers.

- A way to rename versions in the ENVY repository without creating new editions and versioning them.

- Ways of removing source code from ENVY components so that we can deliver libraries to other developers without exposing all of our internal source code.

The material on concepts and on using these tools is appropriate for novice developers and administrators. The material on implementation techniques is very advanced in some areas and is primarily intended for power users and toolsmiths.

User Fields

The ENVY repository is primarily used to store software components, but it can also store additional information, called *user fields*. User fields let end users or development tool builders associate additional information with components in the repository, which can be a powerful mechanism for system extensions. User fields can be associated with any of the basic ENVY components: configuration maps, (sub)applications, classes, compiled methods, and users. We can think of it as a dictionary for each component, with strings or symbols as keys and string values. As we'll see, we can work around the limitation to string values by storing the (string) output of an object serialization tool such as ENVY/Swapper or BOSS.

Types of User Fields

Two types of user fields exist — *inherited* and *local*. Local user fields are associated with one particular edition of a component. An example of a local user field is the notes, or description field of a component. Notes are a standard ENVY feature that let us annotate a particular version or edition (for example, Fixes Bug 1253994-g). The description is specific to the particular edition it's saved with, and won't be visible for earlier or later editions. In terms of the repository, we can think of each edition as having its own dictionary of local user fields. We can see notes in the browser by toggling the button in the lower-right corner.

Inherited user fields, in contrast, are created with a particular edition, but carry forward to all future editions based upon that edition. An example of an inherited user field is the comments field of a component. Viewed in the same area as notes, comments carry forward until they are changed. For example, "This class represents a multiple-choice response to a question." In terms of the repository, we can think of this as each edition having a dictionary of inherited user fields, but looking up keys in its previous editions if the information isn't stored locally. In fact, the implementation is more complex, and this occasionally shows through, as we will see later on.

All components support inherited user fields. Users, because they are not versioned, are the only component not supporting local user fields.

User Fields Protocol

User fields store only strings. The methods for storing and retrieving are simple, but you'll find some variation between components and among versions of ENVY. The basic protocol for inherited user fields is as follows, and applies to configuration maps, applications, subapplications, methods, and users:

- deleteInheritedUserFieldAt: aName — deletes the inherited user field named <aName> from the edition record of the component.

- inheritedUserFieldAt: aName — answers the contents of the inherited user field named <aName> in the edition of the component. If no such entry exists, returns the empty string.

- inheritedUserFieldAt: aName put: aString — sets the contents of the inherited user field <aName> in the edition record of the component to <aString>.

- inheritedUserFieldNames — answers a collection of strings, which are the inherited user field names in the edition record of the component.

The protocol varies slightly for classes because a class can be split up into multiple extensions, each of which can have different user fields. So, the protocol for classes takes an additional parameter for each method (for example, inheritedUserFieldAt:in:), passing along the (sub)application that contains the class edition.

Local User Fields

Local user fields are a little more complicated because the protocol is not as uniformly implemented. In recent versions of ENVY there is protocol analogous to that for inherited user fields. So,

- deleteLocalUserFieldAt: aName — deletes the local user field named <aName> from the edition record of the component.

- localUserFieldAt: aName — answers the contents of the inherited user field named <aName> in the edition of the component. If no such entry exists, returns the empty string.

- localUserFieldAt: aName put: aString — sets the contents of the inherited user field <aName> in the edition record of the component to <aString>.

- localUserFieldNames — answers a collection of strings, which are the inherited user field names in the edition record of the component.

Note, however, that users do not support local user fields because they are not versioned components. In older versions of ENVY (VisualWorks 3.0 is probably the most significant version still in current use) this protocol does not exist. It's still possible to access local user fields; it's just that the public protocol wasn't defined at the component level, so we would need to use record-level protocol. For examples of this, see the methods description and description: in the various component classes (description:in: and descriptionFrom: for Class).

Storing Objects

While user fields in the repository are limited to storing strings, we can also store arbitrary objects using an object serialization mechanism. ENVY even provides public protocol to do this transparently for us. If we use one of the following methods, the object is sent through the default serializer for the dialect (BOSS for VisualWorks, Swapper for VisualAge) and the resulting string is then stored in the user field.

- deleteObjectNamed: aName — deletes the inherited user field named <aName> from the component.

- objectNamed: aName — answers the object in the inherited user field named <aName> in the edition of the component. If no such entry exists, this method returns nil.

- storeObject: anObject as: aName — sets the contents of the inherited user field <aName> in the edition record of the component to <anObject>.

User Field Usage

How are user fields implemented in the repository? Internally, ENVY has a structure called a *disk dictionary* that can associate the keys and values. If a component supports both inherited and local user fields it has a file pointer for each of these fields, each pointing to a disk dictionary. When a new edition of a component is made, the file pointer for the local user fields is set to void (0), representing an empty set of user fields. The disk dictionary for inherited user fields is copied and reinserted into the library; the new edition points to this copy. This means that the semantics of inherited user fields are different from standard object-level inheritance. Rather than being a lookup in the dictionary of the parent component, the parent component's values are copied to the child when it's first created.

It's interesting to note that the fundamental ENVY library schema was established with the first version of ENVY and has not been modified since. To preserve both backward and forward compatibility, all subsequent extensions to the schema have been implemented as user fields. This enables older versions of ENVY to import, export, and clone components, which have been extended in ways the older version doesn't know about. These extensions include the following

- method categories/protocols
- required maps
- application attachments
- file attachments for ENVY/C

For more information on user fields, consult the ENVY documentation, and browse code that uses them in the image. Because many of the internal ENVY structures are represented with user fields, someone using this protocol can do significant damage to the library if he or she modifies fields that begin with "*EM" or similar prefixes. Be careful!

A Script Manager

One of the details that distinguishes Smalltalk as a programming environment is its capability to execute pieces of code without putting them into a larger program. This can take the form of "DoIts," workspaces with useful expressions, or the capability to execute fragments of a method in the debugger. One of the disadvantages of working this way is that the useful code fragments often get lost. The Script Manager goodie lets us keep code fragments in the ENVY repository, categorize them, and easily retrieve them. In addition to being a nifty tool, the implementation of the Script Manager illustrates working with user fields. We will focus primarily on the portions of the code that

Figure 9-1: The Script Manager

interface to ENVY because the user interface portion is dialect-specific, and not particularly related to ENVY. Figure 9-1 shows the Script Manager user interface.

In developing this tool, the one decision that made things click was to define an actual script class, called MedScript. We store the text associated with a script in the repository as user fields attached to an ENVY user. Scripts are logically grouped into folders. We don't create folders as objects, but rather have individual scripts remember the user and folder they are associated with.

```
Object subclass: #MedScript
    instanceVariableNames: 'user folder name text '
    classVariableNames: ''
    poolDictionaries: ''
```

We define class-side methods to create a new script and also to retrieve a script from the repository given a name and a user. The key we use to index the script in the repository is built up out of several components, modeled after the mechanism used for application attachments. We use a special nonprintable character to delimit the folder from the name, and a prefix to be sure no name conflicts occur with other user fields. The construction of this key is shown in Figure 9-2.

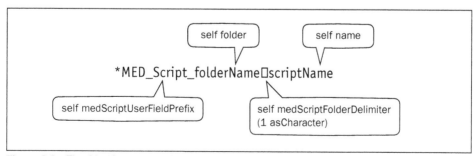

Figure 9-2: The MedScript user field key

Given the name, we can retrieve a script instance with the following code.

```
fromKey: aSymbol
    | index |
    index := aSymbol indexOf: self medScriptFolderDelimiter.
    folder := aSymbol
      copyFrom: (self medScriptUserFieldPrefix size + 1)
      to: index - 1.
    name := aSymbol copyFrom: index + 1 to: aSymbol size.
    text := user inheritedUserFieldAt: aSymbol.
```

```
medScriptFolderDelimiter
    ^1 asCharacter
```

```
medScriptUserFieldPrefix
    ^'*MED_Script_'
```

Basic Operations

We've shown the read operation, but we still need to handle creation, update, and delete. Delete is straightforward; we simply delete the user field.

```
delete
    user deleteInheritedUserFieldAt: self key
```

Creation and update are both the same. We simply save the script and delegate that work to the EmUser object.

```
save
    user
      storeScriptNamed: self name
      inFolder: folder
      script: self text
```

In EmUser, we add the following method.

```
storeScriptNamed: scriptName inFolder: folderName script: scriptString
    | stream userFieldName |
    stream := WriteStream on: ''.
    stream
      nextPutAll: self medScriptUserFieldPrefix;
      nextPutAll: folderName;
      nextPut: self medScriptFolderDelimiter;
      nextPutAll: scriptName.
    userFieldName := stream contents.
    self
      inheritedUserFieldAt: userFieldName
      put: scriptString.
```

One of the reasons we delegate this work to the EmUser object, and pass in our values as parameters, is to make it easier to change script folders and names.

changeFolderTo: newFolderName
```
    user
      storeScriptNamed: self name
      inFolder: newFolderName
      script: self text.
    self delete.
```

changeNameTo: newScriptName
```
    user
      storeScriptNamed: newScriptName
      inFolder: self folder
      script: self text.
    self delete.
```

In both cases we first store the script string under a new key, letting the user do the work of generating the proper key, and then delete the script stored under the current key. Many utility methods end up in the EmUser class because it has direct access to its user fields. To add a folder, for example, we insert a user field with the folder name as key, and an empty string as value. Most of the other methods should be self-explanatory.

addFolderNamed: aString
```
    | stream folderName |
    stream := WriteStream on: ''.
    stream
      nextPutAll: self medScriptUserFieldPrefix;
      nextPutAll: aString;
      nextPut: self medScriptFolderDelimiter.
    folderName := stream contents.
    self inheritedUserFieldAt: folderName put: ''.
```

allFolderNames
```
    ^(self allFolders collect: [:each | each folder])
      asSortedCollection
```

allFolders
```
    ^self allScripts select: [:each | each name isEmpty]
```

allMedScriptsBeginningWith: aString
```
    | scripts |
    scripts := self allScriptsBeginningWith: aString.
    ^self medScriptsFrom: scripts
```

allScriptNames
> ^(self record inheritedUserFields keys select: [:each |
>   each size > 12 and: [
>   (each copyFrom: 1 to: 12) =
>   self medScriptUserFieldPrefix]]) asSortedCollection

allScripts
> | scripts |
> scripts := self allScriptNames.
> ^self medScriptsFrom: scripts

allScriptsBeginningWith: aString
> ^self record inheritedUserFields keys select: [:each |
>   each size > aString size and: [
>   (each copyFrom: 1 to: aString size) = aString]]

deleteFolderNamed: aString
> | folderName |
> folderName := self medScriptUserFieldPrefix , aString.
> (self allScriptsBeginningWith: folderName) do: [:each |
>   self deleteInheritedUserFieldAt: each].

medScriptsFrom: aCollection
> ^aCollection collect: [:each | MedScript user: self key: each]

scriptsInFolder: aString
> ^self allScripts select: [:each |
>   each folder = aString and: [each name notEmpty]]

scriptsInFolders: aCollection
> ^self allScripts select: [:each |
>   (aCollection includes: each folder) and: [
>   each name notEmpty]]

Summary

We've taken a detailed look at an application that uses user fields to keep track of scripts on a per-user basis. It illustrates storing the user fields, grouping them into folders, and managing and retrieving them. While this is a simple example, user fields provide the potential to extend ENVY in many different ways.

ENVY Programming Concepts

These next few sections look at manipulating ENVY structures in considerable detail. Before we dive in, we should talk about some of the internal mechanisms ENVY uses to manipulate software components. Some of these are partially exposed to the user, and some of them are almost completely hidden, but anyone doing tool-building will need to understand at least the terminology of these objects.

This protocol is primarily intended for use by the ENVY browsers and system classes, and for the most part is not clean, well-documented public protocol. Expect to run into hidden source code and some peculiar behavior.

The Browsers

At the user level, all ENVY manipulations go through the browsers. Far more than just a GUI, these browsers contain a lot of important code. If we're programming with ENVY, it's important to understand the browsers.

Essentially, each different browser in the user interface has a corresponding browser class. These are in a deeply nested inheritance hierarchy, underneath EtWindow. These browsers have existed for a long time, and their UI framework is significantly different in places from current Smalltalk frameworks. In VisualAge, these are built at the raw IBM Smalltalk level, using the Common Widgets library and direct hooking of callbacks. In VisualWorks they vary by version. In Version 3.0 and earlier they were built with basic MVC rather than as ApplicationModels, which led to some peculiar behavior. In ENVY for VisualWorks 5i they are now implemented as ApplicationModels, but the widgets are still created and assembled in code rather than from a windowSpec.

To open a browser, we don't explicitly reference the class name. Instead, we create a browser using the expression

```
EtTools browser: <browserSymbol>
```

and then set the ENVY objects it is to browse using some variation of the on: method. For example,

```
((EtTools browser: #methods)
on: aCollectionOfCompiledMethods
    labeled: 'a bunch of methods') open.
```

or

```
((EtTools browser: #class)
on: aClass in: aClass controller) open
```

Toolsmiths often do a lot of work with the browsers, adding menu items, possibly creating new browsers, and so forth. The browsers are also a great resource of information about the system. Because the internals of ENVY are largely undocumented, and much of the source is hidden, it's not exactly easy to figure out what's going on. If we need to implement some functionality, one of the first things we can do is think about similar system functionality. The browser code isn't hidden, so if we can find a method in the browser that is close to what we want to do, that's a valuable starting point.

Finally, the browsers provide a lot of utility functions. For example, EtBrowser implements a variety of prompt: instance methods that are very useful when writing tools that interact with the user. Unfortunately, to use these methods you have to have an instance of a browser to work with, which isn't always convenient. We've made many of these functions available in a more standalone form, as described in "Prompter Utilities."

Timestamps, Versions, and Editions

ENVY identifies components in the library in a variety of ways, but the common factor in all cases is the creation time of that component, represented as an instance of EmTimeStamp.

An EmTimeStamp is the thing that uniquely identifies an edition or a version, by both time of creation and version name. In fact, even though it's called a timestamp, it stores both a timestamp and a version name.

```
Magnitude
    subclass: #EmTimeStamp
    instanceVariableNames: 'seconds versionName'
```

In this class, the seconds instance variable represents an integer number of seconds since the arbitrary zero time of January 1, 1901. This value is set at creation time, and never changes throughout the life of the component. It's also guaranteed to be unique for that particular component. If ENVY ever detects that the timestamp it wants to use is already in use for that component type and name, it will add one-second increments to it until it finds an unused value.

The versionName instance variable represents the name of the version for this component. If this attribute is nil, the component is an open edition. So, if we have an existing version and create a new edition from it, we're creating a new copy of that component, which has a new timestamp and no version name. When we make a version from that edition, the system does it by setting the versionName, which doesn't create a new component, but merely marks the existing component as a version.

Note that every component always has a timestamp. Even a component that does not exist in the current image has the special timestamp Undefined, represented by a timestamp with zero in the seconds instance variable.

Application Classes

One of the things that's confusing for ENVY beginners is that every application and subapplication has a corresponding class, which has the same name as that (sub)application; for example, the application Kernel contains a class called Kernel. We refer to these classes, both for applications and subapplications, as *application classes*. In general, throughout this section we will use the term *application* to mean both applications and subapplications. For more information on application classes, see "Application Classes" later in this chapter.

While application classes are confusing they are also very powerful because they let us easily define methods to control application-level behavior. At the user level, we use these methods to control application loading and unloading. At the programming level we use these classes to manipulate the application itself. Using this class, we can control released classes, configuration expressions, prerequisites, and almost anything else about the application.

Unfortunately, this mechanism is even more confusing at the system programming level than it is for beginners. When dealing with application classes, you have several things to bear in mind:

- These are classes, not instances. Almost everything is done with class methods.

- SubApplication is the superclass of Application. Most of the useful methods are defined in SubApplication and inherited by Application as well as by the actual application classes.

- Very few methods are sent directly to Application or SubApplication. They are inherited and apply to the actual application or to a shadow.

- These classes have several different meanings, depending on how they are used. To understand some of the methods, we need to know how the class is being used. Some methods treat the application class as a factory for retrieving information about the editions of the application (for example, allClassNames, shadows). However, the application class can also represent a particular edition, and other methods access information relevant only to that one edition (for example, addConfigurationExpression:). Finally, some methods treat the application class as a class, not as a stand-in for the application (for example, loaded, removing).

Shadows

Any time the application is loaded there will be a corresponding application class in memory. That class represents the currently loaded edition of the application, and we can use it to manipulate that application edition in the repository.

How do we manipulate other editions of that application? Even worse, how do we manipulate applications that aren't loaded at all? The answer is that we use shadows. We've already seen shadows at the user level in the various editions and shadow browsers. Now we'll see how to manipulate them programmatically.

A shadow is simply an object representing a component as it exists in the repository, rather than as it may exist in memory. In memory, we see a shadow as an instance of one of these shadow classes: EmShadowClass, EmShadowApplication, EmShadowSubApplication, EmShadowCompiledMethod, and EmShadowMetaclass. These classes are not related by inheritance, and instead are subclasses of the items they shadow. For example, EmShadowClass is a subclass of Class. This leads to some duplication of code among shadow classes, but makes it easy for them to accurately reflect the items they represent.

Getting a Shadow

It's easy to obtain a shadow; just ask the appropriate component. For example, we can ask an application for shadows of its classes.

    QuestionModelling classEditionsFor: #Question

Similarly, we can get application shadows by asking the application class for them.

    QuestionUI shadows

For methods, we ask the appropriate class shadow, exactly as if it were a class.

    (QuestionModelling classEditionsFor: #Question) first
        methodDictionary at: #printOn:

No shadow class exists for configuration maps because they never exist as objects in memory. Effectively, the only representation of configuration maps is as a shadow. We can get an instance of EmConfigurationMap with

    EmConfigurationMap editionsFor: 'Questionnaire'

Just because a component is resident doesn't mean we can't get a shadow for it. For example, if we wrote

    (CLDT classEditionsFor: #Object) first

we only expect a single version of the class Object to have been shipped with the base system, and it's almost certainly resident in memory. Nevertheless, we have a shadow of it, and can manipulate its representation in the repository without affecting the copy currently in memory. Figure 9-3 shows a class version in the repository with two copies of that version in an image. One is a resident class that has been loaded, and the other is a shadow. Both reflect the same version.

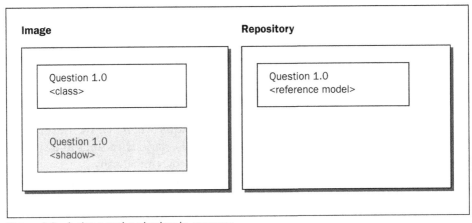

Figure 9-3: A class and a shadow in memory

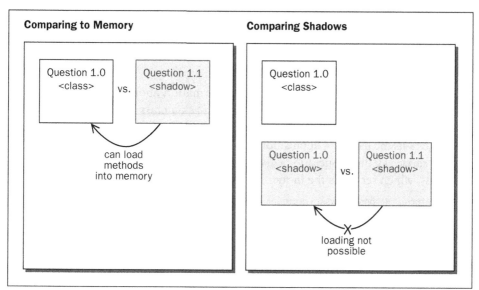

Figure 9-4: Comparing against memory *versus* comparing shadows

We can see a side-effect of this when using differences browsers. If we browse differences from the Application Manager or VisualAge Organizer we get different behavior than if we browse differences from an editions browser. From the Manager/Organizer, we have the option to browse differences between the edition in memory of the selected component(s) and some other edition. This gives us a differences browser, and we can do a merge operation using the load alternatives menu option to load different methods.

On the other hand, if we use an editions browser we can compare two arbitrary editions of components but the resulting differences browser always has the loading options disabled. They're disabled even if one of the two editions we're comparing is currently loaded in memory.

The reason this happens is related to the difference between shadows and resident editions. In the first case, the system knows that it's comparing against what's in memory, so it can always load code into the resident edition. In the second case, neither edition might be loaded, so the system can't assume that loading methods will work. In fact, the system just goes to the repository and gets a shadow of each edition, without checking whether one of them is also loaded or not. This means that when we're comparing two editions from an editions browser, we're always looking at the repository version (in the rare case of an inconsistency between memory and the repository this might be important) and we can never load methods. Figure 9-4 illustrates this difference.

Applications, Classes, and Extensions

When manipulating classes in ENVY, applications also play an important role. Recall that in ENVY a class can be split into a base and multiple extensions, each in a separate application. In memory, though, there's only a single object to represent the class. This means that, for most ENVY operations involving classes, it's not enough to specify just the class or its name; we also need to tell ENVY which application we want to perform this manipulation in. For example, to print a class with its version/edition information, we can use this method.

Object signatureIn: Core -> 'Object V 5.0'

For classes in memory, we can find out information about the applications that define code for that class. For example, we can ask a class for its controller, which gives us the application containing the definition. We can also ask for applications, which gives us the list of all applications containing the definition or extensions. Note that when we say these operations give us the application, they give us the application class, which serves as the in-memory representation of that application.

EtAbstractMethodsBrowser controller => EtDevelopment

EtAbstractMethodsBrowser applications =>(EtDevelopment EtToolsVendorExtensionsApp ...)

Note that we get different results if we ask a shadow the same questions. Each class extension is represented by a different shadow, so its controller is the application that controls this class definition or extension.

| shadow |
shadow := (EtToolsVendorExtensionsApp
    classEditionsFor: #EtAbstractMethodsBrowser) first.
shadow controller => EtToolsVendorExtensionsApp.
shadow applications => (EtToolsVendorExtensionsApp)

Class Protocol

Here's a quick summary of some of the protocol that's useful for dealing with application and class shadows. Much more than this is available, of course, but we've concentrated on those that are most commonly useful and/or most difficult to use. For more information on ENVY protocol, see the appendix and the diagram on the inside back cover. Unless specified these are all class methods for application classes and their shadows. Note that in many cases it makes a difference whether we're sending this to the resident component or a shadow. Typically messages sent to the resident component can return other resident components, whereas methods sent to a shadow will return shadows.

- defined — all the classes with definitions contained in this edition of the application. Returns either classes or class shadows.

- extended — all the classes with extensions contained in this edition of the application. Returns either classes or class shadows.

- classes — all defined and extended classes. Returns either classes or class shadows.

- allClassNames — the names of all defined and extended classes. Returns symbols.

- availableClassNames — the names of classes released in other editions, but not in this one. Returns symbols.

- timeStamps — a dictionary mapping from class names to the timestamp of the currently loaded version of that class in this application.

- releasedClassVersions — a dictionary mapping from class names to the timestamp of the released version of that class in this application. For a shadow, timeStamps and releasedClassVersions will return the same values. For a resident application they may be different.

- classEditionsFor: aSymbol — returns a collection of the class editions (shadows) by that name, sorted by timestamp.

- classEditionNamed: aSymbol at: aTimestamp — returns a shadow of the edition of the named class in this application and corresponding to the timestamp. If no corresponding edition exists, it will return a shadow with timestamp Undefined.

- EmInterface current releasedTimeStampFor: aClass in: anApplication — the current released timestamp for a particular class. This isn't available as direct protocol on the application, but can be accessed through the EmInterface.

- EmInterface current previousVersionOf: aClass in: anApplication — returns the previous version of the class in the given application. This isn't available as direct protocol on the application, but can be accessed through the EmInterface.

- visibleEditionsFor: aClassName — returns all editions of the class loadable for the current user.

- EmClassDevelopment imageBuilder loadClasses: classShadowsArray — loads the given classes. Returns nil on failure.

Application Protocol

For dealing with applications themselves, there's protocol to deal with shadows, subapplications, and loading. These methods can vary between dialects.

- shadows — shadows for all editions of this application.

- residentApplication — returns the resident application, if one exists. This is useful if we don't know whether we have the resident application or a shadow.

- System loadedApplications — returns all applications (but not subapplications) currently loaded in the image. Returns resident applications, not shadows.

- System loadedSubApplications — returns all applications and subapplications currently loaded in the image. Returns resident applications, not shadows.

- Application currentlyLoaded — returns all applications (but not subapplications) currently loaded in the image. Returns resident applications, not shadows.

- SubApplication currentlyLoaded — returns all applications and subapplications currently loaded in the image. Returns resident applications, not shadows.

- EmClassDevelopment imageBuilder loadApplications: arrayOfApplicationShadows — loads the given applications. Returns nil on failure.

Method Protocol

The protocol for dealing with method editions is much simpler, but a few important methods exist.

- Class>>methodsIn: anApplication — returns all the methods in this class contained in the application. Clearly, this method needs to be based on a particular edition of the class, and if the class and application edition are different, it will use the class information. In fact, it doesn't matter at all which edition of the application we use because only the name is used.

- CompiledMethod>>application — for this method edition, returns the application that contains it.

- CompiledMethod>>load — loads this method edition.

Working with Shadows

Once we have a shadow we can manipulate it in many of the same ways we manipulate a real component. Because the shadow inherits from the item it shadows, it has all the attributes of the real thing, although many of them won't be populated, or might be loaded only on demand. For example, a shadow class has a nil method dictionary that will only be loaded if we explicitly ask for it by sending the methodDictionary method.

Shadows can be confusing to work with, particularly shadow classes. One issue is that the normal Smalltalk techniques of manipulating objects in inspectors don't work as well for shadows. First, looking at the fields of the shadow directly doesn't trigger lazy loading, so we have to remember to send methods to them. Worse, evaluating code on class shadows doesn't work unless we're careful.

Consider the expression we use to find a method edition:

```
(QuestionModelling classEditionsFor: #Question) first
    methodDictionary at: #printOn:
```

This works fine if it's executed as a single DoIt. It will also work if we break it up into two expressions and execute them separately in a workspace. First, we'll declare a global variable to store our result. Using globals is bad practice in general, but we're just using it to experiment.

```
Smalltalk declareVariable: #AGlobal.
```

Now let's assign the first part of the expression into the global.

```
AGlobal:=(QuestionModelling classEditionsFor: #Question) first.
```

We evaluate the preceding expression, then, as a separate DoIt, evaluate the following.

```
AGlobal methodDictionary at: #printOn:
```

This works too. But, if we didn't use a global and instead opened an inspector on the result of the first expression, and then evaluated the second expression in the inspector, we'll get a primitive failure trying to execute the compiled version of the DoIt. Actually, it will fail regardless of whether we reference self in the expression or use TempGlobal. See Figure 9-5.

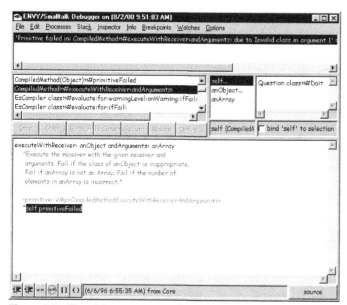

Figure 9-5: The debugger we get from evaluating an expression against a class shadow in an inspector

What's really peculiar is that this will work if we break it up slightly differently:

    (QuestionModelling classEditionsFor: #Question) inspect.

and then in the inspector evaluate

    self first methodDictionary at: #printOn:

The reason for this failure is interesting, and goes back to Smalltalk history. Historically, the original Smalltalk implementations executed fragments of code by compiling them into a method called "DoIt," installing that method into the method dictionary, invoking the method, and then removing it from the method dictionary. If we were evaluating the code in a workspace, the method would be compiled into UndefinedObject. If we were evaluating the code in an inspector, it would be compiled into the class of the object we were inspecting.

This worked, but it had some problems. Multiple simultaneous DoIts could interfere with each other, and cleanup wasn't necessarily reliable. Every once in a while you'd find methods called DoIt, which had been inserted by the system into your classes. Squeak Smalltalk still uses this mechanism today, but both VisualAge and VisualWorks have moved away from it. These dialects support the capability to execute a compiled method against a particular object without having to install it into the method dictionary. They still compile the code into a method and execute it, but without installing it into the class.

So, what does this have to do with the primitive failure?

Well, a shadow doesn't represent the currently loaded version; it represents the version in the repository. This includes everything about the class: the definition, the instance methods, and the class methods. In Smalltalk, class methods aren't stored

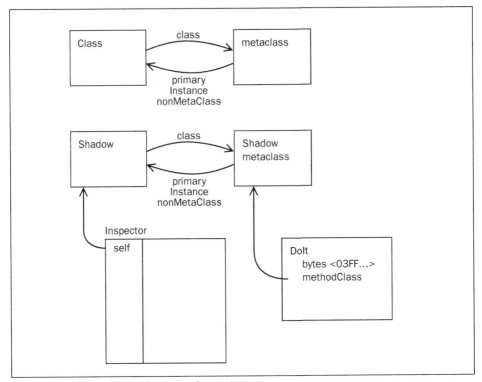

Figure 9-6: What's happening in the inspector

with the class; they're stored with the metaclass. So, if you ask a shadow for its class, the right thing for it to do, from a version-control perspective, is to answer a shadow of its metaclass. This is exactly what happens.

Unfortunately, when you execute code in the inspector, it asks the object in the inspector (which looks like a class) for its class, so it can serve as a context in which to compile the DoIt. The shadow class answers its shadow metaclass, and the expression is compiled there. Now, when we go to execute the DoIt, the class in which it was compiled does not match the class in which it is being executed, and so we get a primitive failure. Figure 9-6 shows these objects and their relationships.

This problem only applies to the compilation process in an inspector. That's why it works if we evaluate these expressions in a workspace. When we break the expression up so that we're inspecting an array rather than a shadow, it also works because it's a real array, and there's nothing peculiar about its class.

By itself this is just a minor quirk, but it illustrates the difficulties we can run into when we try to manipulate shadows. Things don't always work the way we'd intuitively expect, and we shouldn't be surprised or discouraged by these kinds of odd behavior.

Identifying Shadows
One of the biggest problems in working with shadows is keeping track of them. Because shadows look so much like classes, it can be difficult to identify shadows and keep track of which is which.

For example, consider the expression

QuestionModelling classEditionsFor: #Question

which evaluates to

SortedCollection(Question Question Question)

This is a collection of class shadows, but because the shadow inherits from Class, its printString is just its name. We have to inspect the shadows and notice their additional variables in order to determine that they are actually shadows. The only way to tell which shadow it is is to look at the timestamp attribute. Even the printString of a timestamp shows only the date/time information, so to see the version name we have to inspect the timestamp itself. This can make debugging code that works with shadows quite difficult.

One useful tip is how to tell a shadow class from a resident class without inspecting the fields in detail. One way is just to evaluate the expression

aClass class class

For a normal class, the answer is Metaclass. For a shadow, it is EmShadowMetaclass.

Shadow Cache

Finally, note that shadows don't stay in memory indefinitely. ENVY maintains a cache of shadows that have been read from the repository. As long as a shadow remains in this cache it will respond properly to methods, but as soon as anyone sends EmInterface>flushCache, those shadows will be invalid and will stop working. Because the system may flush caches at arbitrary points, we shouldn't rely on shadows staying around for a long time.

We can control the cache to some extent using some of the ENVY API. This is particularly useful if we want to speed up an operation that repeatedly accesses many of the same editions. We can do this by executing our code inside a block that is passed to the following method:

EmLibraryCache cacheEditionsWhileExecuting: [ ]

System and EmInterface

Two other useful objects are worth knowing about in writing ENVY code. The first is the System object, and the second is EmInterface.

Even in relatively straightforward ENVY usage we run into the System object (ENVY.System in VisualWorks 5i). This is a global variable holding an instance of the class EmSystemConfiguration. It provides an interface to otherwise unclassified system capabilities. These include the following:

- Portable dialog boxes (confirm:, prompt:, and so on)
- Global system startup/shutdown hooks
- Finding loaded applications/subapplications
- Identifying the VM and version of ENVY
- Opening system browsers

In general, System is the first place to look for ENVY functionality without an obvious home.

EmInterface is the primary low-level mechanism for talking to the repository. It's mostly internal to ENVY, and it's less likely that we'll need to use this, but occasionally code needs to use EmInterface to get at functionality that is otherwise unavailable. For example, the shadow protocol listed previously includes EmInterface methods to find the released timestamp or the previous version of a class.

EmInterface contains instance methods for the singleton instance, available as follows:

```
EmInterface current
```

Transactions

The ENVY repository is a transactional data store. This is very important for maintaining the integrity of the version information, but most of the time it doesn't matter to us. As an end user, we'll encounter transactions only when something goes wrong and we see an error message about "incorrect use of the transaction protocol." Even when writing basic tools, we mostly call methods that have their own self-contained transaction logic. So, while it's important to be aware of the transactions, it's unlikely we'll need to manipulate them.

Three-Way Differences

Now that we know about the ENVY browsers and the components they manipulate, what can we do with the information? This section describes an example of extending the system by adding a three-way differences browser. This extends the normal ENVY differencing capability to enable a three-way comparison and merge, along with a more sophisticated user interface to support that. We'll see the usage, the internals, and the process of building this browser as an illustration of ENVY tool building. Aside from being a useful addition, this tool is interesting because it does a great deal of manipulating shadows in some very complex ways. Figure 9-7 shows the browser, running under VisualAge.

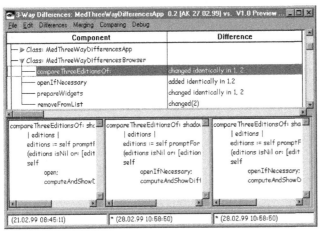

Figure 9-7: The three-way differences browser

What Do You Mean, Three-Way Differences?

The obvious questions about a three-way differences tool are "What does it actually do?" and "Why would I ever need that?" The best way to answer these questions is to look at how you use differences in practice. You'll encounter two main cases.

- **Compare what's changed between two versions in a single stream.** For example, if a bug was fixed between Version 1.1 and Version 1.2 we might browse the differences between them to see what code was affected. In this case, the normal two-way differences are appropriate.

- **Combine two different streams.** At the lowest level, this might be a single class that has been changed by two different developers. To merge the changes, we need to know what each developer did relative to the original version, and what they did relative to each other. This gives us three versions to compare: a base and two different streams derived from it. This also applies at the larger scales of applications and configuration maps. Figure 9-8 illustrates this case, showing a base version and two different derived versions for the class Question.

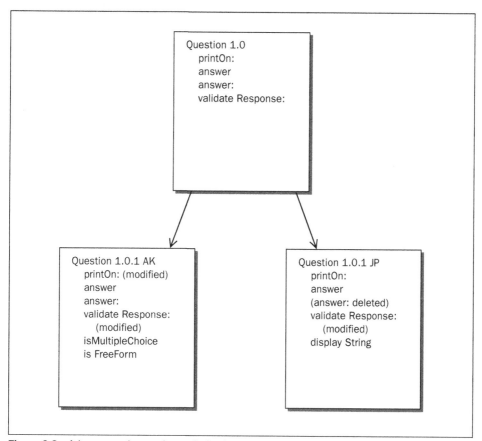

Figure 9-8: A base version and two derived versions

The first case is handled well by the existing changes browsers, but the second is not. If the two variations are directly derived from the same base, we can get an idea of the changes by comparing them against each other, but we often need to pull up other browsers and it can become very confusing. For example, if the text of a method is different between stream A and stream B, does that mean that it was modified in A, modified in B, or modified in both?

Representing Differences

Assuming we believe three-way differences are a good idea, how do we implement it? The most obvious approach is to subclass or otherwise extend the existing differences browser. There's no point writing something new if something existing can do the job. Unfortunately, the existing browsers don't extend well to multiway differences.

The basic browser is EtChangesBrowser. This represents differences between one or more classes. One set of classes is designated as *current*. If we're comparing resident classes against shadows, then the resident classes will be current. If we're comparing two sets of shadows, then whichever was selected first will be considered current. The differences are stored in a differences instance variable, which is a dictionary mapping from the current classes to *difference shadows* between the current edition and the noncurrent edition.

A difference shadow is a way of representing the method-level differences between two class editions. It's another class shadow, but one that doesn't correspond to any existing class edition. Instead, it's based on two different class editions and only methods that are different between these two will appear in the difference shadow. In computing the differences, one of these editions is treated as current, and when there's a difference, the noncurrent edition of that method appears in the difference shadow. When a method does not exist in the noncurrent edition, it appears in the difference shadow with the special timestamp of Undefined. Figure 9-9 shows two different versions and the difference shadow that would be generated by treating Version 1.1 as current and comparing it against Version 1.0.

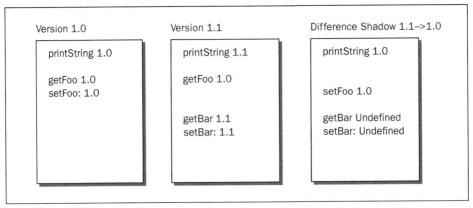

Figure 9-9: A difference shadow

This structure works, but it's very closely tied to the idea of two-way differences. What do we do when two noncurrent versions exist? We could create two different difference shadows, and merge the result into a new structure representing the three-way differences. We can certainly create the difference shadows using

> aClassEdition
>> loadDifferencesFrom: anotherClassEdition
>> in: anApplication

but the merge operation isn't going to be simple, and we're going to need a new structure for the result anyway. Instead of working with difference shadows, let's just create something entirely new and compute the differences ourselves.

So, what do we need in this new structure? We start with a tree of components: configuration maps that contain applications (and possibly a hierarchy of subapplications) that contain classes that contain methods. We need to take three such trees and iterate through the corresponding components in each one, creating a new tree that represents the differences.

It's going to be confusing dealing with three different component trees, so we need to choose some consistent names. Because this browser is primarily intended for the case where we're merging two streams that have diverged from a common base, let's call them

> Base   Stream One   Stream Two

This also suggests the capability to refer to the streams by number, as 0, 1, and 2 respectively. Starting from zero is a little C-like and not something I normally approve of, but in this case it's done to be consistent with human terminology rather than machines, so let's keep it.

We'll need a class representing an individual difference, called MedDifferenceItem, and we'll need a hierarchy of these difference items. In fact, let's use the Composite pattern and create a different kind of difference item for each type of component. We can nest the difference items in a tree that mirrors the component structure. To share behavior, we'll have an abstract superclass for all of them and have the capability to have both compound items (those with children) and leaf items (without children).

We'll need at least the following information:

- name <String> — the name of the component whose differences this represents
- children <SortedCollection> — the differences for our subcomponents, ordered by name (for compound items only)
- parent <MedDifferenceItem | nil> — the parent difference that contains us
- base, streamOne, streamTwo <?> — a specification of the component editions whose difference we represent

Hmmm. We seem to have a problem here. How exactly do we specify which editions we want to difference? Clearly, we could provide shadows, but that introduces other issues. Shadows are very tightly tied to the particular image and library. We can't ever save our list of differences to a file, shadows are tricky to manipulate, and they're hard to create. It would be nice if we could store a simple specification of a component, without it trying to be the component.

Library Specs (Aside)

Smalltalk is a peculiar language. It's very simple; people often talk about how simple the syntax is and how absolutely everything is done by sending messages to objects. The thing is, Smalltalk is *so* simple that we don't even have a way of defining classes or methods in the language. It's all done in terms of sending messages to other objects.

"Normal" computer languages have a meta model represented by the textual form of a program (and they typically throw that model away at run-time). Smalltalk is unusual in that its primary representation is nontextual. A Smalltalk program is defined by a collection of Smalltalk objects in an image, and we create and modify that program by sending messages to those objects. The compiled form of a Smalltalk program is its own meta model, and we don't discard it at run-time. In fact, even the distinction between compile-time and run-time can be vague.

Now, this doesn't mean Smalltalk programs are tied to an image; we can save them into file-out formats, parcels, ENVY export files, ICs, or other representations. The thing is, these are interchange formats. No one writes programs by manipulating these external representations, and it's generally understood that the "real" program is the classes and methods in memory. How do we represent a method in Smalltalk? With a method object, of course.

These ideas carry over into ENVY. When we go to the database to ask for a class or a method, what do we get back? A "shadow." What's a shadow? It's a representation of the programming language construct we want to see, but one that also "is" the programming construct with the same variables and methods as the real thing. This is very powerful, but it can be confusing because we're not used to the idea that we can see and manipulate a class in the image in certain ways, but that the class is still not loaded and somehow not fully real.

Representing versions of objects as the objects themselves can also be a problem because it imposes limits on what we can do with these objects. Shadows become quite heavyweight, are difficult to represent outside of the image, and are subject to arbitrary system actions without warning (for example, flushing the shadow cache). In some circumstances, it would be very nice to be able to represent an arbitrary ENVY software component in a lightweight external way.

Fortunately, we can do this easily by introducing the idea of a specification object, which we call a "Library Spec." This is a simple object, which holds just enough information to be able to retrieve the corresponding component from the library. The original idea for library specs comes from the Bytesmiths Toolkit (formerly available at *www.bytesmiths.com*; for current availability information see the book's Web site). It includes these specifications as a literal array containing the information needed to specify certain components in the library. By extending this idea to a larger range of components and turning specs into full objects we can represent all the components we need in a simple and compact format. This has applications well outside of the three-way differences, but we're going to use it extensively here, and this application motivates the specific features. We also provide compatibility protocol to convert library specs to and from their Bytesmiths Toolkit representation.

So What's in a Library Spec?

A library spec has to contain enough information to uniquely identify a component edition in the library. That information differs by component. The most basic information is the timestamp, which every component needs. For others, the information varies as follows:

- **Configuration Map** — name + configuration map timestamp
- **Application** — name + isSubApplication flag + application timestamp
- **Class** — Application name + isSubApplication flag + class name + class timestamp
- **Method** — Application name + isSubApplication flag + class name + method name + instance/class method flag + method timestamp

At any level, we are effectively specifying the parent component (without a version) plus a name and timestamp for the child component, and any component-specific information needed to uniquely identify it (for example, is this a class or instance method?). We'll need to create a spec class for each type of component, plus an abstract superclass for common behavior.

Library Spec Methods

What do we need from these library specs? First, we need to be able to get the component edition they identify.

- asComponent — returns a shadow for the component edition, which this spec represents.

It'll also be useful to be able to navigate around from this component. That is, we may want to ask for the specification of the parent component, omit or ignore the timestamp so that we get all editions of this component, and construct specifications for child components. To get a flavor of the implementation, let's consider MedClassSpec and look at of some of these methods.

The asComponent method isn't interesting because it simply delegates to the appropriate other "as..." method.

asComponent
```
^self asClass.
```

The real work is done in asClass, which finds and returns the corresponding class shadow. Note that we have to be a little bit careful with our variable and method naming. Methods with names such as class and timeStamp are dangerous because they conflict with the basic Smalltalk system or with ENVY, so we choose unambiguous names like classSymbol and envyTimeStamp.

asClass
```
^self asApplication
  classEditionNamed: self classSymbol
  at: self envyTimeStamp.
```

We implement asClass using asApplication, which ignores the timestamp and returns some edition of the application that contains this class. Because it's fastest to get the resident application, we'll do that if possible.

asApplication
```
| existing |
existing := self asResidentApplication.
existing isNil ifFalse: [^existing].
^self matchingApplications first.
```

If the application isn't found, we need to look it up in the repository. We abstract out classToUseForShadows, which will return either SubApplication or Application as appropriate. The shadowsFor: method is the same as asking an application for its shadows, but can be used for an application that is not resident.

matchingApplications
```
^self classToUseForShadows shadowsFor: self appName.
```

We can also ask for the resident class. This shows the simplest version, although both VisualWorks and VisualAge now include some form of namespaces and/or cross-development tools, which makes this a little bit more complicated for classes that don't reside in the main namespace.

asResidentClass
```
^Smalltalk classAt: self classSymbol ifAbsent: [nil].
```

We also need to be able to create the appropriate specifications. Ideally, we could create them easily from objects in memory, but we should also be able to easily specify a component that is not resident. So, for example, we can create a class spec from a resident class using the following method.

forApplication: anApplication class: aClass
```
^(MedClassSpec new)
  isSubApp: anApplication isSubApplication;
  appName: anApplication name;
  classSymbol: aClass name;
  timeStampInSeconds: (aClass timeStampIn: app) seconds
```

This is convenient because the components are in memory, so we can specify the minimal information and have other required information computed based on the components. If we want to create a specification for a component that is not in memory, or just create specifications more efficiently when we already have the information, we can use a more direct form.

```
forApplicationNamed: appName
    isSubApp: isSubApp
    className: className
    timeStamp: aTimeStamp
        ^(MedClassSpec new)
        isSubApp: isSubApp;
        appName: appName;
        classSymbol: className;
        timeStampInSeconds: (aTimeStamp isNil
            ifTrue: [0]
            ifFalse: [aTimeStamp seconds])
```

Of course we can use these to compute the parent and child specifications for a class spec.

```
parentSpec
    ^MedLibrarySpec
        forApplicationNamed: self appName
        isSubApp: isSubApp
        timeStamp: nil

asMethodSpecForSelector: aSelector
atTime: envyTimeStamp
isInstanceMethod: aBoolean
    ^MedLibrarySpec
        forApplicationNamed: self appName
        isSubApp: isSubApp
        className: self classSymbol
        selector: aSelector
        isInstanceMethod: aBoolean
        timeStamp: envyTimeStamp
```

There are, of course, corresponding methods for the other specification classes, and additional methods in MedClassSpec, but this example illustrates most of the implementation issues. One point worth noting is the implementation of asApplication in MedApplicationSpec. Finding the shadow is relatively straightforward, but if this spec specifies a resident component, we return that component instead. This is particularly important for applications because the resident application will often contain classes that have not been released. If we return the shadow, it will contain only the released versions, rather than new work currently in memory. This will be important when we use the library specs to implement differencing because we want to be able to compare against items in memory.

asApplication
```
| shadow resident |
shadow := self classToUseForShadows
named: self appName
timeStamp: self envyTimeStamp.
resident := shadow residentApplication.
resident isNil ifTrue: [^shadow].
^resident timeStamp seconds = self timeStampInSeconds
  ifTrue: [resident]
  ifFalse: [shadow]
```

Complete code for all of the library spec classes is included in MedLibrarySpecsApp, which is part of the Mastering ENVY/Developer Three-Way Differences Browser configuration map.

Difference Items

That was an interesting side trip, but recall that the problem we were trying to solve was how to represent a tree of three-way differences. Now that we have library specs, it seems like the simplest way to specify the various streams in a difference item is using library specs.

- base, streamOne, streamTwo <MedLibrarySpec> — a specification of the component editions whose difference we represent.

These difference items have two main roles. The first is to actually compute the tree of differences. We'd like to be able to specify a top-level item to compare and then let it compute its own subdifferences. That's complicated, so let's skip over it for the moment. Assuming we've created the tree of differences, what does the browser need from a difference item? Essentially, just the capability to navigate in the tree, to display and compare the source code for particular items, and to load appropriate editions. Navigation in the tree should be easy once we've built it. In addition, we'll need access to source code, which we'll probably want to cache because it's expensive to retrieve and will be frequently used when we're comparing differences. Let's add attributes for the source strings.

- baseSource, streamOneSource, streamTwoSource <String> — the source code for the component editions we represent.

We'd also like an abstract way of asking any difference, regardless of type, for its source code. So, we add methods like the following:

streamOneSource
```
streamOneSource isNil ifTrue: [
  streamOneSource := self findSourceInStream: 1].
^streamOneSource.
```

The implementation of findSourceInStream: varies according to the type of component. In most cases we can just ask a shadow for its source using an appropriate method, but we may also have to handle special cases. For example,

findSourceInStream: streamNumber
    | shadow |
    shadow := self shadowNumber: streamNumber.
    shadow isNil ifTrue: [^'*Undefined*'].
    ^shadow definitionString.

Of course, shadowNumber: is easily implemented in terms of the library specs.

shadowNumber: streamNumber
    | spec |
    spec := self specNumber: streamNumber.
    ^spec isNil
      ifTrue: [nil]
      ifFalse: [spec asComponent].

Finally, we can also ask a difference item for the timestamp of any of its streams (which might be the special Undefined timestamp). This is accomplished simply by asking the appropriate spec for its timestamp.

Computing Differences

We conveniently skipped over actually calculating the differences. In fact, it turns out that this isn't too difficult once we can navigate around within the appropriate components. For example, at the class level we can define the buildDifferences method as follows.

buildDifferences
    | differentMethods |
    differentMethods := self findDifferentInstanceMethods.
    differentMethods do: [:each | self addDifference: each].
    differentMethods := self findDifferentClassMethods.
    differentMethods do: [:each | self addDifference: each].

Actually Computing Differences

Okay, so buildDifferences is a simple method, but it mostly just delegates to findDifferentInstanceMethods. How does that work? That will be component-type specific. The ways two configuration maps can be different aren't the same as the ways two applications can be different, which aren't the same as the ways two classes can be different.

At each level in the component hierarchy we have a different way of dealing with subcomponents, but in many cases the basic idea is the same. This leads us to try and parameterize the operations, using a bit of reflection. We expect to be able to compute a dictionary mapping from component names to their timestamps in a particular stream, and to compute the specific differences for those components. These are passed in as method selectors, which we then perform. So, we calculate these name->timestamp dictionaries for all three streams, and build the set of all component names that appear in any of the streams. Then, for each component name, we calculate the subdifferences for the three timestamps, passing nil for the timestamp if that component doesn't appear in a particular stream.

This method looks very complicated, but in essence all it's doing is finding the three timestamps, checking if they're the same, and if they're not, noting the difference and invoking another method to calculate the subdifferences.

findDifferentSubComponents: timeStampSelector
buildDifferenceUsing: buildDifferenceSelector

```
| base s1 s2 allNames allDifferences |
base := self perform: timeStampSelector with: 0.
s1 := self perform: timeStampSelector with: 1.
s2 := self perform: timeStampSelector with: 2.

allNames := Set new.
allNames addAll: base keys.
allNames addAll: s1 keys.
allNames addAll: s2 keys.

allDifferences := OrderedCollection new.
allNames do: [:each |
  | ts0 ts1 ts2 |
  ts0 := base at: each ifAbsent: [nil].
  ts1 := s1 at: each ifAbsent: [nil].
  ts2 := s2 at: each ifAbsent: [nil].
  (ts0 = ts1 and: [ts1 = ts2]) ifFalse: [
    | args diffs |
    args := Array
      with: each
      with: ts0
      with: ts1
      with ts2.
  diffs := self
    perform: buildDifferenceSelector
    withArguments: args.
  allDifferences add: diffs]].
^allDifferences.
```

A specific invocation of this method might be as follows:

findDifferentClassMethods
```
^self
  findDifferentSubComponents:
  #classMethodTimeStampsForStreamNumber:
  buildDifferenceUsing:
  #buildClassMethodDifferenceFor:baseTime:s1Time:s2Time:
```

Finding Subcomponent Timestamps

The first element to finding the different class methods is finding the timestamps of these methods in each stream. This is done in the following method:

```
classMethodTimeStampsForStreamNumber: streamNumber
    ^self
        methodTimeStampsForStreamNumber: streamNumber
        instanceMethods: false.
```

This method again just delegates to methodTimeStampsForStreamNumber:instanceMethods:. This is quite a complex method, so we've broken it up into chunks with interspersed comments in text.

```
methodTimeStampsForStreamNumber: streamNumber
instanceMethods: aBoolean
    | clsShadow result methodDiskDictionary edition|
    clsShadow := self shadowNumber: streamNumber.
    clsShadow isNil ifTrue: [^Dictionary new: 0].
```

Step one is to locate the class shadow. We have a method to do this automatically as MedDifferenceItem>#shadowNumber:. If this stream has no shadow, then there are no methods, so return a new, empty dictionary.

Here's where it gets ugly. We need to iterate over the methods for this shadow and build up a dictionary whose keys are the method names and whose values are the method timestamps. The obvious way to do this would be something like the following (but note that it's *not* what we're going to end up doing).

```
(clsShadow editionEntryIn: anApplication) loadShadows.
result := IdentityDictionary new..
clsShadow methodDictionary keysAndValuesDo:
    [:methodName :methodShadow |
      result
        at: methodName
        put: methodShadow timeStamp].
^result.
```

Unfortunately, having ENVY build the methodDictionary of shadow-compiled methods (using loadShadows) is very expensive when we're iterating over large numbers of classes. Instead, we'll drop down to the record level and examine the edition entries ourselves. This gets into very low-level ENVY access, and it's not easy to figure out. Of course, programming at this level runs the risk that something will change in ENVY that will break our code, which is a risk we run any time we use nonpublic API.

First, we'll get the edition record. We need an edition, any edition, of the containing application to do that, so we'll get one by sending asApplication to the class spec. Because the class spec doesn't specify enough information to uniquely retrieve a particular application edition, it'll give us the resident edition if one exists, and otherwise some random edition. Then we can ask the class shadow for its edition record in that application.

```
edition := (clsShadow editionEntryIn:
    (self specNumber: streamNumber) asApplication).
```

From the edition entry we can get a *disk dictionary* of either instance or class methods. Disk dictionaries are more or less what they sound like, a persistent dictionary of ENVY records in the repository. The trouble with disk dictionaries is, first of all, we can't inspect them as normal dictionaries; we can only send methods such as keys or forAllEntriesDo:. Even the entries aren't normal associations and are largely opaque. We can ask for the key, but the values are always EmLibraryPointers, and we have to know what to do with the library pointer (that is, what type it really is) to get any useful information out. In this case we know these are method editions, and we can get their timestamps without having to instantiate a method shadow.

```
methodDiskDictionary := aBoolean
    ifTrue: [edition instanceMethods]
    ifFalse: [edition classMethods].
result := IdentityDictionary
    new: methodDiskDictionary endPosition //10.
methodDiskDictionary forAllEntriesDo: [:each |
    result
      at: each key
      put: (EmMethodEdition using: each value) timeStamp].
^result
```

Building Difference Items

After all of that, given a class in a particular stream, we can build ourselves a dictionary from method names to method timestamps. You may note that we still haven't actually built these difference items. Well, as it turns out, we're pretty close. The differences between two class editions are essentially those methods that are different. If the methods are different, they'll have different timestamps (we're going to ignore the case of identical source with different timestamps). So, recall the last section of code in the findDifferentSubComponents method.

```
allNames do: [:each |
    | ts0 ts1 ts2 |
    ts0 := base at: each ifAbsent: [nil].
    ts1 := s1 at: each ifAbsent: [nil].
    ts2 := s2 at: each ifAbsent: [nil].
    (ts0 = ts1 and: [ts1 = ts2]) ifFalse: [
    | args diffs |
    args := Array
      with: each
```

```
      with: ts0
      with: ts1
      with ts2.
   diffs := self
      perform: buildDifferenceSelector
      withArguments: args.
   allDifferences add: diffs]].
```

In this, we iterate over the list of subcomponent names, and for each we look up its timestamp. If all three timestamps are the same, we don't have a difference. If any of them are different, we ask the system to build a difference item using the second method name, which we passed in as a parameter. In the case of building class differences, that method was in class MedClassDifference.

buildClassMethodDifferenceFor: selector
    baseTime: ts0
    s1Time: ts1
    s2Time: ts2

```
^(self
   buildBasicMethodDifferenceFor: selector
   baseTime: ts0
   s1Time: ts1
   s2Time: ts2) beClassMethod.
```

It calls

buildBasicMethodDifferenceFor: selector
    baseTime: ts0
    s1Time: ts1
    s2Time: ts2

```
^(MedMethodDifference new)
   name: selector;
   parent: self;
   baseTimeStamp: ts0;
   streamOneTimeStamp: ts1;
   streamTwoTimeStamp: ts2
```

This illustrates the process of computing method differences based on a class difference. In the same way, we can build class and subapplication differences based on application differences and application differences based on configuration map differences. From the user level, all we have to do is create a difference item for the three component editions we want to compare and ask it to buildDifferences.

The Browser

Now we have a tree of differences we can manipulate, but we need to represent these differences graphically to the user. In the longer term it might be nice to represent them with a graphical tree widget rather than the basic ENVY lists, but for the moment we've just implemented it using the standard ENVY list mechanisms.

Most of the code for this browser actually lies in the library specs and difference items, but a few noteworthy features exist in the browser itself, or are added to the domain objects as a result of browser requirements.

Sorting

Once we have the list of differences, we need to present it in an intuitive order to the user. To do this, we defined a fairly complex sort order for differences. Specifically, we define the default comparison to check first for a component "level" and then by name, as follows:

```
<= aDifferenceItem
    self componentLevel = aDifferenceItem componentLevel
    ifTrue: [^self name <= aDifferenceItem name]
    ifFalse: [^self componentLevel <= aDifferenceItem componentLevel].
```

where the component level is defined as

```
componentLevel
    "1 - config map
    2 - application
    3 - class change
    4 - class internal changes e.g. definition, comment
    5 - class methods
    6 - instance methods"
```

Comparing Source

One of the nice features of the normal differences browsers is its capability to highlight in source code exactly what's changed. We'd like to have a similar feature in the three-way differences as well. Unfortunately, it isn't easy to make a highlighting scheme that can adequately handle three-way changes. We might be able to do it by showing different combinations in different colors, but we'd need three different colors (base *versus* stream one, base *versus* stream two, stream one *versus* stream two) and it would likely take some practice to understand the results. Instead, let's take the easy way out, and let users choose any two of the streams to compare at one time. This means we can also use the standard mechanism to do the highlighting.

The system does text comparison using an instance of EtStringComparer. This takes two strings as inputs and computes the difference between them. We can then highlight these regions in the text widgets using the highlightLine:to:on: method provided by EtBrowser.

Loading/Ignoring

Of course, the browser has to support loading the appropriate changes from different streams. Given the APIs we've discussed, this is not difficult. We simply determine what type of component we're dealing with, and then load it appropriately. We can even use the browser's progress dialog box framework to show the status of large loading operations, such as loading an entire application.

```
loadApplication: anApplication inStream: streamNumber
    | success all |
    success := false.
    browser
        execLongOperation: [:dialog |
          |imageBuilder |
          imageBuilder := EmClassDevelopment imageBuilder.
          imageBuilder progressDialog: dialog.
          success := (imageBuilder loadApplications:
              (Array with: anApplication)) notNil]
        message: ('Loading: %1' bindWith: anApplication name)
        allowCancel: true
        showProgress: true.
    ^success.
```

Once we've loaded a component, we want to remove it from the list of differences, just as in the regular differences browser. If we remove all the child differences, then we also have to remove the corresponding parent difference. Finally, we want to let the user explicitly remove differences when the currently loaded version is the right one.

Summary

At the beginning of this section, we set out to make a three-way differences browser that would merge two divergent streams together. We had to compute the differences, display them in a form that helps them be easily understood, and supports loading components from either stream to merge them. We also set out to explore in practice some of the ENVY concepts and methods we've been describing. In the course of building this tool we looked at shadows and the system's mechanisms for browsing differences. We took a detour into how to specify a component in an abstract way that we could easily manipulate, exploring the use of shadows and navigation among the various ENVY components. We extended these library specs into an abstract representation of differences, which we could compute using further manipulation of shadows and even the ENVY record structures. Finally, we looked at displaying those differences in a convenient form to the user. In the end, we have a usable browser that can handle differences for any level of component and easily merge them.

A Simple Project Management Tool

To support the layered architecture described in "Library Architecture," we'll build a simple, extensible tool for managing the components for a project. We'll look at some of the code, discuss the ideas behind it, illustrate how to extend it, and provide some more examples of how to work with components in ENVY.

Large projects will inevitably start to have many different configuration maps. We still want to preserve our ability to do one-click loading, but it may be awkward to try and organize everything into a hierarchy of required maps. The project management tool will let us define a set of configuration map editions in terms of their library specs, store that in a method, and load it automatically. We'll also incorporate support for the layered architecture by defining the configuration maps for each layer and letting the tool manage the load order automatically.

To build this tool, we'll re-use a number of techniques and objects we've already discussed:

- Library specs to identify configuration maps
- Prompters (from script support) for getting information from the user
- The menu extension API for adding project-specific items to browser menus (we won't be discussing this in detail, but for more information see "The Menu Extension API")
- The ENVY API for getting information about objects and for generating code

MedProject

For each project, we need to know

- a name
- ordered collections of library specs for its components at each layer

We want to be able to store the project definition in a simple form that's easily browsable. We could store the information as user fields, but it's not obvious what component it would be associated with, and it wouldn't be easy to browse. Instead, we'll define the project as a class and add methods to it that define the configuration maps.

```
Object subclass: #MedProject
    instanceVariableNames: "
    classVariableNames: "
    poolDictionaries: "
```

Layers

Recall that in Chapter 4 we described breaking down the architecture into layers, based on rate of change, ownership, dependencies between components, and presence in a packaged run-time image. The tool we're building will support that architecture, with some further breakdown. Specifically, we're going to split the Tools layer into three layers to distinguish between run-time and development-time third-party tools and our own infrastructure. The division is still flexible, and in your own projects you may want to divide slightly differently — perhaps dividing internal application frameworks into run-time and development-time components. The essential principle is to isolate the sections that change frequently and ensure that layers only depend on lower layers to ensure a valid load order. Our division now shows as follows:

1. Kernel — the vendor classes making up the base image

2. Base Support — run-time support for third-party products

3. Tools — development-time support for third-party products

4. Internal Application Frameworks — our project infrastructure

5. Domain Objects — business logic specific to this project

6. GUI — the GUI for this project

Each project contains six methods defining the configuration maps for a specific layer of the architecture: kernel, base support, tools, frameworks , domain, and application:

orderedBaseImageConfigMapDefinitions

```
"This method is auto-generated. Change it at your own risk."

^#(
(#ConfigMap 'ENVY/Image Extended Widgets' 3080465927)
  "ENVY/Image Extended Widgets V 4.5a"
(#ConfigMap 'ENVY/Image Controls' 3081088790)
  "ENVY/Image Controls V 4.5a"
(#ConfigMap 'ENVY/Image OLE' 3052377005)
  "ENVY/Image OLE V 4.02b"
(#ConfigMap 'ENVY/Image OLE Type Information' 3021629992)
  "ENVY/Image OLE Type Information V 4.0"
(#ConfigMap 'AbtOleBase' 3063630843)
  "AbtOleBase V 4.5"
) asOrderedCollection
```

As you can see, the method returns an OrderedCollection of array-format library specs. Because the library spec timestamp is in a machine-readable format, we've set up the code generation to print out the ConfigMap signature as a comment.

Generating the Methods

How do we generate these methods? We have all the necessary infrastructure already available, either in the image or in components we've already developed. This means we can easily define a code-generator utility (called `MedCodeGeneratorUtility`) that can write the source code to, and compile, a method defining the library specs for an architecture layer. The public interface method looks like this:

```
compileDefinitionMethodNamed: methodName
    self project
        compile: (self layerMethodNamed: methodName)
        notifying: nil
        ifNewAddTo: self project class controller
        categorizeIn: (Array with: 'Layer Definitions')
```

We use the ENVY API to compile the source string into a method, and install it in the project definition class. Note the last two keywords in the method call. The ifNewAddTo: keyword tells ENVY which (sub)application to add the method to if it is new. If we are recompiling an existing method, it will be recompiled in the application it is already installed in. The categorizeIn: keyword defines which method categories (protocols) the method should be included in. Because VisualAge supports multiple categories for methods, and VisualWorks does not, we use the dialect-neutral compile:notifying:ifNewAddTo:categorizeIn: method to compile the source string. If we needed to support only one dialect and wanted to take advantage of its facilities, we could use a dialect-specific variant.

In order to generate the code, we first need to know which configuration maps are to be included in the layer definition. To get this information interactively, we use one of the methods from the prompter utility described in "Prompter Utilities."

```
getConfigMapLibrarySpecs
    ^MedPrompters chooseSomeConfigMapsAndEditions
```

Given the configuration map editions we open a new write stream, insert the method header, and dump the library spec descriptions onto the stream.

```
layerMethodNamed: aString
    | specs codeStream |
    (specs := self getConfigMapLibrarySpecs) isNil
        ifTrue: [^self].
    codeStream := self headerStreamNamed: aString.
    self
        writeArrayReturnOn: codeStream;
        writeSpecs: specs on: codeStream;
        writeCodeEndingOn: codeStream.
    ^codeStream contents
```

We won't reproduce all of the code here because it's mostly trivial and the full code is available online. The one important method here is the one dumping the library spec definitions. To do this, we iterate over the array of configuration maps, inserting each one's printString into the stream, and including each one's signature as a comment to make the method text easier to read.

```
writeSpecs: specs on: codeStream
    specs
      inject: codeStream
      into: [:stream :map |
        stream cr;
            tab;
            nextPutAll: map medLibrarySpec asArray printString;
            space;
            nextPutAll: '"', map signature, '"';
            yourself]
```

Loading the Projects

Loading a configuration map is easy. Once we have the shadow, we just send it the message load. To load our project, all we have to do is retrieve all the library specs defining the maps needed, instantiate the configuration map instances from the library specs, and load them one after another.

```
load: aCollectionOfMaps
    Transcript bringToFront.
    aCollection isNil ifTrue: [^false].
    aCollection do: [:each |
      (self loadMap:
        (MedLibrarySpec fromArray: each) asComponent)
            ifFalse: [^false]].
    Transcript cr; show: 'DONE'.
    ^true
```

While loading each map, we inform the developer via the Transcript about what's going on. If the map has not been successfully (fully) loaded, we stop the process.

```
loadMap: aConfigMap
    aConfigMap isNil ifTrue: [^false].
    (aConfigMap loadWithTracing: true) ifFalse: [^false].
    ^true
```

One issue with loading an entire project this way is that we don't get an atomic load of the entire project. The ENVY loading transaction mechanism will not let us load multiple configuration maps in a single transaction. In practice, this is not a major problem. Each configuration map will be loaded in an individual transaction, and is likely independent of the other maps, so we don't run into the possibility of partly loaded code. If a load fails, we can unload or retry without danger, and this same restriction already applies to loading configuration maps with required maps.

If we did want to load the entire project atomically, though, it is possible. Rather than loading configuration maps, we collect up all the applications from all the configuration maps and load them together as one transaction. Note that even this can fail in certain unusual circumstances. For example, VisualWorks DLL/CC installs its own special parser to handle C callout syntax. We cannot load DLL/CC classes, which need recompilation, successfully until after this parser has been fully loaded. In a case such as this we would have no choice but to split the work into two or more loads. To load the applications together, we'd do something like this:

```
load: aCollectionOfMaps
    | apps |
    apps := Set new: aCollection size * 5.
    aCollectionOfMaps do: [:map |
        apps addAll: map shadowApplications].
    EmImageBuilder loadApplications: apps
```

Extracting Information from Projects

Another thing a project tool is useful for is as a way of getting information about the project. For example, we might be computing metrics and want a complete list of all methods in the project. To do this, we'd need to iterate through the tree of components it defines. First, for each configuration map, get its shadow

```
(MedLibrarySpec fromArray: <library spec array>) asComponent
```

and then its applications

```
map shadowApplications
```

This returns only shadows for the released application versions because the configuration map's applications might not be loaded into the image. To get the resident application instances, send the shadows the message residentApplication. This will return the actual application instance, if it's loaded, or nil if it's not.

```
^(map shadowApplications collect: [:app |
    app residentApplication]) select: [:a | a notNil]
```

Once we have the applications, we can ask them for their classes. The ENVY API defines three basic methods (on the SubApplication class) to do this:

- defined — returns the classes defined in the (sub)application
- extended — returns the classes extended in the (sub)application
- classes — returns both defined and extended classes

Because the methods for a specific class may be spread over a number of (sub)applications, we need a way to find out the methods that are defined in a specific application.

```
<class> methodNamesIn: <application>
```

behaves similarly to selectors, and will return the selectors for methods controlled by the application. If we want the CompiledMethod objects, not just method names, we can use

<class> methodsIn: <application>

Summary

In this section we've seen how we can store specifications of components and use this specification to further automate loading an entire project in a single step. We've seen how these specifications support a layered architecture, and how we can use them to extract information about the components that make up a project.

Checkpoints

This section describes a checkpointing facility for ENVY. Normally, ENVY requires us to go through a baselining process to create a version, and only allows versions to be imported/exported. This facility lets us create a version as a snapshot of an edition's state without modifying the edition itself. This can be useful for quick backups and can be very useful for distributed development. Because this is a complex and important facility that delves deeply into ENVY internals, we're going to describe it in two sections — usage and implementation. Even those who aren't interested in the details of the implementation may want to make use of this facility.

Rationale

Normally it is possible to exchange only versioned components between two libraries. The reason for this is that ENVY/Manager identifies components of a given type by their name and timestamp. The timestamp is allocated when the component is first created. If editions of components could be exported between libraries, the same component could exist in more than one library and could then be independently modified and then versioned. The result would be two components that are actually different but that ENVY would think were the same. If we tried to import one of these editions into the library with the other, ENVY would do nothing because it would assume the library already contained that component.

Although this makes sense, it sometimes proves to be very cumbersome for development distributed across multiple libraries. Developers must constantly version components to exchange them. Versioning can sometimes be a very heavyweight operation, especially when it requires many contained components to also be versioned.

We use *checkpoints* to solve the problem of having to version components to send or export them. Checkpoints are versions created *from* editions. Normally editions themselves are versioned and then new editions are created from versions. Checkpoints are versioned, snapshot *copies* of an edition. This means they contain whatever was released into the edition at the time the checkpoint was made. The benefit of creating checkpoints is that open editions of components can be sent at any time. The components that are transferred are indeed versions but the open editions themselves remained untouched. Figure 9-10 shows the difference between checkpointing and a normal baselining procedure.

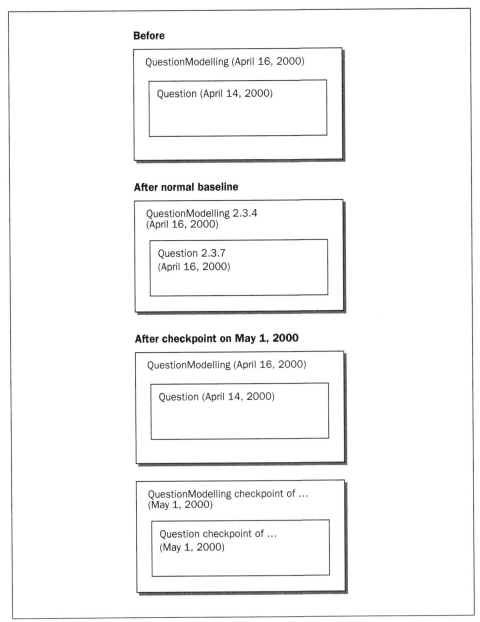

Figure 9-10: Checkpoints *versus* normal baselining

Checkpointed components are automatically given a version name that looks like the following:

```
Checkpoint of (14/12/98 2:32:35) by John Smith [17/12/98 1:59:23]
```

The first time in the version name is the timestamp of the edition that was check-pointed. The second timestamp is the time at which the checkpoint was made. The version name also indicates which user created the checkpoint.

Usage

Checkpoints are created by choosing the Checkpoint menu option in the Application Manager or Configuration Maps Browser. Once checkpoints are created, they are immediately available for export. Typically, once the checkpointed components have been exported, we may want to purge them from the repository to keep the set of edi-tions for a component to a minimal size. If we are keeping checkpoints as a tempo-rary way of marking our state without a full baseline we will probably keep them around for a few iterations, but beyond that there is little to be gained from keeping checkpoints in the repository long-term. If we are checkpointing frequently, the result-ing increase in the number of editions creates unnecessary noise in the user interface that all developers will have to deal with. Also note that any user can create a check-point of a component even if the user does not own or manage that component.

The process of checkpointing a component involves checkpointing not only the component that is sent, but potentially any subcomponent open editions all the way down to the method level. Checkpoints are modified so that they correctly reference the checkpoints of any components they contain rather than the original open edi-tions of those components. Apart from this automatic modification, a checkpoint is identical to the open edition it was created from. Of course, open editions are works in progress, so the open edition may later diverge from the checkpoint.

Checkpointing Issues

Checkpointing represents a significant change from normal ENVY versioning seman-tics, and some of these changes can have an impact on component semantics. This section lists several issues to be aware of when using checkpointing.

First, note that checkpointing works against the repository. The component need not be resident, and even if we do checkpoint a resident application the checkpoint will be a snapshot of that application as it exists in the repository, not as it exists in memory. In other words, if we checkpoint an application and it has subapplications or class edi-tions loaded that are not released, they will not be included in the checkpoint.

Checkpoints only affect components with a strict "part-of" relationship. That is, a checkpoint of a configuration map will affect applications, (sub)applications will affect subapplications and classes, and classes will affect methods. However, prereq-uisites and required maps will not be affected.

This may seem like a minor consideration, but it can result in the exported com-ponents continuing to refer to components in the old library. Consider the case of two configuration maps A and B, where B has A as a required map. If we checkpoint both A and B and export them to another library, the checkpoint of B will still list the open edition of A as a required map, rather than the checkpointed A.

Even with relationships that are followed by the checkpointing code, the "patching up" of relationships only happens within a single *checkpointing session*. Suppose we have open editions of components A, B, and C where A and B both contain C. For example, A and B might be configuration maps and C might be an application. The result of checkpointing A and B together can be different than if A and B are checkpointed independently. If A and B are checkpointed independently, C will be checkpointed twice and the checkpoint of A and the checkpoint of B will contain different checkpoints of C. If A and B are checkpointed in the same operation, C will only be checkpointed once and A and B will both contain the same checkpoint of C. The following paragraphs provide a more detailed example of this, and Figures 9-11 and 9-12 graphically show the differences between checkpointing with contained components like applications and non-contained components like required maps.

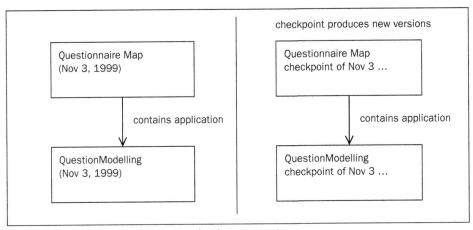

Figure 9-11: Checkpointing with contained components

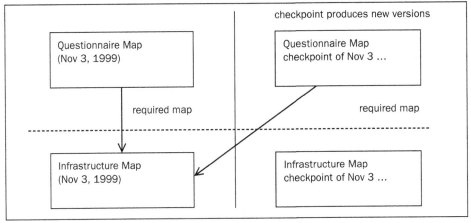

Figure 9-12: Checkpointing required maps

An example will make this clearer:

We have the configuration map:

M1(19/12/98 16:57:46), which contains the applications:

A1(19/12/98 16:57:56) and

A2(20/12/98 11:41:32).

We have another configuration map:

M2(19/12/98 16:57:42), which contains the applications:

A1(19/12/98 16:57:56) and

A3(18/12/98 10:00:25).

M2 also references M1 as a required map.

Checkpointing M1 and M2 together in the same checkpointing session will produce:

M1 Checkpoint of (19/12/98 16:57:46) by John Smith [21/12/98 12:30:46], which contains:

A1 Checkpoint of (19/12/98 16:57:56) by John Smith [21/12/98 12:30:46]

A2 Checkpoint of (20/12/98 11:41:32) by John Smith [21/12/98 12:30:46]

M2 Checkpoint of (19/12/98 16:57:42) by John Smith [21/12/98 12:30:46], which contains

A1 Checkpoint of (19/12/98 16:57:56) by John Smith [21/12/98 12:30:46]

A3 Checkpoint of (18/12/98 10:00:25) by John Smith [21/12/98 12:30:46]

Note that the checkpoints of M1 and M2 share the same checkpoint of A1. If M1 and M2 were checkpointed in two separate operations, A1 would be checkpointed twice and M1 and M2 would contain different checkpoints of A1.

If M1 and M2 were checkpointed and sent to a remote site, then an attempt to load the checkpoint of M2 with required maps would likely fail because M2 requires M1(19/12/98 16:57:46) as a required map and that edition would not be present in that library. We would have the checkpoint of M1, but that is not the required map listed by the checkpoint of M2. M1 and M2 would have to be loaded separately.

The primary purpose of checkpointing is to enable moving components between repositories without having to go through a baselining process. If a large set of components is checkpointed and sent, it may not necessarily form a complete loadable bill-of-materials identical to the open editions they were created from. Although the contents of the components will be identical, they may not load in one single load operation as a result of broken references in required or prerequisite relationships. In practice, this restriction applies only to required maps. Applications contained in configuration maps and subapplications contained in applications will be checkpointed where necessary and correctly referenced by the enclosing or containing checkpointed components.

Why does this limitation exist? You have no simple way to tell if required maps are going to be sent along with any configuration maps that require them. Without additional infrastructure too much burden is placed on the user to have to indicate the complete cycle of required maps in a large chain by checkpointing them all together in a single operation. However, as we'll see in the section on "Zipping Up" later in this chapter, we can tie the checkpoint facility together with our project management facility to provide that information automatically.

Implementation

This section discusses the implementation of the checkpointing feature. Note that the code and issues described here are not for the faint of heart. This code goes deep into the internals of ENVY and illustrates previously unpublished techniques. We would like to express our gratitude to OTI for allowing us to publish this low-level code.

Checkpointing (Sub)Applications

The checkpointing of applications and subapplications is done with the following method, defined for the class SubApplication. The two method arguments, checkpointedApps and checkpointedSubApps, are dictionaries used as recursive checks to ensure that a (sub)application is not checkpointed more than once in a checkpointing transaction.

```
checkpointRememberingApplications: checkpointedApps
    subapplications: checkpointedSubApps
| record shadow fields ws newLineups dd |

self isEdition ifFalse: [^self asShadow].
"ALWAYS answer a shadow for consistency."
```

First, we check if the receiver has already been checkpointed. If it has, it will have already been entered in the checkpointedApps or checkpointedSubApps dictionary.

```
(self isSubApplication
    ifTrue: [checkpointedSubApps]
    ifFalse: [checkpointedApps])
    at: self name ifPresent: [:editions |
        editions
            at: self timeStamp
            ifPresent: [:checkpoint | ^checkpoint]].
```

We inform the user about what's going on, and then make a local copy of the edition record. Into this record we insert the inherited user fields dictionary.

```
EmInterface current messageString:
    ('Checkpointing %1' bindWith: self signature).
record := self editionRecord noLongerExistsInLibrary.
(fields := record inheritedUserFields) notNil ifTrue: [
    record
        at: record inheritedFieldsIndex
        putFilePointer: fields insert].
```

Next, we add a new local user field to store the timestamp of the receiver so that the checkpoint knows which edition it was checkpointed from. If the edition we're checkpointing has local user fields, we create a local copy; otherwise, we initialize the local user fields pointer to point to a new dictionary. We then create a user field record containing the time of the checkpoint, another one containing the ID of the user doing the checkpointing, and insert both into the local user fields dictionary.

Here we see one of a number of performance optimizations. The method at:putFilePointer: is actually a transaction that will cause an update to the library. In this particular case we don't want to do that. We want to construct everything in memory and then write everything out at once when we are finished. For this purpose, we define and use the method at:putPointerFromInMemoryOnly:

```
ws := WriteStream on: (String new: 4).
self timeStamp dumpOn: ws.
(fields := record localUserFields) notNil
    ifTrue: [fields noLongerExistsInLibrary]
    ifFalse: [fields := EmDiskDictionary empty].
record
    at: record localFieldsIndex
    putFilePointer: (fields
      at: self timeStampCheckpointedFromUserFieldKey
      putPointerFromInMemoryOnly: [:ignored |
        (EmUserFieldRecord on: ws contents)
            insertInto: record library];
    at: self userIDCheckpointedByUserFieldKey
    putPointerFrom: [:ignored |
        (EmUserFieldRecord on: EmUser currentID)
            insertInto: record library]).
```

Next, checkpoint each of the receiver's subapplications (and their subapplications and so forth), ensuring that if a subapplication appears in the tree multiple times it will only be checkpointed once.

Even if no subapplications were checkpointed, the checkpoint of the receiver must have its own copy of the expression dictionaries and subapplication dictionaries. Otherwise, it will share them with the receiver, which is definitely not desirable.

Another important point to notice is the use of key to get the symbol for the name of a shadow subapplication. Shadow apps just take whatever object you give them for their name. If you create a shadow with a string name, all types of bad things will happen because comparisons will fail.

```
newLineups := OrderedCollection new: 5.
record subApplicationDictionary
    forAllEntriesDo: [:expressionEntry |
      | newSubs |
      newSubs := Dictionary new: 5.
      (EmDictionaryOfTimeStamps using: expressionEntry value)
        forAllEntriesDo: [:subEntry |
          | sub |
```

```
"Make sure to use #key for a symbol instead of #name for a string."
        sub := (SubApplication shadowClass
            named: subEntry key timeStamp: subEntry value)
        checkpointRememberingApplications: checkpointedApps
        subapplications: checkpointedSubApps.
```

```
"Make sure we use the checkpointed timestamp and not the original timestamp."
        newSubs at: sub name put: sub timeStamp].
```

```
"Make sure to use #name for a string instead of #key for a symbol."
        newLineups add: (Association
            key: expressionEntry name
            value: (EmDictionaryOfTimeStamps
                createFor: newSubs in: record library))].
    dd := EmDiskDictionary empty.
    newLineups do: [:assoc |
      dd appendWith: (dd
        newAssocEntry: assoc key
        value: assoc value)].
    dd forgetCachedSpace.
    record
      at: record subsIndex
      putFilePointer: dd insert.
```

```
    self updateParts: [:partsRecord |
      partsRecord
        updateRecordForPartAt: partsRecord editionsIndex
        ofType: EmEditionsDictionary
        using: [:editionsDict |
        | ts |
        ts := editionsDict nextTimeStamp.
        ts versionName: ('Checkpoint of %1 by %2 %3'
            bindWith: self timeStamp printString
            with: EmUser current fullName
            with: ts checkPointPrintString).
```

```
"NOTE:  shadow should not know any subapplications (subApplications should be nil).
    This is what we want since any subapplications may be checkpointed anyway."
        shadow := self shadowClass
            named: self name
            timeStampWithVersionInfo: ts.
        record
            at: record timeStampIndex putTimeStamp: ts;
            application: shadow;
```

```
"this must come before setting the version name"
        setVersionName: ts versionName.
    editionsDict
        at: ts
        putPointerFrom: [:ignored | record insert]]].
```

Remember the checkpoint in case we need to use it again. We insert it into the appropriate recursion check dictionary.

```
((self isSubApplication
    ifTrue: [checkpointedSubApps]
    ifFalse: [checkpointedApps])
      at: self name ifAbsentPut: [Dictionary new])
    at: self timeStamp
    put: shadow.
^shadow
```

Checkpointing Configuration Maps

Checkpointing configuration maps is similar to checkpointing applications. For this reason, we omit code, which is essentially the same as that listed previously. We define this as a method on EmConfigurationMap.

checkpointRememberingApplications: checkpointedApps
subapplications: checkpointedSubApps

```
| record fields ws dict apps map |
... code omitted...
```

```
"Checkpoint each application and update the checkpoint of the receiver so that it
    references any checkpointed applications.
Even if no applications were checkpointed, the checkpoint of the receiver must have a
    copy of the application editions dictionary, otherwise it will share it with the
    receiver, which is definitely not desirable."
```

```
dict := Dictionary new: self shadowApplications size.
```

```
"NOTE:  Use #checkpointRememberingCheckpointedApplications:subapplications: instead
    of #checkpoint to ensure that if a subapplication appears multiple times across the
    set of the receiver's applications, it will only be checkpointed once."
```

Here we insert the checkpoints of the apps.

```
apps := self shadowApplications collect: [:app |
    app
    checkpointRememberingApplications: checkpointedApps
    subapplications: checkpointedSubApps].
    apps do: [:app | dict at: app name put: app timeStamp].
    record
    at: record applicationEditionsIndex
```

```
putFilePointer: (EmDictionaryOfTimeStamps
    createFor: dict
    in: record library).
```

Here, we are inserting the record for the configuration map checkpoint. We first have to do a lot of work to construct the record in memory, and then afterward write it out to the library. For example, we send nextTimeStamp to get the next timestamp. We can't just use EmTimeStamp now because it may clash if the timestamp is already allocated. We have to send nextTimeStamp to the editions dictionary for configuration maps of that name to get the next available timestamp. We also set the version name, and so on.

```
self class configurationRecordClass
    relocateRootDictionaryUsing: [:diskDict |
    diskDict
        at: self name
        putPointerFrom: [:editionsFP |
            | editionsDict ts |
            editionsDict := EmEditionsDictionary
                updating: editionsFP
                from: diskDict library.
            ts := editionsDict nextTimeStamp.
            ts versionName: ('Checkpoint of %1 by %2 %3'
                bindWith: self timeStamp printString
                with: EmUser current fullName
                with: ts checkPointPrintString).
            map := self class
                named: self name
                timeStampWithVersionInfo: ts.
            map setShadows: apps.
            record
                at: record timeStampIndex putTimeStamp: ts;
                replaceElement: 2 with: ts versionName;
                map: map.
            editionsDict
                at: ts
                putPointerFrom: [:ignored | record insert]]].
    ^map
```

Zipping Up

We've gone this far, so let's go one step further and automate the export process too, tying it in to our simple project management facility. We'll call this *zipping up* — going through all the configuration maps and making checkpoints of all open editions. We can do this using either the required maps mechanism or our project specification. Depending which method we use, the first step is slightly different, but the goal is the same — collect all the configuration maps required for our project. Here's the version using the basic required maps relationships.

```
" Go through a map and all its required maps, checkpointing all maps not currently
    versioned"
| apps subApps toExport allMaps toCheckpoint |
toExport:= MedPrompters chooseAConfigMapAndEdition.
allMaps := toExport withAllPossibleRequiredMaps.
```

Here's the version for the project management tool (note that this code is already included with the project management tool).

```
" Go through a map and all its required maps, checkpointing all maps not currently
    versioned"
| apps subApps toExport allMaps toCheckpoint |
toExport := MedProjectDefinition new
    orderedFrameworkConfigMapDefinitions
      addAll: MedProjectDefinition new
        orderedDomainConfigMapDefinitions;
      addAll: MedProjectDefinition new
        orderedProgramConfigMapDefinitions;
      yourself.
allMaps := toExport
    inject: OrderedCollection new
    into: [:collection :map |
      collection add:
        (MedLibrarySpec fromArray: map) asComponent;
        yourself].
```

Next, we instantiate two dictionaries as recursion stoppers. These dictionaries are passed from configuration map to configuration map and contain entries for all the applications and subapplications that have been checkpointed, respectively. This removes the problem of checkpointing an application more than once simply because it appears in different configuration maps.

```
apps := Dictionary new.
subApps := Dictionary new.
toCheckpoint := allMaps collect: [:each |
    each
      checkpointRememberingApplications: apps
      subapplications: subApps].
```

Once we've checkpointed the maps that aren't versions, we export all maps to another repository. Please note that we use a higher-level method here to avoid going into detail about creating new libraries. It is possible to create the library and name it with some distinguishing features (for example, timestamp), but that code is left as an exercise for the reader.

```
"Export all the maps"
EtTools exportUsing:[:sourceLibrary :destinationLibrary|
    EtTools managerInterface messageString:
      (toCheckpoint size = 1
        ifTrue: ['Exporting: %1' bindWith:
            toCheckpoint first signature]
        ifFalse: ['Exporting configuration maps']).
    EtTools managerInterface
      moveConfigMaps: toCheckpoint
      from: sourceLibrary
      to: destinationLibrary
      withOptions: EtConfigurationMapsBrowser
        currentExportingOptions
      withAllRequiredMaps: EtTools moveAllRequiredMapsToo].
```

After exporting, we should do some clean-up work. Because checkpoints are versions existing in the library, they will show up in all edition lists or browsers. Checkpoints serve a transitory need; after the checkpointed app or map has been exported, checkpoints have outlived their usefulness. For this reason, we purge all checkpoints we have made from the library after we're finished.

In our implementation, we use a user field to tag checkpoints so that we know a) that they are checkpoints and b) that the user field contains the timestamp of the edition it was based on so you can tell (programmatically rather than just by looking at the version name). The methods are isCheckpoint and timeStampCheckpointedFrom, respectively. This enables us (for example) to purge all checkpoints that were based on a particular edition.

```
"purge the checkpoints from the library"
mapsToPurge := toCheckpoint select: [:each |
    each isCheckpoint].
appsToPurge := apps
    inject: Set new
    into: [ :set :editions |
      set addAll: (editions select: [:each |
        each isCheckpoint]); yourself].
subApps
    inject: appsToPurge
    into: [ :set :editions |
      set addAll: (editions select: [:each |
        each isCheckpoint]); yourself].
mapsToPurge do: [:each | each purgeFromLibrary].
appsToPurge do: [:each | each purgeFromLibrary].
```

Checkpoint Summary

In this section we've described a very useful tool for making versions out of editions without going through an entire baseline process. This is particularly useful when exchanging code frequently between libraries at two different sites, but is also useful for backing up code offsite and for other purposes. We've also described the implementation of this tool, which involves complex manipulations of the ENVY record structures that have not previously been published. Despite being an apparently minor change in the ENVY development process, we've found checkpointing to be one of the most useful ENVY add-ons we've come across.

ENVY-izing the Refactoring Browser

The Refactoring Browser is one of the greatest tools ever to be written in and for Smalltalk. It offers a multitude of "refactorings," or sematic-preserving transformations on code. While many of these transformations are relatively simple to do manually, automating them makes doing a series of transformations on code, which would otherwise be tedious and error-prone, very simple. These range from simple tasks such as renaming a local variable or parameter throughout a method to moving an instance variable into a superclass, renaming a method globally throughout the image (including all senders), and adding or removing method parameters. For more information on this browser, and on refactoring in general, see Fowler (1999).

Three kinds of refactorings are available from different browser menus:

- Class-based refactorings operate on classes, instance variables, and class variables and are defined off the class menu.

- The method-based refactorings are defined off the selector menu.

- Finally, the code-based refactorings operate on individual statements and are available through the context-sensitive menus in the text pane. Many of the class-based refactorings are also available in these menus.

One problem, though, was that VisualAge developers didn't like working with the original Refactoring Browser. Not only were they forced to leave their normal browsers to refactor, but they had to work in browsers that weren't organized the same way at all, and used a VisualWorks style and terminology. As an example of how to use the menu extension API, we decided to make much of this functionality available in the standard ENVY browsers. While we were at it, we made sure that the ENVY extensions would function the same in both dialects. We also made slight changes in the functionality to make certain refactorings more "ENVY-aware."

The Refactoring Browser ENVY Extensions are available online with the rest of the code accompanying this book, and we won't go into much detail here about the implementation. We will, however, take a look at the general idea behind the extensions, and some of the techniques we used.

Providing Functionality in the ENVY Browsers

To provide refactoring functionality in the ENVY browsers, we first had to extend the browsers. At appropriate places in the browser hierarchy, we wrote methods extracting the required information about the browser state (selected classes, selected text, and so on) and invoking the refactorings. Most methods were cut and pasted from the Refactoring Browser itself. In some places, though, helper methods were needed, and some methods that were implemented in both places were different. For example, the method selectedClass in the Refactoring Browser returns the selected class *or* metaclass, whereas selectedClass in the ENVY browsers always returns the class. This behavior is implemented in the Refactoring Browser in the method nonMetaClass, and the ENVY browsers implement actualClass to return the selected class *or* metaclass. Once we had the basics up and working, though, we could use the refactorings to help our work, and we progressed at a noticeably increased speed.

We also decided to reduce menu clutter and functional redundancy by not offering a number of refactorings (such as moving a class to another application), which were already available through the standard menus.

Correcting Functionality

Because the Refactoring Browser was conceived to work with or without ENVY, some of the refactorings have to take the "least common denominator" approach, leading to results that ignore ENVY characteristics. For example, take a look at the following hypothetical method on a class Foo:

```
showSourceFor: aSelector in: aBehavior
    Transcript
        cr;
        show: (aBehavior sourceCodeAt: aSelector)
```

The Refactoring Browser offers an ingenious *Move Method to Component* refactoring. This enables us to choose one of the method's arguments, and performs a type analysis to figure out what class the argument is an instance of. It then offers a list of possible class choices, from which we can either choose one or enter a different class. Then it adjusts the arguments, moves the method to the new class, and substitutes a delegator method in the original method.

The result of performing this refactoring on the preceding method would be the following two methods:

Behavior methods:

```
showSourceFor: aSelector
    Transcript
        cr;
        show: (self sourceCodeAt: aSelector)
```

Foo methods:

showSourceFor: aSelector in: aBehavior
   aBehavior showSourceFor: aSelector

After this, we might also take the next refactoring step, inlining showSourceFor:in: in the method that calls it. Once that's done, we could remove showSourceFor:in: because it's no longer necessary.

As we see, the type analysis has shown us that Behavior is the only class in the system that understands the messages sent to it — in this case, sourceCodeAt:. The refactoring engine has moved the method to Behavior, corrected self and argument references, and substituted a delegator method in the original method.

This is where the problem starts. When adding a method to Behavior, the refactoring engine tries to add the method to the application where the class is *defined*. This, of course, is in a subapplication of Kernel. Because we don't want to go around changing system applications, we found it would be a better idea if the new method landed in an extension of the class (Behavior) in the same application as the original method being refactored.

Renaming Versions

In general, we want to use a naming convention that helps us name versions as consistently as possible. Given that, needing to rename a version should be a rare thing. However, knowing how to rename versions can save us a lot of time. Eric Clayberg of Smalltalk Systems/Instantiations contributes this section on how to rename versions and other components directly in the repository. This capability is also built in to the VA Assist Pro add-on product for VisualAge Smalltalk.

Ever named a version incorrectly by mistake and wished you could change it? Ever wanted to baseline your app and adopt a common set of version names before sending it out? Ever wanted to rename a configuration map without having to create a new one and purge the old one? If so, you're going to love these.

If you are a producer of any reusable component — whether you are a third-party vendor or part of a project team — release management is an important consideration. Ideally, when you release a component configuration, you would like to give all of the versions a good, descriptive name. Likewise, you would like all of the classes (or at least the ones that changed since the last release) within the component to have the same version name.

If we look at the base classes, we see that they all share the same version names (for example, V4.0). How do you suppose they all got that way? The brute force approach would be to create new editions of all the classes and then version them all with the same name. We could do it that way, but in doing so we're creating lots of needless editions that contribute nothing other than a new name. Do you think OTI does it that way when they baseline the system? Of course not.

The only thing ENVY cares about is the timestamp of the edition, not the name. A version's name can change and the system still works as before. As far as the manager library is concerned, two versions *may* have the same names as long as the timestamps are different. The restrictions against either renaming an existing version or reusing an existing name are imposed at the browser level. They are artificial (albeit a good idea *most* of the time).

These restrictions can be challenging in certain cases. For example, let's say that you've just finished your product and have carefully versioned all of your classes and applications and finally your master configuration. All is well with the world. Then disaster strikes — you discover a small problem that *must* be fixed. So, you create a new edition of the affected application, make the fix (thus creating a new edition of the affected class), and are now faced with versioning it all off. Guess what? You can't use the same name.

You can deal with this problem in two ways. You can pick a second name (for example, V 4.01 rather than V4.01 — note the extra space after the "V"), but this can quickly get out of hand if you need to rerelease a couple of times to fix a couple of last-minute bugs. The other technique is to export the configuration to a clean manager library, create a *new* edition there, and then rename everything back to the name you really wanted. This method is very painful to say the least!

Wouldn't it be better if there were a way to either re-use an existing name or simply rename an existing version to any other name (including an existing name)? If you answered "yes" to that question, you are in luck. It turns out that you can do this pretty easily if you know where to look.

The folks at OTI and IBM use a number of internal release scripts that allow them to "cheat" when baselining their classes, applications, and configuration maps. The remainder of this section shows you the secrets of doing this yourself.

Enhancing the Menus

We'll start by adding new "Rename Version" commands to the Applications and Classes menus of the Application Manager and the Editions menu of the Configurations Maps Browser. For most browsers, adding new menu items to the existing menus is easily accomplished by using the menu extensions API described in "An Example — The Menu Extensions API" section in Chapter 7 and then overriding the existing addToApplicationsMenu:browser: and addToClassesMenu:browser: methods in the application class for our application.

```
addToApplicationsMenu: aMenu browser: aBrowser
    "Answer the applications menu."
    ^aMenu
      add: #renameApplicationVersions
        label: 'Rename Version...'
        enable: [
          aBrowser isApplicationSelected and: [
            aBrowser selectedApplications conform: [ :app |
```

```
                    aBrowser managerInterface isVersion: app]]]
            before: #versionApplicationsSubMenu;
        yourself
```

addToClassesMenu: aMenu browser: aBrowser

```
    "Answer the classes menu."
    ^aMenu
      add: #renameClassVersions
        label: 'Rename Version...'
        enable: [
            aBrowser selectedClasses notEmpty
                and: [ | selectedApp |
                    selectedApp := self selectedApplication.
                    aBrowser selectedClasses conform: [:class |
                        class isVersionIn: selectedApp]]]
        before: #versionClassesSubMenu;
        yourself
```

addToCMBEditionsMenu: aMenu browser: aBrowser

```
    "Answer the editions menu."
    ^aMenu
      add: #renameConfigMapVersions
        label: 'Rename Version...'
        enable: [
            self isOneEditionSelected
                and: [self selectedEdition isVersion]]
        before: #newMapVersions;
        yourself
```

The enable block can be arbitrarily complicated. In each of the preceding cases, we are checking that at least one item (either an application, a class, or a configuration map edition) is selected and that each selected item is also a version. Notice the use of conform:. This is a very useful collection iterator that returns true if all of the items in the collection answer true for the condition within its block and false if any of the items fails the test. It's equivalent to the ANSI allSatisfy: method.

Renaming Application Versions

The "Rename Version" command we added to our Application Manager's Applications menu invokes the renameApplicationVersions method to do its work. This method is as follows:

renameApplicationVersions

```
    "Rename the selected application versions"
    | versionName |
    versionName := self
```

```
    prompt: 'Enter new version name'
    answer: self selectedApplication versionName.
    versionName isNil or: [versionName isEmpty]) ifTrue: [^self].
    self execShortOperation: [
      self selectedApplications do: [:application |
        application timeStamp versionName = versionName
            ifFalse: [
                application updateEdition: [:editionRecord |
                    editionRecord
                        setVersionName: versionName;
                        insert]]].
    self redrawApplications]
```

The first thing this does is prompt the user for a new version name for the selected applications. The default entry is the current version name of the first selected application. Assuming that a valid version name has been entered, we display the hourglass cursor (via the execShortOperation: method) and loop through all of the selected applications. For each application, we do a quick check to make sure that the current version name is different from the proposed change (there's no sense in doing the work if we don't have to). If the change is needed, we update the application's edition record with the new version name. Finally, we call redrawApplications to update the applications list in the browser.

To get a better handle on what is going on here, it is important to think of the ENVY library as a large, flat-file database. The edition record mentioned previously is a Smalltalk object that directly represents the physical database record within the library.

We would like to point out that we are using a number of private (as well as hidden source) methods to get this done. While that may raise a red flag or two, in this case you have no need to worry because the "API" we are using here hasn't changed in a very long time.

Renaming Class Versions

The "Rename Version" command we added to our Application Manager's Classes menu invokes the renameClassVersions method to do its work. This method is as follows:

```
renameClassVersions
    | application timeStamp versionName |
    application := self selectedApplication.
    timeStamp := self selectedClass timeStampIn: application.
    versionName := self
      prompt: 'Enter new version name'
      answer: timeStamp versionName.
    (versionName isNil or: [versionName isEmpty]) ifTrue: [^self].
    self execShortOperation: [
      self selectedClasses do: [:class |
        class isMetaclass ifFalse: [
```

```
        timeStamp := class timeStampIn: application.
        timeStamp versionName = versionName ifFalse: [
            timeStamp versionName: versionName.
            class updateIn: application with: [:editionsRecord |
                | entry oldLength |
                entry := editionsRecord currentEntry.
                oldLength := entry versionName size.
                entry
                    replaceElement: 2 with: versionName;
                    length: entry length - oldLength +
                        versionName size;
                    yourself]]]].
    self redrawClasses]
```

This method, while more complicated than its predecessor, is structurally very similar. We start by prompting the user for a new version name, this time using the current version name of the first selected class in the context of the currently selected application. Remember that a class can be extended in any number of applications so it is important to change the version name in the proper context.

Once we have a valid version name, we loop through each selected class and test whether its version name (again in the context of the current application) is different from the new version name. Assuming that a change is needed, we again update the class's current edition record with the new version name (by poking in the new version name and updating the record length). Finally, we call redrawClasses to update the classes list in the browser.

You probably noticed that the preceding code is quite a bit more complicated than the application version-changing method presented earlier. In fact, we're engaged in a bit of virtual brain surgery on the ENVY library. If you decide to use the preceding code, we caution you to enter it very carefully. Any deviation from the code (unless you know exactly what you are doing) could result in a corrupted library. You may want to test it out in a scratch library before using it with your production library.

Renaming Configuration Map Versions

The "Rename Version" command we added to our Configurations Maps Browser's Editions menu invokes the renameConfigMapVersions method to do its work. This method is as follows:

```
renameConfigMapVersions
    | edition versionName |
    self changeRequest ifFalse: [^self].
    edition := self selectedEdition.
    versionName := self
        prompt: 'Enter new version name for ', edition signature
        answer: edition versionName.
```

```
(versionName isNil or: [versionName isEmpty]) ifTrue: [^nil].
self execShortOperation: [
  self selectedEdition
    relocateRecordWith: [:editionRecord |
        editionRecord
            replaceElement: 2 with: versionName;
            insert].
  self
    updateEditions: self selectedEditions
    restoreToTop: true]
```

The fundamental mechanism is very similar to the previous two methods. The initial call to changeRequest prevents losing unsaved changes to the notes of the comments field. After prompting the user for a new version name (based upon the current version name), we update the selected edition's edition record with the new name. The final call to updateEditions:restoreToTop: updates the editions list.

Removing Source Code

If we're delivering a tool, we may be delivering it as a repository with code, but still want to hide some or all of the source code. Why hide source? Well, maybe we're deploying a Black Box with no "user-serviceable" parts. We may want to protect code that contains trade secrets, or hide security features (for example, evaluation "time-bomb" code/unlocking code). In many cases, we may simply want to hide the implementation so that we have more freedom to change the internals later on.

ENVY offers a mechanism for removing the source code from compiled methods, but the mechanisms aren't that easy to understand. Let's take a look at the techniques involved, and learn how to do it ourselves.

Mechanics

When we remove source we do not delete it directly from our own repository. (There is a way of doing that, but that's starting to tread on very thin ice.) Instead, the source code is hidden upon export. When the CompiledMethod records are written to a new repository, the source strings are left behind.

We can toggle whether to export the source code or not. It is hidden on an export-by-export basis, controlled by the Configuration Maps Browser's Names->Settings->Remove Source command.

How does ENVY know what source code to remove? Well, we have to tell it. The exact definition of what is to be hidden is stored in a dictionary kept as an inherited user field in the repository. While the dictionary is a standard type, it's interpreted in rather unusual ways. We can get and set this dictionary using the SubApplication class methods removeSourceStructure and removeSourceStructure:.

For each application or subapplication that requires source code removal, there is a dictionary whose keys are the names of the classes that will have their source code removed. For each key, the value is either

- Nil, indicating all the source code for this class should be hidden
- An Association whose key controls instance method hiding and whose value controls class method hiding

In the association, the key is either

- The collection of method selectors of that type that should be hidden
- Nil, indicating that all of that type of method should be hidden

Remember: Because the removeSourceStructure is stored as an inherited user field, it has no version history. To be sure we can recreate this structure as necessary, it's a good idea to write a method that can recreate the dictionary on demand. This is a similar technique to the one described in "toBeLoadedCode."

Let's look at a concrete example to get a better feeling for how the dictionary mechanism works.

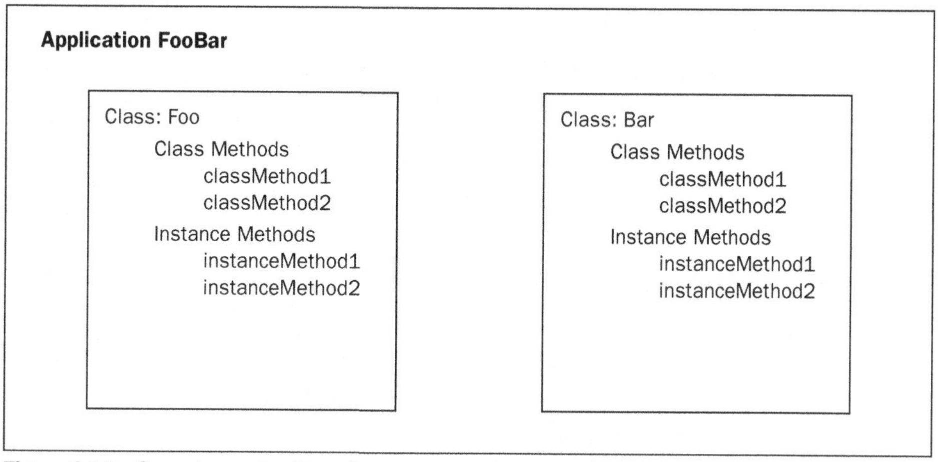

```
Application FooBar

    Class: Foo                              Class: Bar
        Class Methods                           Class Methods
            classMethod1                            classMethod1
            classMethod2                            classMethod2
        Instance Methods                        Instance Methods
            instanceMethod1                         instanceMethod1
            instanceMethod2                         instanceMethod2
```

Figure 9-13: Sample applications for source code removal

As shown in Figure 9-13 our sample application FooBar contains two classes: Foo and Bar. Each class contains two class methods and two instance methods. To remove source code from FooBar, we need to define the removeSourceStructure dictionary.

Example 1: Hide everything in FooBar

```
FooBar removeSourceStructure:
    (Dictionary new
        at: #Foo put: nil;
        at: #Boo put: nil;
        yourself)
```

Example 2: Hide all instance methods in Foo (nothing in Bar)

```
FooBar removeSourceStructure:
```

```
(Dictionary new
   at: #Foo put: (Association key: nil value: #());
   yourself)
```

Example 3: Hide all class methods in Bar (nothing in Foo)

```
FooBar removeSourceStructure:
   (Dictionary new
      at: #Bar put: (Association key: #() value: nil);
      yourself)
```

Example 4: Hide one class and one instance method in Foo

```
FooBar removeSourceStructure:
   (Dictionary new
      at: #Foo
      put: (Association
        key: #(#instanceMethod1)
        value: #(#classMethod2));
      yourself)
```

Importing Without Source

Exporting without source code raises the issue of importing code without source code. This works fine, as long as the source was compiled for the correct virtual machine version (that is, it can be loaded as bytecodes). Otherwise, it will fail to load. This means that if we are providing a sourceless import for multiple platforms, we'll want to make sure those editions have been compiled for each platform so that the bytecodes are available.

A more subtle problem can also occur when importing code without source. If we have imported an application in which the source code has been removed and then attempt to import the exact same application editions from a repository that contains the source, ENVY won't do it. Because the import process is optimized, ENVY sees that the editions are the same, and optimizes out the import process. How can we deal with this problem?

With VisualAge Version 4.5 or later we can use the following undocumented method:

```
EmMethodEdition importSource: true/false
```

If we enable this option, ENVY imports the source code that was missing from the existing method editions. The only catch with this option is that we should try and remember to turn it back off after we're done. Otherwise, the optimization will be disabled for all loads, resulting in slower import times and unnecessary repository growth. Unfortunately, this option is not currently available for VisualWorks/ENVY.

Summary

This chapter has covered a great deal of advanced material with a range of topics. Fundamentally, we've looked at a number of different tools covering different areas of ENVY extensibility:

- A script manager using user fields to keep track of DoIts.

- A three-way differences browser to help merge different streams together — manipulating shadows and library specs to construct differences and building a new browser to compare them.

- A simple project management tool to specify an entire project and automate loading — illustrating storage of library specs, code generation, and loading code from specifications.

- A checkpointing facility for backup and sharing work across repositories — illustrating low-level efficient manipulation of ENVY record structures in the repository.

- Integrating a refactoring facility, encompassing numerous additional options for operations at the class, method, and text levels, into the standard ENVY browsers without modifying either the browser code or the Refactoring Browser code.

- A facility for renaming ENVY versions in place without creating a new edition and baselining it.

- Ways of removing source code from a repository so that we can ship code to developers without exposing all of our internal source code.

Together, these tools cover most of the different areas that are candidates for ENVY extensions. The techniques illustrated can be used as building blocks for a variety of tools and customizations. The material on using these goodies is appropriate for developers or administrators. The material on implementation is intended for toolsmiths and advanced power users.

≡Chapter 10≡

Troubleshooting

This is the chapter to read when you have trouble. We'll discuss dealing with components that won't load, recovering from simple image crashes as well as more complex ENVY crashes, and what you can do to make recovery easier. We'll also discuss more generic project troubleshooting to help you identify potential ENVY-related problems in a project, and suggest some possible remedies. The main topics we won't discuss here are installation and configuration problems, which we covered in Chapter 1.

Component Loading

One of the most common ENVY problems is that component editions will not load. A load may fail for many reasons. Two of the most common reasons are that a component cannot be constructed in the image (for example, the source for a method cannot be compiled or a required superclass is missing), or that loading a component results in the image being inconsistent (for example, a subapplication, class, or method would exist in two different places).

You have three main approaches to correcting a load failure, depending on the situation:

- altering an ENVY system setting that affects loading behavior
- modifying the component editions being loaded
- modifying the image

The two most important ENVY system settings that affect loading are:

```
EmImageBuilder cancelLoadsIfMethodsCollide:
EmImageBuilder cancelLoadsIfMethodsDoNotCompile:
```

When either of these settings has a value of false, the ImageBuilder forces the load to continue. It does this by deleting methods from their class editions so that the methods that do not compile or are the source of conflict will be removed from their class editions. Note that when methods collide, the new methods will supercede the old ones. This is dangerous because it means that the code loaded in the image will not be determined solely by which applications are present, but also by the order in which they were loaded. In general, these types of dependencies are something to avoid, but if we want to load otherwise incompatible components then we don't have a choice.

If these settings are not enough to let the component load, then we'll have to modify it in the library. For example, if the component defines a class whose name conflicts with another class that is already loaded, then we must resolve this conflict manually. We can do this by unloading (and possibly deleting) the class from the resident application. Alternatively, we could delete the class from the application to be loaded. Because that application is not yet resident, we would need to do the modification directly in the repository, using either shadow or editions browsers.

Typical operations to resolve conflicts include the following:

- releasing another edition of a class edition
- releasing another edition of a subapplication
- modifying lineups to change what is loaded
- deleting a class edition from a (sub)application edition
- deleting a subapplication from a lineup

Image Recovery

One of the most common problem scenarios that requires recovery in ENVY is a problem with the development image, either due to a crash or to corruption of some sort. This section discusses techniques for returning the image to a stable state.

Image Crash Recovery

The most basic form of problem recovery in ENVY is recovering from an image crash. Smalltalk is a robust environment, but it's still possible for the environment to crash, either because of bugs, problems in user code, or the operating system.

Fortunately, with ENVY it's relatively simple to recover from a crash and retrieve all of our changes. The process is described in the manuals but we think it's important enough to reiterate and expand on the ideas.

Let's suppose we've been working with some open application and class editions. At some point during development we saved the image, then continued working. Then the image and/or the workstation crashed. Okay, so we restart from the last saved image (we'll deal with the case where that file is corrupt later). This gets us most of the way back, but now this is an old image, and components may be out of date. For any given component, it can be in one of several states:

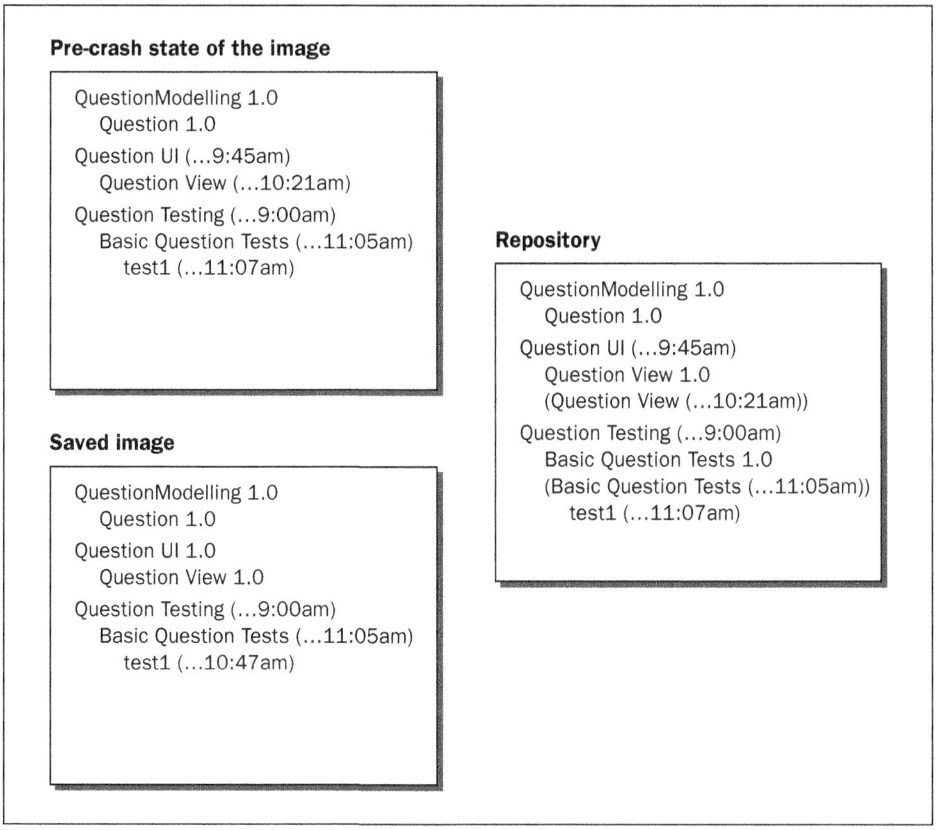

Figure 10-1: Recovering from a crash

- **Versioned, not touched:** We haven't modified these components at all. We don't need to worry about them.

- **Touched since last save:** When we saved the image, these were versions, but in the meantime we've made editions (scratch or otherwise). These editions exist in the repository (unless it's a scratch application edition) but aren't in the image at all. We need to find these components and load them back into the image we're recovering. If the components are applications, we need the open application editions as well as any class editions we had created inside them.

- **Touched before save, modified since:** An open edition was loaded before the last image save, but the edition has been modified since then. The edition exists in the repository and in the saved image, but it's different in each of them. The repository is right. We need to locate components that are different and load the correct version from the repository.

Figure 10-1 shows examples of these cases, illustrating the state in the image that crashed, the image doing the recovery, and the repository. Three applications are shown, each corresponding to one of the three cases. The QuestionModelling application is a version (case 1) and no recovery is necessary. The QuestionUI application has a new open edition in the repository, and the class QuestionView has been modified but not yet released (case 2). We will need to load both the application and the class editions. The application QuestionTesting was an open edition, with an open edition of the class BasicQuestionTests, but it was changed since the last time the image was saved (case 3). We will need to reload the class edition from the repository.

Saving the Image

Should we be saving the image at all? This seems like a pretty basic question, but differing opinions exist. Standard practice is to work in the same image, saving it to disk at various points, ranging from every few minutes to a couple of times a day. The main benefit of this approach is that we can very quickly pick up from where we left off, and continue in the development process. Depending on the environment and exactly what we were doing, we may even be able to save an image with a debugger open and resume debugging later.

The disadvantage to this approach is that we may somehow corrupt the state of the development image. At a minimum, it's likely that the image will eventually build up excess "garbage" such as suspended processes, globals, or half-opened but invisible windows. This causes the image size to increase needlessly and may even interfere with development. Another bad side effect is that because we're saving the image all the time, we may not bother to version and release code properly, meaning that a bad image crash (that is, corruption of the image) will be much harder to recover from.

Because of these disadvantages, a minority of users advocate developing without ever saving the image. In this model, before exiting from Smalltalk, we should always make sure that our changes are easily loadable into a clean image. On startup, reload the current configuration. Because we always load into a clean image, there's never any accumulation of junk and we always know that changes are in the repository. The process of loading into a clean image before packaging becomes trivial.

While it's true that never saving does eliminate some problems, we don't find this argument compelling. Being able to save the image is very convenient for day-to-day work, and we think that occasionally restarting with a clean image and a little bit of discipline can overcome most of the problems. Throughout this book, when it makes a difference, we assume the model containing the image is saved on a regular basis.

ENVY provides a crash-recovery mechanism to handle these cases, which is available on the menu with the somewhat confusing title of Make Image Consistent. This is misleading because it doesn't actually do anything to the image; it just reports on what we need to do to repair the image.

The report lists two different kinds of problems. The first is shown as

```
Scanning doit.log for application and class changes...
    since:  7/23/99 3:38:45 PM ***"
```

This uses the DOIT.LOG file to find all the editions that have been created since the last image save (case 2, previously). Both image saves and creation of new editions are logged in the DOIT.LOG, so it's relatively simple to look through it. In fact, ENVY doesn't even parse the file in any depth; it just looks for the last image save, and then writes out the relevant contents to the Transcript. It's our responsibility to look at this list, which essentially describes a list of application and class editions we'll need to load. Note that if the changes were made in a scratch edition the application edition (obviously) won't show up but the class editions will.

The second section is shown as

```
Checking the consistency of the applications in the image....................................
```

and it actually reports on open class editions that are different in memory from the repository (case 3, previously). This opens up a differences browser for each of the classes involved, showing the differences since the last save. Typically, the repository is right, and we just want to load the saved edition of each class. In the case of a simple image crash, we know the repository is right, so it's simpler to just spawn an editions browser and load the repository's edition rather than going through each change individually.

Once we've gone through both of these sections, the image should be back to normal and we can save it and proceed.

Image Crash Recovery (Part II)

Suppose we tried all of the preceding and it didn't help. What *else* can we do to recover the image?

It depends on why the previous steps didn't work. Checking consistency of open editions in memory against the repository should usually succeed. If there's a failure there, it indicates either an image that is badly damaged or repository problems. In either case, more drastic measures may be called for.

The DOIT.LOG file, on the other hand, might be inaccurate for a variety of reasons. It might simply be missing, truncated, or corrupt. One common case of mild corruption is using the same directory for multiple different images. Usually, this is fine, but all those images will share the same DOIT.LOG file. When we attempt to crash recover, we'll see all of the changes from all those images, which can be a lot of junk to wade through. Finally, the saved image might have been corrupted, forcing us to start from a clean image, complicating the recovery process.

In all these cases, the procedure is more or less the same. If the saved image is corrupt, then the first step is to load in our basic development configuration and save the image. If the log file is corrupt, we can work from our last saved image, which may at least contain some of the unreleased class changes.

Once that's done we need to find class changes. First, we query for any open class editions (using the ENVY menu's option for Query->Open Class Editions). This will list the open editions that might be different in the repository. For each open class edition, we can compare it to itself. This shows the differences between that edition and the repository. As a shortcut, if the repository is right (which is normally the case), we can just reload each edition from the repository to get back the latest changes.

Now we need to find open application editions that were created since our last snapshot. In an ideal setup, this is no problem. All the open (sub)application editions should have been released into the appropriate configuration map or parent application. By reloading into a clean image we've already loaded them. If we have a saved image, we can look through the Application Manager/Organizer and Configuration Maps Browser for unreleased (sub)applications. If we have a saved image with unreleased class changes, then just reloading the top-level component will remove those changes. We'll need to either load changes at a finer granularity or version and release the changes we have already before reloading. Finally, in a less ideal process, we will have to try to remember what we were working on or else go through all the applications we might have changed, browsing editions and looking for ones that seem familiar.

Once we have all the open application editions, we need to look for more recent class editions. We can find these using the More Recent Class Editions menu item from the Application Manager/Organizer. This option lists all the open class editions that are more recent than what's released in that application edition. Chances are that most of these are classes that were being worked on. There may also be old open editions that are nevertheless more recent than what was released. These might have had debugging statements added to them, or represent groups of changes that were abandoned. We'll have to sort through these manually, figuring out which ones actually represent valid changes.

This is more tedious than the normal process, but at the end of it we should be in a position to save our image and/or version/release and then continue working.

ENVY Crash Recovery

A much rarer circumstance than an image crash is an error in ENVY itself. If an ENVY operation fails for some reason, the image may be left in an inconsistent state. The sensible thing to do in this situation is quit the image without saving and recover as described previously. Even if the saved image is corrupt, we should really reload from a clean image. If we've been following good development practices, it'll only take us a few minutes to do that.

Alas, we don't always do the sensible thing. Sometimes it's to save time, or sometimes we're in the middle of a delicate operation. For whatever reason, we may want to try to salvage the image. That's okay, but first we should make very sure that our previously saved image is backed up, and realize that we're treading roughly on some very thin ice. Naturally, the circumstances of this kind of crash vary greatly and all we can do here is provide some general advice.

Any time an operation fails, ENVY knows about it. The next ENVY operation will give a dialog box explaining that a previous operation failed, and that we should really quit without saving. Being both brave and foolish, we proceed anyway, and (given the preceding warnings) it's usually acceptable because we already know there's a problem and are planning to repair it.

Usually, what's happened is that one particular application is in an inconsistent state. We need to get it back to a valid state. Ideally that would be the valid state we had beforehand, but we'll settle for any valid state we can then recover from. We can try several things.

Reload

Obviously, if we can just reload the application(s) then we're happy. So, let's assume that reloading didn't work. The most probable cause of this problem is that something in memory is so messed up that ENVY can't patch it together when reloading.

Unload

If it's wrong in memory, let's get it out of memory. Unload the problem class(es) and try reloading. If that doesn't work, try unloading the entire application. Of course, this isn't always as simple as it sounds. Unloading a class may require unloading subclasses and extensions, and unloading an application may require unloading others that depend on it. Because our image is a mess, any of these operations might also fail. We also may need to get rid of any instances before we can unload classes.

At the end of all that, we've either successfully unloaded, or our image is really in trouble. If we've unloaded, then we may be able to fix the problem just by reloading. If not, we may need to fix the repository version first.

Fix It in the Repository

ENVY makes an important distinction between operations that affect classes in memory and those that affect the repository directly. Most of the time we don't need to think about this distinction; now, however is one of the few times when it really matters. Whether or not we've successfully unloaded, we may need to make some changes to the repository in order to fix things.

In this case, our main weapons are the editions browsers. These let us operate directly on editions in the library. We can't compile or execute code against editions in the library, but we can delete things, change released editions, fiddle with prerequisites, and otherwise make noncode changes. By regressing toward something we think was valid, we should be able to get the code to a loadable state. In the worst case, we give up, get a clean image, and reload a stable version.

Example: Moving Classes

Here's an example of a situation that occurs relatively frequently and is nasty to recover from. Of course, ENVY crashes are rare, and by saying that this occurs frequently, we mean that we've seen it a few times in many years of ENVY usage.

This problem occurs, apparently randomly, when moving classes between two applications. It seems particularly likely to happen when there's a lot of class movement happening at the same time, which is rare, but often occurs when teaching a course on ENVY. The move operation can fail in the middle of a move, leaving the image in a state where the class exists in more than one place. This is a bad thing. We can't just reload because of the name conflict. The error is in two places, so fixing just one of them won't help.

The basic fix is relatively simple. Make sure all the other classes are versioned and released. Unload both of the applications that are causing the problem. Browse the editions (which aren't loaded, so we're modifying the repository directly) and fix the situation by re-releasing the old version of the class and deleting it from the place it was partially moved to. Reload both applications. Try again.

Making Recovery Easier

Usually it's not too hard to recover in ENVY, but following a few guidelines helps make life easier.

- **Version and release frequently.** The fewer changes since the last time we versioned and released classes, the less work it will be to recover from a crash. Along the way, we'll get other desirable side effects such as simpler integration and better communication with other team members. Some people advocate always versioning and releasing before leaving in the evening. That's an extreme position, but it's far better to err on the side of integrating too frequently rather than too infrequently.

- **Avoid scratch editions.** Scratch editions are a very valuable facility. They let the system get out of our way for a while so that we can do what we need to do. They can also be horribly abused. In general, scratch editions are a short-term way to circumvent the privileges and administration structure. Doing long-term work in a scratch edition is almost always a mistake. Even if a scratch edition is the right thing to use it will make integration and crash recovery more difficult. Sure, even in a scratch edition of an application the class editions are still real, but there's nothing to hold them together. We can't compare it to another application edition, and we can't release classes into it until it's made into a real edition. No one else knows there's a scratch edition, so they may create their own scratch edition, or a real one. We're likely to wind up with multiple editions of the same application that need to be integrated. It's possible to integrate in that circumstance, but it's much more difficult than just sharing the (sub)application edition in the first place. A lot of this is general process advice, discussed in the section on "Releasing Application Editions," but it applies very well to keeping our state recoverable.

- **Keep applications manageable.** Chances are we're only working on a relatively small set of classes at one time. If these are reasonably well partitioned into applications, then the possibility for code conflicts and the difficulty of recovery is relatively small. The larger an application gets, the more you have to look at.

- **Version off unused class editions.** As described in the section on "Purge" in Chapter 8, it's often desirable to version off open class editions that are no longer used. An edition that shows up with a name containing "junk" or "obsolete" is much easier to ignore in a list than an open edition with no additional information.

- **Reload into a clean image on a regular basis.** The most drastic recovery is to get a clean image and reload everything. For example, we'll need to do this for a crash that corrupts the saved image on disk. If we reload regularly, we'll have confidence that it can be done, with good procedures for doing it smoothly. Otherwise, there's more risk that the code doesn't actually load cleanly, or has obscure dependencies, so it will take a long time to reestablish a running image.

Repository Recovery

ENVY consolidates all of everyone's development work into the repository — a single, very large file just waiting for something bad to happen to it. The transaction mechanism used by ENVY is robust and it should be nearly impossible to corrupt the library or make it inconsistent through ENVY operations. However, the integrity of the library can be compromised by other means. Most commonly, corruption results from a server crash. Although crashes are rare, they can be catastrophic, so it's important to be prepared.

The first step is to check if something is actually wrong with the repository. Sometimes ENVY gives errors that suggest library corruption in response to network errors, when there's actually nothing wrong with the repository. It's important not to ignore the warning, however, because resuming work after repository corruption has happened can make the problem much, much worse.

Basic Crash Recovery

If the server does crash, the library should immediately be checked when the server is restarted. The best way to lock out all users from the library and prevent any further work is to rename the library to a temporary name. We also strongly recommend making a backup copy of the repository at this point. The library recovery procedures may modify the repository, and having a backup can be extremely important.

Once we've renamed the repository, we can run an image, preferably one that's not connected to the repository at all. We can do that by editing the startup file to specify a nil library (see "The Configuration File") or by disconnecting from the library, using the System->Disconnect from Server... menu item.

As described in the ENVY manuals, run

```
EmLibrary crashRecover: aFileName
```

This examines the recent records in the library, looking for evidence of corruption. It either reports that the library is in a consistent state or truncates the library to the last point at which it believes it to be consistent. If the library has been truncated, we may need to recover some code, as described next, or rewrite it. If the library is consistent we're probably okay, but we may still want to run the second step to verify the entire library.

The second step is running library statistics and it requires us to load the system application EmLibraryStatistics. This application contains a number of classes for analyzing the ENVY repository, primarily extensions to the EmRecord classes. Run the following code fragment.

```
| lib stats |
lib := EmLibrary open: 'complete library path'.
stats := EmLibraryStatistics checkConsistencyOf: lib.
lib close.
^stats
```

This code exhaustively examines the library and produces a report of any corrupt records found. It will take some time to run. This examines the complete repository, but it doesn't attempt to repair the damage. If the library is inconsistent then it should be replaced with a previous backup.

If the library has been damaged in a location that is anywhere but near the end of the library, a severe loss of work may result. Rather than return to a previous backup, one solution may be to ignore the corruption or to try and repair it. What to do depends a lot on the type of records that are corrupted. EmLibraryStatistics contains a further check to find corrupt records in the library. The problem with this is that the information it produces is difficult to interpret.

If we have a corrupt library and wish to salvage work from it, you really have only three options — try to repair the library, try to purge components that are affected by the corruption, or try to export out noncorrupted code into a clean repository. At this point, the prudent thing to do is to contact technical support for assistance.

Recovering Code

If the library has been truncated, we may have code that has been lost. Usually the amount of code is very small and it's better to just rewrite it again. It may be possible, however, to recover some of that code. Basically, we add two new possibilities to the list outlined at the beginning of this chapter as follows:

- Exists in the image; does not exist in the repository.
- Modified, image saved before the repository crashed. The components exist in the repository and in the image, but are different in each of them. The image is right.

Because the source code is stored in the repository, we have a problem. In VisualWorks it may be possible to access the decompiled version of the code and save it. In VisualAge there's no decompiler, so it's not possible to recover the source code. At this point we have to ask ourselves if it's worth trying to recover the code. Chances are that the amount of code is relatively small, and we could recreate the code faster than recovering and verifying it. If we really want to attempt this it should be possible to recover some of the code, but again we probably should contact technical support for assistance.

Project Recovery

Volumes have been written on the topic of identifying and fixing problems with projects and development processes. Here, we'll confine ourselves to discussing problems that are directly related to ENVY usage. Most of the general practices described here are also discussed elsewhere in the book, but here there's an emphasis on recovery. You have a problem with the way you've been doing things. Having read this far, you probably know what you should have done to begin with, but you don't have time to go back and do it right now. What can you do to refactor things enough to address the most serious problems, without stopping work for a month or more to reorganize?

What we discuss here are specific problems, with possible solutions. Naturally, these can't even begin to cover all situations, and you'll have to judge how they apply to your circumstances. Don't take these prescriptions as rules so much as guidelines based on situations we have encountered.

These problems are presented in vaguely pattern-like format, as follows:

Problem: A quick description of the problem.

Details: More detailed description, including possible causes. This lets you judge more precisely if this is your problem.

Solutions: Ways of addressing the problem.

This Week: What you can do in the next few days to start addressing these problems.

See Also: References to other sections in the book that address these issues.

The problems are further broken down by category into coding, integration, packaging, and quality problems.

Coding Problems

These problems reflect day-to-day issues in development, loosely related to writing code.

Changing Users

Problem: We constantly have to change users to get anything done.

Details: Code ownership is inaccurate or fragmented. The people actually doing coding on the class have to change users all the time to release. There may be no clear single owner of a piece of code. In an undisciplined process, developers may change users to create editions of applications they do not manage, possibly leading to the problems described in "Difficult Integration" and "Lost Changes" later in this chapter.

Solutions: The solution depends on why this is happening. If a component formally belongs to one user, but another user is doing most of the work, then the user doing the work may end up changing users frequently to perform administrative operations. Consider changing the ownership to reflect the true situation or having the owner do more of the work. Recall that ENVY supports different owners in different streams, so it's possible to subdivide ownership. For example, we might have one developer working on maintenance and another one on new development. In general, remember that the owner of a class should be the person doing primary development work on that class. Other users can make changes, but the owner must approve them before they can be integrated.

We may have a more fluid situation, where no single person can be considered the primary developer. In this case, we need to carefully consider our process. ENVY is organized around the idea of component ownership. If we don't use this principle, we are circumventing ENVY's normal controls and must account for the risks this entails. In particular, if many users can release a class there's a danger of lost changes as multiple release operations overwrite each other. Frequently changing users also leads to other errors (particularly when users forget to change back) and a lack of traceability. These issues can be dealt with either by enforcing code ownership more strictly or by using additional tools to avoid these problems.

It's possible to build tools that allow nonowners to release classes without having to manually change users. This immediately eliminates the possibility of forgetting to change back. These tools can also perform appropriate safety checks, such as notifying the owners and checking that the version being released is based on the previous released version (that is, we are not overwriting other changes). Commercially, VA Assist Pro includes the features of "super user" mode and "release only clean" for classes, which together provide a reasonably safe way to develop without strict class ownership. Version naming conventions or automatic "notes" mechanisms that identify the developer can improve traceability.

Changing users can also result in integration problems, as described in "Difficult Integration" later in this chapter. Application editions are expected to be shared. If users create their own application editions by changing users, this will make it harder to locate changes.

This Week: Make sure a recent baseline exists. Give developers permission to take ownership (after checking with others) of classes they are doing primary work on. After a few days, check how many conflicts have arisen, and if the problem situations have improved. Examine what simple tools could be used to regulate the situation. Ensure that a disciplined process is in place for creation of application editions.

See Also: See "Resolving Conflicts" in Chapter 3, and "Extreme Programming and ENVY" in Chapter 4 for a discussion of disciplined techniques that do not use class ownership.

Upgrading

Problem: It's difficult to upgrade to a new system version.

Details: A couple of days' work is to be expected when we're upgrading from one version of the base system or a third-party tool to the next, but we're encountering excessive difficulties. This might be because we have many base changes or because we rely too much on internal details of vendor code, which has changed. It might also be because the vendor is doing a poor job of providing backward compatibility in its product. Finally, it may reflect difficulty loading into a new, clean image as described in "Can't Load Into a Clean Image" later in this chapter.

Solutions:

- Reduce dependence on the details of the base by using only documented public protocol as much as possible.

- Don't make base changes except where it's really the right thing to do. This is, of course, a judgment call but you should at least ensure that changes are subject to some oversight.

- This might be a one-time dependency, in which case the only real solution is to accept the difficulty and do the conversion. For example, we might have built custom widgets in older versions of VisualWorks and made them highly dependent on the polling UI mechanism. This can present significant difficulties when converting to the more recent event-driven UI. There's no way to provide full backward compatibility, and this represents a significant improvement in the mechanism. We just have to do the conversion. This is one situation where a consultant who understands the new features we're trying to use may be helpful.

- A good suite of regression tests is very helpful when upgrading. We can quickly pinpoint problem areas and have confidence when the new version is working well.

- If the difficulty reflects an inability to load the code into a new, clean image, we have a serious problem. If we address that problem then upgrades should become much easier.

This Week: In the very short term, all we can really do is defer addressing the problems. Look for appropriate backward-compatibility protocol and assess how much code needs immediate conversion *versus* how much can be done gradually. If there are more fundamental problems, look at short-term measures to address them.

See Also: See "Library Architecture" in Chapter 4.

Integration Problems

These problems are all loosely related to the integration, load building, and versioning process. Because this is the point at which ENVY facilities are most involved, many of the problems with ENVY usage manifest themselves here.

Difficult Integration

Problem: Integration is very difficult.

Details: The ENVY mechanisms are intended to ensure that integration happens throughout the development process, so making a baseline should be a relatively smooth and painless process. Difficulties in integration may be caused by "true" integration problems, where many developers are modifying the same components at the same time in conflicting ways. These need to be addressed through process and partitioning mechanisms. Difficulties may also arise from problems managing the changes, even if they don't conflict. Such problems include the following:

- **Nonshared editions.** The continuous integration process relies on the idea that class editions are private, but application editions are shared. If two developers are working on the same application at the same time, they should be working in the same edition. If each one has a separate edition, avoiding conflicts and merging those changes together is much more difficult. This often arises in conjunction with changing users, where each developer creates application editions as needed, potentially without noticing that an edition already exists.

- **Overuse of scratch editions.** Scratch editions are a valuable tool for making short-term changes. Doing significant amounts of work in scratch editions is similar to nonshared application editions, but worse because the scratch edition isn't even visible to other developers.

- **Lost changes.** If we can't be sure we've integrated everything the process becomes much more difficult. See "Lost Changes" later in this chapter.

- **Too much overlap.** If many developers are working on the same classes, those classes become a bottleneck and a source of problems. This is particularly true for GUI classes because merging changes to these classes is often difficult.

- **Infrequent "Big Bang" integration.** Making a small change and integrating it is usually quite simple. The longer we wait, the more difficult it becomes. Changes should be released regularly throughout a development cycle, and full integrations should be done frequently. Single developers who work in their own stream for long periods can cause significant integration difficulties.

Solutions:

- For (sub)applications under frequent development, create new open editions immediately after versioning. Release them into their parent application or configuration map. Insist that developers work in these editions and that a controlled process exists for creating editions of other applications, ensuring a maximum of one open edition per stream at a time, and that scratch editions are not used for more than a short time.

- For classes that are bottlenecks, identify the problem classes and try to reduce the conflicts. This could be done by splitting out some of the problem methods into extensions, splitting the class into several classes, reducing the need for frequent modifications, or limiting work on those classes to a small number of coordinating developers. We'll need to measure which classes are problems, which could be as simple as asking the developers or building a tool that can highlight classes frequently changed by multiple different developers.

This Week: Put in place the structure just described for ensuring that only one application edition (per stream) is open at a time. Schedule an integration this week, and each week thereafter. Temporarily ban the use of scratch editions. Determine which classes are causing the most integration problems, and consider how to split them up or limit the number of concurrent developers.

See Also: See "Development Process" in Chapter 5.

Slow Integration

Problem: Integration is not necessarily difficult, but it's taking too much time.

Details: Integration takes so long that it is consuming a significant part of the development cycle. Other developers can't work effectively during integration, or they work against the previous build, causing more integration problems for the next cycle. Because integration is a long and painful process, there's pressure to make it less frequent, compounding the difficulty.

Possible causes include the following:

- **Infrequent integration.** The further apart integrations are, the longer they take, and the more complex they become. More frequent releases actually end up consuming less development time.

- **Infrequent release.** The ENVY mechanisms are intended to ensure that integration happens throughout the development process. Developers version and release classes as they finish making incremental changes, so integration should consist primarily of application versioning and testing. If developers do not incrementally release, the integration process becomes slower and more difficult.

- **Inadequate prerelease QA.** If developers consistently test code before releasing, then the integration test should go smoothly. If testing is inadequate, then integration testing takes over the role of incremental testing, and will take much longer. Inadequate testing might happen because of last-minute changes, inability of individual developers to run regression tests, or just because developers "know" their code will work.

- **Complex configurations.** In a large, complex project, the number of configurations to be managed can become very large, to the point where just releasing applications to all the right places takes a significant amount of time.

- **Remote development with overlapping responsibilities.** One special case that can lead to slow integration is off-site developers. A project may have developers working off-site, using separate repositories. While this may make it easier to staff the project, it causes extra work at integration time. Remote developers must use nonshared editions (see "Difficult Integration" earlier in this chapter), requiring a three-way differences check for any application that has also been changed in the main repository. Local and remote developers rarely see each other's changes until a full integration, reducing communication. The problems are reduced if a remote developer owns the application(s) he or she is modifying and no one else makes changes to them, but this requires careful planning and partitioning.

Solutions: Many of the issues are similar to those for difficult integration, and the same solutions apply. Have frequent, smaller integrations, and take steps to streamline them so they do not take up too much time. Ensure that developers release changes in small increments throughout the process, resolving conflicts and testing as they go. It's important to be sure that individual developers have the ability to run at least a reasonable subset of the regression tests so that problems are caught early. Simplify configurations, where possible, and automate repetitive processes to save time and reduce the possibility of error.

This Week: Schedule an integration this week, and each week thereafter. Observe the integration and account for all the time to determine which areas are bottlenecks. Try a temporary policy where developers are required to version and release their changes every day, ensuring that they pass a basic test suite. Examine reassigning remote developer responsibilities to minimize overlap.

See Also: See "Multi-Site Development" in Chapter 4, "Team Development" Chapter 3, "Remote Work" in Chapter 8, and "Checkpoints" in Chapter 9.

Lost Changes

Problem: Changes are being lost. We're never sure if our version contains all the required code.

Details: Possible causes of lost changes include the following:

- **Nonshared application editions.** As described in "Difficult Integration" earlier in this chapter, nonshared editions can cause problems integrating. The integrator must examine each edition, and determine which class editions must be released into the main edition, merging where necessary. Changes can easily be lost.

- **Missing class ownership.** If multiple users can release a class, one may release without noticing changes released by another. This can cause the original changes to be lost.

- **Stream management.** If multiple simultaneous development streams exist, changes made in one stream may not be reflected in another. With many streams, deciding which changes go into which stream can become difficult.

Solutions: Follow the practices described in "Difficult Integration" and "Changing Users" earlier in this chapter. Ensure that application editions are shared, and minimize the use of scratch editions. Either enforce class ownership and ENVY's controls on releasing classes, or modify the system to ensure that changes are not overwritten. Minimize the number of simultaneous streams. Consider carefully tracking changes such as bug fixes and patches to ensure they are propagated to all relevant streams.

This Week: Review the circumstances under which changes have been lost. Look at how this can be prevented in the future. Refer to other relevant problems.

See Also: See "Streams" in Chapter 4.

Packaging Problems

This section describes problems that arise in packaging an image for distribution. It's hard to describe packaging problems in general because such a variety of packaging technologies exists. There are significant differences between packaging code as parcels, ICs, stripped images, and nonstripped images built by remote development tools (XD or OpenTalk). This section attempts to address generic issues, without delving too deeply into all of these variations. In general, we focus on the packaging problems that arise by "stripping" an image, using tools such as the VisualAge Packager or Runtime Packager for VisualWorks to remove unused code from a development image.

Chapter 6 describes packaging issues in more detail, and this section assumes familiarity with the particular packaging process you're using.

Circular Prerequisites

Problem: We're trying to package, we have many circular prerequisite relationships, and we don't know how to get rid of them.

Details: The VisualAge Packager uses the ENVY prerequisite mechanism to determine which classes and methods need to be included in the runtime image. ENVY does not let us define circular prerequisites, but our code may still include references to classes and/or methods that are not in the prerequisite list. This can result in unresolved references when packaging or in run-time errors. Note that this problem does not arise when packaging in VisualWorks because neither parcels nor Runtime Packager use ENVY prerequisites to determine which classes/methods to remove.

Solutions: The ideal solution is to refactor the code into a layered architecture so that prerequisite relationships are correctly organized. Unfortunately, that's a slow process, and it may be difficult to do.

In the short term, we can use a few mechanisms to address these problems as follows:

- **Fix prerequisites.** It may be that all that's needed is minor adjustment of prerequisites, rather than a wholesale reorganization. If fixing it won't require a huge effort, then that's obviously the thing to do.

- **Class extensions.** Often, a conflict occurs because one or two methods in a class refer to classes/methods in other applications. It may be possible to remove the conflicts by moving those methods into a class extension. One common example is the method inspect. It occurs in a domain object but references development-time debug tools. If we define custom inspectors for some of our objects, but want to avoid packaging them, we can do it by moving the inspect method into a debugging tools application, rather than the domain application.

- **Subapplications.** We may have partitioned our applications based on criteria other than coupling or layering. For example, we might have partitioned to split the work between developers, to distinguish between API and internal classes in a library, or we might have started with two independent applications, which have grown to be tightly coupled. In any case, we have two codependent applications. For our purposes, this is acceptable. We don't ever plan on loading just one of them, but the packager doesn't know that and won't handle it correctly. One way of addressing this is to merge the two applications. A simpler way is to move both of them into subapplications and put them underneath the same parent. ENVY does not have prerequisite relationships between subapplications and, for packaging purposes, they all count as part of one big application. Note that we can't easily change an application into a subapplication, so we will probably need to create new applications and move classes around anyway, but in a simpler way.

- **Explicit packaging rules.** ENVY provides a number of ways to explicitly tell the packager which classes and methods to include or exclude. This can address particular problems, but as a workaround for prerequisite errors it's dangerous. We'll need to maintain these packaging rules, which remain a potential source of error.

This Week: Determine the true dependency relationships between applications, based on class references, method usage, and developer knowledge. Where possible, fix prerequisites to reflect this. Examine the remaining dependencies and decide on a mechanism to resolve the problem.

See Also: See "Packaging" in Chapter 6, "Subapplications" in Chapter 4, "Classes and Extensions" in Chapter 2, and "The Art of the Class Extension" in Chapter 7.

Image Size

Problem: Our packaged image is too large.

Details: We can package successfully, but the resulting image is too large for the space constraints. This is a complex problem, but a few root causes exist.

- We didn't package from a clean image, and development-time artifacts crept in.

- Too much is being included unnecessarily.

- Too much is being included necessarily.

Solutions:

- Before packaging, always load the absolute minimum set of applications into a clean image. Do not load any development tools, and do not run any code before packaging (if we want to test that image, we can save the image first and then revert back to it before packaging). This ensures that we don't have extra code, which might be included, and that additional objects (processes, globals, and so forth) aren't created and then unnecessarily included. This is by far the easiest thing we can do to minimize run-time image size.

- Examine the packager's output. This should include a list of everything that was included. Look for things that don't seem necessary, and then use the packager facilities to discover why they were included. Either we'll find that they really are necessary, or that we can fix the thing that causes the unnecessary inclusion. Expect this to take some time.

- As previously, examine the packager's output. Some things will be included because the code really does use them, but small changes to the code could eliminate that dependency. For example, in VisualWorks, we may not need the ability to change the look and feel dynamically at run-time, and we can remove all but one of the UI policies. This could take the most time because it requires us to examine the facilities that our own code uses and evaluate how necessary they are.

This Week: Be sure that the packaging process starts by loading into a clean image. While loading into a clean image, look for applications or configuration maps that don't seem necessary. Set targets for image size. Begin the process of examining the packager's output.

See Also: See Chapter 6, "Packaging and Delivery."

Can't Load Into a Clean Image

Problem: We never load into a clean image, and now we can't.

Details: Our code doesn't load cleanly, so we work based on a reference image.

This problem typically occurs when the integration process is image-based rather than version-based. In a version-based integration process, once a version and new development editions have been created, we announce it to the team, and they load the appropriate editions. In an image-based process, we create the new editions in an image, and then announce it to the team, and they copy the new reference image to their workstations and run from it.

The good thing about image-based integration is that it saves the time for everyone to load, and it ensures that everyone is working from exactly the same configuration. The bad thing is that we may introduce dependencies on a particular image structure into our code, and not notice them for a long time. Suddenly, when we go to package, we notice that our reference image has 3MB of hard-to-locate garbage and we can't load our code into a clean image. With fast machines and the speed of loading incremental changes, there's not a good reason today for doing image-based integration. We have a repository; we should use it.

Solutions: Take a clean image and load the code into it. Note the failure and correct it. Repeat until it loads.

Along the way, we may need to organize the code so that we can load a single configuration map (one-click loading). This greatly simplifies loading for all our developers.

Note that a common source of loading problems is the creation and initialization of globals and/or pool dictionaries. This used to be handled using toBeLoadedCode, which was awkward and hard to debug. More recent versions of ENVY support pragmas to avoid these problems.

This Week: Follow the solutions described in the "Solutions" section.

Quality Problems

This section describes problems with code quality. Our process is generating the code we need; it just doesn't work.

Too Many Defects

Problem: Too many defects exist in our code.

Details: This breaks down into two scenarios, as follows:

- We discover the defects ourselves, but we can't fix them in time. This probably indicates that the code is too difficult to maintain and needs refactoring. Naturally, we never have time to do the refactoring because we're behind on basic issues such as fixing defects.

- Users discover the defects. Because we're not discovering the defects during testing, that probably means our testing and/or requirements are inadequate.

Solutions:

- For the first problem, there's a nice description in Ward Cunningham's Episodes pattern language (http://c2.com/ppr/episodes.html). He very briefly describes a pattern called Motivated Consolidation. There's never extra time available just to refactor code. Therefore, we refactor when it actually saves time. For example, suppose we need to fix one or more defects in a particular area of code that's a mess. Metaphorically, we have to cross a swamp. Is it faster to just hack our way through the swamp, or to drain at least part of the swamp along the way? If it's the latter, then we're refactoring in a way that actually saves time. If it's the former, it isn't worth refactoring that piece of code. Another good reference is Fowler (1999).

- As defects are reported, we should ensure that tests to catch this and any related possible errors we can think of are added to the regression test suite. This ensures that our quality is improving at least a little, and that errors don't recur. In general, we should examine our test building process to see why we're missing so many problems. All of this assumes, of course, that we have a reasonable regression testing system in place. If not, see the "Inadequate Testing" problem next.

- If the problems arise because of misunderstood or missing requirements, then we need to be much clearer about the precise requirements. This could involve getting the users more closely involved with the system building, more frequent rollouts of prototypes or interim versions to users for approval, or more precisely specified up-front requirements.

This Week: Look at the types and frequency of defects. Look for areas of the code that are particular problems and consider refactoring them as you fix outstanding problems. Write some tests.

Inadequate Testing

Problem: We don't have any coordinated regression testing mechanism. Most of our testing is ad hoc.

Details: For whatever reason, we're well into the project, with little or no regression testing in place. We may not even have a regression testing framework.

Solutions: The answer is clear. Put a regression testing framework into place and start writing tests. Concentrate on the areas that are causing the most problems. Emphasize domain tests over GUI tests, and particularly emphasize any stable APIs we may have.

Regression testing slows things down at first, but it's very unlikely we can deliver with reasonable quality without it. Once the system is in place, it will actually improve the speed of development because developers can have more confidence in their code and spend less time on manual testing and debugging.

Sometimes, in a complex deployment environment, it's considered too hard or too expensive to have a full test environment. This is clearly a false economy. We may need to create a scaled-down simulation environment, or otherwise limit testing, but we must have a better way of ensuring the quality of the full product rather than just "deploy and hope."

This Week: Put a test framework in place. You can use a free, minimalist test framework such as SUnit (www.xprogramming.com or http://ansi-st-tests.sourceforge.net/SUnit.html) or a commercial product such as Silvermark's Test Mentor (www.silvermark.com) or OTF (www.mcgsoft.com). Start writing some basic test cases. Examine what you can easily test and make a plan for the more difficult areas.

See Also: See "Extreme Programming and ENVY" in Chapter 4 for an example of a very testing-focused methodology.

Summary

This chapter has gone into some depth on various aspects of troubleshooting. Unfortunately, troubles are so ingenious that we can only cover a small portion of the possible difficulties you'll run into. We hope this section helps you out of at least the basic difficulties you encounter, and leaves you prepared for the truly nasty problems.

Some of the important details to remember from this chapter are as follows:

- If components won't load we may be able to force a load by changing some system settings, or we may need to modify the components or the image.
- ENVY includes features for recovery from image crashes and repository crashes.
- You have many different ways to approach project issues, most of which are focused on process but can take advantage of Smalltalk and ENVY features.

≡Appendix≡

A Selected Annotated API of ENVY System Classes

In this book we've talked a lot about programming using ENVY System classes. At the simplest level this involves implementing methods such as loaded or removing on our own application classes. At the most complex level, we've seen code to create checkpoint versions directly out of application editions in the repository. All of this requires manipulating the classes that make up ENVY itself.

This kind of programming can be quite difficult. Although we refer to this as an API, many of these classes and methods are not well documented and have changed over time. The most difficult part of writing ENVY system code is understanding the relationships between components and finding the methods necessary to manipulate these relationships. This is complicated by a few factors. First, the components are not directly related through instance variables; rather, many of the most important relationships are implicit in methods. Further, these methods are not concentrated in the components themselves, but are spread out over three distinct groups of classes: the browsers, the "helper" classes such as EmInterface, and the components themselves.

In the earliest versions of ENVY almost everything was done directly in the browser code. Over time much of the code was moved to the components themselves or to utility classes such as EtTools and EmInterface. This reduced code duplication but the utility classes became very complex, with many methods that manipulate different types of components, making it harder to find any given piece of functionality. Many operations require a combination of these different types of classes. Finally, these classes have many methods, serving many different purposes, and the method categories are not very helpful in distinguishing these purposes.

In an attempt to make ENVY system programming easier, this appendix presents many of the most important classes and methods in ENVY, along with explanations of their use. You'll also find many examples of using these APIs in the code that accompanies this book, as well as further discussion of these issues in the "Writing Scripts" section in Chapter 8.

We will first deal with the three basic components unique to ENVY: (Sub)Application, EmConfigurationMap, and EmUser, and then look at enhancements that ENVY adds to classes and methods.

Application and SubApplication

In ENVY, applications and subapplications are represented and manipulated as application classes (see "Application Classes" in Chapter 9). These classes inherit from Application or from SubApplication respectively. There are a number of peculiar aspects to these classes that can be confusing for both novices and advanced users.

First, the class SubApplication is actually the superclass of the class Application. In practice this can be ignored most of the time, but it does mean that many of the more general methods for manipulating applications are found in the SubApplication class.

Second, application classes are (usually) singletons, where the singleton is represented by the class. We never manipulate instances of application classes, and all of their methods are class methods. We say that these are usually singletons because the application class for the resident application is a singleton, but we may have multiple shadows present for that same application class.

Third, and more important, is the fundamental confusion between the different components represented by the application class. This class fulfills several different roles.

- It is a class, which exists in its own right.
- It represents an application edition in memory, either resident or as a shadow.
- It represents the application in general, with no particular edition.

The same object fulfills all of these roles, and its methods have implicit assumptions about the role the class is playing. We can group the application class's methods into four main categories, based on which of these roles the class plays in that method, as follows:

- **Factory methods for retrieving applications and subapplications.** These are normally sent to SubApplication or Application directly, and the application class plays no role at all. For example, currentlyLoaded.
- **Methods for the application class.** These are sent to the class directly and treat it as a class. For example, loaded and removing.
- **Methods affecting the application edition.** These are normally sent to the application class directly, with SubApplication or Application treated as an abstract superclass. The class represents a particular application edition, and these methods often modify the repository. For example, addConfigurationExpression.
- **Methods affecting the application as a whole.** These are normally sent to the application class, and treat it as a factory for retrieving information about its editions. For example, allClassNames, residentApplication, and shadows.

All of these methods are grouped together in the protocol for the classes Application and SubApplication. The following sections break these methods down further according to the components they manipulate. The majority of the methods expect to be sent to an application edition. Where this is not the case, we've identified that in the method description.

Protocols

Within ENVY, all of the system methods are categorized according to the application that contains them, along with a distinction between API methods and internal methods (represented by the protocols EM-API and EM-Internal). While this is helpful, it doesn't go nearly far enough if we are to understand the different roles these methods play. Here, we've attempted to classify the Application and SubApplication methods into the following categories. Note that many of these methods apply to both applications and subapplications, and we've used the generic term *application* inclusively.

- Classes
- Applications/Subapplications
- Configuration Expressions
- Editions/Timestamps
- Menus
- Pre/Post Loading/Removing
- Shadows
- Startup/Shutdown
- User Fields/Library Objects
- Users
- Version/Edition Status

Classes

allClassNames Returns all the known class names ever defined in any edition of this application sorted alphabetically.

allClassNamesIn: aSymbol (Sent to Application/SubApplication) Returns all the known class names ever defined in any edition of the (sub)application named aSymbol sorted alphabetically.

allLocalClasses Returns all the public classes local to this application edition's root application.

allNames Returns all the known class names ever defined in any edition of this application sorted alphabetically.

areReleased: Returns whether each class in classes is a version in this application editions and is also the same as the released version in the receiver.

availableClassNames Returns the names of classes released in other editions of this application but not in this edition, sorted alphabetically.

classes Returns all the classes contained in this application edition. This includes defined classes, extended classes, and classes that are listed but without a released edition (that is, undefined classes).

defined Returns the set of classes defined in this application edition. Note that within an image any class is defined in exactly one place.

extended Returns the set of classes extended in this application edition.

findAllInconsistentClasses (sent to an open application edition) Checks all of the class editions in this application edition and returns shadow classes for any class edition that is inconsistent with its methods.

isReleased: aClass Returns whether the current edition of aClass is the released version in this application edition.

moreRecentClassEditions Returns shadows for any class editions owned by the current user that are more recent than the ones currently loaded in this application edition. The result is a dictionary in which keys are a shadow of the loaded classes that have such editions, and the values are collections of shadow classes for the more recent editions.

releaseClass: aClassEdition Release the version corresponding to aClass in this application edition.

releaseEachClassIn: aCollectionOfClasses For each class in aCollectionOfClasses, set the released timestamp in this application edition to be the timestamp of that class (that is, release the class).

moreRecentClassEditions Returns shadows for any class editions owned by the current user that are more recent than the ones currently loaded in this application edition. The result is a dictionary in which keys are a shadow of the loaded classes that have such editions, and the values are collections of ShadowClasses for the more recent editions.

releasedClassVersions Returns a dictionary of the class names for this application edition associated with their released timestamp.

undefined Returns the set of shadow classes for all the known class names that have yet to be defined or loaded in this application edition.

Class Visibility

allVisibleClasses Returns all the public classes visible in the scope of this application edition's root application.

isClassVisible: Returns whether aClass is visible in this application edition. A class is visible if it's a public class defined by this edition or by one of its prerequisites or subapplications. If a class is private it is visible if it has the same root application as the receiver.

Applications/SubApplications

allParents Returns a collection of all the parents of this application edition. These are listed in inverse hierarchical order, that is, the root application is last.

allPossibleSubApplications Returns *all* of this application's possible subapplications (that is, shadows for all subapplications required by any of the configuration expressions. This will also traverse subapplications recursively. The order of the results is undefined.

allSubApplications Returns the hierarchy of subapplications visible to this application edition. Starts with the subapplications of this edition, sorted alphabetically; then adds all of their subapplications, and so on.

currentlyLoaded (Sent to Application/SubApplication) If sent to Application, returns all applications in the image. If sent to SubApplication returns all applications and subapplications. In either case this starts with Kernel and traverses up through the prerequisite relationships. Within a layer of prerequisites the applications are sorted alphabetically and are immediately followed by their subapplications. The list returned by this method is read-only. In VisualAge this is obsolete; use EmSystemConfiguration->loadedSubApplications instead.

default Returns the default (sub)application, which is the one used when filing in code. Obsolete; use EmSystemConfiguration->defaultApplication instead.

hasSubApplications Returns whether the receiver has subapplications.

loadSubApplication: shadowSub in: existingExpression Loads the shadow subapplication into the receiver, but first checks to see if it can be added to the existing configuration expression existingExpression (given that it isn't there already). If it is successfully loaded, this method then adds it to the existing expression. The receiver must be an open application edition and the current user must be the manager of that edition.

parent Returns the receiver's parent application (either an application or a subapplication).

parent: anApplication Sets the receiver's parent application (either an application or a subapplication) to be anApplication and sets its root application to be the root application of anApplication.

releasedSubApplications Returns a dictionary containing this application edition's subapplication names associated with their released timestamps. This will use the configuration expression that currently applies to this edition.

releasedSubApplicationsFor: aConfigurationExpression Returns this application edition's subapplication names associated with their released timestamps for aConfigurationExpression; if it is unaware of the expression, this methods answers an empty collection.

releaseSubApp Releases this subapplication edition into its parent. This method is derived from EtApplicationManager->releaseSubApplicationsAction. If more than one configuration expression can apply to the image, then this method prompts the user to determine which configuration is being updated.

releaseSubApplication: aSubApp in: aConfigurationExpression Makes the current timestamp of aSubApp be the released one in the existing configuration expression aConfigurationExpression (adding aSubApp to the lineup if it does not exist). The receiver must be an open edition and the current user must be its manager. If the expression does not exist, nothing will happen.

removeSubApplication: aSubApplication Removes aSubApplication from this application edition in the image and from all of its subapplications.

rootApplication Returns the application in which the receiver is a part.

subApplications Returns the subapplications that are a direct part of the receiver.

subApplications: subApps Changes the receiver's set of subapplications to be subApps.

withAllPossibleSubApplications Returns the receiver with *all* its possible subapplications, that is, shadows for all subapplications required by any of the receiver's (or its subs and so on) configuration expressions. The order is unknown.

withAllSubApplications Returns the receiver with all its subapplications.

Configuration Expressions

Configuration expressions are the syntax supporting the conditional loading mechanism of subapplications. Although they are rarely set programmatically, a few methods are interesting.

allConfigurationExpressions Returns this application edition's configuration expressions in the order in which they are evaluated.

configurationExpression Returns the configuration expression for this application edition.

Editions/TimeStamps

classEditionNamed: aSymbol at: aTimeStamp Returns a class edition named aSymbol for the edition at aTimeStamp in this application edition.

classEditionsFor: aSymbol Returns class editions for aSymbol in this application edition, sorted chronologically.

editionTimeStampsFor: aSymbol Returns timestamps for each edition of aSymbol sorted chronologically, latest first.

timeStampFor: aClassOrName Returns the timestamp for aClassOrName in this application edition.

timeStampFor: aClassOrName is: aTimestamp Sets the edition of aClassOrName in this application edition.

timeStamps Returns the editions of the classes for which this application has extensions.

Menus

addToSystemMenu A hook to allow this application to add code to the system menu. The default behavior is to do nothing.

Pre/Post Loading/Removing

failedRemove A hook to notify the application that an error occurred in attempting to unload the application. This gives the application an opportunity to put itself back into a stable state, reversing the effects of anything done in the removing method. The default behavior is to make the application a scratch edition if it was a version and to otherwise do nothing.

loaded A hook to notify the application that it has been loaded. This is called each time the receiver is loaded. The default behavior is to do nothing.

removing A hook to notify the application that it is about to be unloaded. To help ensure a successful unload, this method should remove instances of any of the application classes that may exist in class, pool, or global variables. Note that failedRemove will be called if the unload operation fails.

toBeLoadedCode Returns the "to be loaded" code for this application edition, which is evaluated before the application is loaded. This code is typically used to define global or pool variables that must be created before the application is loaded in order for the application code to compile correctly. This functionality has largely been replaced by pragmas; consider using those instead.

toBeLoadedCode: Sets the "to be loaded" code for this application edition.

wasRemovedCode Returns the "was removed" code, which is evaluated once this application edition is successfully removed to remove any global or pool dictionaries created by this application edition. This functionality has largely been replaced by pragmas; consider using those instead.

wasRemovedCode: Remembers aString as the "was removed" code for this application edition.

Shadows

hasResidentApplication Sent to an application shadow or a resident application. Returns true if a resident copy of this application exists in the image.

residentApplication Sent to an application shadow or to a resident application. Returns the resident edition of this application if it exists.

shadowAt: Returns a shadow for this application with the given timestamp. This creates the shadow directly in memory, so there is no guarantee that this corresponds to anything in the repository, and the attributes of the shadow will not be populated.

shadowClass Returns the class used to represent shadows of this type of object. For applications this will be either EmShadowSubApplication or EmShadowApplication.

shadows Returns shadow applications for each edition of this application sorted in descending timestamp order.

shadowsFor: aName (Sent to Application/SubApplication) Returns shadow applications for each edition of the application named aName sorted in descending timestamp order.

shadowsWithSubs Returns shadow applications for each edition of this application in descending timestamp order. Each shadow will know if it has subapplications but these will only be created when asked for.

shadowsWithSubsFor: aName (Sent to Application/SubApplication) Returns shadow applications for each edition of aName sorted in descending timestamp order. Each shadow will know if it has subapplications but these will only be created when asked for.

Startup/Shutdown

exiting A hook to notify the application that the image is exiting. This is called once before the image is exited.

postExiting A hook to notify the application that the image is really about to exit now. This is called after all of the exiting methods have been called. This is called once before the image is exited.

preStartUp A hook to notify the application that the image is about to start up. This method is run before any application startUp methods have been run. This method should not depend on any other applications in the system.

restart A hook to notify the application that the image is about to restart. This is called each time the image is restarted after being shut down.

runtimeStartUp A hook to notify the application that the image is starting up, but sent only at run-time. This lets an application define different development-time and run-time startup sequences.

saving A hook to notify the application that the image is about to be saved.

shutDown A hook to notify the application that the image is about to be shut down (either being saved or exited).

startUp A hook to notify the application that the image is starting up.

User Fields/Library Objects

allObjectNames Returns all the names of the objects in the receiver's object store.

atObjectNamed: aName put: anObject Stores a dumped representation of anObject in the object store for the receiver. Returns the timestamp for the new edition of the object, or nil if an error occurs.

applicationComment Returns the comment entered for the receiver. The comment is inherited from the previous edition of the receiver.

applicationComment: aString Associates aString as the comment for the receiver. All new editions will share this comment until they change it themselves.

deleteInheritedUserFieldAt: aName Deletes the inherited user field named aName from the loaded edition of this application edition.

deleteLocalUserFieldAt: aName Deletes the local user field named aName from the loaded edition of this application edition.

deleteObjectNamed: aName Deletes the object named aName from the receiver.

description Returns the note entered for the receiver.

description: aString Stores aString as the note for the receiver.

inheritedUserFieldAt: aName Returns the inherited user field named aName for this application edition. If no such field exists, returns an empty string.

inheritedUserFieldAt: aName put: aString Sets the inherited user field named aName in this application edition to aString.

inheritedUserFieldNames Returns a collection of the inherited user field names in this application edition.

latestObjectNamed: aName Returns the latest edition of the library object named aName.

localUserFieldAt: aName Returns the contents of the local user field named aName in the loaded edition of the receiver application. If no such field exists, returns an empty string.

localUserFieldAt: aName put: aString Sets the contents of the local user field named aName in this application edition to aString.

localUserFieldNames Answers a collection of the local user field names in this application edition.

objectNamed: aName Returns the object in the library named aName. If the object is not found, this method returns nil.

objectNamed: aName at: aTimestamp Returns the edition of the library object named aName stored at aTimestamp.

storeObject: anObject as: aName Stores anObject as a library object named aName. Use this image's serialization mechanism (BOSS or ENVY/Swapper) to convert anObject to a string.

timeStampsForObjectNamed: aName Returns the edition timestamps for the object named aName sorted chronologically.

Users

addGroupMember: anEmUser Adds the user to the application group for this application edition.

allClassNamesOwnedBy: anEmUser Returns all the class names (sorted alphabetically) owned by anEmUser.

allLoadedClassesOwnedBy: anEmUser Returns all the loaded classes owned by anEmUser.

canReleaseEachClassIn: aCollectionOfClasses Returns whether the current user can release each class in aCollectionOfClasses into this application edition. This is allowed if this is an open edition, the current image owner is the owner of each class, and each class is a version but not the released version.

classOwnershipDictionary Answers a dictionary. The keys are the symbols of the classes contained in this application edition and the values are the unique names of the users who own the classes.

groupMembers Returns the users who are group members in this application edition.

manager Returns the manager of this application edition.

manager: anEmUser Changes the manager of the receiver to be anEmUser if allowed. Returns whether it succeeded.

ownerOf: aClassOrName Returns the user who owns aClassOrName in the receiver. If the class or owner does not exist, then this method returns nil.

ownerOf: classOrClasses to: anEmUser Takes an argument that is either a single class or a collection of classes. Changes the owner of each class to be anEmUser if allowed. Returns whether it succeeded.

ownerOfEachIn: aCollectionOfClasses Returns all users who own at least one class in aCollectionOfClasses.

removeGroupMember: anEmUser Removes the user from this application edition's group. Fails and returns false if the user still owns classes in this application edition.

userIsManager Returns whether the current user is the manager of this application edition.

userThatReleased: Answers the user that released aClassOrName in the receiver. If aClassOrName is not released then this method answers nil; otherwise, the method answers the owner.

Version/Edition Status

allPurgedNames (Sent to Application/SubApplication) Returns all the known names of purged applications sorted alphabetically.

asScratch If this application edition is a version, marks it as a scratch edition.

asShadow Returns a shadow copy of this application edition.

becomeDefault Changes this application to be the default. Only applies to resident applications.

EmConfigurationMap

The configuration map and its protocol are significantly different from the Application and SubApplication protocol.

Protocols

- Accessing
- Applications
- Configuration Expressions
- Differencing
- Loading
- Required Maps
- User Fields
- Users
- Version/Edition status

EmConfigurationMap Class

configurationMapNames Returns all of the configuration map names in the library.

create: aName Creates a new configuration map named aName.

editionsDictionaryFor: aName Returns a dictionary of configuration map editions for aName keyed by timestamp.

editionsFor: aName Returns all of the configuration map editions for aName sorted by descending timestamp.

editionTimeStampsFor: aName Returns timestamps for each edition of aName sorted chronologically, latest first.

initialVersionName Returns the initial version name for configuration maps.

named: aName timeStamp: aTimestamp Answers a new configuration map named aName with timestamp aTimestamp. There is no requirement that this map exist in the library.

purgeAllFromLibrary: aCollectionOfNames Purges all editions of the configuration maps named in aCollectionOfNames from the library.

purgedConfigurationMapNames Returns all of the purged configuration map names in the library.

purgedEditionsFor: Returns all of the editions of the purged configuration map named aName, sorted chronologically.

purgeFromLibrary: aName Purges all editions of the configuration map named aName from the library.

salvageFromLibrary: aName Salvages all purged editions of the configuration map named aName that can be recovered.

Accessing

previousTimeStamp Returns the previous timestamp for this configuration map edition.

purgeFromLibrary Purges this edition from the library. If this is the only version of the receiver, this method purges the entire configuration map.

salvageFromLibrary Salvages the receiver from the library.

signature Returns the name of the configuration map concatenated with its timestamp or version name.

Applications

addApplication: anApplication Adds the current edition of anApplication to this configuration map edition (this may replace a previous edition). Reports an error if the receiver is a version. Returns whether it was successful.

applicationEditions Returns a dictionary of the application editions contained in this configuration map edition; keyed by timestamp.

applicationNames Returns the application names contained in this configuration map edition, sorted alphabetically.

areApplicationsLoaded Answers whether all of this configuration map edition's applications are loaded.

removeApplication: anApplication Removes anApplication from the receiver. Reports an error if the receiver is a version. Returns whether it was successful.

shadowApplications Returns a sorted collection containing shadow applications for the application editions of the receiver.

shadowApplicationsWithoutVersionNames Returns a sorted collection containing shadow applications for the application editions of the receiver. NOTE: The shadows will not have any version name information set because they will be created from the application editions dictionary. This method should only be used when the version names of the shadow apps are unimportant, for example, when loading. The shadows are not sorted in any particular order.

Configuration Expressions

addConfigurationExpression: newExpression Adds the configuration newExpression to the receiver, which must be an edition managed by the current user. If newExpression exists, forget its current lineup. The newExpression must not contain double-byte characters.

copyConfigurationExpression: existingExpression toCreate: newExpression Copies the configuration for existingExpression, creating a new configuration for newExpression. The receiver must be a configuration map edition managed by the current user. If the existingExpression is unknown, an empty lineup will be inserted for newExpression, and if it already exists then its lineup will be erased. The expressions must not contain double-byte characters.

deleteConfigurationExpression: existingExpression Deletes the configuration for existingExpression from the receiver, which must be a configuration map edition managed by the current user.

Differencing

differencesWith: aConfigurationMap Finds the released applications in aConfigurationMap that are not the same as the released applications in the receiver. For each of these, this method creates an edition containing the methods that are different. Answers a dictionary whose keys are applications and whose values are dictionaries of class editions containing the methods that are different.

Loading

load Loads all of the applications of the receiver. If this succeeds then this method marks the receiver that it has been loaded and answers true; otherwise, it answers false.

loadWithRequiredMaps Loads the receiver and all its required maps for the first lineup encountered where the expression evaluates to true. Loading a required map may in turn load other required maps.

loadWithRequiredMapsAndTracing: includeTracing Like loadWithRequiredMaps, but if includeTracing is true then this method writes to the Transcript explicitly so the user sees the progress.

loadWithRequiredMapsAndTracing: reportProgressTo: Like the previous method but reports progress so that it can be used with execLongOperation:.

loadWithTracing: Like load, but if includeTracing is true then this method writes to the Transcript explicitly so the user sees the progress.

loadWithTracing: reportProgressTo: Like the previous method but reports progress so that it can be used with execLongOperation:.

unload Unloads the applications for this configuration map edition. Answers whether the operation was successful.

Required Maps

allPossibleRequiredMaps Returns all of the required maps referenced by any of this edition's configuration expressions. The order is undefined and may include multiple editions of the same required map.

allRequiredMaps Answers all the required maps of this edition in the order in which they should be loaded. If a cyclic reference is encountered, answers an association mapping the two configuration maps involved together. For each map, this uses the first encountered lineup with an expression that evaluates to true to obtain its required maps. The result may include different editions of the same required map.

hasValidLineup Answers whether this edition has a required maps lineup that is valid for this image.

requiredMaps Answers the required maps of this configuration map edition using the first valid lineup for this image.

requiredMapsConfigurations Answers an array of associations that describe all the possible required map configurations for this edition. The key is the configuration expression of the lineup and the value, which is an array of associations whose keys are configuration map names and whose values are the timestamps of the released editions. The required maps are ordered in the sequence in which they should be loaded.

User Fields

comment Returns the comment entered for the receiver. The comment is inherited from the previous edition of the receiver.

comment: aString Associates aString as the comment for the receiver. All new editions will share this comment until they change it themselves.

deleteInheritedUserFieldAt: aName Deletes the inherited user field named aName from the loaded edition of this application edition.

deleteLocalUserFieldAt: aName Deletes the local user field named aName from the loaded edition of this application edition.

deleteObjectNamed: aName Deletes the object named aName from the receiver.

description Returns the note entered for the receiver.

description: aString Stores aString as the note for the receiver.

inheritedUserFieldAt: aName Returns the inherited user field named aName for this application edition. If there is no such field, returns an empty string.

inheritedUserFieldAt: aName put: aString Sets the inherited user field named aName in this application edition to aString.

inheritedUserFieldNames Answers a collection of strings, which are the inherited user field names in the edition of the receiver configuration map.

localUserFieldAt: aName Returns the contents of the local user field named aName in the loaded edition of the receiver application. If no such field exists, it returns an empty string.

localUserFieldAt: aName put: aString Sets the contents of the local user field named aName in this application edition to aString.

localUserFieldNames Answers a collection of strings, which are the local user field names in this configuration map edition.

objectNamed: aName Returns the object in the library named aName. If the object is not found, this method returns nil.

objectNamed: aName ifAbsent: aBlock Returns the object in the library named aName. If the object is not found, this method returns the result of evaluating aBlock.

storeObject: anObject as: aName Stores anObject as a library object named aName. Use this image's serialization mechanism (BOSS or ENVY/Swapper) to convert anObject to a string.

Users

manager Returns the user that manages this configuration map edition.

manager: anEmUser Sets the user that manages this configuration map edition.

Version/Edition Status

isEdition Answers whether the receiver is an open edition.

isVersion Answers whether the receiver is a version.

newEdition If the receiver is a version, creates a new edition from it.

EmUser Class

EmUser has few interesting instance methods, mostly confined to accessors and standard user field protocol, so we omit these and concentrate on the class methods.

allUsers Returns a collection of all users.

called: aName Returns the user object whose unique name is aName. If the user is not found, this method returns a user whose fullName reflects that it is missing. See also named:, which uses the full name rather than the unique name.

called: aName ifAbsent: aBlock Returns the user object whose unique name is aName. Evaluates aBlock if the user is not found.

current Returns the current user of the image.

current: anEmUser Sets the current user of the image.

currentID Answers the unique name of the current user of the image. Answers an empty string if the current user is not set.

exists: Returns whether a user with a unique name of aName already exists in the library.

isCurrentSupervisor Answers whether the current user of the image is the library supervisor.

named: fullName Returns the user object named fullName. Reports an error if the user is not found. See also called:, which uses the unique name rather than the full name.

named: fullName ifAbsent: aBlock Returns the user object named fullName. Evaluates aBlock if the user is not found.

purgeAllFromLibrary: uniqueNames Purges all the users with unique names in uniqueNames from the library. Reports an error if uniqueNames includes the current user.

purgeFromLibrary: uniqueName Purges the user called uniqueName from the library. Reports an error if uniqueName is the current user.

resetImageOwner Resets the owner of the image to be undefined. The next time the image is started, a prompter will ask for the image owner.

Class and CompiledMethod

Classes and methods are both basic Smalltalk objects, and not ENVY components. Nevertheless, ENVY adds protocol to both classes. Both classes and class extensions are represented in the same way, so most methods apply to both.

Class

allMethodNames Returns the names of all the methods for this class.

allSelectorsFor: anApplication Returns the names of all methods for this class in anApplication.

applicationFor: aSymbol Returns the application that controls the method named aSymbol.

applications Returns all the applications that control methods in this class.

asEditionIn: anApplication Creates a shadow of this class, which is controlled by anApplication. This is an in-memory operation, and does not imply creating an edition in the repository.

controller Returns the application that controls this class or class extension.

defaultSignature Returns a string with the timestamp or version name of this class in the application that controls this class.

definitionTimeStamp Returns a string with the timestamp or version name of this class in the application that controls the class definition.

description: aString in: anApplication Stores aString in the notes field for the part of this class associated with anApplication.

developerIn: anApplication Returns the user who is the developer of this class in anApplication.

hasMethodsIn: anApplication Returns true if this class has any methods controlled by anApplication.

isEditionIn: anApplication Returns true if the portion of this class contained in anApplication is an open edition.

isLoaded Returns true if this class is the resident class for this name in the image.

isVersionIn: anApplication Returns true if the portion of this class contained in anApplication is a version in the image.

isReallyVersionIn: anApplication Returns true if the portion of this class contained in anApplication is a version in the repository. This will differ from isVersionIn: only if the repository and the image are out of sync.

isReleasedIn: anApplication Returns true if the portion of this class contained in anApplication is released.

isUndefinedIn: anApplication Returns true if this class is undefined in anApplication.

methodsIn: anApplication Returns all of the methods for this class controlled by anApplication.

methodNamesIn: anApplication Returns all of the method names for this class controlled by anApplication.

ownerIn: anApplication Returns the class owner for the portion of this class controlled by anApplication.

residentClass Returns the resident class for this class name.

signatureIn: anApplication Returns a string describing the class timestamp or version name for the portion of this class controlled by anApplication.

timeStampIn: anApplication Returns the timestamp for the portion of this class controlled by anApplication.

versionNameIn: anApplication Returns the version name for the portion of this class controlled by anApplication, or an empty string if that is an open edition.

CompiledMethod

editionStamp Returns a string with the timestamp of this method edition.

editionStampWithCategories Returns a string describing this method edition and including its categories.

isLoaded Returns whether the receiver is loaded in the image.

isPrimitive Answers true if the receiver is a user or a system primitive.

isPrivate Returns whether the method is private, not public.

isPublic Returns whether the method is public, not private.

isResident Returns whether the receiver represents the currently resident edition of the method.

loadPrevious If the receiver has a previous edition, this method loads it if it still exists in the library and returns true; otherwise, it returns false.

removeSource Permanently removes the source string for the receiver from the current manager library.

setSource: aString Sets the source code to this method edition to aString.

signature Returns a name for the method.

sourceString Returns the source code for the receiver.

testVisibilityIn: anApplication Reports any references to variables, classes, and pools anApplication cannot see.

timeStamp Returns the edition timeStamp for the receiver.

Helper Classes

A number of ENVY operations aren't implemented as methods on components, but on various helper classes.

EtTools

browser: aSymbol Opens an ENVY browser whose type is determined by aSymbol. For example, ((EtTools browser: #application) on: Kernel) open. See resetBrowserMappings for possible browser types.

changeDefaultLibrary Prompts the user to change the current ENVY repository.

changeUser Prompts the user to change the current image owner.

checkConsistency Performs a consistency check of the repository.

exportUsing: aBlock Prompts for a library and passes the current and the selected library to the block. This also wraps the operation in a progress dialog box.

importChoosing: chooseBlock message: messageBlock using: importBlock Provides a framework for controlling import operations. The chooseBlock controls how the components to be imported are chosen, the messageBlock controls what is displayed on the Transcript, and the importBlock controls how the import operation happens. See the method comment for detailed information.

resetBrowserMappings Resets the definitions of which browser symbol corresponds to which browser class. This is most useful as a way of knowing which browser symbols are available.

EmInterface

loadPreviousMethodEditionFor: aCompiledMethod Loads the previous edition of aCompiledMethod. Answers true if successful.

previousVersion: anApplication Returns a shadow application representing the previous version of anApplication. If it does not have one, returns nil.

previousVersionOf: aClass in: anApplication Returns a shadow class that represents the previous version of aClass in anApplication. If no previous version exists or it cannot be found, it returns nil. The previous version might not be found if this component was not originally from this repository, or if the previous version has been purged.

versionApplication: anApplication withName: aString If anApplication is an open edition, version it. Answers true if successful.

extend: aClass in: anApplication Creates an extension of aClass in anApplication, if possible.

System

allClasses Returns all the classes in the image.

defaultApplication Returns the application into which filed-in code will be placed.

defaultApplication: anApplication Sets anApplication to be the application into which filed-in code will be placed.

loadedApplications Returns a collection of all applications loaded in the image. See also Application currentlyLoaded.

loadedSubApplications Returns a collection of all subapplications loaded in the image. See also SubApplication currentlyLoaded.

≡Glossary≡

Application – A collection of classes and class extensions. An application corresponds to what are commonly called *modules* or *packages* in other systems.

Application Attachment – A file that is stored inside the ENVY repository as a user field (for example, C source code or files containing pictures used by the associated code).

Application Browser – A browser that shows the details of one application or subapplication.

Application Class – A special ENVY-generated class that exists for each application/subapplication and has the same name as the application/subapplication.

Application Editions Browser – A browser that shows all of the editions of an application in the repository.

Application Group – The list of developers who work in an application. Only members of this group can own classes in the application. This list can change from edition to edition.

Application Lineup – The definition of configuration information used to specify conditional loading of subapplications. *See* Lineup.

Application Manager (the user) – The user responsible for the overall status of a particular application. The manager is a member of the application group and is responsible for assigning ownership of the classes to the other group members. The manager is also responsible for versioning the application edition. The application manager can change from edition to edition.

Application Manager (the browser) – A browser that controls applications, the classes they contain, their prerequisites, and the application group. This fulfills many of the same functions as the VisualAge Organizer. It will usually be clear from the context whether something refers to the user who manages an application or this browser.

Applications Browser – A browser that shows all of the applications and subapplications resident in the image.

Atomic Load – The characteristic of ENVY loads that, under almost all circumstances, a load will either succeed in its entirety or fail without making any changes to the image.

Baselining – Making a version of the top-level component in a project, which involves versioning and/or releasing all of its subcomponents. For example, we can make a baseline of a configuration map by ensuring that all classes are versioned and released, that all the released application editions have been versioned, and then versioning the configuration map.

Class Browser – A browser that shows one particular class. This gives a class-centric view, and does not visually distinguish between methods in the class definition and methods in extensions.

Class Developer – Any user who develops new editions of a class. If a developer creates a class edition, only he or she may modify and version it.

Class Extension – A group of methods added to a class in an application other than the one that contains the class definition. Class extensions can only add methods; they cannot change methods in other applications or change the class definition.

Class Owner – The application group member responsible for the integrity and well-being of a class or class extension in an application. The owner of a class or class extension can change from edition to edition.

Class Ownership – ENVY's conflict-resolution mechanism. Any user can create class editions and version those editions, but only the owner can release those versions into the containing application.

Classes Browser – A browser organized around a list of all the classes resident in the image.

Clone – The process of copying the ENVY library and discarding unused open editions.

Comment – An explanatory string associated with a component and stored in an ENVY user field.

Component – Any of the ENVY software components: configuration maps, applications, subapplications, classes, class extensions, and methods.

Conditional Loading – Using application lineups or required maps to load different code depending on the load environment (for example, the operating system or the Smalltalk implementation).

Configuration Expression – A Smalltalk expression that evaluates to true or false, determining whether a particular application lineup or set of required maps will be loaded.

Configuration Map – A component containing applications. Usually the top-level component of a project is a configuration map.

Configuration Map Browser – A browser that shows configuration map editions, their contained applications, notes, and required maps.

Configuration Map Manager – The user responsible for managing the integrity of a particular configuration map edition. The manager is responsible for releasing the appropriate application editions to the configuration map and for versioning the configuration map.

Continuous Integration – A development process in which integration happens in small increments throughout development. Application editions are shared, and developers constantly release classes into the shared edition and use one-click loading to resynchronize with the reference model.

Controller – An application that contains a class or class extension is said to control it, and is called the controller of that class or class extension.

Defined Class – A new class added to the system by an application. A class can be defined in only one loaded application.

Edition – The general term for both versions and open editions.

EMSRV – A server process used to control access to the ENVY repository in a multi-user environment.

Export – The process of transferring ENVY component versions from the repository attached to this image into another repository.

Extended Class – *See* Class Extension.

File-In – The process of reading Smalltalk source code representing one or more ENVY components from a file.

File-Out – The process of writing Smalltalk source code representing one or more ENVY components to a file.

Hierarchy Browser – A browser organized around the inheritance hierarchy of a particular class.

Image – The set of code present in a running development environment. Typically this can also be saved to an image file and restarted, preserving the exact state of the environment.

Image Component (IC) – A VisualAge mechanism for storing compiled Smalltalk code in a sharable library.

Image Owner – The user who is working in a particular image. This is used to determine permissions for operations and to set the owner and/or developer for components and editions created from this image.

Import – The process of transferring ENVY component versions from another repository into the one attached to this image.

Kernel – The ENVY application that contains the fundamental system classes (for example, Object).

Library – The multi-user repository that stores all of the ENVY components, source code, compiled code, and associated data.

Library Supervisor – A special administrative user who is initially the owner of all system components and who has the right to create and modify other users. The Library Supervisor does not have any other special privileges and is not analogous to a UNIX "root" user.

Lineup – A mechanism for specifying multiple configurations. A lineup contains a set of configuration expressions and specifications of component editions. When a configuration expression evaluates to true, the associated set of editions is loaded. *See* Application Lineup *and* Required Maps.

Load – The act of making a runnable, in-memory copy of a component from the repository.

Method List Browser – A browser that shows a list of methods, independent of the class or classes that contain them. This browser is most frequently seen in lists of senders or implementors of a message name.

Note – An explanatory string associated with an ENVY component edition and stored as a user field.

One-Click Loading – The act of loading a component that has been configured so the appropriate editions of all subcomponents are automatically loaded at the same time. This is done by releasing open application editions into the parent configuration map and open subapplication editions into the parent application. This enables a single load operation to synchronize the state of an entire project.

Open Edition – An ENVY component that has not yet been versioned. Open editions can be modified, and are identified by the timestamp at which they were created.

Packaging – The process of preparing a Smalltalk application for distribution as a standalone program.

Parcel – A VisualWorks mechanism for storing compiled code and optionally source code into a standalone format, which can be loaded very rapidly.

Pragma – A declarative notation that acts as a special instruction to ENVY or to the Smalltalk system in general. For example, ENVY supports pragmas to declare and initialize pool dictionaries, avoiding the need for explicit initialization code.

Prerequisites – For an application, the other applications that must be loaded for this application to function.

Previous Version – The version from which this component edition was created.

Purge – Remove an application or configuration map edition from the repository. This does not reclaim space, so the purged edition can be restored.

Reference Model – The hierarchy or group of hierarchies of components that entirely defines a particular project in the repository. Development can be thought of as a succession of deviations from this model, followed by releasing changes into the reference model.

Releasing – Making a component edition the default to be loaded when its parent component is loaded.

Repository – *See* Library.

Required Maps – For a configuration map, a list of other configuration maps that should be loaded before this map is loaded. These can be specified by lineups to make use of conditional loading. Note that this differs from application lineups because the configuration map loads are independent. A failed load will not reverse the effects of previous loads.

Resident – A runnable version of a component that is present in the image; in other words, the thing we think about as the component itself.

Restore – Recover an application or configuration map edition that has been purged.

Scratch Edition – A temporary application edition, used to allow short-term modifications to applications for which the user would otherwise not have permission to modify.

Shadow – An in-memory representation of a component edition from the repository.

Stripping – The process of removing unused code from an image as part of packaging.

Subapplication – A subapplication is an application contained within another application or subapplication. This facility lets users organize classes within an application or separate out platform-specific code.

Syncing Up – Loading component editions from the repository to bring ourselves back into sync with the reference model.

System Administrator – *See* Library Supervisor.

Timestamp – A signature associated with a new edition of a component. It is comprised of the date and time the edition was created, for example, (11/29/99 18:19:00).

Transcript – The development tool window that contains a log of messages associated with the global variable Transcript.

Unload – Remove a resident component from the image.

Undefined – A special timestamp for components that do not have a version released into a particular application edition.

User Field –A field associated with any ENVY component that can be used to associate arbitrary additional information with that component.

Version – A component that has been given a version name and cannot be further modified. Versions are identified by their version name.

Versioning – The act of making an edition into a version.

Version/Release All – An ENVY option for versioning all of the open class editions within an application and releasing all of them at once. Note that this affects *all* open class editions in the application, not merely the selected editions.

VisualAge – The generic name for a number of IBM development environments.

VisualAge Generator – A 4GL environment from IBM that generates applications from visually defined specifications. The development environment is based on VisualAge Smalltalk and includes ENVY.

VisualAge Java – A Java development environment from IBM, with very similar development concepts to VisualAge Smalltalk, particularly with respect to team programming.

VisualAge Organizer – A VisualAge browser that controls applications, the classes they contain, their prerequisites, and the application group. This fulfills many of the same functions as the Application Manager.

VisualAge Smalltalk – IBM's Smalltalk development environment.

VisualWorks – Cincom's Smalltalk development environment, a direct descendant of Xerox Smalltalk-80.

═══References═══

Alpert, Sherman R., Kyle Brown, and Bobby Woolf. 1998. *The Design Patterns Smalltalk Companion*. Reading, Massachusetts: Addison-Wesley.

Beck, Kent. 1997. *Smalltalk Best Practice Patterns*. Upper Saddle River, New Jersey: Prentice-Hall PTR.

Beck, Kent. 1999. *eXtreme Programming eXplained: Embrace Change*. Reading, Massachusetts: Addison-Wesley.

Fowler, Martin. 1999. *Refactoring: Improving the Design of Existing Code*. Reading, Massachusetts: Addison-Wesley.

Gamma, Erich, Richard Helm, Ralph Johnson, and John Vlissides. 1994. *Design Patterns: Elements of Reusable Object-Oriented Software*. Reading, Massachusetts: Addison-Wesley.

Jeffries, Ron, Ann Anderson, and Chet Hendrickson. 2000. *Extreme Programming Installed*. Reading, Massachusetts: Addison-Wesley.

McConnell, Steve. 1996. *Rapid Development: Taming Wild Software Schedules*. Redmond, Washington: Microsoft Press.

≡≡Index≡≡

Printed in the United States
By Bookmasters